THE BEST
PUB
QUIZ
BOOK

Ever! 2

1 85868 425 0

Project Editor: Simon Kirrane
Production: Alexia Rencricca

Questions set by The Puzzle House

Printed and bound in Great Britain

THE BEST
PUB
QUIZ
BOOK

Ever! 2

CARLTON

Contents

INTRODUCTION

Way back in 1996 *The Best Pub Quiz Book Ever!* was first published; it was followed, rather rapidly, by the tongue-twisting *The Best Pub Pop Quiz Book Ever!* and then by the soccer-mad *The Best Football Quiz Book Ever!*. That the public cannot get enough of their quizzes and that the idea of doing them in a pub is not a fad but an institution is now a fact that manifests itself in the seemingly self-contradictory *The Best Pub Quiz Book Ever! 2*. Still, needs must, necessity is the mother of invention and I'll take the high road, but the fact and the book remain, and so here, as it was in the first place and will be in the second. Welcome.

The aim of this fine tome is to guide you through the pitfalls of pub quizzardry to the land of Pub Facts (and I'm not talking warm beer) where you can safely head up a quiz at your local hostelry and thereby gain the undying gratitude of the stout yeoman of the bar and love of the locals.

There is a guide to the rear of the book that will show you the way forward but some initial pointers for you to note are that the whole ideal of the pub quiz is one of entertainment. It may engender well-placed pedantry and overzealous Zimmer rattling but it will be fun, fun, fun. Keep this as your philosophy and you won't go far wrong.

Talk the idea through with your landlord and have the quiz at your local where you know everyone and everyone knows you and where you can escape home all the quicker if the locals fall upon you with cries and hollers and flaming torches. Start slowly and build up your quiz nights carefully, controlling and feeding the voracious appetites of the regulars until you have them eating quiz out of the palms of your hands. Finally and quite seriously. No, really. When setting a quiz make sure you note down all the questions and then the answers and then double check that everything is present and correct. If an answer gives you pause to think then double-check it and make sure it's the right answer and moreover the *only* right answer. Also while every effort has been undertaken to ensure that the answers given are the correct answers there is a possibility, however slight, that the answer given is incorrect. If, however, you have checked this then you can begin your quiz with quiet confidence, or even loud and booming confidence. At any rate, you can begin.

The best of luck.

Easy Questions

Let's look at the facts for a minute:

easy adj. **1** not difficult. **2** free from pain, care, or anxiety.
3 tolerant and undemanding; easy-going **4** readily
influenced; pliant: an *easy victim*.... We'll leave the dictionary
definition there. You should have got the message, but just in
case you haven't I'll underline it, metaphorically of course, in
double-line puce ink. This section of the quiz book is not
difficult: it is, like, so many pub regulars, simple. Not hard. If
this section were an aeroplane it would be made out of balsa
wood, driven by an elastic band and piloted by a five-year-old.
People who find difficulty in this section should be asked to
leave the pub because they're under age (by around 17 years)
or over the limit (by about 30 units). To further clarify: people
who cannot answer the following questions should not be
asked to participate in the quiz AT ALL:

What is your name?
How old are you?
2 + 2 = ?
Fill in the missing number: 1, 2, 3, ?, 5
Finish this sentence: "Mine's a..."

As Shirley Crabtree (AKA 'Big Daddy', grapple fans) sang:
Easy!...Easy!...Easy!...Easy!...Easy!...Easy!...Easy!...Easy!...
Easy!...(*repeat to fade*)

1   Who married Patsy Kensit in April 1997?
2   Which singer's daughter is called Lourdes Maria?
3   Who has a backing group called the Waves?
4   Who took "Wannabe" to No. 1 in 1996?
5   Who is lead singer with Wet Wet Wet?
6   Who won the Eurovision Song Contest with "Puppet on a String"?
7   Who sang "Strangers in the Night"?
8   Who is the brother of the late Karen Carpenter?
9   Who wrote "Words", a 90s hit for Boyzone?
10 Which singer/songwriter received a knighthood in January 1997?
11 Who was Bernie Taupin's most famous songwriting partner?
12 Who is Mick Jagger's second wife?
13 Who changed his name from Gordon Sumner to top the charts?
14 Who was the only female singer managed by Brian Epstein?
15 Who was the female vocalist with the Pretenders?
16 Who co-starred with Whitney Houston in *The Bodyguard*?
17 Who wrote the music for *Jesus Christ Superstar*?
18 Who were known on TV as Dave Tucker and Paddy Garvey?
19 Who sang that they were "Back For Good" in 1995?
20 Whose "new" single, "Free As A Bird", charted in 1995?
21 The title from which TV drama gave Jimmy Nail a hit in 1994?
22 Who was the subject of the biopic *What's Love Got to Do With It*??
23 Whose first solo No. 1 was "Sacrifice/Healing Hands"?
24 Who was the British Monkee?
25 Who played Wimbledon's Centre Court without a racket in 1996?
26 Who had a hit with "Radio Ga Ga"?
27 Who was the father of the former Mrs Lisa Marie Jackson?
28 Which 80s duo included Andrew Ridgeley?
29 Who had his first UK solo No. 1 with "I Just Called To Say I Love You"?
30 Who was lead singer with Culture Club?

Quiz 2 Pot Luck 1

Answers - see page 12

LEVEL 1

1   On which day are hot cross buns traditionally eaten?
2   How many signs of the zodiac are there?
3   In which decade of the 20th century was Muhammad Ali born?
4   What word can go after "hobby" and before "radish"?
5   How is Maurice Cole better known?
6   Which soccer club has had Royal and Woolwich as part of its name?
7   Who wrote the novel *Lucky Jim*?
8   On a Monopoly board, what colour is Old Kent Road?
9   Who invented Braille?
10 In song, who was born "on a mountain top in Tennessee"?
11 What is Kampuchea now called?
12 Which Richard starred in "The Good Life"?
13 Lance Cairns played cricket for which country?
14 What word can go before "draft", "flow" and "shadow"?
15 Traditionally, what colour is willow pattern?
16 In which country is the city of Addis Ababa?
17 Which Boys recorded "Barbara Ann" in the 60s?
18 Which cartoon character has an anchor tattooed on his arm?
19 What is the square root of 4?
20 Iceberg and Dorothy Perkins are examples of what?
21 Ivor Allchurch is associated with which sport?
22 Which film ends with "tomorrow is another day"?
23 A revolving firework is named after which saint?
24 Who murdered Abel?
25 In 1974, parts of Somerset and Gloucestershire made which new county?
26 Which Italian phrase used in English means in the fresh or cool air?
27 In which TV series did the characters Edina and Saffron appear?
28 Which Ben won an Oscar for Best Actor in *Gandhi*?
29 How many degrees in a right angle?
30 Which group had a No. 1 with "Hey Jude"?

Answers

Around the UK (see Quiz 4)

1 Strathclyde. 2 Leeds. 3 Clwyd. 4 M1. 5 Anglesey. 6 Northern Ireland.
7 One - Devon. 8 Lake District. 9 Scarborough. 10 Scotland. 11 Humber.
12 Birmingham. 13 Edinburgh. 14 East. 15 M11. 16 Regent's Park.
17 M4. 18 Isle of Wight. 19 Bognor, Lyme. 20 Ealing, Enfield.
21 Liverpool. 22 Guernsey. 23 The Mall. 24 Blackpool. 25 Fife.
26 Dartford. 27 M6. 28 Suffolk. 29 Glasgow. 30 North.

Quiz 3 TV: Soaps

Answers - see page 9

Answers - see page 9

LEVEL 1

1 Who left "EastEnders" for France with two of her three children?
2 What is the name of Maureen's mum in "Coronation Street"?
3 Who is the Street's repetitive butcher?
4 In which soap did Dave Glover perish in a fire?
5 Which "Coronation Street" MacDonald twin went to prison?
6 In which soap does Sinbad appear?
7 What is EastEnder Tiffany's daughter called?
8 What was Ivy Tilsley's surname when she died?
9 Former members of which soap starred in a BT ad in 1997?
10 In "Neighbours" what was the surname of Scott, Paul, Lucy and Julie?
11 Who was Frank Tate's murdered wife in "Emmerdale"?
12 What is the name of Jack and Vera Duckworth's wayward son?
13 Where was David Wicks heading for when he left "EastEnders"?
14 Who is Bianca's mum in "EastEnders"?
15 Who married Shane in "Home and Away"?
16 What is the name of the Barbara Windsor character in "EastEnders"?
17 In the Street what is Curly's real name?
18 Where was Curly's wife Raquel heading for on leaving Weatherfield?
19 Which Street character had a fling with gangster Fraser Henderson?
20 Which soap pub is famous for its Newton & Ridley beer?
21 "Home and Away" is set near which Australian city?
22 What is Phil and Kathy Mitchell's son called?
23 Who is the most senior of the Archer family?
24 In which soap would you see the character Tinhead?
25 Which soap is set in Erinsborough?
26 What was the name of Joan Collins's character in "Dynasty"?
27 Who sponsored "Coronation Street" in 1997?
28 Which soap is "Knot's Landing" a spin off from?
29 Which soap is set in Borsetshire?
30 Which dish is the Rover's Return's Betty Williams famous for?

Answers

Pop: Who's Who? (see Quiz 1)
1 Liam Gallagher. 2 Madonna. 3 Katrina. 4 The Spice Girls. 5 Marti Pellow. 6 Sandie Shaw. 7 Frank Sinatra. 8 Richard. 9 The Bee Gees. 10 Paul McCartney. 11 Elton John. 12 Jerry Hall. 13 Sting. 14 Cilla Black. 15 Chrissie Hynde. 16 Kevin Costner. 17 Andrew Lloyd Webber. 18 Robson and Jerome. 19 Take That. 20 The Beatles. 21 "Crocodile Shoes". 22 Tina Turner. 23 Elton John. 24 Davy Jones. 25 Cliff Richard. 26 Queen. 27 Elvis Presley. 28 Wham! 29 Stevie Wonder. 30 Boy George.

Quiz 4 Around the UK

LEVEL 1

Answers - see page 10

1. Glasgow is the administrative centre of which Scottish region?
2. Which is further north, Liverpool or Leeds?
3. What before the 1996 reorganization was the only Welsh county to begin with C?
4. Which motorway would you travel on from London to Leeds?
5. How is the Welsh island Ynys Mon also known?
6. In which part of the UK is Newry?
7. How many counties have a border with Cornwall?
8. In which District are Ullswater and Bassenthwaite?
9. Which resort beginning with S lies between Whitby and Bridlington?
10. In which country is Prestwick Airport?
11. On which river does Hull lie?
12. Which city's major station is New Street?
13. In which city is Princes Street a major shopping thoroughfare?
14. On which coast of Scotland is Dundee?
15. Which motorway would you travel on from London to Cambridge?
16. London Zoo is in which Park?
17. Which motorway stretches from the outskirts of London into Wales?
18. On which island are Shanklin and Sandown?
19. Which two south-coast resorts include the name Regis?
20. Which two London Boroughs begin with E?
21. In which city is Lime Street station and the Albert Dock?
22. On which Channel Island is St Peter Port?
23. Which road leads from Trafalgar Square up to Buckingham Palace?
24. St Annes lies to the south of which major seaside resort?
25. Which is the only Scottish region beginning with F?
26. Which tunnel is a major link around the M25?
27. Which motorway would you travel on from Birmingham to Lancaster?
28. Which county lies between Norfolk and Essex?
29. In which city is Sauciehall Street?
30. Does London's Euston station serve the north, south, east or west of the country?

Answers

Pot Luck 1 (see Quiz 2)

1 Good Friday. **2** 12. **3** 40s. **4** "Horse". **5** Kenny Everett. **6** Arsenal.
7 Kingsley Amis. **8** Brown. **9** Louis Braille. **10** Davy Crockett.
11 Cambodia. **12** Briers. **13** New Zealand. **14** "Over". **15** Blue.
16 Ethiopia. **17** The Beach Boys. **18** Popeye. **19** 2. **20** Rose. **21** Football.
22 *Gone With The Wind*. **23** Catherine. **24** Cain. **25** Avon. **26** Al fresco.
27 "Absolutely Fabulous". **28** Kingsley. **29** 90. **30** The Beatles.

Quiz 5 Pot Luck 2

Answers - see page 15

1   Which UK car manufacturer produced the Cambridge?
2   Which Welsh comedian was a member of the Goons?
3   Gubby Allen is associated with which sport?
4   What word can go after "roller" and before "board"?
5   In which country is the city of Acapulco?
6   How many millimetres in three centimetres?
7   Who wrote the novel *Jane Eyre*?
8   The character Elsie Tanner appeared in which TV soap?
9   Who had an 80s No. 1 with "You Win Again"?
10 In which decade of the 20th century was Woody Allen born?
11 Al is the chemical symbol for which element?
12 In which TV series did the characters James, Siegfried and Tristan appear?
13 What title did the eldest son of the king of France hold?
14 Ben Gurion airport is in which country?
15 How is Sophia Scicoloni better known?
16 Which Tim became Britain's most expensive soccer keeper in 1993?
17 Bob Cratchit appears in which Charles Dickens novel?
18 What does the C stand for in ACAS?
19 What is the administrative centre for the county of Avon?
20 Which quizmaster says, "I've started so I'll finish"?
21 What colour appears along with white on the Polish flag?
22 Which Glenda starred in "Elizabeth R"?
23 What is 3 cubed?
24 DEAR CASH is an anagram of which indoor game?
25 What is measured in amperes?
26 What is the study of the earth's crust and rocks called?
27 What term describes instruments that produce sound when struck?
28 Which Tony had a 50s hit with "Stranger In Paradise"?
29 What was the name of the painter and decorator in "Brush Strokes"?
30 How many sides does a trapezium have?

Answers

Pot Luck 3 (see Quiz 7)

1 Parlophone. 2 Logie. 3 40s. 4 "Cracker". 5 Dirk Bogarde. 6 Aston Villa. 7 Agatha Christie. 8 Golf. 9 Queen Elizabeth I. 10 "Hound Dog". 11 Caffeine. 12 Dennis the Menace. 13 Rossiter. 14 "Show". 15 Rouge. 16 Stephen Sondheim. 17 Déjà vu. 18 1,000. 19 Canada. 20 "'Allo 'Allo". 21 Tuesday. 22 Hanks. 23 Grey and red. 24 Salvation Army. 25 Fred Flintstone. 26 Eyes. 27 Police. 28 Egypt. 29 Lent. 30 Dark blue.

Quiz 6 Hobbies & Leisure 1

Answers - see page 16

LEVEL 1

1 How many different coloured squares are there on a chessboard?
2 What would you buy from a Gibbons' catalogue?
3 Whose three-dimensional cube became a 70s and 80s craze?
4 If 3 is on the top side of a dice, what number is on the hidden side?
5 What does a snorkel help you do?
6 What is the art of knotting cord or string in patterns?
7 In Scrabble what is the value of the blank tile?
8 What does the musical term largo mean?
9 What fairground attraction did George Ferris construct in the 1890s?
10 Jokers apart, how many red cards are there in a standard pack?
11 What does a twitcher look for?
12 Which game features Miss Scarlet and the Reverend Green?
13 What do we call the art of paper-folding, which originated in Japan?
14 How many discs does each player have to start with in draughts?
15 What type of dancing was originally only performed by men, usually dressed in white, with bells and garlands?
16 If you practise calligraphy what do you do?
17 If you're involved in firing, throwing and glazing what do you do?
18 Which game has a board, cards and wedges?
19 In which leisure pursuit might you do a Turkey Trot or a Bunny Hug?
20 How many people can you normally fit in a go-kart?
21 What is a John Innes No. 1?
22 If you combined k and p to make cables what would your hobby be?
23 What was developed to experience the excitement of surfing on land?
24 Which exercises are designed to increase oxygen consumption and speed blood circulation?
25 What is a whist competition or tournament called?
26 A Royal Flush is the best hand you can get in which card game?
27 Which British game is known as checkers in the USA?
28 Which card game has a pegboard used for scoring?
29 Where on your body would you wear flippers?
30 Which playing card is the Black Lady?

Answers

Living World (see Quiz 8)
1 Elm. 2 Fish. 3 Constriction. 4 Eagle. 5 Two. 6 Breed of terrier.
7 Snake. 8 Below. 9 Its colour. 10 Tree. 11 Southern. 12 Beaver.
13 Vixen. 14 Its tail. 15 Caterpillar. 16 Canada. 17 Deer. 18 Fungus.
19 America. 20 Skunk. 21 Shark. 22 White. 23 Liver. 24 Red.
25 Venom. 26 Fish. 27 Two. 28 Kangaroo. 29 Swim - type of tuna fish.
30 Australia.

Quiz 7 Pot Luck 3

Answers - see page 13

1 On which label did the Beatles have their first hit record?
2 What was the television pioneer John Baird's middle name?
3 In which decade of the 20th century was Paddy Ashdown born?
4 What word can go after "nut" and before "jack"?
5 How is Derek Jules Gaspard Ulrich Van Den Bogaerde better known?
6 Which soccer team does Nigel Kennedy support?
7 Who wrote the novel *The Murder Of Roger Ackroyd*?
8 Peter Allis is associated with which sport?
9 Who is the US state of Virginia name after?
10 Which Elvis song has the words "you ain't never caught a rabbit"?
11 Which stimulant is found in tea and coffee?
12 Who has a dog called Gnasher?
13 Which Leonard starred in "The Rise And fall Of Reginald Perrin"?
14 What word can go before "down", "jumping" and "off"?
15 Which make-up item is the French word for red?
16 Who wrote "Send In The Clowns"?
17 Which French phrase used in English means already seen?
18 What number is represented by the Roman numeral M?
19 The airline Labrador Airways is from which country?
20 In which TV series did the character René Artois appear?
21 Which day of the week is Shrove once a year?
22 Which Tom won an Oscar for Best Actor in *Forrest Gump*?
23 What two colours of squirrel are found in Britain?
24 The *War Cry* is the magazine of which organization?
25 Whose catchphrase is "Yabba-dabba-doo!"?
26 In Cockney rhyming slang what are mince pies?
27 Who had a 70s No. 1 with "Message In a Bottle"?
28 In which country is the city of Alexandria?
29 Ash Wednesday is the first day of which period of fasting?
30 On a Monopoly board, what colour is Mayfair?

Answers

Quiz 8 Living World

LEVEL 1

Answers - see page 14

1 Which tree can be Dutch, English or wych?
2 What type of creature is a stingray?
3 How does a boa kill?
4 Which bird can be bald, golden or harpy?
5 How many humps does a Bactrian camel have?
6 What sort of animal is a Dandie Dinmont?
7 What is a mamba?
8 Would a tuber grow above or below the ground?
9 What is a chameleon famous for being capable of changing?
10 What is a monkey puzzle?
11 To which hemisphere do penguins belong?
12 Which creature constructs dams and lodges?
13 What is a female fox called?
14 What does a rattlesnake rattle when it is disturbed?
15 What is the larva of a butterfly or moth called?
16 Which country were Newfoundland dogs originally from?
17 The moose or elk are species of which creature?
18 What sort of plant is a common puffball?
19 On which continent is the opossum found in its natural habitat?
20 Which American creature is renowned for its foul-smelling defence mechanism?
21 What can be great white, tiger or whale?
22 What colour is a West Highland terrier?
23 Bile is a secretion of which organ of the body?
24 What colour are the bracts of a poinsettia?
25 What is snake poison called?
26 A shoal is a group of what type of creatures?
27 How many sets of teeth do most mammals have?
28 Which is larger, the wallaby or the kangaroo?
29 Does a skipjack, jump, skip or swim?
30 Where are emus found in their natural habitat?

Quiz 9 Pot Luck 4

1   In which month is Epiphany?
2   Who went with Christopher Robin to Buckingham Palace?
3   In which TV series did Mrs Slocombe and Mr Humphries first appear?
4   What word can go after "sand" and before "account"?
5   In which country is the city of Amritsar?
6   Which Amateur Association has the abbreviation AAA?
7   Who wrote the novel *Rebecca*?
8   The characters Jason and Sable appeared in which TV soap?
9   Moving clockwise on a dartboard what number is next to 1?
10 In which decade of the 20th century was Richard Attenborough born?
11 What is the name of Del Trotter's local?
12 How many yards in a chain?
13 The zodiac sign Pisces covers which two calendar months?
14 Steve Backley is associated with which branch of athletics?
15 How is Charles Holley better known?
16 Who was the first German to be *Football Writers'* Player of the Year?
17 In the Bible, which Book immediately follows Genesis?
18 What is 80 per cent of 400?
19 Frigophobia is the fear of what?
20 In the 80s, who had a No. 1 with "Eternal Flame"?
21 Charles de Gaulle airport is in which country?
22 Which Andrew starred in "Fawlty Towers"?
23 What device goes across a guitar fretboard to raise the pitch?
24 In printing, uppercase are what type of letters?
25 Beta is the second letter of which alphabet?
26 In which game would you find a night watchman?
27 Which Italian dictator was the founder of Fascism?
28 Which UK car manufacturer produced the Anglia?
29 Who played the characters of Simon Templar and Maverick?
30 In song, in which Row was Mother Kelly's doorstep?

Quiz 10 UK Football

Answers - see page 20

LEVEL 1

1 Which Steve scored Leicester's 1997 League Cup Final winner?
2 What was Daniel Amokachi's first English league club?
3 Who followed Ossie Ardiles as manager of Spurs?
4 Who was Arsenal's regular keeper in the 1970-71 double season?
5 Which player was nicknamed "The Divine Ponytail"?
6 Which was the first English club to install an artificial pitch?
7 Who was Blackburn's benefactor of the 90s?
8 Robins, Valiants and Addicks are all nicknames of which team?
9 How many England caps did Steve Bruce win?
10 What colour are Colombian international shirts?
11 Who moved from Aston Villa to Bari for over £5 million in 1991?
12 What was Darren Anderton's first league club?
13 Which Ted scored nine goals in an FA Cup game for Bournemouth?
14 Keeper Chris Woods set a British record for clean sheets at which club?
15 Who became the first female football club managing director?
16 Who was manager when Ipswich first won the FA Cup?
17 Stan Collymore won his first England cap while at which club?
18 Which former Manchester United star also turned out for Fulham and Hibs?
19 Peter Schmeichel plays for which country?
20 What was Gazza's first London club?
21 Which Marco was three times European Footballer of the Year?
22 Tony Parkes was caretaker manager of which Premiership club?
23 Which Premiership team had three points deducted in 1996-7?
24 What has been Bolton's home ground for most of the 20th century?
25 Vinny Jones has played for which country?
26 At which club did Alan Shearer start his league career?
27 Who was Celtic's boss when they first won the European Cup?
28 Which Italian side did Gazza play for?
29 Which club did Alex Ferguson leave to go to Manchester United?
30 Which Spurs keeper scored in a 60s Charity Shield game?

Answers

50s Films (see Quiz 12)
1 *The Ten Commandments*. 2 Charlton Heston. 3 Dog. 4 *Peter Pan*.
5 *Ben Hur*. 6 David Niven. 7 Walt Disney. 8 World War II. 9 Burton.
10 *The Bridge on the River Kwai*. 11 Elvis Presley. 12 Seatbelts.
13 Zanuck. 14 Chevalier. 15 Frank Sinatra. 16 Deborah Kerr. 17 Marlon
Brando. 18 *Rebel Without a Cause*. 19 Brigitte Bardot. 20 Gene Kelly.
21 Circus. 22 Lavender Hill. 23 Grace (Kelly). 24 *Vertigo*. 25 Humphrey
Bogart. 26 Dirk Bogarde. 27 *Annie Get Your Gun*. 28 Doris Day.
29 *Carousel*. 30 None.

Quiz 11 Pot Luck 5

LEVEL 1

1   St Winifred's School Choir sang about which relative?
2   Which colour describes Victorian photographs?
3   In which decade of the 20th century was Joan Baez born?
4   What word can go after "egg" and before "board"?
5   How is Rocco Marchegiano better known?
6   In the 90s, which London club had the "Famous Five" strike force?
7   Who wrote the novel *The Water Babies*?
8   What colour is a female blackbird?
9   What does VE stand for in VE Day?
10 What type of pastry is used to make profiteroles?
11 In the group's name, what comes after Bonzo Dog?
12 Which Nicholas starred in "Goodnight Sweetheart"?
13 In which country is the city of Antwerp?
14 How many degrees in a semicircle?
15 In the 80s, who had a No. 1 with "One Moment In Time"?
16 Which BBC TV gardener died suddenly of a heart attack in 1996?
17 If Boxing Day is a Friday what day is December 1?
18 Which Al won an Oscar for Best Actor in *Scent Of A Woman*?
19 What is the female equivalent of the rank of Earl?
20 What word can follow "light", "green" and "slaughter"?
21 Dennis Amis is associated with which sport?
22 What is a scout rally called?
23 Puccini died in which century?
24 Whose catchphrase was "Stop messing about"?
25 Au is the chemical symbol for which element?
26 What, according to proverb, breeds contempt?
27 Which French phrase used in English means a false step or mistake?
28 In which TV series did the characters Steed and Emma Peel appear?
29 What is the square root of 9?
30 What does the C stand for in the business organization the CBI?

Quiz 12 50s films

LEVEL 1

1   Which film told of Moses leading the Israelites to the Promised Land?
2   Who starred as Moses in the film?
3   What or who is Lady in *Lady and the Tramp*?
4   Which film of J.M. Barrie's book was described as "a painful travesty"?
5   Which 11-Oscar-winning film of 1959 cost four million dollars?
6   Who was the star of *Around the World in Eighty Days*?
7   Which film company released *Sleeping Beauty*?
8   The action of *South Pacific* takes place during which war?
9   Which Welsh actor Richard starred in *The Robe*?
10 Which 1957 film had the whistled "Colonel Bogey" as its theme?
11 Who played the pop star in *Jailhouse Rock*?
12 What completes the line from "All About Eve", "Fasten your _____, it's going to be a bumpy night"?
13 What was the surname of film the director Darryl F?
14 Which Maurice starred in *Gigi*?
15 Which US singer had an acting role in *From Here to Eternity*?
16 Which actress starred in *From Here to Eternity* and *The King and I*?
17 Who played the starring role of Terry in *On the Waterfront*?
18 Which film catapulted James Dean to stardom?
19 Which French star appeared in *And God Created Woman* set in St Tropez?
20 Which dancer/singer was the "American in Paris"?
21 Which entertainment features in *The Greatest Show on Earth*?
22 Which Ealing comedy Mob organized a bullion robbery?
23 Which future Princess starred in Hitchcock's *Rear Window*?
24 Which Hitchcock film features a detective who was afraid of heights?
25 Who played the boozy Charlie Allnut in *The African Queen*?
26 Which British actor was Simon Sparrow in the Doctor films?
27 Which musical told of the life of Annie Oakley?
28 Which singer/actress starred opposite Rock Hudson in *Pillow Talk*?
29 Which film featured "You'll Never Walk Alone"?
30 How many Oscars did *High Society* win?

Quiz 13 Pot Luck 6

Answers - see page 23

1   If it's Friday and it's five o'clock, what else is it in children's TV terms?
2   Which two colours are most frequently confused in colour blindness?
3   In which decade of the 20th century was Roger Bannister born?
4   What word can go after "neighbour" and before "wink"?
5   In the 90s, who had a No. 1 with "Always On My Mind"?
6   Moving anticlockwise on a dartboard, what number is next to 4?
7   Who wrote the novel *Lady Chatterley's Lover*?
8   Dennis Andries is associated with which sport?
9   In which country is the city of Bulawayo?
10 In which TV series did Sharon, Tracey and Dorian appear?
11 How many pints in a gallon?
12 What was the name of Dick Turpin's horse?
13 In which decade did Radio 1 start?
14 Wilkins Micawber appears in which Charles Dickens novel?
15 How is Allen Konigsberg better known?
16 Who was the only Robbie in England's Euro 96 squad?
17 Which group of workers does ABTA represent?
18 The character Pete Beal appeared in which TV soap?
19 What can be cardinal or ordinal?
20 In *Cinderella*, what was the pumpkin turned in to?
21 What is the administrative centre for the county of Cornwall?
22 Which Henry starred in "Happy Days"?
23 The airline Luxair is from which country?
24 How does 7.20 p.m. appear on a 24-hour clock?
25 Which Frank created Billy Bunter?
26 In pre-decimal money how many farthings were in a penny?
27 The film *The Great Rock 'n' Roll Swindle* was about which group?
28 Whose catchphrase is "It's the way I tell 'em!"?
29 Which military tune is sounded at the start of the day?
30 How many sides has a rhombus?

Answers

Pop: The 60s (see Quiz 15)

1 The Beach Boys. 2 Monkees. 3 Elvis Presley. 4 Paperback Writer.
5 The Bee Gees. 6 The Kinks. 7 Supremes. 8 The Hollies. 9 Her feet.
10 Helen Shapiro. 11 Yes. 12 Springfield. 13 Matchstick. 14 Jim Reeves.
15 The Tremeloes. 16 Liverpool. 17 Frank Ifield. 18 Dozy. 19 Proby.
20 San Francisco. 21 Dave Clark. 22 Bob Dylan. 23 Faithfull. 24 US.
25 Martin. 26 Move. 27 Herman. 28 Lonnie Donegan. 29 John Lennon.
30 The Twist.

Quiz 14 TV: Who's Who?

Answers - see page 24

LEVEL 1

1 Who formed the Black Abbots and had a TV Madhouse?
2 Which Paula presented "The Tube" and "Big Breakfast"?
3 What is the profession of Miriam Stoppard?
4 What do Jilly Goolden and Oz Clarke of "Food and Drink" sample?
5 Which Jeremy has fronted "Newsnight" and "University Challenge"?
6 Which Gaby presented the first series of "Whatever You Want"?
7 Barry Norman fronts a long-running show on which subject?
8 Which Sue co-presented ITV's 1997 "Election Night" programme?
9 What are the first names of Wood and Walters?
10 Which David presents sports programmes such as skiing and snooker?
11 Which part of the UK is GMTV's Lorraine Kelly from?
12 Which Mr Whiteley presents "Countdown"?
13 Which Alan replaced the late Geoff Hamilton on "Gardener's World"?
14 What is the surname of the actor David and his brother, the newsreader John?
15 Which Michael has been from "Pole to Pole"?
16 Which outspoken American interviewed the Duchess of York?
17 Which Eamonn spoke the first words on GMTV?
18 Who is Mrs Lenny Henry?
19 Which talented cartoonist presents "Animal Hospital"?
20 Which knight presents a breakfast programme on Sundays?
21 Which Carol was the first woman on Channel Four?
22 Who presented "Blue Peter" and "Duncan Dares"?
23 Which Julia reads the news for ITN?
24 Which Terry helped present "Animal Magic" and "The Really Wild Show"?
25 Which Jill replaced Sue Cook on "Crimewatch UK"?
26 What type of programme is Sophie Grigson most likely to present?
27 Which Chris was on "Tiswas" and has been "on TV"?
28 Bill Giles provides information about what on TV?
29 Which Matthew presents "Stars in Their Eyes"?
30 Which Carol was the first presenter of the midweek Lottery?

Quiz 15 Pop: The 60s

Answers - see page 21

LEVEL 1

1 Who went "Surfin' USA"?
2 Micky Dolenz found fame in which simian-sounding group?
3 Who was Crying In the Chapel?
4 Which Beatles hit starts "Dear Sir or Madam, will you read my book"?
5 Brothers Barry, Maurice and Robin formed which group?
6 Who mocked the clothes conscious with "Dedicated Follower of Fashion"?
7 Diana Ross fronted which Tamla group?
8 Which group loved Jennifer Eccles?
9 Which part of her body did Sandie Shaw bare on stage?
10 Who sang "Don't Treat Me Like A Child" while still at school?
11 Were the Everley brothers actually brothers?
12 Which Dusty was Going Back?
13 Status Quo first charted with Pictures of what type of Men?
14 Which country-style singer was known as Gentleman Jim?
15 Who backed Brian Poole?
16 Which city did the Searchers come from?
17 Which Australian yodelled "I Remember You"?
18 Who completed the line-up with Dave Dee, Beaky, Mick and Tich?
19 Which trouser splitting singer had the initials PJ ?
20 Which city did the Flowerpot Men want to go to?
21 Whose Five were in Bits And Pieces?
22 Critics said Donovan was a British copy of which US performer?
23 Which Marianne was linked with Mick Jagger?
24 Which country did Roy Orbison come from?
25 Which George produced the Beatles' records?
26 Which group recorded "Flowers In The Rain"?
27 Who was backed by Hermits?
28 Who managed to get to No. 1 with a song about a dustman?
29 Which John wanted to Give Peace A Chance at the end of the 60s?
30 Which dance was Chubby Checker doing at the start of the 60s?

Quiz 16 Pot Luck 7

Answers - see page 22

1 What nationality was Herb Alpert's Flea?
2 What is alopecia?
3 Sue Barker played which sport?
4 What word can go after "lance" and before "punishment"?
5 How is Frederick Austerlitz better known?
6 Which defender won 43 England caps while with Blackpool?
7 Who wrote the novel *Tinker, Tailor, Soldier, Spy*?
8 On which lake was Donald Campbell killed?
9 Beauty of Bath and Discovery are types of what?
10 In which decade of the 20th century was Tony Benn born?
11 Who died after being wounded in the heel by an arrow from Paris?
12 Which Nick starred in "Heartbeat"?
13 Which of the Beatles was the shortest?
14 What word can go before "auction", "courage" and "uncle"?
15 Which duo had a 70s hit with "Welcome Home"?
16 The band leader Glen Miller died in what type of tragedy?
17 In which British cathedral is the Whispering Gallery?
18 Who was the first presenter of "Blockbusters"?
19 In rhyme, where do you go to see a fine lady on a white horse?
20 Warm weather in autumn is described as what type of summer?
21 On a Monopoly board, what colour is Trafalgar Square?
22 What type of play is performed at Oberammergau?
23 In the song "Aquarius" which planet does Jupiter align with?
24 Which French phrase used in English means each dish individually priced?
25 In which TV series did Tinker and Lady Jane appear?
26 In the 90s, who had a No. 1 with "Sacrifice"?
27 Which Anthony won an Oscar for Best Actor in *The Silence Of the Lambs*?
28 What term describes the highest point of a triangle?
29 In which country is the city of Casablanca?
30 Who loads his van "Early in the morning, Just as day is dawning"?

Quiz 17 Food & Drink 1

Answers - see page 27

1   What colour is crème de menthe?
2   Which county does Wensleydale cheese traditionally come from?
3   What type of vegetable is a Maris Piper?
4   What are the two main ingredients of a vinaigrette dressing?
5   What is the fruit flavour of Cointreau?
6   What type of food is coley?
7   What is basmati?
8   Which food accompaniment is Dijon famous for?
9   What is a small segment of garlic called?
10   What is the main ingredient of a traditional fondue?
11   What type of food is pitta?
12   Which shellfish are in Moules Marinière?
13   What is the top layer of a Queen of Puddings made from?
14   What type of meat is brisket?
15   What colour is paprika?
16   What is the chief vegetable ingredient of coleslaw?
17   At which stage of a meal would you have an hors d'oeuvre?
18   What type of drink is Darjeeling?
19   If a coffee was drunk au lait, what would it have added to it?
20   What is a tortilla?
21   What is a vol-au-vent made from?
22   Is a schnitzel sweet or savoury?
23   What colour is the flesh of an avocado?
24   Which red jelly is a traditional accompaniment to lamb?
25   What type of drink is Perrier?
26   What is mulligatawny?
27   What is filo?
28   What sort of fish is a kipper?
29   If a drink was served "on the rocks" what would it have in the glass?
30   What colour is the sauce served over a prawn cocktail?

Quiz 18 Pot Luck 8

Answers - see page 28

1   In the 90s, who had a No. 1 with "Pray"?
2   In the Bible, which Book immediately follows Matthew?
3   In which decade of the 20th century was Stuart Pearce born?
4   What word can go after "pad" and before "smith"?
5   In which country is the city of Crakow (or Kraków)?
6   In which TV series did the character Margaret Meldrew appear?
7   Who wrote the novel *Polo*?
8   In which month is St David's Day?
9   "Bush bush!" are the last words of which song?
10 What colour is the wax covering Edam cheese?
11 How did Marc Bolan die?
12 At the rate of 17·5 per cent, what VAT would be added to a £100 item?
13 Thermophobia is the fear of what?
14 Trevor Bailey is associated with which sport?
15 How is John Barry Prendergast better known?
16 In the UK's first million-pound soccer deal, which club bought Trevor Francis ?
17 In South Africa what does ANC stand for?
18 What part of the body did Adam not have that all other men do?
19 In which decade did Channel 4 start?
20 C is the chemical symbol for which element?
21 Which UK car manufacturer produced the Imp?
22 Which Su stared in "Hi-De-Hi!"?
23 Who was Jan's singing partner?
24 RED ANGER is an anagram of which job?
25 How many ounces in a pound?
26 Who produced Ike and Tina Turner's "River Deep, Mountain High"?
27 Which country was Nerys Hughes born in?
28 Moving clockwise on a dartboard what number is next to 5?
29 The character Meg Richardson appeared in which TV soap?
30 What is a Pontefract cake made of?

Answers

The 50s (see Quiz 20)
1 Conservative. **2** Campbell. **3** George VI. **4** Agatha Christie. **5** Suez.
6 Miss World. **7** Graham. **8** Winston Churchill. **9** Richards. **10** Eden.
11 Golding. **12** Car crash. **13** Eva Péron (Evita). **14** Reaching Everest's summit. **15** X certificate. **16** Marciano. **17** Dan Dare. **18** Australia.
19 Cuba. **20** Diamonds. **21** Smog. **22** London. **23** Anne Frank.
24 "The Goon Show". **25** Hutton. **26** Liberace. **27** Munich. **28** Gaitskell.
29 Kelly. **30** Wright.

Quiz 19 The Royals

Answers - see page 25

1   In which decade did Prince Charles marry Lady Diana Spencer?
2   What was Sarah Duchess of York's maiden name?
3   Prince Michael's title is of which county?
4   Who is the elder of Prince Andrew's daughters, Beatrice or Eugenie?
5   What is Princess Anne's son's first name?
6   Which royal title do Princess Anne's children have?
7   What was the occupation of Princess Margaret's first husband?
8   What was the name of the king who abdicated in 1936?
9   What was the surname of the woman he married a year later?
10 What was the name of the first monarch of the 20th century?
11 Which Duchess comforted a weeping Jana Novotna at Wimbledon?
12 Which royal yacht will be out of service from the end of the 1990s?
13 What is the Queen's residence in Norfolk called?
14 Which school did Prince William attend in his teens?
15 Who is next in line to the throne after Prince William?
16 With which royal did Captain Peter Townsend have a romance?
17 What was the name of the king immediately before Elizabeth II?
18 Which royal has a daughter called Zara?
19 Which royal couple organized a large golden-wedding anniversary celebration in 1997?
20 Which royal highlighted the problems of landmines in Angola?
21 Who had a father called Prince Andrew and has a son called Prince Andrew?
22 In which cathedral did Charles and Diana marry?
23 In which decade did Elizabeth II come to the throne?
24 How many children did she have when she became Queen?
25 Whose country home is at Highgrove?
26 Which birthday did the Queen Mother celebrate in 1996?
27 How many grandchildren does she have?
28 Who is the Queen Mother's younger daughter?
29 Which Princess is married to Angus Ogilvy?
30 What was Lord Mountbatten's first name?

Answers

Food & Drink 1 (see Quiz 17)

1 Green. 2 Yorkshire. 3 Potato. 4 Oil, vinegar. 5 Orange. 6 Fish.
7 Rice. 8 Mustard. 9 Clove. 10 Cheese. 11 Bread. 12 Mussels.
13 Meringue. 14 Beef. 15 Red. 16 Cabbage. 17 Beginning. 18 Tea.
19 Milk. 20 Pancake. 21 Pastry. 22 Savoury. 23 Green. 24 Redcurrant.
25 Mineral water. 26 Soup. 27 Pastry. 28 Herring. 29 Ice cubes.
30 Pink.

Quiz 20 The 50s

LEVEL 1

1 In 1959, which party was elected for the third time in a row in Britain?
2 Which Donald set a world water speed record in the Lake District?
3 Which monarch died at Sandringham in 1952?
4 *The Mousetrap* opened its London stage run, but who wrote it?
5 Colonel Nasser nationalized which canal?
6 The first of which contest was won by a woman from Sweden in 1951?
7 Which American evangelist Billy led a London crusade?
8 Which 77-year-old was returned as British Prime Minister?
9 Which Sir Gordon won the Derby for the first time?
10 Which Anthony became British Prime Minister in the 50s?
11 *Lord of the Flies* was written by which author William?
12 How did James Dean die?
13 Who died in the 50s and was played on film by Madonna in the 90s?
14 What was the peak of Edmund Hilary's achievements in 1953?
15 Which film classification was introduced to show films were unsuitable for the under 16s?
16 Which Rocky retired undefeated as a professional boxer?
17 Which character in children's comics was the "Pilot Of The Future"?
18 Robert Menzies was PM of which country throughout the 50s?
19 Fidel Castro seized power in which country?
20 What, according to Marilyn Monroe, were a girl's best friend?
21 What was a London pea-souper?
22 The 1951 Festival of Britain was centred on which city?
23 The diary of which young girl hiding from the Germans was published?
24 Which radio show featured Bluebottle and Eccles?
25 Which Len captained England as they won the Ashes?
26 Which entertainer said, "I cried all the way to the bank"?
27 Manchester United's Bobby Charlton survived a plane crash in which city?
28 Which Hugh became leader of the Labour Party?
29 Which Grace married Prince Rainier of Monaco?
30 Which Billy became the first English soccer player to win 100 caps?

Quiz 21 Pot Luck 9

LEVEL 1

1 How many zeros in a million written in digits?
2 Which TV series featured the characters Raquel and Uncle Albert?
3 Packham's Triumph and Conference are types of what?
4 What word can go after "bottle" and before "manager"?
5 How is George Ivan Morrison better known?
6 Which footballing Jack was nicknamed the Giraffe?
7 Who wrote the novel *Rumpole of the Bailey*?
8 What is East Pakistan now called?
9 On which hill did Fats Domino find his thrill?
10 In which decade of the 20th century was Ian Botham born?
11 In which country is the city of Durban?
12 Which Kevin stared in "Inspector Morse"?
13 What note is written in the space above the bottom line of the treble clef?
14 What word can go before "brother", "orange" and "thirsty"?
15 Brian Barnes is associated with which sport?
16 Which is greater 2/3 or 1/2?
17 The character Sheila Grant appeared in which TV soap?
18 Who joins Ginger, Baby, Sporty and Posh to make up the Spice Girls?
19 Which French phrase used in English means have a good journey?
20 In 1974 parts of Durham and Yorkshire made which new county?
21 Bob Woolmer played cricket for which country?
22 What was advertised as "your flexible friend"?
23 Which British film won nine Oscars in 1997?
24 Which planet in our solar system has the fewest letters in its name?
25 Which Daniel won an Oscar for Best Actor in *My Left Foot*?
26 What is the square root of 16?
27 In which activity do you purl and cast off?
28 In the Bible, who was paid 30 pieces of silver?
29 What colour is the famous big book in "This Is Your Life"?
30 In the 60s, who had a No. 1 with "House Of The Rising Sun"?

1   What name is given to a small, portable computer?
2   COBOL is common business-orientated what?
3   A molecule of water contains how many atoms of oxygen?
4   The study of fluids moving in pipes is known as what?
5   What is the process by which plants make food using light?
6   In a three-pronged plug what is the colour of the live wire?
7   Which small portable tape players were introduced by Sony?
8   Frank Whittle first produced what type of engine?
9   What is the chemical symbol for lead?
10 What do the initials LCD stand for?
11 Gouache is a type of what ?
12 In the 30s the Biro brothers produced the first low-cost what?
13 What device produces the air/petrol mix used in internal combustion engines?
14 Which Alfred invented dynamite and gelignite?
15 Sellafield is in which county in England?
16 What name is given to a screen picture that represents a standard computer function?
17 Which vehicle did J.C. Bamford give his name to?
18 What fuel is used by a Bunsen burner?
19 Which Michael invented the dynamo and the transformer?
20 What sort of pressure does a barometer measure?
21 In which decade did colour programmes first go out on British TV?
22 Which Chicago tower built in the 70s became the world's tallest building?
23 Clarence Birdseye developed processes for doing what to food?
24 Where in the Ukraine did a nuclear reactor explode in 1986?
25 Coal is composed of which element?
26 Watt, a unit of power, is named after which scientist?
27 In computing, WYSIWYG stands for "what you see is ..." what?
28 Which Bill founded Microsoft?
29 Which Sir Francis gave his name to a scale of wind force?
30 What does a Geiger counter measure?

Quiz 23 Pot Luck 10

Answers - see page 29

1   In the 70s, which future MP had a shaved head to play a Tudor monarch?
2   Who is Gail's second husband in "Coronation Street"?
3   In which decade of the 20th century was Cliff Richard born?
4   The zodiac sign Taurus covers which two calendar months?
5   In the Bible, which book immediately follows the first book of Samuel?
6   Wally Barnes is associated with which sport?
7   Who wrote the novel *Kidnapped*?
8   What word can go after "boxing" and before "puppet"?
9   The campaign ASH stands for Action on what?
10 In which TV series did Superintendent Jane Tennison appear?
11 How many centimetres in seven metres?
12 In the 80s, who had a No. 1 with "Who's That Girl"?
13 The character Scott Robinson appeared in which TV soap?
14 In which country is the city of Fez?
15 How is John Lydon better known?
16 Barry Venison and Dean Saunders played for which Turkish team?
17 On a Monopoly board, what colour is the Angel, Islington?
18 Which UK car manufacturer produced the Elan?
19 Which saint's day follows Christmas Day?
20 Who in "Coronation Street" died of a heart attack after a road-rage incident?
21 What is the administrative centre for the county of Bedfordshire?
22 Which Melvyn starred in "It Ain't Half Hot, Mum"?
23 What term describes a triangle with two equal sides?
24 Who originally recorded "Light My Fire"?
25 Entebbe airport is in which country?
26 Which rugby league team are the Eagles?
27 In which decade did the writer Laurie Lee die?
28 Moving anticlockwise on a dartboard what number is next to 19?
29 What is the name of Dot Cotton's nasty son in "EastEnders"?
30 What colour is quartz citrine?

Answers

Pot Luck 9 (see Quiz 21)

1 Six. 2 "Only Fools and Horses". 3 Pears. 4 "Bank". 5 Van Morrison.
6 Charlton. 7 John Mortimer. 8 Bangladesh. 9 Blueberry. 10 50s.
11 South Africa. 12 Whately. 13 F. 14 "Blood". 15 Golf. 16 2/3.
17 "Brookside". 18 Scary. 19 Bon voyage. 20 Cleveland. 21 England.
22 Access Card. 23 *The English Patient*. 24 Mars. 25 Day-Lewis.
26 4. 27 Knitting. 28 Judas Iscariot. 29 Red. 30 The Animals.

Quiz 24 Movies: Superstars

LEVEL 1

Answers - see page 30

1   Who played the head of the Corleone family in *The Godfather*?
2   Which Welsh actor starred opposite Debra Winger in *Shadowlands*?
3   Who played Han Solo in *Star Wars*?
4   Which Jack starred with Shirley Maclaine in *Terms of Endearment*?
5   Which Eddie's most famous role is in *Beverley Hills Cop*?
6   Which British Michael won an Oscar for *Hannah and her Sisters*?
7   Which Jack's films vary from *Some Like It Hot* to *The Odd Couple*?
8   Which Mrs Bruce Willis starred in *Ghost*?
9   Which Katherine has received a record 12 Oscar nominations?
10 Who starred in and wrote the song "Evergreen" for *A Star is Born*?
11 Which Warren starred in *Dick Tracy* and *Bugsy Malone*?
12 Which Paul was in *The Sting* and *The Color of Money*?
13 Although born in the US, where was Mel Gibson brought up?
14 Who won Oscars for *Philadelphia* in '93 and *Forrest Gump* in '94?
15 Who was the female Kramer in *Kramer v Kramer*?
16 In which decade did Sylvester Stallone first play Rambo?
17 Which country was Sean Connery born in?
18 Which Al won an Oscar for his role in *Scent of a Woman*?
19 Who was in *Rain Man* and was one of Four Good Men?
20 What "Color" is in the title of Whoopi Goldberg's first major film?
21 Which Nick starred in *The Prince of Tides*?
22 Which Bruce is co-owner of "Planet Hollywood"?
23 Who starred in *Every Which Way But Loose* and *The Outlaw Josey Wales*?
24 Which superstar played the title role in *Hook*?
25 Who married her seventh husband in Michael Jackson's garden?
26 Which Kevin played the President in *JFK*?
27 Whose film and TV appearances range from *Ben Hur* to "The Colbys"?
28 Who was in *Bugsy Malone* and *Taxi Driver* as a child and went on to *The Accused*?
29 Which Robert starred with Dustin Hoffman in *All the President's Men*?
30 Which Michelle played Catwoman in *Batman Returns*?

Answers

Technology & Industry (see Quiz 22)
1 Laptop. **2** Language. **3** One. **4** Hydraulics. **5** Photosynthesis. **6** Brown.
7 Walkmans. **8** Jet. **9** Pb. **10** Liquid crystal display. **11** Paint. **12** Biro
(ball-point pen). **13** Carburettor. **14** Nobel. **15** Cumbria. **16** Icon. **17** JCB.
18 Gas. **19** Faraday. **20** Atmospheric. **21** 60s. **22** Sears Tower.
23 Freezing it. **24** Chernobyl. **25** Carbon. **26** James Watt. **27** What you
get. **28** Gates. **29** Beaufort. **30** Radioactivity.

Quiz 25 Pot Luck 11

Answers - see page 35

LEVEL 1

1   Which TV show has an anagram puzzle called the Conundrum?
2   Who were the first team to win the FA Premiership?
3   In which decade of the 20th century was Elton John born?
4   In which country is the city of Kathmandu?
5   In which TV programme did Florence and Zebedee appear?
6   Ca is the chemical symbol for which element?
7   Who wrote the novel *Dracula*?
8   What is 1/3 as a percentage to two decimal places?
9   The character Len Fairclough appeared in which TV soap?
10   Which song features "the girl with kaleidoscope eyes"?
11   Which fruit do Macintosh computers use as a logo?
12   Which Jan starred in "Just Good Friends"?
13   Ken Barrington is associated with which sport?
14   What word can go before "thorn", "sand" and "silver"?
15   Miss Havisham appears in which Charles Dickens novel?
16   Which instrument was Nat King Cole famous for playing?
17   Who won an Oscar for Best Actor in *Rain Man* in 1989?
18   Who sang "On The Good Ship Lollipop"?
19   Which present-day country do we associate with the Magyars?
20   Which Damon was BBC Sports Personality of the Year in 1994?
21   Doctors Jack Kerruish and Beth Glover appeared in which TV series?
22   What make of car was the 1906 Silver Ghost?
23   In which month is St Swithin's Day?
24   What word can go after "slip" and before "rage"?
25   How is the actor Michel Shalhoub better known?
26   What colour was Gazza's hair during Euro 96?
27   In the 70s, who had a No. 1 with "We Don't Talk Anymore"?
28   The Kalahari desert is in which continent?
29   Which magician hosted "Every Second Counts"?
30   Which duke is associated with Arundel Castle?

Quiz 26 Sport: Who's Who?

LEVEL 1

Answers - see page 36

1   Which Ben won the US Masters in 1995?
2   Was Geoff Boycott left- or right-handed as a batsman?
3   Which Spaniard won the Tour de France from 1991 to 1995?
4   Which Chris was WBO super middleweight champion in 1991?
5   Who was the first jockey to go through a seven-race card?
6   Who is the Crafty Cockney?
7   Who was the manager that took Chesterfield to the FA Cup semis?
8   Which Nigel was Formula 1 world champion in the 80s?
9   Which country does Greg Norman come from?
10 Which Australian tycoon was responsible for World Series Cricket?
11 Who was West Indian skipper for the 1996 World Cup?
12 Who was the National Hunt champion jockey from 1986 to 1992?
13 Who was Smokin' Joe?
14 In the 90s, who tried to claim 5 per cent of his transfer fee from Forest to Liverpool?
15 Woodforde and Woodbridge are partners in which sport?
16 Which snooker star was born on August 22 1957 in Plumstead?
17 Which golfer Sandy won the British Open in the 80s?
18 Who was the jockey who rode Aldaniti to Grand National success?
19 Who succeeded Jack Charlton as soccer boss of the Republic of Ireland?
20 Which England captain had his name linked with the Princess of Wales?
21 Who announced in September '96 that he would race for the TWR Arrows?
22 Who was the first male Brit to make Wimbledon's last eight in the 90s?
23 Who retired aged 30 after winning the Premiership with Man. Utd?
24 Which Jo played Wightman Cup tennis for Britain through the 80s?
25 Who was manager of Nottingham Forest throughout the 80s?
26 In February '96, which English jockey suffered severe head injuries in a Hong Kong race?
27 Which unseeded MaliVai reached the 1996 Wimbledon men's final?
28 In 1997, who scored the quickest ever FA Cup Final goal?
29 Who was the England cricket skipper in the ball-tampering claims of 1994?
30 Which scrum-half Gareth forged a partnership with Barry John for Cardiff and Wales?

Answers

TV Times 1 (see Quiz 28)
1 Robinson. 2 Gower, Lineker. 3 Cookery. 4 Detective. 5 "Songs of Praise".
6 "The X Files". 7 Doctor. 8 Feltz. 9 "999". 10 David. 11 Motoring.
12 Four. 13 Hamilton. 14 David Coleman. 15 "Peak Practice".
16 Pathologist. 17 Oxford. 18 Hospital. 19 Deayton. 20 "Absolutely
Fabulous". 21 "Newsnight". 22 Bean. 23 9 p.m.. 24 Victor Meldrew.
25 "Ballykissangel". 26 Three. 27 Norden. 28 After. 29 Thaw.
30 Yorkshire.

Quiz 27 Pot Luck 12

Answers - see page 33

1   In Cockney rhyming slang, what are 'plates of meat'?
2   The character Michelle Fowler appeared in which TV soap?
3   Is France ahead of or behind Greenwich Mean Time?
4   What word can go after "safety" and before "aid"?
5   How is Eugene Vincent Craddock better known?
6   Who managed the first English side to win soccer's European Cup?
7   Who wrote the novel *The Hobbit*?
8   Bill Beaumont is associated with which sport?
9   What does the C stand for in CBE?
10 In which decade of the 20th century was Barbara Cartland born?
11 Nellie and Adrian Boswell appeared in which TV series?
12 How many inches in six feet?
13 In the 90s, who had a No. 1 with "Ride On Time"?
14 When did the Super League begin in rugby league?
15 As which outspoken pensioner is Caroline Aherne better known?
16 In which play does the skull of Yorick appear?
17 In Bill Hayley's "See You Later, Alligator" what three words come before crocodile?
18 What is the capital of the Falkland Islands?
19 Who made up the trio with Emerson and Lake?
20 What number is cubed to give the answer 8?
21 In which country is the city of Kiev?
22 Which Bill starred in "Last Of The Summer Wine"?
23 Phobophobia is the fear of what?
24 Which UK car manufacturer produced the Midget?
25 Who had a No. 1 with "Three Steps To Heaven" after his death?
26 Which county have Gallian and Fairbrother played cricket for?
27 Which English king was known as the Unready?
28 Moving clockwise on a dartboard what number is next to 6?
29 Which BBC programme features Sheepdog Championships?
30 Which ex-Chancellor Norman lost his seat in 1997's general election?

Quiz 28 TV Times 1

Answers - see page 34

1 Which Anne presents "Watchdog"?
2 Which David and Gary are team captains on "They Think It's All Over"?
3 What sort of TV programmes does Sophie Grigson present?
4 What is the profession of Frost in "A Touch of Frost"?
5 What is the BBC's long-running hymn-singing programme called?
6 In which programme do Mulder and Scully appear?
7 What is the occupation of Bramwell?
8 What is the surname of a presenter called Vanessa?
9 Which show about emergencies has the name of a phone number?
10 Which Dimbleby presents the BBC's "Question Time"?
11 What is the programme "Top Gear" about?
12 In 1997, how many episodes of "Coronation Street" were there each week?
13 Which Geoff presented "Gardener's World" until his death in 1996?
14 Which chairman of "A Question of Sport" retired in 1997?
15 Which programme features the doctors of Cardale?
16 What is the profession of Sam Ryan in "Silent Witness"?
17 In which city does "Inspector Morse" take place?
18 What is the setting for "ER"?
19 Which Angus chairs "Have I Got News For You"?
20 In which sitcom did Saffron and Bubble appear?
21 Which late-evening current-affairs programme does Jeremy Paxman often present?
22 Which Sean starred on TV as Sharpe?
23 What time is the late-evening weekday news on BBC1?
24 Whose famous catchphrase is "I don't believe it!"?
25 Which comedy series was about an English priest in Ireland?
26 How many times per week is "Blue Peter" broadcast?
27 Which Denis presents "It'll Be Alright on the Night"?
28 Is the weather forecast immediately before or after "News At Ten"?
29 Which John played Kavanagh QC?
30 In which county does "Heartbeat" take place?

Quiz 29 Pot Luck 13

Answers - see page 39

1 Which Michael won an Oscar for Best Actor in *Wall Street*?
2 What sort of animal was Terry Hall's puppet Lennie?
3 In which decade of the 20th century was Jose Carreras born?
4 What word can go after "monk" and before "cake"?
5 In the 90s, who had a No. 1 with "Think Twice"?
6 How would 14 be written in Roman numerals?
7 Who wrote the novel *War And Peace*?
8 Who plays rugby union at the Recreation Ground, London Road?
9 In which UK No. 1 did Elvis Presley sing in German?
10 Whom did Margaret Thatcher follow as Conservative Party leader?
11 Quicksilver is another name for which element?
12 Which Jean starred in "Bread"?
13 Are the North Downs north of London?
14 In which country is the city of Kualalumpur?
15 How is Edward Stewart Mainwaring better known?
16 What colour are the shorts of Germany's international soccer side?
17 Dave Bedford is associated with which sport?
18 In the Bible, which book immediately follows St John's Gospel?
19 What word can follow "fruit", "rabbit" and "Suffolk"?
20 Where on the body could a cataract form?
21 Private Pike appeared in which TV series?
22 The airline Aeroflot is from which country?
23 Who wrote the Messiah?
24 What is the square root of 25?
25 Which planet is named after the Roman god of war?
26 Which scandal made US President Richard Nixon resign?
27 On a Monopoly board, what colour is Bond Street?
28 Which two brothers hosted BBC's and ITV's 1997 election-night coverage?
29 Kurt Cobain was in which grunge group?
30 The character Cliff Barnes appeared in which TV soap?

Quiz 30 Euro Tour

Answers - see page 40

1   Reykjavik is the capital of which country?
2   Which is farther south - Corsica or Sardinia?
3   Which river runs through Belgrade, Budapest and Vienna?
4   Which Peter spent a Year In Provence?
5   The Acropolis overlooks which capital city?
6   Which is the highest mountain in the Alps?
7   Do the stripes go horizontally or vertically on the Austrian flag?
8   Belgium's coast touches which sea?
9   What is the currency of Greece?
10 Which capital takes its name from a prince of Troy?
11 Which ocean is Europe's northern boundary?
12 Which mountains divide Spain from France?
13 Ankara is the capital of which country?
14 What is the currency of Denmark?
15 Which tiny European country has the European Court of Justice?
16 Which two colours make up the Greek flag?
17 Nero fiddled while which city burnt?
18 Which of the three Baltic states of the former USSR does not begin with L?
19 What is the tourist area of southern Portugal called?
20 What is the capital of Malta?
21 Which mountains are Europe's eastern boundary?
22 What is the currency of Austria?
23 The Black Forest is a mountain range in which country?
24 Which country has the regions Lazio and Calabria?
25 What is the colour of the middle of the French flag?
26 Which Sea is Europe's southern boundary?
27 Which two major European rivers begin with R?
28 What would an English-speaking person call Bretagne?
29 Sofia is the capital of which country?
30 Which country has the markka or finnmark as its currency?

Answers

Pop: No. 1s (see Quiz 32)

1 Yellow. 2 "Love Is All Around". 3 1950s. 4 "Earth Song". 5 Brother.
6 "White Cliffs Of Dover". 7 Freddie Mercury. 8 Your Daughter.
9 "Mr Blobby". 10 Kate Bush. 11 Man. Utd. 12 Blondie. 13 Elton John.
14 "Without You". 15 Cliff Richard. 16 Gabrielle. 17 Massachusetts.
18 Take That. 19 "Yellow Submarine". 20 Abba. 21 Paul Simon.
22 Country. 23 Wham!. 24 Scaffold. 25 Village People. 26 The Shadows.
27 Waltz. 28 David Bowie. 29 Rednex. 30 Two.

Quiz 31 Pot Luck 14

Answers - see page 37

LEVEL 1

1 Live Aid raised money for famine relief in which country?
2 Margo and Jerry Leadbetter appeared in which TV series?
3 In which decade of the 20th century was Kenneth Branagh born?
4 What word can go after "blue" and before "hound"?
5 Nigel Benn is associated with which sport?
6 In which country is the city of Nice?
7 In the 70s, which Suzi had a No. 1 with "Devil Gate Drive"?
8 Which UK car manufacturer produced the Oxford?
9 80 per cent of Earth's atmosphere is formed by which gas?
10 How many yards in a mile?
11 Cu is the chemical symbol for which element?
12 Agnetha Faltskog was a singer with which group?
13 Who first presented BBC 2's "University Challenge"?
14 What does the A stand for in CIA?
15 How is Burl Ivanhoe better known?
16 Who in 1991 became the youngest ever Welsh soccer international?
17 Romano and Desiree are types of what?
18 Who wanted the head of John the Baptist?
19 In song, what do you pack up in your old kit bag?
20 What part did Boris Karloff play in the 30s film *Frankenstein*?
21 What name is given to angles of less than 90 degrees?
22 Which Chris starred in "The Brittas Empire"?
23 In legend, who was the wife of King Arthur?
24 Which Beatle played guitar left-handed?
25 The character Donald Fisher appeared in which TV soap?
26 Which units are used to measure sound intensity?
27 What name is given to trimming hedges into shapes?
28 "(They Long To Be) Close To You" was the first hit for which group?
29 What was the first quiz to be seen on Channel 4?
30 Moving anticlockwise on a dartboard what number is next to 17?

Quiz 32 Pop: No. 1s

Answers - see page 38

LEVEL 1

1   What colour was Bombalurina's teeny-weeny polka-dot bikini?
2   *Four Weddings And A Funeral* made which song a No. 1?
3   In which decade did Elvis have his first UK No. 1?
4   Which Song was a UK Christmas No. 1 in 1995 for Michael Jackson?
5   Which relative features in a Hollies song title?
6   Which other song was on Robson and Jerome's "Unchained Melody"?
7   Whose death gave "Bohemian Rhapsody" a second visit to No. 1?
8   Whom should you bring to the slaughter, according to Iron Maiden?
9   What was the imaginative title of Mr Blobby's first No. 1?
10 Who charted with a song about Heathcliff and Cathy?
11 Which soccer team were involved in "Come On You Reds"?
12 Who had No. 1s with "Call Me" and "Atomic"?
13 Who sang with Kiki Dee on "Don't Go Breaking My Heart"?
14 Which song was a No. 1 for both Nilsson and Mariah Carey?
15 Which English Sir has had No. 1s in the 50s, 60s, 70s, 80s and 90s?
16 Who had Dreams in 1993?
17 Which US state was the title of a Bee Gees No. 1?
18 Which band were Back For Good in 1995?
19 Which Beatle No. 1 featured the word Yellow in the title?
20 "The Winner Takes It All" was yet another No. 1 for which group?
21 Who wrote Simon and Garfunkel's "Bridge Over Troubled Water"?
22 What type of House did Blur take to the top of the charts?
23 George Michael first hit No. 1 as a member of which duo?
24 Who took "Lily The Pink" to No. 1?
25 Who thought it was fun to stay in the YMCA?
26 Whose first UK No. 1 was "Apache"?
27 In psychedelic '67, which old-time dance gave Englebert Humperdinck a huge hit?
28 Who teamed up with Queen for "Under Pressure"?
29 Who had a No. 1 with "Cotton Eye Joe"?
30 In the Frankie Goes To Hollywood hit, how many tribes were there?

Answers

Euro Tour (see Quiz 30)

1 Iceland. 2 Sardinia. 3 Danube. 4 Mayle. 5 Athens. 6 Mont Blanc.
7 Horizontally. 8 North Sea. 9 Drachma. 10 Paris. 11 Arctic.
12 Pyrenees. 13 Turkey. 14 Krone. 15 Luxembourg. 16 Blue and white.
17 Rome. 18 Estonia. 19 The Algarve. 20 Valetta. 21 Urals.
22 Schilling. 23 Germany. 24 Italy. 25 White. 26 Mediterranean.
27 Rhine, Rhone. 28 Brittany. 29 Bulgaria. 30 Finland.

Quiz 33 Pot Luck 15

Answers - see page 43

1 Which vitamin deficiency was responsible for scurvy?
2 Which Doctor had a dog called K9?
3 Gary and Yvonne Sparrow appeared in which TV series?
4 What word can go after "honey" and before "wax"?
5 How is the comedian Thomas Derbyshire better known?
6 Steve Ogrizovic set an appearance record at which soccer club?
7 Who wrote the novel *Pride and Prejudice*?
8 Roger Black is associated with which sport?
9 How many seconds in one hour?
10 In which decade of the 20th century was Prince Charles born?
11 Who tried to mend his head with vinegar and brown paper?
12 Which Karl starred in "Brush Strokes"?
13 Where does an arboreal creature live?
14 Which descriptive word is linked with the singer John Baldry?
15 Which Henry won an Oscar for Best Actor in *On Golden Pond*?
16 What kind of bomb contains hydrogen sulphide?
17 What is the flavour of Pernod?
18 Little Nell appears in which Charles Dickens novel?
19 What word can go before "leader", "main" and "master"?
20 In which month is Hallowe'en?
21 How many people make up the panel of BBC's "Question Time"?
22 Which is smaller 5/10 or 3/4?
23 What is a hora?
24 Who sang the theme from *Goldfinger*?
25 The character Brian Tilsley appeared in which TV soap?
26 In boxing, what is the maximum number of rounds in a contest?
27 The letter S is on which row of a keyboard?
28 In the 70s, who had a No. 1 with "Mama Weer All Crazee Now"?
29 In which country is the city of Palermo?
30 Which cartoon series features Pebbles and Bam Bam?

Pot Luck 16 (see Quiz 35)
1 Black. 2 Football. 3 60s. 4 Purple. 5 July and August. 6 Cumbria.
7 H.E. Bates. 8 "Heartbeat". 9 10. 10 The Beach Boys. 11 Nine.
12 Sleepy. 13 1960s. 14 Cocktail. 15 Big Daddy. 16 Paris St Germain.
17 Germany. 18 14. 19 The Beatles. 20 Rural England. 21 Majorca.
22 Craig. 23 Two. 24 Creedence Clearwater Revival. 25 Kiwi fruit.
26 "Neighbours". 27 Faldo. 28 Reliant. 29 Makepeace. 30 Jones.

41

Quiz 34 Books

LEVEL 1

1   Charles Dodgson wrote his classic children's story under what name?
2   Which Frederick wrote *The Day of The Jackal*?
3   Fitzwilliam Darcy appears in which novel?
4   Whom did Bertie Wooster have as his manservant?
5   Which Irving Welsh novel was about Scottish heroin addicts?
6   Which county in England did Laurie Lee come from?
7   Which Arthur wrote the children's classic *Swallows and Amazons*?
8   Which James became Britain's most read vet?
9   Who created Thomas the Tank Engine?
10   Which French detective was created by Georges Simenon?
11   What was the first name of the girl who went to live at Green Gables?
12   Who created the Discworld books?
13   Which Ian created James Bond?
14   Which creatures are the central characters in *Watership Down*?
15   Who wrote *Rebecca*?
16   What was the name of the boy in *The Jungle Book*?
17   What term is used for writing a novel that will go out under someone else's name?
18   Which novelist born in 1886 had the initials H.G.?
19   What is Joseph Heller's novel with a number in its catchy title?
20   Which children's publisher has a black-and-red insect as its logo?
21   Who created Inspector Adam Dalgleish?
22   Which Douglas wrote *The Hitch Hiker's Guide To The Galaxy*?
23   Brother Cadfael belonged to which order of monks?
24   What sex was Richmal Crompton, author of the William books?
25   Which fictional barrister referred to his wife as "she who must be obeyed"?
26   Which country was Stephen King born in?
27   Which Victor wrote the novel *Les Miserables*?
28   Which Tory fundraiser wrote *Not A Penny More Not A Penny Less*?
29   Who wrote *Murder On the Orient Express*?
30   John Grisham's novels centre on which profession?

Answers

Movies: Who's Who? (see Quiz 36)

1 Brooke Shields. **2** Agutter. **3** Austria. **4** Stone. **5** Sigourney. **6** Nielsen.
7 Christopher Reeve. **8** France. **9** Kiefer. **10** Kathleen. **11** Alfred
Hitchcock. **12** Kirk. **13** Rosanna. **14** Barrymore. **15** Cher. **16** *The Doors*.
17 Madonna. **18** Woodward. **19** Sissy. **20** Curtis. **21** Woody Allen.
22 Bridges. **23** Schindler. **24** Tatum. **25** Keanu. **26** Basinger. **27** Jane.
28 Omar Sharif. **29** Bacall. **30** Gere.

Quiz 35 Pot Luck 16

Answers - see page 41

LEVEL 1

1 What colour was the contestant's chair in "Mastermind"?
2 Steve Bloomer is associated with which sport?
3 In which decade of the 20th century was Diana, Princess of Wales born?
4 On a Monopoly board, what colour is Pall Mall?
5 The zodiac sign Leo covers which two calendar months?
6 In 1974 parts of Cumberland and Westmorland made which new county?
7 Who wrote the novel *The Darling Buds Of May*?
8 Nick and Kate Rowan appeared in which TV series?
9 How many sides does a decagon have?
10 Which group featured Brian Wilson?
11 How many spaces in a noughts-and-crosses frame?
12 Which of the Seven Dwarfs was always feeling tired?
13 In which decade did man first land on the moon?
14 What word can go after "prawn" and before "dress"?
15 How is Shirley Crabtree better known?
16 David Ginola joined Newcastle from which team?
17 The airline Lufthansa is from which country?
18 Moving clockwise on a dartboard what number is next to 11?
19 In the 60s, who had a No. 1 with "Can't Buy Me Love"?
20 The CPRE is the Council for the Preservation of what?
21 In which country is the city of Palma?
22 Which Wendy starred in "Butterflies"?
23 How many pints in a quart?
24 Which group had Clearwater as their middle name?
25 What is another name for Chinese gooseberries?
26 Madge and Harold Bishop appeared in which TV soap?
27 Which Nick was BBC Sports Personality of the Year in 1989?
28 Which UK car manufacturer produced the Robin?
29 Who was the female half of Dempsey and Makepeace?
30 Which Tom led the most weeks in the singles chart list for 1968?

Pot Luck 15 (see Quiz 33)

Answers

1 C. 2 Doctor Who. 3 "Good Night Sweetheart". 4 "Bees". 5 Tommy Cannon. 6 Coventry. 7 Jane Austen. 8 Athletics. 9 3,600. 10 40s. 11 Jack (in "Jack and Jill"). 12 Howman. 13 In a tree. 14 Long. 15 Fonda. 16 Stink bomb. 17 Aniseed. 18 *The Old Curiosity Shop*. 19 "Ring". 20 October. 21 Four. 22 5/10. 23 Dance (Jewish). 24 Shirley Bassey. 25 "Coronation Street". 26 15. 27 Middle. 28 Slade. 29 Italy. 30 "The Flintstones".

Quiz 36 Movies: Who's Who?

Answers - see page 42

LEVEL 1

1 Which actress married André Agassi in 1997?

2 Which Jenny played Roberta in *The Railway Children*?

3 In which country was Arnold Schwarzenegger born?

4 Which Sharon played opposite Michael Douglas in *Basic Instinct*?

5 What did Susan Weaver change her first name to?

6 Which Leslie stars in *The Naked Gun* series of films?

7 Which Superman actor was seriously injured in a riding accident?

8 In which country was Gerard Dépardieu born?

9 Who is Donald Sutherland's actor son?

10 Which Ms Turner was the speaking voice of Jessica Rabbit?

11 Who directed *Psycho* and *The Birds*?

12 What is the first name of Michael Douglas's father?

13 What is the first name of Ms Arquette, star of *Desperately Seeking Susan*?

14 Which Drew was in *E.T.* and *Batman Forever*?

15 Which chart-topper was in *Silkwood* and *Moonstruck*?

16 In which film did Val Kilmer play the rock star Jim Morrison?

17 Which star of *Evita* was the first wife of the actor Sean Penn?

18 Which Joanne is Mrs Paul Newman?

19 How is Mary Elizabeth Spacek better known?

20 Which Tony is the father of Jamie Lee?

21 Which actor/director was born Allen Konigsberg in 1935?

22 What is the surname of the father and son actors Lloyd, Jeff and Beau?

23 Which character did Liam Neeson play in *Schindler's List*?

24 Who is the Oscar-winning daughter of Ryan O'Neal?

25 Which actor Reeves starred in *Bram Stoker's Dracula*?

26 Which Kim was the Bond girl in *Never Say Never Again*?

27 Who is Bridget Fonda's actress/fitness fanatic aunt?

28 Which talented bridge player played the title role in *Doctor Zhivago*?

29 Which Lauren was married to Humphrey Bogart?

30 Which Richard starred opposite Julia Roberts in *Pretty Woman*?

Books (see Quiz 34)

Answers

1 Lewis Carroll. 2 Forsyth. 3 *Pride and Prejudice*. 4 Jeeves.
5 *Trainspotting*. 6 Gloucestershire. 7 Rackham. 8 Herriot. 9 Rev Awdry.
10 Maigret. 11 Anne. 12 Terry Pratchett. 13 Fleming. 14 Rabbits.
15 Daphne Du Maurier. 16 Mowgli. 17 Ghosting. 18 Wells. 19 *Catch-22*.
20 Ladybird. 21 P D James. 22 Adams. 23 Benedictine. 24 Female.
25 Horace Rumpole. 26 US. 27 Hugo. 28 Jeffrey Archer. 29 Agatha
Christie. 30 Legal profession.

Quiz 37 Pot Luck 17

LEVEL 1

1   In the 90s, who had a No. 1 with "Some Might Say"?
2   Ted Bovis and Gladys Pugh appeared in which TV series?
3   In which decade of the 20th century was Bobby Charlton born?
4   What word can go after "bowling" and before "house"?
5   Bill Voce is associated with which sport?
6   In which country is the city of Saragossa?
7   Who wrote the novel *Wuthering Heights*?
8   H is the chemical symbol for which element?
9   Which Joan had a 60s hit with "There But For Fortune"?
10 The letter W is on which row of a typewriter or computer keyboard?
11 In cooking, Florentine means garnished with which vegetable?
12 Which Edward starred in "Callan"?
13 What is the square root of 36?
14 Who had a little buddy called Boo Boo?
15 The character Reg Holdsworth appeared in which TV soap?
16 Who described a wine as "sweaty gym shoes on hot tarmac"?
17 What is the administrative centre for the county of Devon?
18 What word can go before "ball", "drunk" and "line?"
19 How is Dora Broadbent better known?
20 Which Scottish soccer keeper Andy played for Oldham in the 80s?
21 Which children's TV show is based on the Guinness Book of Records?
22 At 17·5 per cent, how much VAT is added to an item priced at £300?
23 Who was singer/songwriter with the Boomtown Rats?
24 Which Robert won an Oscar for Best Actor in *Raging Bull*?
25 What is the only English anagram of WRONG?
26 Which major battle took place between July and November 1916?
27 What is the term for written or recorded defamation?
28 What are the two colours of a standard "Blue Peter" badge?
29 What is 5/8 minus 1/4?
30 Who partnered Jennifer Warnes on "Up Where We Belong"?

Quiz 38 TV Game Shows

Answers - see page 48

LEVEL 1

1　Which Gaby Roslin game show has contestants aiming to fulfil an ambition?
2　Who co-presents "Through the Keyhole" with David Frost?
3　Which TV wine expert is the presenter of "The Great Antiques Hunt"?
4　Which show introduced by Fern Britton features celebrity chefs?
5　Where does Dale Winton organize a TV Sweep?
6　Which Shane hosts "Lucky Numbers"?
7　What does Bruce Forsyth say to Play Right in the game show?
8　Which transport was used in "Treasure Hunt" with Anneka Rice?
9　What did "Strike It Lucky" change its name to?
10　Who was host in the 90s revival of "Take Your Pick"?
11　In which show did Bruce Forsyth say "What's on the board Miss Ford"?
12　What Factor was the subject of the contest to find a "superperson"?
13　Which inter-town Euro contest was hosted by Eddie Waring and Stuart Hall?
14　What was the weapon used in "The Golden Shot"?
15　Which game show is based on snooker?
16　Who introduced the very first edition of "Countdown"?
17　Which game show was based on a whodunnit board game?
18　Which show saw famous folk in a giant noughts-and-crosses board?
19　Which Mr Walker introduces "Catchphrase"?
20　Which quiz game was built around the game of darts?
21　How many contestants appear on a single panel on "Blind Date"?
22　Which Terry was the first host of "Blankety Blank"?
23　Which magician presented "Every Second Counts"?
24　What is the subject of the panel game "Going For A Song"?
25　On which Channel is "The Great Garden Game" broadcast?
26　Which Bob has presented "Call My Bluff"?
27　Which Michael first presented "Blockbusters" with older contestants?
28　What is Today in the show with Martyn Lewis?
29　Who replaced Bruce Forsyth in the 1990s "Generation Game"?
30　How many are reduced to One in the show with William G. Stewart?

Pot Luck 18 (see Quiz 40)
1 *William Tell Overture.* **2** Ceefax. **3** 40s. **4** "Clip". **5** Richard Burton.
6 Crewe. **7** Daniel Defoe. **8** Equestrianism. **9** Exchange Rate Mechanism.
10 "Just Good Friends". **11** Triumph. **12** Birmingham. **13** Open spaces.
14 U2. **15** 20. **16** "EastEnders". **17** Doncaster. **18** Mendel.
19 "Amazing Grace". **20** Circumference. **21** Germany. **22** Lindsay.
23 *The Three Musketeers.* **24** Stars. **25** First and fifth (the last). **26** Six.
27 Crosby. **28** 1,000. **29** Hairdresser. **30** D.

Quiz 39 Sporting Chance 1

Answers - see page 45

LEVEL 1

1   Which country does Ian Baker-Finch come from?

2   How many reds are there at the start of a snooker game?

3   What does BDA stand for?

4   What sport do the Buffalo Bills play?

5   In which sport is the Giro D'Italia - the Tour of Italy?

6   Which sport combines cross-country skiing and rifle shooting?

7   What is the nickname of the heavyweight James Douglas?

8   Which rugby league team are the Bears?

9   How often is golf's US Masters held?

10 James Whittaker captained which side to the County Championship?

11 How many people are there in a hurling team?

12 Shannon Miler is famous for which sport?

13 In golf, what is the term for one under par for a hole?

14 In boxing, what is the lowest weight category?

15 Hale Irwin is famous for which sport?

16 Which England captain helped set up Kerry Packer's cricket "circus"?

17 The Mackeson Gold Cup is run at which course?

18 Dave Whitcombe plays darts for which country?

19 In the 90s, who lost the two major English finals and were relegated?

20 In 1996, which country was expelled from rugby's Five Nations?

21 AXA Equity & Law League cricket games are played on which day?

22 Wentworth golf course is in which county?

23 Which newspaper supported a darts tournament from 1948 to 1990?

24 Which ball in snooker is worth seven points?

25 A cricket umpire raises both arms above his head to signal what?

26 On what day of the week is the Prix De L'Arc de Triomphe race held?

27 Aikido is the ancient Japanese art of what?

28 Which county cricket club has its home at Grace Road?

29 Was Bertie Blunt the name of the rider or the horse that won the 1996 Badminton Horse Trials?

30 In what decade did David Gower first play cricket for England?

1   Which classical overture became the "Lone Ranger" theme?
2   What is the BBC's teletext service called?
3   In which decade of the 20th century was Bill Clinton born?
4   What word can go after "paper" and before "board"?
5   How was Richard Jenkins better known?
6   Gresty Road is the home ground of which soccer club?
7   Who wrote the novel *Robinson Crusoe*?
8   Caroline Bradley is associated with which sport?
9   In monetary terms, what does ERM stand for?
10 The characters Vince and Penny appeared in which TV series?
11 Which UK car manufacturer produced the Herald?
12 What is the administrative centre for the county of West Midlands?
13 Agoraphobia is the fear of what?
14 In the 90s, who had a No. 1 with "The Fly"?
15 Moving anticlockwise on a dartboard what number is next to 1?
16 The character Frank Butcher appeared in which TV soap?
17 Which rugby league added Dragons to their name in the 90s?
18 Which Gregor was noted for experiments in genetics?
19 In song, which two words go before, "how sweet the sound, That saved a wretch like me"?
20 What is the boundary of a circle called?
21 In which country is the city of Stuttgart?
22 Which Robert starred in "Citizen Smith"?
23 Which book includes the words "All for one and one for all"?
24 Which are there more of on the USA flag - stars or stripes?
25 In a limerick, which lines should rhyme with the second line?
26 How many pockets does a snooker table have?
27 Who sang with Stills, Nash and Young?
28 How many milligrams in a gram?
29 What is Fiona Middleton's job in "Coronation Street"?
30 In music, what note is written on the line above the middle line of the treble clef?

Quiz 41 The 60s

Answers - see page 51

LEVEL 1

1 Who made the "wind of change" speech?
2 George Cohen was a member of the world's winners at which sport?
3 Which call-girl Christine was involved in a government scandal?
4 Which future Princess of Wales was born in the 60s?
5 Edwin Aldrin became the second person to walk where?
6 Who played piano while Peter Cook sang?
7 Whom did Anthony Armstrong-Jones marry in 1960?
8 How did the English comic Tony Hancock die?
9 Whom did Richard Burton marry in Canada in 1964?
10 Gaddafi seized power in which country?
11 Which D.H. Lawrence book from the 20s featured in an Old Bailey obscenity trial?
12 Bob Dylan starred at a 1969 rock Festival on which British isle?
13 Which doctor's report led to the cutting of the railway network?
14 George Blake gained notoriety as what?
15 Which Francis sailed solo round the world?
16 Who became the youngest ever USA President?
17 Who was involved with John Lennon in a "bed-in" for peace?
18 Which President originally blocked Britain's entry into the EEC?
19 Which country banned a tour by England's cricketers?
20 Which country made the first manned space flight?
21 The Torrey Canyon was what type of transporter?
22 George Brown was a prominent MP for which party?
23 Which Private magazine signalled the satire boom?
24 Which theatre that "never closed" finally did close?
25 US President Johnson was known by which three initials?
26 Nuclear war threatened in 1962 over Soviet missiles in which country?
27 Which English footballer retired in 1965 at the age of 50?
28 Which Anglo-French supersonic airliner took to the skies?
29 Who was manager of the Beatles until his death in 1967?
30 Which ex-Nazi leader Adolf was tried and hanged?

Quiz 42 Pot Luck 19

LEVEL 1

Answers - see page 52

1   Elvis Costello was born in which country?
2   What word can go before "ground", "pedal" and "water"?
3   Two US cops, Christine and Mary Beth, appeared in which TV series?
4   What is Abyssinia now called?
5   How is actor William Claude Dukinfield better known?
6   Johan Cruyff started his career at which club?
7   Who wrote the novel *Middlemarch*?
8   Cambridge Gage and Victoria are types of what?
9   Which French phrase in English means a road closed at one end?
10 In the 90s, who had a No. 1 with "Never Forget"?
11 Which is greater 1/3 or 4/8?
12 Which Clive starred in "Dad's Army"?
13 In which decade of the 20th century was Eric Clapton born?
14 What word can go after "fish" and before "print"?
15 Chris Brasher is associated with which sport?
16 On a Monopoly board, what colour is Bow Street?
17 In schools, what do the initials GCSE stand for?
18 In which country is the city of Tangier?
19 Which five words traditionally closed the original Sooty show?
20 Who recorded the album *Money For Nothing*?
21 Geoff Miller played cricket for which country?
22 Ornithophobia is the fear of what?
23 What is 4 cubed?
24 What note is written in the space below the middle line of the treble clef?
25 Which Jack won an Oscar for Best Actor in *One Flew Over The Cuckoo's Nest*?
26 Is Barbados ahead of or behind Greenwich Mean Time?
27 Pearl celebrates which wedding anniversary?
28 Which TV quiz show always pits one contestant against two?
29 Which Alice declared: School's Out?
30 The character Charlene Mitchell appeared in which TV soap?

Answers

Pop: Singers (see Quiz 44)
1 Madonna. 2 Donny. 3 Gilbert O'Sullivan. 4 Dana. 5 Stansfield.
6 Holder. 7 Enya. 8 Kenny Rogers. 9 Marc Bolan. 10 Smokey Robinson.
11 Pretenders. 12 John Denver. 13 Bryan Adams. 14 Phil Collins.
15 Cliff Richard. 16 Boy George. 17 Nick Berry. 18 "Reet Petite".
19 Chris de Burgh. 20 Sting. 21 Jason Donovan. 22 Moyet.
23 Wet Wet Wet. 24 Wales. 25 Nat King Cole. 26 M. 27 Englebert
Humperdinck. 28 Bob Marley. 29 UB40. 30 Frank Sinatra.

Quiz 43 Time And Space

Answers - see page 49

LEVEL 1

1 Which planet is closest to the sun?

2 Which Big theory explains the formation of the universe?

3 What is another name for the star constellation the Plough?

4 Which Helen became the first Briton in space?

5 What is the term for a giant group of stars held together by gravity?

6 In 1981, *Columbia I* was the first flight of which distinctive craft?

7 What can be a red dwarf or a white dwarf?

8 Which planet is the largest in our solar system?

9 Who or what was Hale-Bopp?

10 In 1986, what happened to *Challenger 52* after take-off?

11 Cape Canaveral took on board the name of which US President?

12 Where is the Sea of Tranquillity?

13 What is the name of the force that keeps planets moving round the sun?

14 Tiros, Echo and Sputnik were types of what?

15 What is the name for the study of the structure of the universe?

16 Which John was the first American to orbit Earth?

17 What was the name of the project that first put man on the moon?

18 Alphabetically, which is last in the list of planets in our solar system?

19 What is Yuri Gagarin's famous first?

20 Approximately how long does it take the Earth to travel round the sun?

21 Which bright comet visits Earth every 76 years?

22 Which country launched the Pioneer space probes?

23 What is the popular name for the star Sirius?

24 Quasi-stellar sources are in short usually known as what?

25 Who is the long-time presenter of "The Sky At Night"?

26 The moons of Uranus are named after which playwright's characters?

27 Jodrell Bank is in which English county?

28 What units are used for measuring distance in space?

29 What was the first animal in space?

30 Our solar system lies in which galaxy?

Answers *The 60s* (see Quiz 41)

1 Harold Macmillan. 2 Football. 3 Keeler. 4 Lady Diana Spencer.
5 On the moon. 6 Dudley Moore. 7 Princess Margaret. 8 Committed
suicide. 9 Elizabeth Taylor. 10 Libya. 11 *Lady Chatterley's Lover.*
12 Isle of Wight. 13 Beeching. 14 A spy. 15 Chichester. 16 John Kennedy.
17 Yoko Ono. 18 De Gaulle. 19 South Africa. 20 USSR. 21 Oil tanker.
22 Labour. 23 *Private Eye.* 24 Windmill. 25 LBJ. 26 Cuba. 27 Stanley
Matthews. 28 Concorde. 29 Brian Epstein. 30 Eichmann.

Quiz 44 Pop: Singers

Answers - see page 50

LEVEL 1

1 Who sang "Like A Virgin"?

2 Which Osmond sang "Puppy Love" and "Young Love"?

3 Who was Alone Again (Naturally)?

4 Which Irish singer won Eurovision with "All Kinds of Everything"?

5 Which Lisa sang on the "Five Live EP"?

6 Which Noddy sang lead with Slade?

7 Which female singer went solo from Clannad?

8 Who sang "Coward Of The County"?

9 Who sang lead with T. Rex?

10 Under what name did high-voiced William Robinson Jnr sing?

11 Chrissie Hynde was lead singer with which group?

12 Which writer and guitarist sang "Annie's Song"?

13 "(Everything I Do) I Do It For You" was a monster hit for whom?

14 Who had a No. 1 with "A Groovy Kind Of Love"?

15 Who had a Christmas No. 1 with "Saviour's Day"?

16 Who sang lead with Culture Club?

17 Who sang "Every Loser Wins"?

18 Which song gave Jackie Wilson a No. 1 years after his death?

19 Who sang "The Lady In Red"?

20 Who was lead singer with the Police?

21 Who hit No. 1 with "Any Dream Will Do"?

22 Which Alison revived "Love Letters" and "That Old Devil Called Love"?

23 Marti Pellow sang lead with which group?

24 Which country does Shirley Bassey come from?

25 Who sang "Mona Lisa" and "When I Fall In Love"?

26 Heather Small sang lead with which people?

27 Who had a huge 60s hit with "Release Me"?

28 Who sang with the Wailers?

29 Ali Campbell sings lead with which group?

30 Which singer is known as Old Blue Eyes?

Quiz 45 Pot Luck 20

Answers - see page 55

LEVEL 1

1 Eric Clapton, Ginger Baker and Jack Bruce formed which group?
2 What are Maplin's entertainment staff called?
3 How many square feet in a square yard?
4 What word can go after "free" and before "corporal"?
5 In 1974 parts of Yorkshire and Lincolnshire made which new county?
6 He is the chemical symbol for which element?
7 Who wrote the novel *Dead Cert*?
8 Moving clockwise on a dartboard what number is next to 15?
9 Which cosmetic company had an ad which featured a distinctive doorbell?
10 Which rugby league team are the Blue Sox?
11 In the 80s, who had a No. 1 with "Karma Chameleon"?
12 Galileo Galilei airport is in which country?
13 In which decade of the 20th century was Steve Davis born?
14 David Broome is associated with which sport?
15 How is the actor James Baumgartner better known?
16 Who was Liverpool's regular soccer keeper throughout the 80s?
17 The letter E is on which row of a typewriter or computer keyboard?
18 Which Linford was BBC Sports Personality of the Year in 1993?
19 Mr Bumble appears in which Charles Dickens novel?
20 Which UK car manufacturer produced the Victor?
21 In which country is the city of Toulouse?
22 Which Pam starred in "The Darling Buds Of May"?
23 What is the administrative centre for the county of Berkshire?
24 How many degrees in a circle?
25 The zodiac sign Aquarius covers which two calendar months?
26 Who had a hit with "I Want To Know What Love Is"?
27 What term describes vegetables cut thinly and slowly cooked in butter?
28 What sport does Murray Walker commentate on?
29 The character Clayton Farlow appeared in which TV soap?
30 Which Holly was in Frankie Goes To Hollywood?

Answers

Pot Luck 21 (see Quiz 47)

1 Farrow. 2 St Paul's. 3 Bowls. 4 "Ball". 5 Matt Monro. 6 Wolves. 7 Arthur C. Clarke. 8 November. 9 Frank Zappa. 10 Wayne. 11 90. 12 James. 13 30s. 14 Greenwich Mean Time. 15 Yorkshire. 16 Pasta shapes. 17 Acker Bilk. 18 Canada. 19 "Box". 20 Take That. 21 "Chef". 22 7. 23 Toby. 24 Tenth. 25 "Knots Landing". 26 U2. 27 April 23. 28 Three. 29 Rodgers. 30 Threat.

Quiz 46 Crime & Punishment

Answers - see page 56

1   Jack the Ripper operated in which city?
2   What nationality was the fictional sleuth Hercule Poirot?
3   Who was Burke's body-snatching partner?
4   Who wrote the comic opera *Trial By Jury*?
5   What is the name of a secret crime society based in Hong Kong?
6   Al Capone was imprisoned in the 30s for what offence?
7   Which notorious American island prison closed in March, 1963?
8   How were the US outlaws Parker and Barrow better known?
9   Which criminal was released by Pontius Pilate instead of Jesus?
10 Which Myra was involved in the Moors Murders?
11 Policemen got the nickname Peelers from whom?
12 How did Frederick West take his life?
13 When did the Knave of Hearts steal the tarts?
14 In which city was John Lennon murdered?
15 Which Kray twin was the first to die?
16 What is the Flying Squad in cockney rhyming slang?
17 What name is given to the crime of deliberately burning someone else's property?
18 Which Nick got nicked for the Barings Bank scam?
19 In which decade was the Great Train Robbery?
20 Whom did Dr Crippen murder?
21 In the US, which Charles led his "family" in ritual killings?
22 Which Arsenal boss got the boot after a bung?
23 Why does Ruth Ellis have her place assured in British crime history?
24 Lee Harvey Oswald was accused of murdering which famous American?
25 Klaus Barbie became known as the Butcher of where?
26 In England and Wales how many people sit on a jury?
27 Peter Sutcliffe became known as what?
28 Ernest Saunders was involved with the fraud trial at which drinks company?
29 Rudolf Hess spent the last years of his life at which prison?
30 Sweeney Todd operated in which London Street?

Quiz 47 Pot Luck 21

Answers - see page 53

1   Which Mia married André Previn?
2   Which church appeared on the Thames TV logo?
3   David Bryant is associated with which sport?
4   What word can go after "beach" and before "gown"?
5   How is the singer Terrence Parsons better known?
6   Stan Cullis took which English soccer club to the championship?
7   Who wrote the novel *2001: A Space Odyssey*?
8   In which month is St Andrew's Day?
9   Who was the long-time leader of the Mothers Of Invention?
10 Which John won an Oscar for Best Actor in *True Grit*?
11 What number is represented by the Roman numerals XC?
12 Which Polly starred in "The Liver Birds"?
13 In which decade of the 20th century was Sophia Loren born?
14 What does the abbreviation GMT stand for?
15 For which county does Darren Gough play cricket?
16 What are farfalle, pansotti and rigati?
17 Which musician wrote and recorded "Stranger On The Shore"?
18 In which country is the city of Vancouver?
19 What word can follow "letter", "tool" and "witness"?
20 In the 90s, who had a No. 1 with "Never Forget"?
21 Lenny Henry was Gareth Blackstock in which TV series?
22 What is the square root of 49?
23 What is the dog called in a Punch and Judy show?
24 Tin denotes which wedding anniversary?
25 The character Karen Fairgate appeared in which TV soap?
26 Which group made the album *The Joshua Tree*?
27 What date is St George's Day?
28 In song, how many times is Happy Birthday referred to before naming the person?
29 Which Anton starred in *May To December*?
30 What is the only English anagram of HATTER?

1. In which series did the London copper say "Evening, all"?
2. Which veteran presented "Gardening Club" in the 50s and 60s?
3. Who had a sidekick called Tonto?
4. "All Gas and Gaiters" was one of the first sitcoms to poke fun at whom?
5. Who was the female half of Mork and Mindy?
6. Which blonde actress played Purdey in "The New Avengers"?
7. Which Pamela was a regular on "Not the Nine O'Clock News"?
8. What is the world's longest-running current-affairs programme?
9. Which sitcom featured Bernard Hedges of Fenn Street School?
10. In which century was "Poldark" set?
11. Which king was played by Keith Michell in 1970?
12. Was it Starsky or Hutch who started a trend for chunky cardigans?
13. Which series featured the Cartwrights of the Ponderosa?
14. Which 60s sitcom was about the oil rich Clampett family?
15. In "A Family at War" where did the Ashtons live?
16. Which show recreated the era of music hall?
17. Which Saga was the last the BBC produced in black and white?
18. What were the real-life surnames of Terry and June?
19. Which 50s/60s medical drama was set in Oxbridge General Hospital?
20. What breed of dog was Rin-Tin-Tin?
21. What type of programme did Fanny Cradock present?
22. Whose Half Hour featured "the lad himself"?
23. Which future James Bond starred as Ivanhoe in the 50s?
24. Which Irishman presented "This is Your Life" from the 1950s?
25. Which Hattie starred in sitcoms with Eric Sykes?
26. How many Goodies were there?
27. Which Irish comic finished his act with "May your God go with you"?
28. Why was "Mastermind" an incongruous title for the first three series?
29. In which sitcom did Lucille Ball and her husband Desi Arnaz play Lucy and Ricky Ricardo?
30. Which 60s pop singer played the title role in "Budgie" in the 70s?

Quiz 49 Pot Luck 22

Answers - see page 59

LEVEL 1

1 How many yards in an acre?

2 Which Alf became mayor of Weatherfield in 1973?

3 In which decade of the 20th century was Margaret Thatcher born?

4 In the 90s, who had a No. 1 with "Fairground"?

5 Who plays rugby union at Welford Road?

6 In the Bible, which book immediately follows Exodus?

7 Who wrote the novel *The Runaway Jury*?

8 In which country is the city of Sao Paulo?

9 Joe and Annie Sugden appeared in which TV series?

10 Moving anticlockwise on a dartboard, what number is next to 5?

11 Who sang with Dolly Parton on "Islands In The Stream"?

12 On a Monopoly board, what colour is Park Lane?

13 Charles Buchan is associated with which sport?

14 What word can go after "double" and before "section"?

15 What name is given to a yacht with two hulls?

16 In song, which road is taken to get to Scotland "afore ye"?

17 In theatre, what is traditionally the main colour in a Pierrot costume?

18 Which UK car manufacturer produced the Princess?

19 How is actor Ronald Moodnick better known?

20 "You don't win anything with kids" was Alan Hansen's quote about which team?

21 Who in the 50s had "Rock Island Line" as his first million-seller?

22 Which Harry starred in "Men Behaving Badly"?

23 The airline Qantas is from which country?

24 What is 75 per cent of 200?

25 What name is given to a thin Mexican pancake?

26 Which English city has Oxford Road, Victoria and Piccadilly railway stations?

27 What is the former Prime Minister John Major's constituency?

28 Who called his autobiography From *Drags To Riches*?

29 Which Cat sang "I Love My Dog"?

30 The character Hattie Tavernier appeared in which TV soap?

Pot Luck 23 (see Quiz 51)

Answers

1 George Bush. 2 "Paper." 3 "Fawlty Towers". 4 Tomato. 5 Edith Piaf.
6 Glasgow. 7 John Buchan. 8 Liverpool. 9 Status Quo. 10 30s. 11 1/3.
12 Johnson. 13 March and April. 14 "Yard". 15 Boxing. 16 Stationery
Office. 17 Switzerland. 18 Tom Jones. 19 Knight. 20 "Jim Fixed It For
Me". 21 Meteors. 22 Portillo. 23 Scofield. 24 Hypotenuse. 25 Nickel.
26 "Brookside". 27 US. 28 Two turtle doves. 29 "Dad's Army".
30 Jimmy Nail.

Quiz 50 60s Films

Answers - see page 60

1 Who won a BAFTA for his role in *Lawrence of Arabia* but not an Oscar?

2 Who starred in *Funny Girl* and *Lawrence of Arabia*?

3 Who starred in *Mary Poppins* and *The Sound of Music*?

4 What is the job of Bert, alias Dick Van Dyke, in *Mary Poppins*?

5 In which Disney film does "The Bare Necessities" appear?

6 Which daughter of Charlie Chaplin appeared in *Doctor Zhivago*?

7 Who was Butch Cassidy in *Butch Cassidy and the Sundance Kid*?

8 Which classic had the line "This is Benjamin. He's a little worried about his future"?

9 Who played Eliza Doolittle in *My Fair Lady*?

10 In which city does *One Hundred and One Dalmatians* take place?

11 Which 1963 BAFTA winner shared its name with a 60s Welsh singer?

12 How many "years BC" were in the title of the 1966 Raquel Welch film?

13 Which "The Upper Hand" actress starred in *Goldfinger*?

14 In which film does 007 seek a diamond smuggler?

15 How many were there in the Dirty band led by Charles Bronson?

16 Which Romeo and Juliet type of musical won most Oscars in the 60s?

17 In which 1968 musical did Bill Sikes murder Nancy?

18 What was Paul Scofield A Man For in 1966?

19 Who co-starred with Jon Voight as Ratso Rizzo in *Midnight Cowboy*?

20 Who is the incompetent Inspector in the *Pink Panther* films?

21 Which *Carry On* film tells of the all-female Glamcabs firm?

22 Who starred in *The Alamo* and *True Grit*?

23 In *Easy Rider* what are the riders riding?

24 In which 60s film did the deranged character Norman Bates appear?

25 Which Mrs Richard Burton starred in *Who's Afraid of Virginia Woolf*?

26 Which Goon starred in *Dr Strangelove*?

27 Who co-starred with Walter Matthau in *The Odd Couple*?

28 Tommy Steele sang the title song in Half a what in 1967?

29 Who was a GI and was the star of a film with that in the title?

30 Which blonde's last film was *The Misfits* in 1960?

The Media 1 (see Quiz 52)

1 The *Sun*. 2 Anglia Television. 3 Channel 5. 4 Central. 5 Associated Television. 6 Radio 4. 7 The *Mail on Sunday*. 8 British Broadcasting Corporation. 9 1930s. 10 BBC 2. 11 Prime Minister. 12 Welsh. 13 Channel 4. 14 British Sky Broadcasting. 15 Camcorder. 16 Sunday. 17 News. 18 Adverts. 19 Drama-documentary. 20 *Today*. 21 1960s. 22 BBC 2. 23 London Weekend Television. 24 GMTV. 25 "Today" 26 Granada. 27 HTV. 28 "New At Ten". 29 Independent. 30 BBC 1 and BBC 2.

Answers

Quiz 51 Pot Luck 23

Answers - see page 57

LEVEL 1

1   Who was the outgoing American President when Bill Clinton took office?
2   What word can go before "bag", "clip" and "tiger"?
3   Manuel and Sybil appeared in which TV series?
4   Love apple is an old-fashioned name for what?
5   How was the singer Edith Giovanna Gassion better known?
6   In which city was Kenny Dalglish born?
7   Who wrote the novel *The Thirty-Nine Steps*?
8   What is the administrative centre for the county of Merseyside?
9   Veteran rockers Rossi and Parfitt are in which group?
10 In which decade of the 20th century was Mary Quant born?
11 Which is smaller 3/8 or 1/3?
12 Which Don starred in "Miami Vice"?
13 The zodiac sign Aries covers which two calendar months?
14 What word can go after "farm" and before "stick"?
15 Joe Bugner is associated with which sport?
16 In HMSO what does SO stand for?
17 In which country is the city of Zürich?
18 "It's Not Unusual" was the first No. 1 for which singer?
19 Which chess piece can change direction in a normal move?
20 What is the inscription on a "Jim'll Fix It" medal?
21 Meteorophobia is the fear of what?
22 Which Cabinet member Michael lost his Enfield seat at the 1997 general election?
23 Which Paul won an Oscar for Best Actor in *A Man For All Seasons*?
24 What name is given to the longest side of a right-angled triangle?
25 Ni is the chemical symbol for which element?
26 The character Beth Jordache appeared in which TV soap?
27 Which country did the Righteous Brothers come from?
28 In song, what did my true love send me on the second day of Christmas?
29 Which sitcom was set in Walmington-on-Sea?
30 In the 90s, who had a No. 1 with "Ain't No Doubt"?

Answers

Pot Luck 22 (see Quiz 49)

1 4,840. 2 Roberts. 3 20s. 4 Simply Red. 5 Leicester. 6 Leviticus.
7 John Grisham. 8 Brazil. 9 "Emmerdale". 10 12. 11 Kenny Rogers.
12 Dark Blue. 13 Football. 14 "Cross". 15 Catamaran. 16 Low Road.
17 White. 18 Austin. 19 Ron Moody. 20 Man. Utd. 21 Lonnie Donegan.
22 Enfield. 23 Australia. 24 150. 25 Tortilla. 26 Manchester.
27 Huntingdon. 28 Danny La Rue. 29 Stevens. 30 "EastEnders".

Quiz 52 The Media 1

Answers - see page 58

LEVEL 1

1 Which British daily paper was founded in the 1960s?
2 Which independent TV company serves East Anglia?
3 Which Channel began broadcasting in March 1997?
4 Which company took over ATV's Midlands broadcasting?
5 What did ATV stand for?
6 On which Radio station is "The Archers" broadcast?
7 What is the Daily Mail's sister Sunday paper called?
8 What does BBC stand for?
9 In which decade did the BBC begin a TV broadcasting service?
10 Which channel was the third UK terrestrial channel?
11 Which political role did the Italian TV magnate Silvio Berlusconi have in 1994?
12 S4C broadcasts in which minority UK language?
13 On which channel is "Brookside" broadcast?
14 What is BSkyB an abbreviation of?
15 What is a video recorder and a recording device in one unit called?
16 Which day of the week is the *Observer* published?
17 What type of information does CNN broadcast?
18 In early ITV what was shown in a "natural break"?
19 What kind of programme is a drama-doc?
20 Which daily UK paper was founded in the 80s and ceased in the 90s?
21 In which decade did colour broadcasting begin?
22 On which channel were colour broadcasts first seen in the UK?
23 In broadcasting what did LWT stand for?
24 Which 90s breakfast TV station was originally known as Sunrise TV?
25 What is Radio 4's early-morning news programme called?
26 Which TV company was named after a Spanish city loved by its founder?
27 Harlech Television's name was shortened to what?
28 What was the UK's first 30 minute TV news programme begun in '67?
29 What did I stand for in IBA before 1991?
30 Which TV channels does the TV licence fund?

Answers

60s Films (see Quiz 50)
1 Peter O'Toole. 2 Omar Sharif. 3 Julie Andrews. 4 Chimney sweep.
5 *The Jungle Book*. 6 Geraldine. 7 Paul Newman. 8 *The Graduate*.
9 Audrey Hepburn. 10 London. 11 Tom Jones. 12 One Million.
13 Honor Blackman. 14 *Diamonds Are Forever*. 15 Dozen. 16 *West Side Story*. 17 *Oliver!*. 18 All Seasons. 19 Dustin Hoffman. 20 Clouseau.
21 Cabby. 22 John Wayne. 23 Motorbikes. 24 *Psycho*. 25 Elizabeth Taylor. 26 Peter Sellers. 27 Jack Lemmon. 28 Sixpence. 29 Elvis Presley.
30 Marilyn Monroe.

Quiz 53 Famous Names

LEVEL 1

1   Michael Hutchence dated which model Helena before Paula Yates?

2   What name did Pamela Anderson add to her own when she wed rock star Tommy?

3   Which Johnny's name was once linked to the model Kate Moss?

4   Which Mrs Carling publicly criticized the Princess of Wales?

5   Which former Pakistan cricket captain married Jemima Goldsmith?

6   Mandy Allwood's expectation of how many babies made the news in 1996?

7   Which Gareth's summer miss of 1996 made him a household name?

8   What is the first name of the TV presenter Ms Frostrup?

9   What is Mrs Michael Jackson II's first name?

10   In '97 Man. Utd's David Beckham was dating one of which pop band?

11   What is the profession of Claudia Shiffer's ex, David Copperfield?

12   Which actress married Richard Burton twice?

13   Which star of *Evita* married the actress Melanie Griffith?

14   Which Royal Prince's name was linked with photographer Koo Stark?

15   Which former son-in-law of the Queen remarried in 1997?

16   Which tenor left his wife for a Miss Mantovani?

17   Although a top model, Jerry Hall is also famous as which star's wife?

18   Which comedian Paul split with wife Caroline Quentin in 1997?

19   Which singer was the second Mrs Andrew Lloyd Webber?

20   What is the first name of David Emanuel's fashion designer ex-wife?

21   Nicky Clarke's name is famous in which fashion field?

22   Trudie Styler married which singer/rainforest conservationist in 1992?

23   Which star of "Minder" has been married to the actress Rula Lenska?

24   Which model Elle is an ex-flame of the actor Kevin Costner?

25   What is the first name of Tony Blair's wife?

26   Which Francesca partnered Robson Green on TV and Ralph Fiennes in real life?

27   Who has been the husband of Rachel Hunter and Alana Hamilton?

28   Who is the wife of Derek Redmond and mother of Elliot?

29   What is the first name of Chelsea Clinton's mother?

30   Which actress, a.k.a. Dorien, had a rose named after her at the 1997 Chelsea Flower Show?

Answers

Record Breakers (see Quiz 55)

1 Somerset. 2 Cycling. 3 Faldo. 4 Alan Shearer. 5 Hingis. 6 Wigan. 7 Swimming. 8 Javelin. 9 Clive Lloyd. 10 Glenn Hoddle. 11 Underwood. 12 Sampras. 13 Joe Davis. 14 Badminton. 15 Ian Rush. 16 Shriver. 17 Rhodes. 18 Connors. 19 Andrew. 20 Offiah. 21 Brazil. 22 147. 23 Brian Lara. 24 Hastings. 25 English Channel. 26 Nicklaus. 27 Mark and Steve. 28 Scotland. 29 All Blacks. 30 Wales.

Quiz 54 Pot Luck 24

LEVEL 1

Answers - see page 64

1 Who was the first female presenter of "Desert Island Discs"?
2 Which UK car manufacturer produced the Zodiac?
3 What is Formosa now called?
4 What word can go after "sea" and before "heart"?
5 In the 90s, who had a No. 1 with "Stay Another Day"?
6 The letter M is on which row of a typewriter or computer keyboard?
7 Who wrote the novel *Lord Of The Flies*?
8 What is a third of 1,200?
9 Gary, Tony, Deborah and Dorothy appeared in which TV series?
10 In which decade of the 20th century was Jimmy Connors born?
11 Which Noel wrote the play Hay Fever?
12 Who formed a trio with Paul and Mary?
13 The character Annie Walker appeared in which TV soap?
14 Who created the detective Miss Marple?
15 Which prime minister held office first - Wilson or Heath?
16 What is 1/2 plus 2/8?
17 What is the administrative centre for the county of Dorset?
18 With which event in athletics was Geoff Capes associated?
19 How is the TV personality Annie Rice better known?
20 Which keeper John won championships at Arsenal and Leeds?
21 How many metres in four kilometres?
22 Which George starred in "Minder"?
23 Who wrote the song recorded for Dunblane?
24 Adnams brewery is located in which county?
25 Which Liverpudlian grandfather told "Thomas The Tank Engine" tales on TV?
26 In which country is South America's highest mountain?
27 Moving clockwise on a dartboard what number is next to 9?
28 In which country is the city of Istanbul?
29 Who has presented "Through The Keyhole" with Loyd Grossman?
30 Which standard begins, "They asked me how I knew, my true love was true"?

Answers

Pot Luck 25 (see Quiz 56)

1 USA. 2 "Half". 3 20s. 4 Blue. 5 David Niven. 6 Germany. 7 Thomas Hardy. 8 Little Jimmy Osmond. 9 Marlon Brando. 10 Huddersfield.
11 Orwell. 12 Willis. 13 Le Bon. 14 "Weight". 15 Horse racing.
16 Imperial. 17 "Home and Away". 18 F. 19 Sahara. 20 8.
21 Bryan Ferry. 22 "Porridge". 23 Custer. 24 Spain. 25 Red.
26 Amazon. 27 Cloud. 28 Square. 29 Bruce Forsyth. 30 Albert.

Quiz 55 Record Breakers

LEVEL 1

1　Ian Botham first played for which county?
2　Eddie Merckx was a record breaker in which sport?
3　In 1977, which Nick became the youngest ever Ryder Cup player?
4　Who set a new transfer record when he was bought and sold by Blackburn?
5　In the 90s which Martina became Wimbledon's youngest ever senior champ?
6　Which team set a record run as rugby league champs in the 90s?
7　In which sport was Mark Spitz a record-breaker?
8　In which event did Fatima Whitbread set a 1986 world record?
9　Who holds the record for most games as West Indian cricket captain?
10　In 1996, who became England's youngest ever soccer boss?
11　Which Rory played rugby union 85 times for England?
12　In tennis, which Pete set a men's record season earnings in 1995?
13　Who won the first 15 World Pro Snooker championships?
14　Gillian Clark made record England appearances in which sport?
15　Which Liverpool record-scorer moved to Leeds in 1996?
16　Which Pam was Martina Navratilova's doubles partner in the 80s?
17　Which Wilfred set a record as England's oldest player of Test cricket?
18　Which Jimmy was first to 100 tennis singles titles in a career?
19　In 1994, which Rob scored a record 27 points in a rugby union game for England?
20　Which Martin left Widnes for Wigan in a record rugby transfer?
21　Which team won soccer's World Cup for a record fourth time in 1994?
22　What is the maximum break in snooker?
23　Who became the first player to score over 500 in first-class cricket?
24　Which Gavin became Scotland's most capped rugby union player?
25　Matthew Webb was the first person to swim what?
26　Which Jack was first to six triumphs in golf's US Masters?
27　What is the name of cricket's Aussie Waugh brothers?
28　Which country is Stephen Hendry from?
29　Sean Fitzpatrick played for which international team?
30　Billy Meredith was playing soccer for which country when aged 45?

Answers

Quiz 56 Pot Luck 25

Answers - see page 62

LEVEL 1

1   In which country is the city of Albuquerque?
2   What word can go before "baked", "measures" and "time"?
3   In which decade of the 20th century was Doris Day born?
4   What colour is Noddy's hat?
5   How is the actor James David Graham Nevins better known?
6   Who did Denmark beat in soccer's '92 European Championship Final?
7   Who wrote the novel *Tess of the D'Urbervilles*?
8   In the 70s, who had a No. 1 with "Long-Haired Lover From Liverpool"?
9   Who won an Oscar for Best Actor in *The Godfather*?
10 Which rugby league side added Giants to their name in the 90s?
11 Which 20th-century novelist used a Suffolk river as a pen name?
12 Which Bruce starred in "Moonlighting"?
13 Which Simon was vocalist with Duran Duran?
14 What word can go after "paper" and before "lifter"?
15 Henry Cecil is associated with which sport?
16 In the royal address HIH what does I stand for?
17 The character Shannon Reed appeared in which TV soap?
18 In music, what note is written on the top line of the treble clef?
19 Timbuktu is on the edge of which desert?
20 What is the square root of 64?
21 Who was singer with Roxy Music?
22 The characters Fletcher and Godber appeared in which TV series?
23 Which general made a last stand at Little Big Horn?
24 The airline Iberia is from which country?
25 On a Monopoly board, what colour is Strand?
26 What was Sharron Davies's name in Gladiators?
27 What is the only English anagram of COULD?
28 What type of a rectangle has four equal sides and angles?
29 Who introduced "the eight who are going to generate"?
30 What is Frank Sinatra's middle name?

Quiz 57 The 70s

Answers - see page 67

LEVEL 1

1 Which Spaniard won a British Open at golf?
2 Whom did Ted Heath replace as British PM?
3 The tennis superstar Bjorn Borg came from which country?
4 In the UK, the age of majority was lowered from 21 to what?
5 The song "Bright Eyes" was about what type of animal?
6 Haile Selassie was deposed in which country?
7 Which rock legend died at his mansion Graceland?
8 D-Day in 1971 introduced what to Britain?
9 Which athlete Sebastian broke three world records in six weeks?
10 Which art historian Sir Anthony was revealed to be a spy?
11 Idi Amin became President of which country?
12 Who vanished after the murder of Lady Lucan's nanny?
13 The Ayatollah Khomeini drove the Shah from which country?
14 Which Princess was named Sportswoman of the Year?
15 Which legendary artist Pablo died in 1973?
16 Which organization bombed pubs in Guildford and Birmingham?
17 In 1971, 200,000 people demonstrated in the US against which war?
18 Bobby Fischer became a world champion in which game?
19 Olga Korbut delighted the world in what?
20 Whose Silver Jubilee celebrations led to a week of festivities in 1977?
21 In 1976 Jeremy Thorpe resigned as leader of which party?
22 Which Richard was re-elected as President of the US?
23 Which James became motor racing's Formula 1 world champion?
24 Who became the first female leader of a British political party?
25 Which former British monarch passed away?
26 The monarchy returned to Spain after the death of which general?
27 Whom did Princess Anne marry in 1973?
28 Which author Aleksandr was expelled from the USSR?
29 Which commodity quadrupled in price after Israeli-Arab conflict?
30 Second Division Sunderland beat which soccer giants to win the FA Cup?

Quiz 58 Pot Luck 26

LEVEL 1

Answers - see page 68

1 Tony Blair is MP for which constituency?

2 What is sauerkraut?

3 The characters Rigsby and Miss Jones appeared in which TV series?

4 What word can go after "pine" and before "turnover"?

5 Jeremy Bates is associated with which sport?

6 What's the fruity link with the name of William III of England?

7 Who wrote the novel *For Whom the Bell Tolls*?

8 In the Bible, which book immediately follows Luke?

9 How many pounds in a stone?

10 In which decade of the 20th century was George Best born?

11 Which Top group are destined to be last in an alphabetical list?

12 In history, which harbour in the US had a famous Tea Party?

13 Is Uruguay ahead of or behind Greenwich Mean Time?

14 The character Jenna Wade appeared in which TV soap?

15 On a dartboard what number is opposite 20?

16 Which UK car manufacturer produced the Avenger?

17 In which country is the city of Auckland?

18 On a Monopoly board, what colour is Piccadilly?

19 How is comic great Arthur Jefferson better known?

20 Glenn Hoddle finished his playing career with which club?

21 Sydney Carton appears in which Charles Dickens novel?

22 In which month is St Patrick's Day?

23 Which Annette starred in "One Foot in the Grave"?

24 What is a quarter of 180?

25 Dr Hook sang about whose mother?

26 In which series did a dog called Rowf play the piano?

27 Who was awarded a supper of brown bread and butter?

28 Which Steve was BBC Sports Personality of the Year in 1988?

29 On TV what sort of animal was Dylan?

30 In the 70s, who had a No. 1 with "Dancing Queen"?

Pot Luck 27 (see Quiz 60)

1 "Candle In the Wind". **2** "Emmerdale". **3** Middle. **4** "Stand". **5** Ernie Wise. **6** Lev Yashin. **7** Jeffrey Archer. **8** Olympic. **9** Carmichael. **10** Radius. **11** Osborne. **12** Barker. **13** 70s. **14** Stone. **15** Rugby (Union). **16** Iraq. **17** Oxygen. **18** "Yesterday". **19** Rex Harrison. **20** Cherry. **21** Four. **22** Mutley. **23** "Soldier Soldier". **24** Inspector Morse. **25** Gabrielle. **26** Mellor. **27** "The Magic Roundabout". **28** "Emmerdale". **29** December and January. **30** Brown.

Answers

Quiz 59 Pop: Charts

Answers - see page 65

LEVEL 1

1   Whose first chart success was "Your Song"?

2   Which David has charted with both Bing Crosby and Mick Jagger?

3   Which Frank Sinatra hit has charted on more than ten occasions?

4   Roy "Chubie" Brown charted with which group in 1995?

5   Which Rod has had over 50 chart hits?

6   Which Mariah spent most weeks in the charts in 1994?

7   "Red Red Wine" was the first No. 1 for which group?

8   Which Welsh singer Tom had most weeks in the chart back in 1968?

9   In the 80s, which Paul first charted with "Wherever I Lay My Hat"?

10   Where in London did the Kinks watch the Sunset?

11   Which song was No. 1 for Jimmy Young and Robson and Jerome?

12   Who were Alone in the charts, 30 years after their first hit?

13   Which New Kids had seven singles in the charts in 1990?

14   Who was the leader of the gang in the glam rock 70s?

15   Who was in the charts with "Crying" in 1961 and 1992?

16   In which decade did Belinda Carlisle first hit the UK charts?

17   Debbie Harry fronted which chart busters in the late 70s early 80s?

18   Whose first chart entry was "Space Oddity"?

19   Which Olivia charted with John Travolta and ELO?

20   Which Ben E. King classic made No. 1 25 years after it was recorded?

21   Which Rick went to No. 1 with his first hit "Never Gonna Give You Up"?

22   "Waterloo" was the first chart success for which group?

23   Which Judy Collins song amazingly charted eight times in the 70s?

24   "Song For Whoever" was the first hit for which Beautiful group?

25   Which John had three No. 1s following his murder?

26   Which 60s female vocalist came back in the 80s with the Pet Shop Boys?

27   Which early hit did Cliff Richard rerecord with the Young Ones?

28   Boyzone charted with "Words" in the 90s, but who made the original?

29   In which decade did Stevie Wonder first hit the UK charts?

30   In which decade did charts start to be compiled in the UK?

The 70s (see Quiz 57)

1 Severiano Ballesteros. **2** Harold Wilson. **3** Sweden. **4** 18. **5** Rabbit.
6 Ethiopia. **7** Elvis Presley. **8** Decimal coins. **9** Coe. **10** Blunt.
11 Uganda. **12** Lord Lucan. **13** Iran. **14** Anne. **15** Picasso. **16** IRA.
17 Vietnam. **18** Chess. **19** Gymnastics. **20** Queen Elizabeth II. **21** Liberal.
22 Nixon. **23** Hunt. **24** Margaret Thatcher. **25** Edward VIII. **26** Franco.
27 Captain Mark Phillips. **28** Solzhenitsyn. **29** Oil. **30** Leeds.

Quiz 60 Pot Luck 27

Answers - see page 66

1　Which Elton John song includes the words "Goodbye Norman Jean"?
2　Which TV soap was described by Les Dawson as "Dallas with dung"?
3　The letter A is on which row of a keyboard?
4　What word can follow "band", "hat" and "grand"?
5　How is Ernest Wiseman better known?
6　Which Russian keeper was known as the Black Spider?
7　Who wrote the novel *The Fourth Estate*?
8　Which International Committee has the initials IOC?
9　Which Hoagy penned "Stardust"?
10　What is the distance from any point on the circumference to the centre of a circle?
11　Which John wrote the play *Look Back In Anger*?
12　Which Ronnie starred in "Open All Hours"?
13　In which decade of the 20th century was Spice Girl Emma born?
14　What word can go after "sand" and before "mason"?
15　Maurice Colclough is associated with which sport?
16　In which country is the city of Baghdad?
17　O is the chemical symbol for which element?
18　In the song title what goes after "Yester-Me Yester-You"?
19　Who won an Oscar for Best Actor in *My Fair Lady*?
20　From which fruit is the drink kirsch made?
21　In ten-pin bowling, how many pins are there in the back row?
22　What is Dick Dastardly's dog called?
23　The characters Paddy Garvey and Dave Tucker appeared in which TV series?
24　Who is Colin Dexter's most famous creation?
25　Who had a 1993 hit with "Dreams"?
26　Which media man and MP David lost his Putney seat in 1997?
27　In which series did Zebedee appear?
28　The character Dolly Skilbeck appeared in which TV soap?
29　The zodiac sign Capricorn covers which two calendar months?
30　On a Monopoly board, what colour is Whitechapel?

Quiz 61 TV: Sitcoms

Answers - see page 71

LEVEL 1

1 In "Dad's Army" who called Sgt Wilson Uncle Arthur?
2 What is the nationality of Margaret Meldrew?
3 Which family lived in Nelson Mandela House, Peckham?
4 Which space-age sitcom stars Craig Charles and Chris Barrie?
5 Which Scottish pop star played Adrian Mole's mum?
6 Which Felicity was the star of "Solo"?
7 Who plays Jean, husband of Lionel, in "As Time Goes By"?
8 Where did Hester and William Fields head for in the 80s/90s sitcom?
9 Which 70s character wore a knitted tanktop, long mac and a beret?
10 Which sitcom featured Mimi La Bonc and a painting by Van Clomp?
11 What was the occupation of Gladys Emmanuel in "Open All Hours"?
12 In which show does Tracey have a husband Darryl and son Garth?
13 Where were Miss Tibbs, Miss Gatsby and Major Gowen permanent guests?
14 In the 80s how were Candice, Amanda, Jennifer and Shelley known?
15 On which birthday did Tom Good begin "The Good Life"?
16 Whose dreams of his mother-in-law featured a hippopotamus?
17 Which 70s sitcom saw Wendy Richard as Miss Brahms?
18 Which Birmingham comic starred as Bob Louis in "The Detectives"?
19 What was the profession of Tom and Toby in "Don't Wait Up"?
20 How were the mature Dorothy, Blanche, Rose and Sophia known?
21 How was Bombadier Beaumont known in "It Ain't Half Hot Mum"?
22 In which show did Paul Nicholas play Vince Pinner?
23 What is the first name of Mr Bucket in "Keeping Up Appearances"?
24 Which sitcom was set in HMP Slade?
25 Which blonde does Leslie Ash play in "Men Behaving Badly"?
26 "Drop the Dead Donkey" takes place in what type of office?
27 In which show did Baldrick first appear?
28 Which sitcom chronicled the life of Zoë and Alec Callender?
29 Which show's theme song was "Holiday Rock"?
30 Which decade does Gary return to in "Goodnight Sweetheart"?

On the Map (see Quiz 63)

Answers

1 England. 2 Mountain. 3 Bath. 4 Suez Canal. 5 Downing Street.
6 America. 7 Canterbury. 8 They're not surrounded by water. 9 Norwich.
10 K2. 11 The Cenotaph. 12 Belgium. 13 Washington DC. 14 Ayers Rock.
15 Halifax. 16 Munich. 17 Hadrian's Wall. 18 Red. 19 The Queen
Mother. 20 Antarctica. 21 New South Wales. 22 Japan. 23 Sicily.
24 Midlands. 25 Niagara. 26 Paris. 27 Arab. 28 Holland.
29 Sandwich. 30 Mediterranean.

Quiz 62 Pot Luck 28

Answers - see page 72

LEVEL 1

1　Who is R2D2's robot companion in *Star Wars*?
2　In the "Street" what was Betty Williams's surname before she married Billy?
3　In which decade of the 20th century was Tim Henman born?
4　What word can go after "pike" and before "nurse"?
5　How is the rock guitarist William Perks better known?
6　Martin Edwards is soccer chairman of which club?
7　Who wrote the novel *Three Men In A Boat*?
8　Arachnophobia is the fear of what?
9　The character Nick Cotton appeared in which TV soap?
10　What is Persia now called?
11　Which Daniel sang "I Just Want To Dance With You"?
12　Which comic got major stars to act in "a play what I wrote"?
13　How many grams in a kilogram?
14　Queen Anne Boleyn was said to possess an extra what on her body?
15　Who was Queen of the Greek Gods?
16　Which is greater 6/8 or 2/3?
17　Which Kylie topped the most weeks in the singles chart list for 1988?
18　Moving clockwise on a dartboard what number is next to 16?
19　Henry Cotton is associated with which sport?
20　What word can go before "hound", "pressure" and "vessel"?
21　Cambridge Favourite and Cambridge Vigour are types of what?
22　Which Amanda starred in "Peak Practice"?
23　In which country is the city of Bangalore?
24　Wayne Daniel played cricket for which country?
25　What is 5 cubed?
26　What is the only English anagram of CLERIC?
27　What note is written in the space above the middle line of the treble clef?
28　Which UK car manufacturer produced the Cowley?
29　The character Frank Spencer appeared in which TV series?
30　In the 90s, which comic duo had a No. 1 with "The Stonk"?

70s Films　(see Quiz 64)
1　Pink Panther. 2　*Star Wars*. 3　*Jaws*. 4　Fifties. 5　*The Godfather*.
6　*Superman*. 7　Spielberg. 8　Chicago. 9　Gibb. 10　*The Muppet Movie*.
11　*Jesus Christ Superstar*. 12　Streisand. 13　*Towering Inferno*. 14　Airport. 15　Los Angeles. 16　King Kong. 17　Roger Moore. 18　*M*A*S*H*.
19　McQueen. 20　*One Flew Over the Cuckoo's Nest*. 21　Rocky. 22　*Poseidon Adventure*. 23　Hall. 24　Glenda Jackson. 25　Alice. 26　*Cabaret*.
27　Dudley. 28　Vietnam. 29　On the Roof. 30　Cop.

Quiz 63 On the Map

LEVEL 1

1   If you were in France and crossed La Manche, where would you be?
2   In Scotland what does Ben mean in a place name?
3   Which Somerset city has a Spa railway station?
4   Which Canal links the Mediterranean and the Red Sea?
5   In which London street is the Chancellor of the Exchequer's official residence?
6   In which continent is the Hoover Dam?
7   In which city is England's oldest cathedral?
8   What do the Isle of Ely and the Isle of Dogs have in common?
9   In which city is the University of East Anglia?
10 By which letter and number is Mount Godwin-Austen known?
11 Which war memorial is in Whitehall?
12 Which country has the international vehicle registration letter B?
13 Which capital city stands on the Potomac river?
14 Which Australian rock is sacred to the aborigines?
15 The capital of Nova Scotia shares its name with which Yorkshire town?
16 Which German city hosted the 1972 Olympics?
17 What was manmade and stretches from Tyne and Wear to Cumbria?
18 On the London Underground what colour is the Central Line?
19 Glamis Castle was the childhood home of which royal?
20 Which continent is the iciest?
21 Which Australian state is made up of three words?
22 In which country is Mount Fuji?
23 On which island is the volcanic Mount Etna?
24 In which area of the UK is the Black Country?
25 On which river are the Niagara Falls?
26 In which city would you find the Champs Elysées?
27 What does A stand for in the Middle Eastern UAE?
28 In which country is the port of Rotterdam?
29 Which of the Cinque Ports shares its name with a snack food?
30 Which European Sea's name means "Middle of the earth"?

Quiz 64 70s Films

Answers - see page 70

1   Which Pink character appeared in three top films of the 70s?
2   Which 1977 film was rereleased 20 years later?
3   Which film was described as 'shark stew for the stupefied'?
4   In which decade does the action of *Grease* take place?
5   Which 1972 movie detailed the career of the Corleone family?
6   In which film did Clark Kent combat the Spider Lady?
7   Which Steven directed *Close Encounters of the Third Kind*?
8   In which gangster city does the action of *The Sting* take place?
9   Which brothers wrote most of the songs for *Saturday Night Fever*?
10 Which 1977 Movie had a frog as one of its main stars?
11 Which was the first Rice/Lloyd Webber musical made into a film?
12 Which Barbra starred in *A Star Is Born*?
13 Which film was based on *The Tower* and *The Glass Inferno*?
14 Which disaster movie was described as "Grand Hotel in the sky ..."?
15 In which Californian city did *Earthquake* take place?
16 Which gorilla was the star of a 1976 remake of a 30s classic?
17 Who played James Bond in *Moonraker*?
18 Which 1970 war film led to a long-running TV spin off with Alan Alda?
19 Which Steve starred in *Papillon*?
20 Which 1975 Jack Nicholson film takes place in a mental hospital?
21 Which boxer did Sylvester Stallone create on the big screen?
22 Which disaster movie tells of a capsized luxury liner?
23 Which Annie was an Oscar winner for Woody Allen?
24 Which future British MP won an Oscar for *Women in Love* in 1970?
25 Who Doesn't Live Here Any More in the 1974 movie?
26 Which Liza Minnelli Oscar-winning film was set in pre-war Germany?
27 Which Mr Moore starred opposite Bo Derek in *10*?
28 Which Asian war was *The Deer Hunter* about?
29 Where was the Fiddler in the 1971 film?
30 What was the profession of "hero" Doyle in *The French Connection*?

Quiz 65 Pot Luck 29

Answers - see page 75

1 June Croft is associated with which sport?
2 Which major landmark is seen at the start of "News At Ten"?
3 In the 90s, who had a No. 1 with "Vogue"?
4 Which Nigel was BBC Sports Personality of the Year in 1992?
5 Prince Michael of Moldavia appeared in which TV soap?
6 In which country is the city of Berne?
7 Who wrote the novel *Cider With Rosie*?
8 The zodiac sign Gemini covers which two calendar months?
9 What does the Q stand for in IQ?
10 In which decade of the 20th century was Bob Dylan born?
11 Who was the outgoing American President when George Bush took office?
12 Which Helen starred in "Prime Suspect"?
13 Indira Gandhi International airport is in which country?
14 What word can go after "top" and before "trick"?
15 How is John Ravenscroft better known?
16 What colour are Holland's international soccer shirts?
17 Who sang with Frederick about a Little Donkey?
18 What did Wigan's name become for the 1997 rugby league season?
19 What is the administrative centre for the county of Buckinghamshire?
20 The character Captain Kirk appeared in which TV series?
21 Is Turkey ahead of or behind Greenwich Mean Time?
22 What were the two colours of Andy Pandy's costume?
23 Who backed Buddy Holly?
24 What does 1/2 x 1/2 equal?
25 On a Monopoly board, what colour is Euston Road?
26 Which is closer to the sea - London or New York?
27 Who predicted that everyone would be famous for 15 minutes?
28 Who won an Oscar for Best Actor in *Ben Hur*?
29 What is the square root of 100?
30 "U Can't Touch This" was the first chart success for which rapper?

Answers

Pot Luck 30 (see Quiz 67)

1 Top letters row. 2 Gaynor. 3 Magnesium. 4 "Pole". 5 Eric Morecambe.
6 Benfica. 7 James Herriot. 8 Greece. 9 Read the news. 10 36.
11 Saddam Hussein. 12 Merseyside. 13 20s. 14 Golf. 15 "Coronation
Street". 16 Daryl Hall. 17 60/100. 18 9. 19 Triumph. 20 "Room".
21 Spain. 22 Elphick. 23 B. 24 Second. 25 Phil Collins. 26 Norwich.
27 13. 28 Cassandra. 29 Books. 30 "Steptoe And Son".

Quiz 66 Hobbies & Leisure 2

LEVEL 1

Answers - see page 76

1 If you practised callisthenics what type of activity would you be doing?
2 If you were watching someone on a PGA tour what would you be watching?
3 Which board game has a Genus Edition?
4 Which toy was Hornby most famous for?
5 What do you hit with a racket in badminton?
6 What was the traditional colour for Aran wool?
7 What sort of toy was a Cabbage Patch?
8 In which board game do you draw the meaning of a word?
9 Which game is also the name of a gourdlike vegetable?
10 How many balls are used in a game of billiards?
11 How many members make up a water polo team?
12 What type of food would you get at Harry Ramsden's?
13 Which game has lawn and crown green varieties?
14 In which sport would you wear blades or quads?
15 In DIY, which is shinier - emulsion or gloss?
16 Which is normally larger, a pool table or a billiards table?
17 In Scrabble what colour are the double-word-score squares?
18 In which county is Alton Towers?
19 Which London museum is named after a queen and her cousin?
20 In which sport would you use a sabre, foil or épée?
21 Which is the most versatile piece on a chessboard?
22 Which game is called the national pastime in the USA?
23 Which Lancashire seaside resort has a famous Pleasure Beach?
24 Which Manchester TV studio became a tourist attraction in the 80s?
25 Which actress Jane pioneered her workout plans for others to use?
26 What type of tourist attraction is at Whipsnade Park?
27 What is Barbie's boyfriend called?
28 Which city boasts the Jorvik Viking Centre?
29 Which total is aimed for in pegging in a game of cribbage?
30 In snooker what is the white ball called?

Answers

History: Who's Who? (see Quiz 68)

Quiz 67 Pot Luck 30

Answers - see page 73

LEVEL 1

1 The letter R is on which row of a typewriter or computer keyboard?
2 Which Gloria recorded "I Will Survive"?
3 Mg is the chemical symbol for which element?
4 What word can go after "flag" and before "cat"?
5 How is Eric Bartholomew better known?
6 Eusebio played for which Portuguese club?
7 Who wrote the book *Vet In A Spin*?
8 The airline Olympic is from which country?
9 What did Gordon Honeycombe do in his TV appearances?
10 How many feet in a dozen yards?
11 Who was leader of Iraq during the 1991 Gulf War?
12 In 1974 parts of Lancashire and Cheshire made which new county?
13 In which decade of the 20th century was Bob Monkhouse born?
14 Laura Davies is associated with which sport?
15 The character Bet Gilroy appeared in which TV soap?
16 Who is John Oates's musical partner?
17 Which is smaller 60/100 or 8/10?
18 How many zeros in a billion written in digits?
19 Which UK car manufacturer produced the Dolomite?
20 What word can follow "box", "cloak" and "waiting"?
21 In which country is the city of Bilbao?
22 Which Michael starred in "Boon"?
23 In music, what note is written on the middle line of the treble clef?
24 Paper celebrates which wedding anniversary?
25 In the 80s, who had a No. 1 with "A Groovy Kind Of Love"?
26 What is the administrative centre for the county of Norfolk?
27 Moving anticlockwise on a dartboard what number is next to 6?
28 What is the first name of Rodney Trotter's wife?
29 Bibliophobia is the fear of what?
30 The father and son Albert and Harold appeared in which TV series?

Quiz 68 History: Who's Who?

LEVEL 1

Answers - see page 74

1. Who was British monarch throughout the Second World War?
2. Which US President was assassinated at the theatre?
3. Which ruler was stabbed to death in Rome in March 44 BC?
4. Who was Queen Elizabeth I's husband?
5. Who led the British forces at the Battle of Waterloo?
6. Who was Queen of England for nine days?
7. Which monarch was forced to sign the Magna Carta?
8. Which teenage girl led the French army against the English in the 15th century?
9. Who was Henry VIII's first wife?
10. Who was the famous General killed at Khartoum?
11. Which King Henry ordered the murder of Thomas Becket?
12. Which unpleasant-sounding Ivan was crowned first Tsar of Russia?
13. What was the name of the first King of England and Scotland?
14. Who was the Younger PM who introduced income tax?
15. From 1714 to 1830 all British monarchs were called what?
16. Who had his tomb in the Valley of Kings discovered in the 1920s?
17. Who was the famous captain of the ship the *Golden Hind*?
18. Inigo Jones followed which profession?
19. Who were massacred by the Campbells at Glencoe?
20. Of British monarchs, have more been called William or Edward?
21. In which battle was Admiral Horatio Nelson fatally wounded?
22. Who took the rap for the failed pot to blow up James I?
23. By what name was Richard I known?
24. How did Charles I die?
25. Whom does the Albert Hall in London commemorate?
26. To which monarch did Nell Gwyn display her oranges?
27. Which William ordered the building of the Tower of London?
28. Which Queen Marie lost her head in the French Revolution?
29. King George II gave his name to which American state?
30. Which monarch has ruled longest in the UK?

Quiz 69 World Soccer

Answers - see page 79

LEVEL 1

1 Which German player effectively created the sweeper role?
2 Which country does Patrick Berger play for?
3 What is the colour of the strip of the Welsh national team?
4 Which Billy was Northern Ireland manager throughout the 80s?
5 Boca Juniors come from which country?
6 Which striker's England goal tally was one short of Bobby Charlton's?
7 Franco Baresi played 450 plus games for which Italian club?
8 What was the Brazil v. Italy 1994 World Cup Final score at full time?
9 Jan Ceulemans played for which country?
10 At which Dutch club did Denis Bergkamp start his career?
11 In October 1995, who was the first Brazilian to sign for Middlesbrough?
12 What is the nationality of the FA Cup Final's fastest ever goal-scorer?
13 Carlos Alberto was skipper of which World Cup-winning country?
14 George Weah plays for which country?
15 Which Lothar is Germany's most capped player?
16 Who followed Cruyff as coach at Barcelona?
17 Which country hosted the 1994 World Cup?
18 Which Republic star Liam played for Juventus and Sampdoria?
19 The Stadium Of Light is home of which Portuguese club?
20 What was the "colour" of the type of goal that decided Euro 96's Final?
21 Which Scottish boss died of a heart attack during a game against Wales?
22 In which country did Pele wind down his playing career?
23 Who scored England's first and last goals in Euro 96?
24 Which country does Faustino Asprilla play for?
25 Which national team was managed by Roy Hodgson?
26 Which country hosted the 1966 World Cup?
27 Alfredo di Stefano was a regular European Cup Final scorer for which club?
28 Which Russian winger played for Man. Utd and Everton?
29 Who was the first person to have been in charge of England and Australia?
30 Gazza has played club football in which three European countries?

Quiz 70 Pot Luck 31

LEVEL 1

1 Which prime minister held office first - Eden or Macmillan?
2 Which Don made the album *American Pie*?
3 Who won an Oscar for Best Actor in *The King And I*?
4 Who plays rugby union at Kingsholm Road?
5 The character Mrs Mangel appeared in which TV soap?
6 Sharron Davies is associated with which sport?
7 Who wrote the novel *Animal Farm*?
8 What does the M stand for in MIRAS?
9 In the Bible, which book immediately follows the Acts of the Apostles?
10 Who had a No. 1 with "I'd Do Anything For Love (But I Won't Do That)"?
11 In which country is the city of Calgary?
12 Which Martin starred in "The Chief"?
13 In which decade of the 20th century was Sue Lawley born?
14 What word can go after "sign" and before "office"?
15 Which Marvin Heard It Through the Grapevine?
16 Which Virginia was BBC Sports Personality of The Year in 1977?
17 Which George wrote the play *Pygmalion*?
18 Uriah Heep appears in which Charles Dickens novel?
19 What colour is in Cilla Black's maiden name?
20 Which prime minister supported Huddersfield Town?
21 How would 71 be shown in Roman numerals?
22 Jack Regan and George Carter appeared in which TV series?
23 Joy, Babs and Teddy formed which sisters?
24 In which month is St George's Day?
25 Which bird gave Fleetwood Mac their first No. 1?
26 For which county does Mike Atherton play cricket?
27 Which lumbering animals appear in the *Fantasia* ballet dance?
28 What instrument did Fats Waller play?
29 What is the only English anagram of CAUTION?
30 In which decade did Labour gain its biggest parliamentary majority?

Quiz 71 Animal World

Answers - see page 77

LEVEL 1

1 In mammals, the Asian elephant is second but man has the longest - what?
2 A papillon is a breed of what?
3 What is the term for a group of beavers?
4 Alphabetically, which animal always comes first?
5 Dromedary and Bactrian are types of what?
6 What is a male fox called?
7 How many teats does a cow usually have?
8 In Britain, which is the only venomous snake?
9 What type of leaves does a koala feed on?
10 The cairn terrier was originally bred in which country?
11 What type of animal is a natterjack?
12 What type of "ology" is the study of animals?
13 What colour are the markings on a skunk?
14 A jenny is a female what?
15 What is the term for a group of elephants?
16 Which monkey has a blue and red face?
17 What type of animal is an ibex?
18 Which animal lives in an earth or sett?
19 What type of animal eats meat?
20 What name is given to a baby kangaroo?
21 Which creature provides a mole's main source of food?
22 What type of animal was Baloo in *The Jungle Book*?
23 The common and the grey are types of which creature that breed around the coast of Britain?
24 What kind of Naked creature did Desmond Morris write about?
25 A leveret is a young what?
26 Which animal's home is called a drey?
27 Which creature is the fastest land mammal?
28 Which is the largest land animal?
29 What is the term for a group of foxhounds?
30 The wild dog the dingo comes from which country?

World Soccer (see Quiz 69)
1 Franz Beckenbauer. 2 Czech Republic. 3 Red. 4 Bingham. 5 Argentina.
6 Gary Lineker. 7 AC Milan. 8 0-0. 9 Belgium. 10 Ajax. 11 Juninho.
12 Italian. 13 Brazil. 14 Liberia. 15 Matthaus. 16 Bobby Robson.
17 USA. 18 Brady. 19 Benfica. 20 Golden. 21 Jock Stein. 22 USA.
23 Alan Shearer. 24 Colombia. 25 Switzerland. 26 England. 27 Real
Madrid. 28 Andrei Kanchelskis. 29 Terry Venables. 30 England, Italy,
Scotland.

Answers

Quiz 72 Pot Luck 32

LEVEL 1

Answers - see page 78

1   The characters Alf, Else and Rita appeared in which TV series?
2   Which all-girl group had a Manic Monday in 1986?
3   Which UK car manufacturer produced the Hornet?
4   What word can go after "king" and before "man"?
5   How is the TV writer Lynda Titchmarsh better known?
6   Which Liverpool manager was born at Bootle in October 1948?
7   Who wrote the novel *Gridlock*?
8   What is the Roman numeral for one thousand?
9   How many gills in a pint?
10 In which decade of the 20th century was Mick Jagger born?
11 What are the two main parties in the US?
12 What name is given to a two-coloured oblong cake covered with almond paste?
13 In which country is the city of Dresden?
14 Which Brothers sang about the Price of Love?
15 Who wanted to ask the Wizard of Oz for courage?
16 In past times, what would a gentleman keep in his fob pocket?
17 What kind of creature is a cabbage white?
18 Who sang with the Miami Sound Machine?
19 Peter Docherty is associated with which sport?
20 What word can go before "holiday", "relations" and "school"?
21 Moving clockwise on a dartboard what number is next to 4?
22 Which Nigel starred in "Don't Wait Up"?
23 What type of triangle has equal sides and angles?
24 What is locked up in a tantalus?
25 Which planet is also referred to as the morning star?
26 Alvin, Theodore and Simon formed which group?
27 What name is given to a starter dish of sliced raw vegetables?
28 In the 90s, who had a No. 1 with "Goodnight Girl"?
29 The character Shane Parrish appeared in which TV soap?
30 Claustrophobia is the fear of what?

Pot Luck 31   (see Quiz 70)

1 Eden. **2** Maclean. **3** Yul Brynner. **4** Gloucester. **5** "Neighbours".
6 Swimming. **7** George Orwell. **8** Mortgage. **9** Romans. **10** Meat Loaf.
11 Canada. **12** Shaw. **13** 40s. **14** "Post". **15** Gaye. **16** Wade. **17** Bernard Shaw. **18** *David Copperfield*. **19** White. **20** Harold Wilson. **21** LXXI.
22 "The Sweeney". **23** The Beverley Sisters. **24** April. **25** Albatross.
26 Lancashire. **27** Hippos. **28** Piano. **29** Auction. **30** 1990s.

Quiz 73 Pop: Albums

Answers - see page 83

LEVEL 1

1 Who recorded *Rubber Soul*?

2 What goes after "What's The Story" in the title of Oasis's album?

3 Which Phil recorded *No Jacket Required*?

4 Who recorded *Dark Side of the Moon*?

5 Which Rod had six consecutive No. 1 albums in the 70s?

6 Who recorded *Purple Rain*?

7 Which group had a Night at the Opera and a Day at the Races?

8 Who recorded *Blue Hawaii*?

9 Paul McCartney was in which group for *Band On the Run*?

10 Who called their greatest hits album *End Of Part One*?

11 Which legendary guitarist recorded *From The Cradle*?

12 Who recorded *Off The Wall*?

13 Mike Oldfield presented what type of Bells?

14 Who recorded *The Colour Of My Love*?

15 Which Cat spent most weeks in the album charts in 1972?

16 Who recorded *Breakfast In America*?

17 Which Abba album had a French title?

18 Neil Diamond's film soundtrack album was about what type of singer?

19 Which easy-listening bandleader James has made over 50 albums?

20 Who recorded *Brothers In Arms*?

21 Which group were of a Different Class in 1995?

22 In the 90s, who broke out with *The Great Escape*?

23 Which Bruce spent most weeks in the album charts in 1985?

24 Who recorded *Bridge Over Troubled Water*?

25 In the 70s who recorded *Goodbye Yellow Brick Road*?

26 Which Simply Red album featured "For Your Babies" and "Stars"?

27 *Rumours* provided over 400 weeks on the album chart for whom ?

28 Who recorded *Bat Out Of Hell*?

29 Which Michael - not Jackson - spent most weeks in the 1991 charts?

30 What was Definitely the first No. 1 album from Oasis?

Quiz 74 Pot Luck 33

Answers - see page 84

1   Desmond Douglas is associated with which sport?
2   What is Siam now called?
3   In which decade of the 20th century was Bonnie Langford born?
4   In which country is the city of Faisalabad?
5   Audrey Fforbes-Hamilton appeared in which TV series?
6   Alicante and Marmande are types of what?
7   Who wrote the novel *Black Beauty*?
8   In France, what is the abbreviation for Monsieur?
9   Which Michael declared "Love Changes Everything"?
10 Which Nigel was BBC Sports Personality of the Year in 1986?
11 What is the square root of 121?
12 Which John starred in "Bergerac"?
13 The airline Aer Lingus is from which country?
14 What word can go after "paper" and before "reaction"?
15 What is the administrative centre for the county of Essex?
16 Is Bermuda ahead of or behind Greenwich Mean Time?
17 In the 80s, who had a No. 1 with "Imagine"?
18 The zodiac sign Sagittarius covers which two calendar months?
19 How is the Hollywood actor John Charlton Carter better known?
20 Which Spanish club did Mark Hughes play for?
21 On a Monopoly board, what colour is Regent Street?
22 The character Amy Turtle appeared in which TV soap?
23 Was Neptune a Roman or Greek god?
24 Who won an Oscar for Best Actress in *The Silence of the Lambs*?
25 What is the traditional accompaniment to haggis on Burns Night?
26 How many minutes in half a day?
27 Which trumpeter Kenny performed with his Jazzmen?
28 How many walls surround a squash court?
29 The resort of Morecambe is in which county?
30 A4 is a size of what?

Answers

Performing Arts (see Quiz 76)

1 Ballet. 2 Drury Lane. 3 Opera. 4 Moscow. 5 Gilbert and Sullivan.
6 French. 7 None. 8 The Proms. 9 Glenn Miller. 10 Opera. 11 Milan.
12 Violin. 13 Music Hall. 14 USA. 15 Circus. 16 Good luck.
17 Nashville. 18 Tom Stoppard. 19 Three. 20 Rudolph, Margot.
21 English. 22 Harmonica. 23 Lipman. 24 Brass. 25 New York.
26 Greece. 27 Tchaikovsky. 28 The Met. 29 Sydney. 30 Miller.

Quiz 75 TV Times 2

LEVEL 1

1　Which Clive chaired "Whose Line is it Anyway"?

2　Which 80s drama centred on Liverpudlian Yosser Hughes?

3　In which US city did the action of "Cheers" take place?

4　Which Doctor abandoned his Casebook in the 90s revival of the series?

5　Who played Jeeves to Hugh Laurie's Bertie Wooster?

6　In "Neighbours" Erinsborough is a suburb of which city?

7　On which night does "Noel's House Party" take place?

8　What were Rita Garnett's parents called?

9　In which series did Richard de Vere buy Grantleigh Manor?

10　Which animals did Barbara Woodhouse usually appear with?

11　Which soap was a spin-off from "Dallas"?

12　What is "Jimmy's"?

13　Who plays the Chef at the Le Château Anglais in Oxfordshire?

14　Which British actress played Alexis Carrington in "Dynasty"?

15　Which two Michaels have hosted "Give Us A Clue"?

16　What was James's wife called in "All Creatures Great and Small"?

17　Which Kate is famous for her news reports from Tiananmen Square ?

18　What is Charlie Fairhead's job at Holby City Hospital?

19　In "Dallas" which character returned from the dead in the shower?

20　Which Doctor has had assistants called Vicki, Jo, Melanie and Ace?

21　Which 90s series featured Guy Lofthouse and Guy MacFadyean?

22　Where was "Harry's Game" set?

23　What is the House in TV's "House of Cards"?

24　Which drama features Claude Jeremiah Greengrass?

25　Which comedy show is TV's answer to radio's "News Quiz"?

26　Who is the male presenter of BBC TV's "Children in Need"?

27　Which two comedians were famous for their 'head-to-head' scenes?

28　Which TV war reporter became an MP in 1997?

29　Which all-round entertainer's catchphrase is "Awight!"?

30　Which soap was trailed as "sex, sun and sangria"?

1   Diaghilev was associated with which branch of the arts?
2   In which London lane is the Theatre Royal?
3   Guiseppe Verdi is most famous for which type of musical work?
4   In which city is the Bolshoi Theatre?
5   Who wrote *HMS Pinafore*?
6   What was the nationality of the pianist and composer Claude Debussy?
7   How many symphonies did Beethoven write after the ninth?
8   Which series of concerts is held in late summer at the Albert Hall?
9   Which dance band leader disappeared during World War II?
10 In which branch of the arts did Joan Sutherland achieve fame?
11 In which Italian city is La Scala?
12 Which musical instrument does Stephane Grappelli play?
13 What type of entertainment did the Americans call vaudeville?
14 If you receive a Tony you have been performing in which country?
15 What kind of entertainment did Barnum call "the Greatest Show on Earth"?
16 What do you wish a performer when you say "break a leg"?
17 What is the name of the music centre that is the capital of Tennessee?
18 Which playwright married the TV doctor, Miriam?
19 How many sisters were in the title of the play by Chekhov?
20 What were the first names of Nureyev and Fonteyn?
21 What was Elgar's nationality?
22 Which musical instrument does Larry Adler play?
23 Which actress Maureen is the wife of the playwright Jack Rosenthal?
24 The cornet belongs to which family of musical instruments?
25 In which city is Broadway?
26 A balalaika originates from which country?
27 Which composer had the first names Peter Ilyich?
28 What is New York's Metropolitan Opera more popularly called?
29 Which Australian city has an imaginatively designed Opera House ?
30 Which Arthur wrote *The Crucible*?

Quiz 77 Pot Luck 34

Answers - see page 87

1   In rugby, what did Keighley add to their name in the 90s?
2   Dipsophobia is the fear of what?
3   In which decade of the 20th century was John Thaw born?
4   What word can go after "soap" and before "office"?
5   How is the 60s singer James Marcus Smith better known?
6   Kendall, Walker and Royle have all managed which club?
7   Who wrote the novel *Tom Sawyer*?
8   How many yards in a furlong?
9   The characters Bill and Ben Porter appeared in which TV series?
10 In the 80s, who had a No. 1 with "Papa Don't Preach"?
11 What is the only English anagram of TEND?
12 Edwina Currie represented which political party?
13 Which country does the drink ouzo come from?
14 How many times do you sing "jingle" in a chorus of jingle bells?
15 The character Doreen Corkhill appeared in which TV soap?
16 Moving anticlockwise on a dartboard what number is next to 15?
17 In which country is the city of Gothenburg?
18 Mal Donaghy is associated with which sport?
19 What word can follow "filter", "graph" and "rice"?
20 In which city did Tony Bennett leave his heart?
21 By what name is endive known in the US?
22 Which Nigel starred in "Yes Minister"?
23 Which UK car manufacturer produced the Prefect?
24 What is 60 per cent of 3,000?
25 Who was singing about his Ding-a-Ling in 1972?
26 What is the sum of a century plus a gross?
27 A mazurka is a type of what?
28 On the Swedish flag what is the colour of the cross?
29 The soldier Robert Clive has his name linked with which country?
30 Who led the Family Stone?

Answers

Pot Luck 35 (see Quiz 79)
1 Seaweed. 2 Cher. 3 Obtuse. 4 Black. 5 Faith. 6 Boxing. 7 Douglas Adams. 8 A knot. 9 Honor Blackman. 10 Four. 11 Abba. 12 Defence. 13 30s. 14 "Blind". 15 "The Upper Hand". 16 Andrew. 17 Wilde. 18 Germany. 19 Charles Aznavour. 20 Paul Ince. 21 "Coronation Street". 22 Middle letters row. 23 Bolton. 24 Zirconium. 25 None. 26 The maiden all forlorn. 27 North Sea. 28 "Cook". 29 A flitch. 30 Blur.

Quiz 78 80s Films

LEVEL 1

Answers - see page 88

1 Which Attenborough brother directed *Gandhi*?

2 What is the nationality of the hero of *Crocodile Dundee*?

3 Which Raging animal is in the title of the 1980 Robert De Niro film?

4 The Return of what was the third of the *Star Wars* trilogy?

5 Whose Choice won Meryl Streep an Oscar in 1982?

6 Which British film was about the 1924 Olympics?

7 The Adventures of which Baron proved to be one of the greatest cinematic flops in history?

8 Which Crusade featured in the title of the 1989 *Indiana Jones* movie?

9 In which city does *Beverly Hills Cop* take place?

10 What sort of People were the stars of the 1980 Donald Sutherland film?

11 Which Henry and Katharine won Oscars for *On Golden Pond*?

12 In which film did Bob Hoskins play opposite a cartoon character?

13 Who renewed his battle against the Joker in 1989?

14 How many Men starred with a baby in the 1987 movie?

15 In which 1982 film did Dustin Hoffman appear in drag?

16 In which US state was the Best Little Whorehouse in 1982?

17 Which organization is *Married to the Mob* about?

18 Which country did the DJ say Good Morning to in the 1987 film?

19 Which continent featured in the Robert Redford/Meryl Streep film about Karen Blixen?

20 Whom was the chauffeur Driving in the 1989 film?

21 Which financial location was the subject of a Michael Douglas film?

22 Which Warren Beatty film of the 80s was set in communist Russia?

23 The Kiss of whom provided William Hurt with an Oscar?

24 Who and her Sisters were the subject of a Woody Allen movie?

25 Which Kevin appeared in *A Fish Called Wanda*?

26 If Billy Crystal was Harry, who was Sally in 1989?

27 Where was the American Werewolf in the 1981 film?

28 *The Killing Fields* deals with events in which neighbour of Vietnam?

29 Which Helena starred in *A Room With a View*?

30 Where was the Last Exit to in 1989?

Answers

Celebs (see Quiz 80)

1 Christy. 2 Roger Moore. 3 Swedish. 4 Gaby Roslin. 5 Monaco.
6 Andrew. 7 Ekland. 8 Henshall. 9 Gazza. 10 None. 11 Max. 12 Boys
- in a Wonderbra ad. 13 Ivana. 14 Zandra. 15 Antonia. 16 The Spice Girls.
17 Tennis. 18 Japanese. 19 Versace. 20 Helvin. 21 Lumley. 22 Collins.
23 Laura Ashley. 24 Frost. 25 Tara. 26 The car keys. 27 Hugh Grant.
28 Jasper. 29 Ronald. 30 Princess of Wales.

Quiz 79 Pot Luck 35

Answers - see page 85

1　Agar-agar is a type of gelatine made from what?
2　Who won an Oscar for Best Actress in *Moonstruck*?
3　What type of angles are greater than 90 but less than 180 degrees?
4　What colour goes before Sabbath and Box in group names?
5　Which Adam starred in "Love Hurts"?
6　Terry Downes is associated with which sport?
7　Who wrote the book *The Hitch Hiker's Guide To the Galaxy*?
8　What is a sheep-shank?
9　Who played Pussy Galore in *Goldfinger*?
10　How many portraits are carved into Mount Rushmore?
11　In the 70s, who had a No. 1 with "Knowing Me Knowing You"?
12　Which Ministry is the MoD?
13　In which decade of the 20th century was Paul Daniels born?
14　What word can go after "colour" and before "spot"?
15　The character Charlie Burrows appeared in which TV series?
16　Alphabetically, who is the first of the Apostles?
17　Which Oscar wrote the play *The Importance of Being Earnest*?
18　In which country is the city of Hanover?
19　How is Charles Aznavurjan better known?
20　Who was the first black soccer player to captain England?
21　The character Stan Ogden appeared in which TV soap?
22　The letter D is on which row of a typewriter or computer keyboard?
23　Which Michael sang "How Am I Supposed To Live Without You"?
24　Zr is the chemical symbol for which element?
25　How many Tory MPs were left in Scotland after the 1997 general election?
26　In "The House That Jack Built", who milked the cow with the crumpled horn?
27　The River Tay flows into which sea?
28　On TV what does Fern Britten say after "Ready Steady"?
29　What is the term given to a side of unsliced bacon?
30　"There's No Other Way" was the first top ten hit for which group?

Answers

Pot Luck 34 (see Quiz 77)

1　Cougars. 2　Drinking. 3　40s. 4　"Box". 5　P.J. Proby. 6　Everton. 7　Mark Twain. 8　220. 9　"2 Point 4 Children". 10　Madonna. 11　Dent. 12　Conservative. 13　Greece. 14　Six. 15　"Brookside". 16　10. 17　Sweden. 18　Football. 19　"Paper". 20　San Francisco. 21　Chicory. 22　Hawthorne. 23　Ford. 24　1,800. 25　Chuck Berry. 26　244. 27　Dance. 28　Yellow. 29　India. 30　Sly.

Quiz 80 Celebs

Answers - see page 86

LEVEL 1

1   What is the first name of the supermodel Ms Turlington?
2   Which former James Bond parted from his wife Luisa in the 1990s?
3   Which language other than English does Ulrika Jonsson speak?
4   Who is the daughter of the veteran broadcaster Clive Roslin?
5   Royals Albert, Caroline and Stephanie are from which principality?
6   What is the first name of Mr Parker-Bowles?
7   Which Swedish Britt was married to Peter Sellers?
8   Which musical star Ruthie became engaged to the actor John-Gordon Sinclair?
9   Which controversial footballer married Sheryl Failes?
10 Of Paula Yates and Bob Geldof's three children, how many are boys?
11 What is the first name of the publicist Mr Clifford?
12 To whom did Eva Herzigova most famously say hello?
13 What is the first name of Ivanka Trump's mother?
14 What is the first name of the flamboyant fashion designer Ms Rhodes?
15 Which Ms Da Sancha's affair with David Mellor caused his resignation?
16 Which quintet first advertised Pepsi in mid-1997?
17 Brooke Shields and Tatum O'Neal both married which type of sporting stars?
18 What is the nationality of the fashion designer Kenzo?
19 Who designed Liz Hurley's infamous "safety pin" dress?
20 Which model Marie was married to the photographer David Bailey?
21 Which actress Joanna was a model for the designer Jean Muir?
22 Which four-times-married actress Joan wrote *My Secrets*?
23 What was the designer Laura Mountney's married and business name?
24 Which political interviewer David is married to the daughter of the Duke of Norfolk?
25 What is the first name of the royal skiing companion Palmer-Tomkinson?
26 When Paula Hamilton advertised VW cars what were the only possessions of her ex's she kept?
27 Which English actor was arrested in Hollywood in a Divine situation?
28 What is Sir Terence Conran's designer son called?
29 What is the first name of Fergie's dad?
30 Andrew Morton became a celeb due to a biography of whom?

Answers

80s Films (see Quiz 78)
1 Richard. 2 Australian. 3 Bull. 4 The Jedi. 5 Sophie's. 6 *Chariots of Fire*.
7 Munchhausen. 8 Last. 9 Los Angeles. 10 Ordinary. 11 Fonda, Hepburn.
12 *Who Framed Roger Rabbit?*. 13 Batman. 14 Three. 15 *Tootsie*. 16 Texas.
17 Mafia. 18 Vietnam. 19 Africa. 20 Miss Daisy. 21 Wall Street.
22 *Reds*. 23 The Spider Woman. 24 Hannah. 25 Kline. 26 Meg Ryan.
27 London. 28 Cambodia. 29 Bonham-Carter. 30 Brooklyn.

Quiz 81 Pot Luck 36

Answers - see page 91

LEVEL 1

1 Clive Rice played cricket for which country?
2 James Grieve and Lord Lambourne are types of what?
3 Which UK car manufacturer produced the Hunter?
4 In which month is All Saints' Day?
5 How is Francis Avallone better known?
6 Which team did Coventry beat in their 80s FA Cup Final triumph?
7 Who wrote the novel *A Clockwork Orange*?
8 In which country is Ho Chi Minh City?
9 What word describes a straight line crossing the centre of a circle?
10 In which decade of the 20th century was Jim Davidson born?
11 Which Bill topped the most weeks in the chart list for 1956?
12 Which Tom starred in "Magnum PI"?
13 Richard Dunwoody is associated with which sport?
14 What word can go after "salad" and before "gown"?
15 How many square inches in a square foot?
16 In *Snow White*, what do the dwarfs tell you to do while you work?
17 Who was queen of the Roman Gods?
18 If February 1 is a Thursday in a non-leap year, what day is March 1?
19 The butler Hudson appeared in which TV series?
20 Haematophobia is the fear of what?
21 On a Monopoly board, what colour is Vine Street?
22 In the 60s, who had a No. 1 with "Honky Tonk Women"?
23 Which is greater 2/3 or 7/10?
24 What word can go before "all", "cast" and "take"?
25 What is South West Africa now called?
26 The character Lofty Holloway appeared in which TV soap?
27 Gazpacho is a type of what?
28 In which city does Batman operate?
29 Which Mike was the musical force behind the Wombles?
30 In ancient China, which precious green stone vase was buried with the dead?

Answers

Pot Luck 37 (see Quiz 83)
1 Italy. 2 Jerry Lee Lewis. 3 60s. 4 "Cream". 5 Chester. 6 Equestrianism.
7 Raymond Chandler. 8 Tyne and Wear. 9 "Worzel Gummidge". 10 Wolves.
11 Bottom. 12 Beaver. 13 12. 14 South Africa. 15 Maria Callas. 16 The
Republic. 17 *Nicholas Nickleby*. 18 Mme. 19 "Neighbours". 20 Bucks Fizz.
21 McColgan. 22 MacNee. 23 Sudan. 24 Citrus. 25 Altitude.
26 Liza Minnelli. 27 Jimmy Carter. 28 Sand. 29 Ahead. 30 Trumpet.

1   The green jacket is presented to the winner of which event?
2   Which country did the cricketer Graham Roope play for?
3   In boxing, what weight division is directly below heavyweight?
4   In horse racing, in which month is the Melbourne Cup held?
5   The 1994 Winter Olympic Games took place in which country?
6   Who won the Wimbledon women's singles most times in the 80s?
7   Which two USA cities stage major marathons?
8   Phil Hubble is associated with which sport?
9   How often is cycling's Tour of Spain held?
10 The golfer Nick Price comes from which country?
11 A cricket umpire extends both arms horizontally to signal what?
12 The boxers Ray Leonard and Ray Robinson were both known as what?
13 In which sport did Michelle Smith find fame?
14 In golf, what is the term for two under par for a hole?
15 What sport do the Pittsburgh Steelers play?
16 The Harry Vardon Trophy is presented in which sport?
17 Which country won the 1996 cricket World Cup Final?
18 Which county cricket club has its home at Old Trafford?
19 What is the nickname of rugby union's William Henry Hare?
20 In horse racing, which of the five Classics is held at Doncaster?
21 In boxing, what do the initials WBA stand for?
22 Allison Fisher is connected with which sport?
23 At which French course is the Prix du Jockey-Club held?
24 Who captained the 1997 visiting Aussie cricket team?
25 LOVELY is an anagram of which tennis term?
26 Which sport takes place in a velodrome?
27 In equestrianism, which Nick won the Volvo World Cup in 1995?
28 Martine Le Moignay is associated with which sport?
29 The terms serve, dig and spike relate to which sport?
30 Which rugby league team are the Tigers?

Answers

The 80s (see Quiz 84)

1 Lester Piggott. 2 Argentina. 3 October. 4 Marathon. 5 Bob Geldof.
6 Poland. 7 Mike Gatting. 8 Shergar. 9 Ronald Reagan. 10 Brighton.
11 Whitbread. 12 Foot. 13 Yuppies. 14 London. 15 Steel. 16 Egypt.
17 McEnroe. 18 Terry Waite. 19 Democrat. 20 Grade. 21 Arthur Scargill.
22 Livingstone. 23 AIDS. 24 Greenham. 25 Extraterrestrial. 26 Lawson.
27 Conservative. 28 *Mary Rose*. 29 India. 30 William.

Quiz 83 Pot Luck 37

Answers - see page 89

LEVEL 1

1　Gnocchi is a food from which country?
2　In the 50s, who had a No. 1 with "Great Balls Of Fire"?
3　In which decade of the 20th century was Jill Dando born?
4　What word can go after "ice" and before "cheese"?
5　What is the administrative centre for the county of Cheshire?
6　Liz Edgar is associated with which sport?
7　Who wrote the book *The Big Sleep*?
8　In 1974 parts of Northumberland and Durham made which new county?
9　Aunt Sally and Dolly Clothes-Peg appeared in which TV series?
10　In rugby league what did Warrington add to their name for 1997?
11　The letter X is on which row of a typewriter or computer keyboard?
12　Which gnawing Canadian animal has bright-orange teeth?
13　What is the square root of 144?
14　Jan Smuts airport is in which country?
15　How is the opera singer Maria Kalogeropoulos better known?
16　Frank Stapleton became highest scorer for which international side?
17　Wackford Squeers appears in which Charles Dickens novel?
18　In France, what is the abbreviation for Madame?
19　The twins Caroline and Christina Alessi appeared in which TV soap?
20　"Making Your Mind Up" was the first No. 1 for which group?
21　Which Liz was BBC Sports Personality of The Year in 1991?
22　Which Patrick starred in "The Avengers"?
23　In which country is the city of Khartoum?
24　What is the only English anagram of RUSTIC?
25　What term describes the measurement of height?
26　Who won an Oscar for Best Actress in *Cabaret*?
27　Who was the outgoing American President when Ronald Reagan took office?
28　What is the main ingredient in glass?
29　Is Zambia ahead of or behind Greenwich Mean Time?
30　What instrument did Eddie Calvert play?

Answers

Pot Luck 36 (see Quiz 81)

1 South Africa. 2 Apple. 3 Hillman. 4 November. 5 Frankie Avalon.
6 Spurs. 7 Anthony Burgess. 8 Vietnam. 9 Diameter. 10 50s. 11 Haley.
12 Selleck. 13 Horse Racing. 14 "Dressing". 15 144. 16 Whistle.
17 Juno. 18 Thursday. 19 "Upstairs Downstairs". 20 Blood. 21 Orange.
22 Rolling Stones. 23 7/10. 24 "Over". 25 Namibia. 26 "EastEnders".
27 Soup. 28 Gotham. 29 Batt. 30 Jade.

Quiz 84 The 80s

Answers - see page 90

1   Which British jockey was jailed for tax evasion in 1987?
2   General Galtieri was ousted as president of which country?
3   In which month was the hurricane of 1987 that swept Britain?
4   Which London race was held for the first time?
5   Who was the founder of Band Aid?
6   The Solidarity movement opposed communists in which country?
7   Which England cricket captain rowed with a Pakistani umpire?
8   Which Derby winning horse was kidnapped while in Ireland?
9   Which ex-movie actor became President of the US?
10 The IRA bombed a Tory Party conference at which seaside venue?
11 Which Fatima won Olympic gold for Britain in the javelin?
12 Which Michael became leader of the Labour Party?
13 Young upwardly mobile persons became known as what?
14 In which city were Prince Charles and Lady Diana Spencer married?
15 Which David stood down as Liberal leader in 1988?
16 Army officers assassinated President Sadat of which country?
17 Which John ended Borg's Wimbledon dominance?
18 Who was the special representative of the Archbishop of Canterbury taken
    hostage in Beirut?
19 What did the D stand for in the newly formed political party?
20 Which Michael took over as head of Channel Four?
21 Who was leader of the NUM in the mid-80s strikes?
22 Which Ken emerged as leader of the Greater London Council?
23 "Don't Die Of Ignorance" was a slogan linked with which disease?
24 Which Common witnessed protest against nuclear cruise missiles?
25 What does ET stand for in the Spielberg movie?
26 Which Nigel resigned as Mrs Thatcher's Chancellor ?
27 Which party had a landslide victory in Britain in the 1983 elections?
28 Which Tudor ship was raised from the seabed?
29 There was a chemical leak at Bhopal - in which country?
30 Which Prince was the first-born child of the Princess of Wales?

Answers

Sporting Chance 2 (see Quiz 82)

1 US Masters. **2** England. **3** Cruiserweight. **4** November. **5** Norway.
6 Martina Navratilova. **7** Boston and New York. **8** Swimming. **9** Annually.
10 Zimbabwe. **11** A wide. **12** Sugar Ray. **13** Swimming. **14** Eagle.
15 American Football. **16** Golf. **17** Sri Lanka. **18** Lancashire. **19** Dusty.
20 St Leger. **21** World Boxing Association. **22** Snooker. **23** Chantilly.
24 Mark Taylor. **25** Volley. **26** Cycling. **27** Skelton. **28** Squash.
29 Volleyball. **30** Castleford.

Quiz 85 Pop: Superstars

Answers - see page 95

LEVEL 1

1 "You Can't Hurry Love" was the first No. 1 for which male singer?

2 Who is the Boss?

3 Which Eurovision Song Contest entry gave Cliff Richard a UK No. 1?

4 Who was a "Rocket Man" in the 70s?

5 Ziggy Stardust was the creation of which performer?

6 Whose autobiography was titled *Moonwalk*?

7 Who penned "Sultans Of Swing"?

8 The death of whose son inspired the song "Tears In Heaven"?

9 Which Peter was a founder member of Genesis?

10 Which supergroup took "Innuendo" to No. 1 in the UK?

11 Whose name had turned into a symbol for "Most Beautiful Girl In The World"?

12 Including membership of a group, which Paul has 20-plus UK No. 1s?

13 Which female star recorded "Chain Reaction"?

14 "Holiday" was the first hit in the UK for which solo performer?

15 Who created the fashion for wearing only one glove?

16 Which George sang "Careless Whisper"?

17 In the 80s, which Barbra was "A Woman In Love"?

18 Who was nicknamed the Pelvis in the 50s?

19 Who - after his death - had a No. 1 called "Living On My Own"?

20 Who was Tina Turner's first husband?

21 Who was Dancing in the Street with Dave Bowie for Live Aid ?

22 Who used to sing with the Faces?

23 Which country queen first hit the charts with "Jolene"?

24 Whose first UK Top Ten hit was "Dancing in the Dark" in 1985?

25 Elton John and who duetted on "Don't Let The Sun Go Down On Me"?

26 In which film did Madonna sing "Another Suitcase In Another Hall"?

27 In the 90s, who sang "I've Got You Under My Skin" with Bono?

28 Which group had a No. 1 with "Night Fever"?

29 What was the 1990 duet hit single for Tina Turner and Rod Stewart?

30 "Cracklin' Rosie" was the first hit of which singer/writer?

Answers

TV: Cops & Robbers (see Quiz 87)

1 "EastEnders". 2 "Cracker". 3 Hill Street. 4 Adam. 5 Chef. 6 New York.
7 Poirot. 8 "Prime Suspect". 9 He was a ghost. 10 Sherlock Holmes.
11 Pierce Brosnan. 12 East Anglia. 13 Juliet Bravo. 14 Jim. 15 "The Bill".
16 Kojak. 17 Hamish Macbeth. 18 Maigret. 19 Inspector Wexford.
20 "Miami Vice". 21 Bergerac. 22 Boon. 23 Ironside. 24 Red.
25 Miss Marple. 26 London. 27 Roderick. 28 Singing. 29 "Z Cars".
30 Jimmy Nail.

Quiz 86 Pot Luck 38

Answers - see page 96

1 Which Rik starred in "The New Statesman"?
2 What word can follow "clip", "dart" and "side"?
3 In which country is the city of Kingston?
4 Moving anticlockwise on a dartboard what number is next to 9?
5 How is Desmond Dacres better known?
6 What was the first Scottish soccer side that Chris Waddle played for?
7 Who wrote the novel *Tilly Trotter*?
8 Hippophobia is the fear of what?
9 Glen Campbell sang about what type of Cowboy?
10 Zn is the chemical symbol for which element?
11 The characters Peter and Annie Mayle appeared in which TV series?
12 Peter Elliott is associated with which sport?
13 In which decade of the 20th century was Anna Ford born?
14 What word can go after "Victoria" and before "tomato"?
15 How many cubic feet in a cubic yard?
16 "Vision Of Love" was the first Top Ten hit for which Mariah?
17 What other fruit is crossed with a plum to produce a nectarine?
18 What do you have a pocket full of if you play ring-a-ring-o'-roses?
19 What note is written in the space below the top line of the treble clef?
20 Ruby denotes which wedding anniversary?
21 Which UK car manufacturer produced the Viva?
22 What is the name of Queen Victoria's house on the Isle Of Wight?
23 Which Cockney duo sang "There Ain't No Pleasing You"?
24 Chapatti is unleavened bread originally from which country?
25 What is three eighths of 96?
26 Which old English coin was known as the tanner?
27 The River Mersey flows into which sea?
28 Alphabetically, which is the first of the days of the week?
29 In the 90s, who had a No. 1 with "I Will Always Love You"?
30 The character Derek Wilton appeared in which TV soap?

Quiz 87 TV: Cops & Robbers

Answers - see page 93

1   Michael French left which soap to star as Slade in "Crime Traveller"?

2   Which series featured Eddie "Fitz" Fitzgerald?

3   Which police station's Blues were led by Captain Frank Furillo?

4   What is the first name of P.D. James's Commander Dalgliesh?

5   In "Pie in the Sky" which profession did Henry combine with policing?

6   In which city was "Cagney and Lacey" set?

7   Which European sleuth's assistant was Captain Hastings?

8   Which series about a woman detective was written by Lynda La Plante?

9   Why was Marty Hopkirk an unusual detective?

10   Which Victorian sleuth was portrayed on TV by Jeremy Brett?

11   Which future 007 played Remington Steele?

12   In which area of the UK was "The Chief" set?

13   In the 80s what was the call sign of Inspector Jean Darblay then Inspector Kate Longton?

14   What was the first name of Rockford of "The Rockford Files"?

15   Which show features "Tosh" Lines, Jim Carver and June Ackland ?

16   Which New York cop ate lollipops?

17   Which policeman had a West Highland terrier called Wee Jock?

18   Which French detective had a pipe, raincoat and trilby?

19   Which Ruth Rendell detective lived in Kingsmarkham?

20   Which Florida-based drama had a theme song by Jan Hammer?

21   In the 80s who was rooting out villains in Jersey?

22   Which Midlands troubleshooter had a sidekick called Rocky?

23   Which wheelchair-bound detective was played by Raymond Burr?

24   What colour is Inspector Morse's Jaguar?

25   Which elderly female sleuth was played by Joan Hickson from 1984?

26   In which city did the action of "Between the Lines" take place?

27   What is the first name of Inspector Alleyn, created by Ngaio Marsh?

28   What was unusual about the detective in the Dennis Potter drama?

29   "Softly Softly" was the sequel to which TV police classic series?

30   Which Geordie actor starred as "Spender"?

Answers

Pop: Superstars (see Quiz 85)

1 Phil Collins. 2 Bruce Springsteen. 3 "Congratulations". 4 Elton John.
5 David Bowie. 6 Michael Jackson. 7 Mark Knopfler. 8 Eric Clapton.
9 Gabriel. 10 Queen. 11 Prince. 12 McCartney. 13 Diana Ross.
14 Madonna. 15 Michael Jackson. 16 Michael. 17 Streisand. 18 Elvis
Presley. 19 Freddie Mercury. 20 Ike Turner. 21 Mick Jagger. 22 Rod
Stewart. 23 Dolly Parton. 24 Bruce Springsteen. 25 George Michael.
26 *Evita*. 27 Frank Sinatra. 28 The Bee Gees. 29 "It Takes Two".
30 Neil Diamond.

Quiz 88 Pot Luck 39

Answers - see page 94

1   The three Christian brothers founded which group?
2   The zodiac sign Cancer covers which two calendar months?
3   In which decade of the 20th century was Bruce Forsyth born?
4   What word can go after "biscuit" and before "organ"?
5   The characters Jim and Annie Hacker appeared in which TV series?
6   Poseidon was the Greek god of what?
7   Who wrote *The Hound of the Baskervilles*?
8   Mike Gibson is associated with which sport?
9   Which angles are more than 180 but less than 360 degrees?
10 Which country did Clannad come from?
11 Who won an Oscar for Best Actress in *Gone With The Wind*?
12 Shortbread is a speciality of which country?
13 Alphabetically, what is the last of the calendar months?
14 Which profession is represented by the NAS/UWT?
15 How is the country singer Brenda Gail Webb better known?
16 Who was the first rock star to become chairman of a soccer club?
17 What is the fifth book of the Old Testament?
18 In which country is the city of Kyoto?
19 In the 90s, who had a No. 1 with "I Believe"?
20 The *Victory* was whose flagship?
21 In comics, on TV and in film, how is Bruce Wayne better known?
22 Which Dennis starred in "On The Up"?
23 Who recorded "Deeply Dippy"?
24 In which century was the Manchester Ship Canal opened?
25 Prime Minister Stanley Baldwin represented which political party?
26 The airline Aus-air is from which country?
27 Which is smaller 2/3 or 1/4?
28 The character David Wicks appeared in which TV soap?
29 Who took "Downtown" into the charts in the 60s and the 80s?
30 What is the middle colour of the Italian flag?

Quiz 89 Food & Drink 2

LEVEL 1

1　What colour wine goes into sangria?
2　Which country does Calvados come from originally?
3　What is the outer layer of a baked Alaska made from?
4　What colour is usually associated with the liqueur Chartreuse?
5　What is the main ingredient of a caramel sauce?
6　What are the two main vegetable ingredients of bubble and squeak?
7　What are large tubes of pasta called, usually eaten stuffed?
8　What is espresso?
9　Is Greek yoghurt thick, or does it have a pouring consistency?
10　Mozzarella cheese is used on top of which snack-food favourite?
11　Rick Stein's TV programmes are chiefly about which food?
12　Which nuts are used in marzipan?
13　Which county is traditionally famous for its hotpot?
14　Chapatti is an item from which country's cuisine?
15　Italian egg-shaped tomatoes are named after which fruit?
16　What colour is demerara sugar?
17　What sort of fruit would go into a Dundee cake?
18　What colour is an extra-virgin olive oil?
19　A crown roast would be made up from which meat?
20　Morel and oyster are which types of vegetable?
21　What sort of drink would fino or oloroso be?
22　What is a crouton made from?
23　Is green bacon smoked or unsmoked?
24　What is a Blue Vinney?
25　Which spice would a steak au poivre have on its outside?
26　Would a brut champagne be sweet or dry?
27　Which herb is used in pesto sauce?
28　Would a three-star brandy be very good, average or rather inferior?
29　Does a raw apricot have equal, more or fewer calories than a fresh one?
30　Which fruit could be honeydew or cantaloupe?

1 In which decade did the driving test introduce a written section?
2 What is an Eskimo canoe called?
3 Which is Germany's main airport?
4 What name is given to a cigar-shaped airship?
5 Which musical features a song about a "surrey with a fringe on top"?
6 The Montgolfier brothers flew in what type of craft?
7 Which motor company made the first production-line car?
8 What shape is the bottom of a punt?
9 E is the international vehicle registration letter of which country?
10 Whose 60s report axed many railway lines in Britain?
11 Orly airport is in which city?
12 In which country did the Toyota Motor Corporation originate?
13 Eurostar goes from which London station?
14 In song, "my old man said follow" which vehicle?
15 A Chinook is what type of vehicle?
16 What colour is the Circle Line on a London Underground map?
17 In which century was the Suez Canal opened?
18 What is the Boeing 747 usually known as?
19 What is the international vehicle registration letter of Germany?
20 The SNFC operates in which country?
21 What is the usual colour of an aeroplane's black box?
22 In the 1820s, who designed the locomotive the Rocket?
23 Which country does a sampan come from?
24 In which decade did Concorde enter commercial service?
25 What type of transporter was the ill-fated *Herald Of Free Enterprise*?
26 The major cargo port of Felixstowe is in which county?
27 Which Sir Freddie saw his airways company collapse in 1982?
28 What type of cars did the de Lorean factory produce?
29 Which brothers pioneered the first powered flight?
30 S is the international vehicle registration letter of which country?

Quiz 91 Pot Luck 40

Answers - see page 97

1 In verse, which bells said "You owe me five farthings"?
2 Which Rosemary had a 50s No. 1 with "This Ole House"?
3 The characters Rick, Neil and Vyvyan appeared in which TV series?
4 What word can go after "board" and before "service"?
5 How is the singer Thomas Woodward better known?
6 In 1995, which striker moved from QPR to Newcastle for £6 million?
7 Who wrote the novel *My Family and Other Animals*?
8 How many gallons in a bushel?
9 Who was Herge's most famous comic creation?
10 In which decade of the 20th century was Keith Floyd born?
11 In song what name follows "There's an old mill by a stream"?
12 Which David starred in "Poirot"?
13 Which Natalie sang "Miss You Like Crazy"?
14 The letter K is on which row of a typewriter or computer keyboard?
15 In America, what is the traditional Thanksgiving Day dessert?
16 How many of Henry VIII's wives were executed?
17 "Byker Grove" was set in which city?
18 The character Jacqui Dixon appeared in which TV soap?
19 How does 10.45 p.m. appear on a 24-hour clock?
20 What word can go before "frost", "knife" and "pot"?
21 Josh Gifford is associated with which sport?
22 On a Monopoly board, what colour is Leicester Square?
23 Which UK car manufacturer produced the Kitten?
24 Hydrophobia is the fear of what?
25 In which country is the city of Leipzig?
26 Moving clockwise on a dartboard what number is next to 17?
27 In the 80s, who had a No. 1 with "I Should Be So Lucky"?
28 Which athlete Brendan was BBC Sports Personality of the Year in 1974?
29 What is the only English anagram of OCHRE?
30 What type of apes live on the rock of Gibraltar?

1   Who was Ginger Rogers' most famous screen partner?

2   Who played Rick Blaine in *Casablanca*?

3   Which tramp's hat and cane were sold for £55,000 in the early 90s?

4   Who won an Oscar in 1934 when she was six years old?

5   Which Katharine starred in many films with Spencer Tracy?

6   Which blonde starred as Lorelei Lee in *Gentlemen Prefer Blondes*?

7   Who starred in *It Happened One Night* and *Gone With the Wind*?

8   Who was the female member of the Road films trio?

9   Who acted with her fourth husband in *All About Eve*?

10 Who played the title role in *Citizen Kane*?

11 Whose real name was Marion and was most famous for his westerns?

12 Which silent-movie star was born Rodolpho Alphonso Guglielmi di Valentina d'Antonguolla?

13 Which Hollywood star Barbara was in "The Thorn Birds" and "The Colbys" on TV?

14 Which diminutive star Mickey played a cigar-smoking midget in his first film at the age of seven?

15 Which Gregory won an Oscar for *To Kill a Mockingbird*?

16 Which Dracula star was born Bela Ferenc Denszo Blasko?

17 Which Steve of *The Great Escape* did his own racing stunts?

18 Which Vivien was once Mrs Laurence Olivier?

19 Which half of Laurel and Hardy was born in the Lake District?

20 Which famous co-star of Doris Day died of AIDS in 1985?

21 In which country was Cary Grant born?

22 Which Judy started out as part of the Gumm Sisters Kiddie Act?

23 What was the first name of the father and son actors Fairbanks?

24 Which Berlin-born star's first major film was *The Blue Angel* in 1930?

25 Which actor/singer in *High Society* died on a golf course?

26 Which James is credited with the catchphrase "You dirty rat!"?

27 Which Robert is known for his languid, sleepy eyes?

28 In which European capital city was Greta Garbo born?

29 What were the first names of sisters Fontaine and De Havilland?

30 Which Gary, of *High Noon* was the archetypal strong silent type?

Answers

Travel and Transport (see Quiz 90)

1 1990s. 2 Kayak. 3 Frankfurt. 4 Zeppelin. 5 *Oklahoma*. 6 Hot-air balloon. 7 Ford. 8 Flat. 9 Spain. 10 Dr Beeching. 11 Paris. 12 Japan. 13 Waterloo. 14 Van. 15 Helicopter. 16 Yellow. 17 19th. 18 Jumbo jet. 19 D. 20 France. 21 Orange. 22 George Stephenson. 23 China. 24 1970s. 25 Ferry. 26 Suffolk. 27 Laker. 28 Sports cars. 29 Wright Brothers. 30 Sweden.

1 Which pianist Russ had a 50s No. 1?
2 The character Dave Glover appeared in which TV soap?
3 In which decade of the 20th century was Michael Fish born?
4 Dusty Hare is associated with which sport?
5 Of which country is NBC a major broadcasting company?
6 What number is represented by the Roman numeral D?
7 Who wrote the novel *Dr No*?
8 What is the administrative centre for the county of Hampshire?
9 The characters Ted and Rita Simcock appeared in which TV series?
10 In the 90s, who had a No. 1 with "These Are the Days of Our Lives"?
11 Who plays rugby union at the Franklins Garden, Weedon Road?
12 In mythology, was Aphrodite a Greek or Roman goddess?
13 In music, what note is written on the line below the middle line of the treble clef?
14 What word can go after "trade" and before "Jack"?
15 How is Huey Louis Clegg better known?
16 Who were runners-up in soccer's 1994 World Cup?
17 Which Sam Cooke song includes the words "draw back your bow"?
18 What name is given to small cubes of fried bread served with soup?
19 Balaclava was a battle in which war?
20 What is the square root of 169?
21 In which country is the city of Malaga?
22 Which Robin starred in "Poldark"?
23 Which group backed Steve Harley?
24 Which boxer Barry was BBC Sports Personality of the Year in 1985?
25 Which constellation has three stars forming a "belt"?
26 What colour is umber?
27 Who won an Oscar for Best Actress in *Mary Poppins*?
28 What is 1/4 plus 1/8?
29 Which county does Alec Stewart play cricket for?
30 Which Elvis recorded "Oliver's Army"?

Pot Luck 42 (see Quiz 95)

Answers

1 Kiki Dee. 2 "Absolutely Fabulous". 3 Burma. 4 "Nap". 5 David Soul.
6 Alex Ferguson. 7 Arthur Hailey. 8 Uranium. 9 Whigfield. 10 50s.
11 1. 12 Bolam. 13 Being alone. 14 Worcester. 15 Percentage.
16 Triumph. 17 November. 18 Cricket. 19 "Pudding". 20 "Coronation
Street". 21 Dodd. 22 Rhinos. 23 Ahead. 24 Harold Wilson. 25 112.
26 Denmark. 27 Vingt. 28 Air Commodore. 29 Silver. 30 Val Doonican.

Quiz 94 Plant World

LEVEL 1

Answers - see page 104

1. Which green plant is widely seen on St Patrick's Day?
2. Which term describes a plant crossed from different species?
3. Where in London are the Royal Botanical Gardens?
4. If a leaf is variegated it has two or more what?
5. What is the flower truss of a willow tree called?
6. Which flower became the emblem of the Labour Party in the 80s?
7. Which part of a tree is cork made from?
8. Which former Tory minister shares his name with a type of tree?
9. Which Busy plant is also called Impatiens walleriana?
10. Which part of a plant may be called tap?
11. Which word describes a plant which can withstand the cold and frost?
12. Which "trap" shares its name with a planet?
13. What name is given to a plant which completes its life cycle in less than a year?
14. Are conifers evergreen or deciduous?
15. Which London borough hosts an annual flower show?
16. The thistle may be a weed to some but it's the symbol of which country?
17. What does a fungicide do to fungi?
18. Which garden vegetable - often used as a fruit - has edible stems and poisonous leaves?
19. What is the study of plants called?
20. A type of crocus produces which yellow spice or flavouring?
21. What are the fruits of the wild rose called?
22. Which holly trees are the only ones to bear berries?
23. Which plant associated with the seaside is used to make laver bread?
24. The cone or flower cluster of which plant is used to make beer?
25. Which tree can be white or weeping?
26. Archers made their bows from which wood commonly found in churchyards?
27. Does a crocus grow from a bulb or a corm?
28. On which continent did potatoes originate?
29. The maple is the national emblem of which country?
30. Is the cocoa tree native to North or South America?

The Media 2 (see Quiz 96)

Quiz 95 Pot Luck 42

Answers - see page 101

Answers - see page 101

LEVEL 1

1 Who sang with Elton John on "True Love"?
2 The character Patsy Stone appeared in which TV series?
3 In which country is the city of Mandelay?
4 What word can go after "kid" and before "kin"?
5 How is David Soulberg better known?
6 Who was the first manager to twice win the English soccer double?
7 Who wrote the novel *Airport*?
8 U is the chemical symbol for which element?
9 In the 90s, who had a No. 1 with "Saturday Night"?
10 In which decade of the 20th century was Ruby Wax born?
11 On a dartboard what number is opposite 19?
12 Which James starred in "The Likely Lads"?
13 Monophobia is the fear of what?
14 What is the administrative centre for the county of Hereford and Worcester?
15 Which term describes a way of representing a number as a fraction of one hundred?
16 Which UK car manufacturer produced the Toledo?
17 In which month is Thanksgiving Day in the USA?
18 Rachel Heyhoe Flint is chiefly associated with which sport?
19 What word can follow "milk", "summer" and "Yorkshire"?
20 The character Maud Grimes appeared in which TV soap?
21 Which comedian Ken sang "Love Is Like A Violin"?
22 In rugby league, what did Leeds add to their name in the 1990s?
23 Is Greece ahead of or behind Greenwich Mean Time?
24 Who was the outgoing PM when Edward Heath took office?
25 How many pounds in a hundredweight?
26 The airline Danair is from which country?
27 What is French for twenty?
28 Which RAF rank is the higher - Air Commodore or Group Captain?
29 In heraldry what is argent?
30 Which relaxed Irish singer recorded "Walk Tall"?

Quiz 96 The Media 2

Answers - see page 102

LEVEL 1

1   On which Radio station does Jimmy Young have a morning show?
2   If laughter is "canned" what is it?
3   Which part of the country does Meridian serve?
4   On which Radio station is "Desert Island Discs"?
5   What is the nationality of the media mogul Rupert Murdoch?
6   What does NBC stand for in the US?
7   In broadcasting what is an OB?
8   A simulcast is a simultaneous broadcast on which two media?
9   What is Channel 4's teletext service called?
10   Which Kelvin left the *Sun* to run Live! TV?
11   Which term describes a broadcast, transmitted as it takes place?
12   What is sitcom an abbreviation of?
13   TVS broadcasts in which part of the UK?
14   Which video format was outrivalled by the now established VHS?
15   Which independent radio station broadcasts classical music?
16   Which UK daily newspaper is printed on pink newsprint?
17   Which listings magazine was originally "the official organ of the BBC"?
18   What did Chris Evans leave because he didn't want to work on Fridays?
19   Which size of newspaper is smaller, tabloid or broadsheet?
20   Which radio station is known by the initials GLR?
21   Of Radios 1,2,3,4, and 5 which is broadcast only on medium wave?
22   Which day of the week has an omnibus edition of "The Archers"?
23   Which country had an official newspaper *Pravda*?
24   Which city's name was dropped from the *Guardian* in 1959?
25   On which channel is the National Lottery draw seen live?
26   In which decade did BBC 2 open?
27   How many nights per week is "Newsnight" normally broadcast?
28   Which Danny was sacked by the BBC for criticizing football referees?
29   Which country, population only 738, has only one newspaper *L'Osservatore Romano*, yet prints more than 70,000 copies?
30   What shape is the logo for Channel 5?

Answers

Plant World (see Quiz 94)

1 Shamrock. 2 Hybrid. 3 Kew. 4 Colours. 5 Catkin. 6 Red rose. 7 Bark.
8 Redwood. 9 Busy Lizzie. 10 Root. 11 Hardy. 12 Venus Flytrap.
13 Annual. 14 Evergreen. 15 Chelsea. 16 Scotland. 17 Kills it.
18 Rhubarb. 19 Botany. 20 Saffron. 21 Hips. 22 Females. 23 Seaweed.
24 Hop. 25 Willow. 26 Yew. 27 Corm. 28 America. 29 Canada.
30 South.

Quiz 97 Speed Stars

Answers - see page 107

LEVEL 1

1. Which Pat was flat racing's champion jockey in 1993?
2. Mick the Miller was a champion in which sport?
3. Which Liz won the 1991 New York Marathon?
4. Which country did motor racing's Nelson Piquet come from?
5. Which Carl won Olympic 100 metre gold in 1984 and 1988?
6. The quick bowler Shaun Pollock plays for which country?
7. Mike Hazelwood is associated with which sport?
8. Which athlete Diane was cleared of charges of drugs taking in March '96?
9. Which snooker player was known as Hurricane?
10. Which Graham was Formula 1 World Champion in the 60s?
11. Which speed race goes from Putney to Mortlake?
12. Steve Cram comes from which town in the north-east?
13. Sanath Jayasuriya raced to a 48-ball century in '96 for which country?
14. Which country is Jacques Villeneuve from?
15. Which Kriss broke a British 20-year record in the 400m hurdles?
16. Where is the San Marino Grand Prix raced?
17. Which team scored in the first minute of the 1997 FA Cup Final?
18. In motor racing, who lost his place with the Williams team in the year he finished World Champion?
19. Which Barry was a 70s motorcycling world champion?
20. In what sport has Sarah Hardcastle won Olympic medals?
21. Which record-breaking athlete became a Tory MP in the 90s?
22. Which German won nine Grand Prix victories in 1995?
23. The Curragh race course is in which Irish county?
24. Which Zola controversially ran for Britain in the 80s ?
25. Which county does Sally Gunnell come from?
26. Which snooker player was nicknamed Whirlwind?
27. Which Ben was stripped of 100m Olympic Gold after a drugs test?
28. Which country did motor racing's Ayrton Senna come from?
29. Which sport takes place on the Cresta Run?
30. Who won Olympic 100 metres gold in 1992 for Britain?

Answers

Pop: Musicals (see Quiz 99)

1 *Cats.* **2** Travolta. **3** Crawford. **4** Barbara Dickson. **5** *Chess.* **6** Sensible. **7** *Carousel.* **8** Madonna. **9** Joseph. **10** "Don't Cry For Me, Argentina". **11** Grease. **12** Abba. **13** Banderas. **14** Cliff Richard. **15** Andrew Lloyd Webber. **16** Townshend. **17** Tim Rice. **18** Technicolor. **19** Magaldi. **20** *Les Miserables.* **21** *Phantom of the Opera.* **22** Electric Light Orchestra. **23** Summer. **24** *Sunset Boulevard.* **25** Jason Donovan. **26** Paige. **27** Essex. **28** *Cabaret.* **29** *Oliver!.* **30** Ball.

Quiz 98 Pot Luck 43

Answers - see page 108

LEVEL 1

1   The warmth rating of what is measured in togs?
2   The character Von Klinkerhoffen appeared in which TV series?
3   In which decade of the 20th century was Chris Tarrant born?
4   Which book is known as the NEB?
5   In the 60s, who had a No. 1 with "Eleanor Rigby"?
6   Gold denotes which wedding anniversary?
7   Who wrote the novel *Schindler's Ark*?
8   Totnes and Tiverton castles are both in which county?
9   In architecture, what is a water spout carved as a grotesque face?
10 In the US, who was Senator McCarthy trying to identify in his "witch-hunts"?
11 In mythology, who had a face that launched a thousand ships?
12 In the 80s, who joined forces with the Dubliners for "The Irish Rover"?
13 Patsy Hendren is associated with which sport?
14 What word can go after "home" and before "house"?
15 How is the singer Paul Hewson better known?
16 In October 1995, Middlesbrough's club shop sold 2,000 shirts of which international side?
17 The zodiac sign Virgo covers which two calendar months?
18 What is the total if VAT at 15% is added to a £500 item?
19 In London what are Harlequins and Saracens?
20 In 1965, "Times They Are A-Changin'" was whose first Top Ten hit?
21 In which country is the city of Marrakesh?
22 Which Julia starred in "Fresh Fields"?
23 In economics, what does the B stand for in PSBR?
24 Gouda cheese comes from which country?
25 Which Henry claimed that "History is bunk"?
26 Who won an Oscar for Best Actress in *Sophie's Choice*?
27 What is the only English anagram of INCH?
28 Which Rod topped the most weeks in the chart list for 1976?
29 The character Annalise Hartman appeared in which TV soap?
30 With which sport is Dickie Jeeps associated?

Quiz 99 Pop: Musicals

Answers - see page 105

LEVEL 1

1   The song "Memory" comes from which musical?
2   Which John starred in the film of *Grease*?
3   Which Michael had a hit with "Music Of The Night"?
4   Who sang with Elaine Paige on the single "I Know Him So Well"?
5   Which musical did the song come from?
6   Which Captain had an unlikely No. 1 with "Happy Talk"?
7   The song "You'll Never Walk Alone" comes from which musical?
8   In the film *Evita*, who sang "You Must Love Me"?
9   Phillip Schofield and Jason Donovan have played which biblical character?
10   In which song are the words, "I kept my promise, Don't keep your distance"?
11   Which musical features Danny and Sandy in the rock 'n' roll 50s?
12   Tim Rice and writers from which supergroup wrote *Chess*?
13   Which Antonio featured in the film *Evita*?
14   Who starred in the 60s film *Summer Holiday*?
15   Who provided the music for *Cats*?
16   Which Pete wrote the rock/opera *Tommy*?
17   Who wrote the lyrics for *Jesus Christ Superstar*?
18   What word describes Joseph's Dreamcoat?
19   Which character did Jimmy Nail play in *Evita*?
20   Which Victor Hugo novel became a musical?
21   Which stage musical is set in the Paris Opera House?
22   Which Orchestra feature on the No. 1 hit "Xanadu"?
23   Which type of Nights are in the title of a No. 1 single from *Grease*?
24   In which musical does the character Norma Desmond appear?
25   Who had a UK No. 1 with "Any Dream Will Do"?
26   Which Elaine played Grizabella the Glamour Cat?
27   Which Cockney David played Che on stage in *Evita*?
28   Which musical does the song "Cabaret" come from?
29   "As Long As He Needs Me" comes from which musical?
30   Which Michael first starred in *Aspects Of Love*?

Answers

Speed Stars (see Quiz 97)

1 Eddery. 2 Greyhound racing. 3 McColgan. 4 Brazil. 5 Lewis. 6 South Africa. 7 Water skiing. 8 Modahl. 9 Alex Higgins. 10 Hill. 11 University boat race. 12 Gateshead. 13 Sri Lanka. 14 Canada. 15 Akabusi. 16 Imola. 17 Chelsea. 18 Damon Hill. 19 Sheene. 20 Swimming. 21 Sebastian Coe. 22 Michael Schumacher. 23 Kildare. 24 Budd. 25 Essex. 26 Jimmy White. 27 Johnson. 28 Brazil. 29 Bobsleigh. 30 Linford Christie.

Quiz 100 Pot Luck 44

LEVEL 1

1   How many feet in a nautical mile?
2   In which country is the city of Osaka?
3   Brian Huggett is associated with which sport?
4   What word can go before "hole", "pie" and "post"?
5   Hoss and Little Joe Cartwright appeared in which TV series?
6   Who was drummer with the Who?
7   Who told a tale in "A Whiter Shade Of Pale"?
8   If the first of June is a Monday what day is the 1st of July?
9   What sport is played by the San Francisco 49ers?
10 In the Bible, what is the first book of the New Testament?
11 How many minutes in a day?
12 Which June starred in "Happy Ever After"?
13 On a Monopoly board, what colour is Oxford Street?
14 Peggotty appears in which Charles Dickens novel?
15 Which UK car manufacturer produced the Cresta?
16 Which song mentions a jolly swagman?
17 The letter U is on which row of a typewriter or computer keyboard?
18 In legend, which bird rises from its own ashes?
19 In computing, what does the A stand for in RAM?
20 Alphabetically, what is the first sign of the zodiac?
21 What name is given to the horizontal bar of a window?
22 Which phrase from French is used for a false step or a gaffe?
23 What day of the week did the Boomtown Rats not like?
24 What does a misogynist hate?
25 Which Foreign Secretary lost his seat in the 1997 general election?
26 Moving clockwise on a dartboard, what number is next to 19?
27 Chris Old is associated with which sport?
28 Xenophobia is the fear of what?
29 The character Dennis Watts appeared in which TV soap?
30 In the 80s, who had a No. 1 with "True Blue"?

Quiz 101 Children's TV

Answers - see page 111

LEVEL 1

1   Which series dealt with International Rescue and their super aircraft?
2   Where would you find a rabbit called Dylan and Ermintrude the cow?
3   In "The Muppets" what was Fozzie?
4   Which continent did Paddington Bear come from?
5   What sort of animals were Pinky and Perky?
6   Which programme began "Here is a house. Here is a door. Windows: one, two, three, four"?
7   What was the number plate on Postman Pat's van?
8   Which show featured Zippy, George plus Rod, Jane and Freddy?
9   Which show features the tallest, the fastest, the biggest of everything?
10 What sort of animal was Skippy?
11 Which Gerry and Sylvia pioneered supermarionation?
12 How was Granny Smith, played by Gudrun Ure, better known?
13 Which podgy cartoon Captain's ship was the *Black Pig*?
14 Which long-running programme did Tim Vincent leave in 1997?
15 Which Tank Engine is blue and has the number 1 on it?
16 Which Maggie co-presented "Multi-Coloured Swap Shop"?
17 Whose vocabulary was limited to words like "flobbalot"?
18 Whose friends were Teddy and Looby Loo?
19 Which show awarded cabbages to its losers?
20 Which school did Tucker, Zammo and Tegs attend?
21 Which country did Ivor the Engine come from?
22 Who was the first presenter of "Newsround"?
23 What was ITV's answer to "Blue Peter" called ?
24 In which show did Uncle Bulgaria, Tomsk and Tobermory appear?
25 Which Johnny was the first presenter of "Animal Magic"?
26 What was Worzel Gummidge?
27 What day of the week was "Live and Kicking" broadcast?
28 Which show featured Dill the dog and Parsley the lion?
29 What sort of creature was Basil Brush?
30 What form of entertainment are Hanna-Barbera famous for?

Answers

The 90s   (see Quiz 103)

1 The Queen. **2** Driving test. **3** Margaret Thatcher. **4** Mel and Kim.
5 Channel tunnel. **6** John McCarthy. **7** George Bush. **8** Hadlee. **9** The BBC.
10 Imran Khan. **11** Glasgow. **12** MPs. **13** Bobby Robson. **14** Comet.
15 David Mellor. **16** Michael Heseltine. **17** Ireland. **18** Atlanta in 1996.
19 Laura Davies. **20** The Referendum Party. **21** John Smith.
22 Ladies' public toilets. **23** Chris Patten. **24** Freddie Mercury.
25 O.J. Simpson. **26** Estée Lauder. **27** Carson. **28** Eric Cantona.
29 Windsor. **30** Camelot.

Quiz 102 Pot Luck 45

LEVEL 1

Answers - see page 112

1 Which Bette won an Oscar for Best Actress in *Dangerous*?
2 What is 10 cubed?
3 What is the administrative centre for the county of Shropshire?
4 What word can go after "music" and before "mark"?
5 How is Marvin Lee Addy better known?
6 Duncan Ferguson moved to Everton from which soccer club?
7 Who wrote the novel *The Shining*?
8 Tom Thumb and Little Gem are types of what?
9 In France, what is the abbreviation for Mademoiselle?
10 In which decade of the 20th century was Michaela Strachan born?
11 Brian Jacks is associated with which sport?
12 What does the Y stand for in NIMBY?
13 C.J. Parker and Lt Mitch Bucannon appeared in which TV series?
14 In the 80s, who had a No. 1 with "West End Girls"?
15 What did Castleford's name become for the 1997 rugby league season?
16 The airline El Al is from which country?
17 Who was the outgoing American President when Jimmy Carter took office?
18 What is Ceylon now called?
19 Mike Proctor played cricket for which country?
20 What word can follow "clay", "racing" and "wood"?
21 In which country is the city of Poona?
22 Which Paul starred in "Just Good Friends"?
23 Which Donna sang "Love To Love You Baby"?
24 Which Paul was BBC Sports Personality of the Year in 1990?
25 Diamond denotes which wedding anniversary?
26 Which army rank is the higher - colonel or brigadier?
27 The character Kim Tate appeared in which TV soap?
28 What is the only English anagram of ACHES?
29 What was Lot's wife turned into?
30 A merino is what kind of creature?

Quiz 103 The 90s

Answers - see page 109

LEVEL 1

1   Who described 1992 as an "annus horribilis"?
2   Which widely taken test had a theory element introduced in 1996?
3   Who became the first Prime Minister to be made a baroness?
4   Dying of cancer at 22, Mel Appleby had been part of which pop duo?
5   In which tunnel was there a major fire in autumn 1996?
6   Which former Beirut hostage wrote a book with Jill Morrell?
7   Who lost when Bill Clinton first became US President?
8   Which New Zealander Richard became the first to 400 Test wickets?
9   Before he was elected an MP in 1997, who was Martin Bell's employer?
10 Which Pakistan cricketer was named in the Botham/Lamb libel case?
11 Which Scottish city was the Cultural Capital of Europe in 1990-1?
12 Who voted themselves a 26-per-cent pay rise in 1996?
13 Who managed England's soccer team in Italia 90?
14 Hale-Bopp hit the headlines in the 90s, but who or what was it?
15 Which former "Minister of Fun" resigned over a scandal with an actress?
16 Who was John Major's Deputy Prime Minister?
17 Which country dominated the Eurovision Song Contest in the 90s?
18 Which Olympics were blighted by the Centennial Park bomb?
19 Which golfer became the first British woman in history to earn a million
    from her sport?
20 Which Party did Sir James Goldsmith found before the 1997 election?
21 Who immediately preceded Tony Blair as leader of the Labour Party?
22 In 1997 the WI campaigned for more private space in which public places?
23 Who was the last British Governor of Hong Kong?
24 Which member of Queen died?
25 Which ex-footballer's trial was a long-running saga on US TV?
26 Which cosmetic house signed up Liz Hurley in 1995?
27 Which Willie announced his retirement from horse racing in 1997?
28 Which French footballer moved from Leeds to Man. Utd?
29 Which royal castle caught fire in 1992?
30 Which company won the contract for the National Lottery?

Quiz 104 World Tour

LEVEL 1

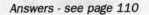

Answers - see page 110

1 The capital of Western Australia shares its name with which Scottish city?
2 How is Peking now more commonly known?
3 In which country would you see an emu fly?
4 Is French Provence nearer the Channel or the Mediterranean?
5 In which country do people speak Afrikaans?
6 Which bay to the west of France is notorious for its rough seas?
7 What is the principal language of Bulgaria?
8 If you were visiting the home of Parmesan cheese, in which country would you be?
9 Which country used to be called the DDR?
10 In which city is the Wailing Wall?
11 Is the Orinoco in North or South America?
12 How many consonants are there in Mississippi?
13 Which country has the international vehicle registration letter I?
14 Which major town of Morocco shares its name with a famous film?
15 In which country is Bavaria?
16 Which drug is Colombia's chief export?
17 On which long African river is the Aswan Dam?
18 Which Spanish city hosted the 1992 Olympics?
19 In which city is the University of Essex?
20 An Indian city gave its name to which style of riding breeches?
21 Andorra lies between which two countries?
22 Which country's national sport is Sumo wrestling?
23 The Cape of Good Hope is at the tip of which continent?
24 Which city has the cathedrals of Notre Dame and Sacre Coeur?
25 Which falls lie on the Zambesi river?
26 Which US state, capital Phoenix, is called the Grand Canyon state?
27 Which Baltic state has Tallinn as its capital?
28 Which is the only country in the world to begin with Q?
29 In which continent is Mount McKinley?
30 Which currency would you spend in Pakistan?

Answers

Pot Luck 45 (see Quiz 102)

1 Davis. **2** 1,000. **3** Shrewsbury. **4** "Hall". **5** Meat Loaf. **6** Rangers. **7** Stephen King. **8** Lettuce. **9** Mlle. **10** 60s. **11** Judo. **12** Yard. **13** " Baywatch". **14** Pet Shop Boys. **15** Castleford Tigers. **16** Israel. **17** Gerald Ford. **18** Sri Lanka. **19** South Africa. **20** "Pigeon". **21** India. **22** Nicholas. **23** Summer. **24** Gascoigne. **25** Sixtieth. **26** Brigadier. **27** "Emmerdale". **28** Chase. **29** Pillar of salt. **30** Sheep.

Quiz 105 Pot Luck 46

Answers - see page 115

Answers - see page 115

LEVEL 1

1 In the 70s, who had a No. 1 with "Bright Eyes"?
2 What word can go before "ache", "ring" and "wig"?
3 Mark James is associated with which sport?
4 Blake and Krystle Carrington appeared in which TV series?
5 In tennis, what name is given to a score of 40-40?
6 Maastricht airport is in which country?
7 Who wrote the novel *The Invisible Man*?
8 What is 4/10 minus 2/5?
9 In Greek mythology, who was god of the sun?
10 In which decade of the 20th century was Phillip Schofield born?
11 Which UK car manufacturer produced the Capri?
12 Which Paul starred in "The Good Life"?
13 How would 42 be shown in Roman numerals?
14 What word can go after "special" and before "line"?
15 How is the singer Kim Smith better known?
16 Which club did Roy Keane play for before his move to Man. Utd?
17 What does E stand for in PEP?
18 In which country is the city of Port Elizabeth?
19 In which month is Christmas in Australia?
20 The zodiac sign Scorpio covers which two calendar months?
21 How is Christopher John Mottram better known?
22 Ra is the chemical symbol for which element?
23 The character Jean Crosbie appeared in which TV soap?
24 What type of Love was a hit for Soft Cell in 1981 and 1991?
25 How many kilograms in seven tonnes?
26 Is Greenland ahead of or behind Greenwich Mean Time?
27 The letter Y is on which row of a typewriter or computer keyboard?
28 Who won ice figure skating gold for Britain in 1980?
29 What is the administrative centre for the county of Cleveland?
30 Moving anticlockwise on a dartboard what number is next to 11?

Pot Luck 47 (see Quiz 107)

1 Hockey. 2 "Dallas". 3 60s. 4 Trinidad. 5 Tammy Wynette.
6 Federation. 7 Salman Rushdie. 8 Switzerland. 9 Billy Ocean.
10 Cobbler. 11 James Callaghan. 12 Brambell. 13 American Football.
14 Wednesday. 15 Their relatives. 16 Fish. 17 12·50. 18 Christie.
19 "Coronation Street". 20 A car. 21 Dumb. 22 Upper arm. 23 Rivet.
24 Italy. 25 Sheep. 26 Dougal. 27 Red. 28 Simply Red. 29 Trent Bridge.
30 McGee.

Answers

Quiz 106 90s Films

Answers - see page 116

 LEVEL 1

1   In which film did Hannibal Lecter feature?
2   Which Steven Spielberg film was described as "65 million years in the making"?
3   Which film gave Macaulay Culkin his first huge success?
4   Which English film swept the Oscar board in 1997?
5   In which film did Robin Williams dress as a Scottish housekeeper?
6   Which actor was the ghost in the film of the same name?
7   Who did Kevin Costner protect in *The Bodyguard*?
8   Which musical instrument was the title of a 1993 Oscar winner?
9   Which comedy was described as "Five good reasons to stay single"?
10   In which film was Robin Williams the voice of the genie?
11   Which hero was Prince of Thieves in 1991?
12   Which creatures had the prefix Teenage Mutant Ninja?
13   In which film is Peter Pan a father and a lawyer?
14   Which Disney film was about the heroine who saved Captain Smith?
15   In which movie did Nigel Hawthorne play an English monarch?
16   Which 1990 Western had Kevin Costner as actor and director?
17   Which Disney film included "The Circle of Life" and "Hakuna Matata"?
18   Who played Eva Duarte in a 1996 musical?
19   In which film did Susan Sarandon play a nun who visits a prisoner on Death Row?
20   Which Disney Story was the first to be wholly computer-generated?
21   Which 1993 Spielberg film was largely shot in black and white?
22   In which film did Mel Gibson play the Scots hero William Wallace?
23   Which Whoopi Goldberg film was subtitled "Back in the Habit"?
24   Which western actor directed and starred in *Unforgiven*?
25   Which British actor Jeremy won an Oscar for *Reversal of Fortune*?
26   Which Tom was the star of *Forrest Gump*?
27   Which film had the song "Streets of Philadelphia"?
28   Which Jamie starred in *Fierce Creatures*?
29   Who played James Bond in *Goldeneye*?
30   Which US President did Anthony Hopkins play on film in 1995?

Quiz 107 Pot Luck 47

Answers - see page 113

LEVEL 1

1 Janet Sixsmith is associated with which sport?
2 J.R. Ewing and Miss Ellie appeared in which TV series?
3 In which decade of the 20th century was Rory Bremner born?
4 In which country is the city of Port of Spain?
5 How is the country singer Virginia Pugh better known?
6 In the initials FIFA, what does the first F stand for?
7 Who wrote the controversial novel *The Satanic Verses*?
8 Which country's stamps have featured the word Helvetia?
9 In the 80s, who had a No. 1 with "When The Going Gets Tough, The Tough Get Going"?
10 What is the only English anagram of CLOBBER?
11 Who was the outgoing PM when Margaret Thatcher took office?
12 Which Wilfred starred in "Steptoe And Son"?
13 What sport is played by the Miami Dolphins?
14 Alphabetically, what is the last of the days of the week?
15 A nepotist favours what type of people?
16 Billingsgate Market was famous for what sort of food?
17 What is 1/8 as a percentage to two decimal points?
18 Which Julie won an Oscar for Best Actress in *Darling*?
19 The character Denise Osbourne appeared in which TV soap?
20 Who or what was Genevieve in the classic film of the same name?
21 A lift for food in a restaurant is known as what kind of waiter?
22 The humerus is in what part of the body?
23 Countersunk, flat-headed and snap-head are common types of what?
24 Which country did Galileo come from?
25 In Australia what is a jumbuck?
26 What is the name of the "Magic Roundabout" dog?
27 On a Monopoly board, what colour is Fleet Street?
28 Which group were simply Holding Back the Years in the 1986 charts?
29 In May 1997 which cricket ground was given a £4 million grant?
30 Which Debbie married Paul Daniels?

Answers

Pot Luck 46 (see Quiz 105)
1 Art Garfunkel. 2 "Ear". 3 Golf. 4 "Dynasty". 5 Deuce. 6 The Netherlands. 7 H G Wells. 8 0. 9 Apollo. 10 60s. 11 Ford. 12 Eddington. 13 XLII. 14 Branch. 15 Kim Wilde. 16 Nottingham Forest. 17 Equity. 18 South Africa. 19 December. 20 October & November. 21 Buster Mottram. 22 Radium. 23 "Brookside". 24 Tainted. 25 7,000. 26 Behind. 27 Top letters row. 28 Robin Cousins. 29 Middlesbrough. 30 8.

115

1   How many court cards are there in a standard pack?
2   In which game would you have a pitcher's mound and an outfield?
3   How many cards are needed for a game of canasta?
4   Which card game is also called vingt-et-un?
5   What is the name of the hedgehog in Sega's computer game?
6   Which London Palace has a famous maze?
7   Where are the Crown Jewels housed?
8   What colour flag is awarded by the EC to beaches of a certain standard?
9   What would you collect if you collected Clarice Cliff?
10 Near which city is Cadbury World?
11 What is the junior version of Lego called?
12 Where in Scotland is an Old Blacksmith's shop a tourist attraction?
13 What type of wildlife attraction is Longleat famous for?
14 Which Rosemary is famous for her keep-fit books and videos?
15 Which Norfolk seaside resort has a famous Pleasure Beach?
16 In knitting, which yarn is thicker, double-knitting or four-ply?
17 In chess, which piece can be called two different things?
18 How many cards do you deal to each player in rummy?
19 In Scrabble what colour are the triple-word score squares?
20 Which is the oldest swimming stroke?
21 What type of competition might you watch at a gymkhana?
22 If you like bonsai what would you be interested in?
23 Is volleyball normally played indoors or outdoors?
24 What would your hobby be if you bought a first day cover?
25 Which sport was originally called "football in the water"?
26 Which UK city would you visit to see Roman Baths and a famous Pump Room?
27 If you collected lepidoptera what would you collect?
28 In ice hockey what shape is a puck?
29 Europe's first Disney theme park was built near which city?
30 What type of museum has Imperial in front of its name in London?

Quiz 109 Pot Luck 48

Answers - see page 119

LEVEL 1

1 The airline Finnair is from which country?

2 If a price is £1,200 with VAT, what is the value minus VAT at 20 per cent?

3 In which decade of the 20th century was Shane Richie born?

4 Colin Milburn is associated with which sport?

5 In which month is VE Day?

6 Moving anticlockwise on a dartboard, what number is next to 16?

7 Who wrote the novel *A Town Like Alice*?

8 In which country is the city of Salonika?

9 Which UK car manufacturer produced the Alpine?

10 The character Alan B'Stard appeared in which TV series?

11 In the 90s, who had a No. 1 with "Do The Bartman"?

12 How many acres in a square mile?

13 In billiards how many points are scored for a cannon?

14 A car must have its first MOT by what age?

15 How is Richard Penniman better known?

16 What was the first English club that Matt Le Tissier played for?

17 Jacob Marley appears in which Charles Dickens novel?

18 What is an ampersand used to mean?

19 Which liberation organization had the initials PLO?

20 A cricket umpire raises his index finger above his head to indicate what?

21 Zoophobia is the fear of what?

22 Which Arthur starred in "Dad's Army"?

23 In heraldry what is or?

24 Gorgonzola cheese comes from which country?

25 In computing, what does the O stand for in ROM?

26 Which American city was devastated by the earthquake of 1906?

27 What name is given to the vertical bar of a window?

28 What did former US President Jimmy Carter grow on his farm?

29 Which county have Boycott and Illingworth played cricket for?

30 The character Henry Ramsay appeared in which TV soap?

Quiz 110 Communications

LEVEL 1

1   What does 'e' stand for in e-mail?
2   What was the world's first stamp called?
3   Which country has most first-language speakers of English?
4   What does the abbreviation BT stand for?
5   If A is for Alpha and B is for Bravo, what is C for ?
6   What did Samuel Morse design for communications?
7   When a number of computers are connected what are they called?
8   Which punctuation mark and letters indicate a UK Internet user?
9   How much do you pay for phone calls which begin with 0800?
10 In speech how should you - officially, at least - address a pope?
11 The Braille alphabet is made up of raised what?
12 Oftel is an independent watchdog relating to which service?
13 What does Hon. mean in the form of address Right Hon.?
14 A physician is addressed as Doctor; how is a male surgeon addressed?
15 The Greek letter beta corresponds with which letter of our alphabet?
16 Sputnik 1 was the first artificial what?
17 Which country has *Le Monde* as a major national newspaper?
18 What is Reuters?
19 In communication terms what is the *Washington Post*?
20 In which city is the headquarters of the *Scotsman* newspaper?
21 On inland phone calls when does the cheaper evening rate begin, Monday to Friday?
22 Phone calls made to 0345 numbers are charged at what rate?
23 If a skull and crossbones is seen on a container what does it mean?
24 To use a French road called a "péage" what must you do?
25 Which BT number do you dial to find your last caller's number?
26 Is it possible for a fax and a phone line to have the same number?
27 On the Internet what does the abbreviation WWW stand for?
28 An autoroute in France and an autobahn in Germany is what?
29 Which BT number do you ring for operator services?
30 What is the smallest denomination of postage stamp you can buy?

Answers

TV Times 3 (see Quiz 112)

1   Anne Robinson. **2** The A-Team. **3** Bruce Forsyth. **4** Australia.
5   "A Question of Sport". **6** "Question Time". **7** "Soldier Soldier".
8   Rubber. **9** Damon Hill. **10** 1940s. **11** Esther Rantzen. **12** Arthur Fowler.
13 Scotland. **14** Hughie Green. **15** Michael Barry. **16** Corbett.
17 Auf Wiedersehen Pet. **18** "Ballykissangel". **19** 1950s. **20** Picnic baskets.
21 "Yes Minister". **22** Jeremy Beadle. **23** Sunday. **24** "London's Burning".
25 Jo Brand. **26** Delia Smith. **27** Sharron Davies. **28** Madeley, Finnigan.
29 Carolgees. **30** "Lovejoy".

Quiz 111 Pot Luck 49

1   Which boxer Henry was BBC Sports Personality of the Year in 1970?
2   The character Jackie Merrick appeared in which TV soap?
3   What are the words in the shortest verse of the Bible?
4   In the royal address HSH what does S stand for?
5   How is the guitarist Huddie Ledbetter better known?
6   Which Tom was the first player to be twice Footballer of the Year?
7   Who wrote the novel *Around The World In Eighty Days*?
8   Which Whitney led the most weeks in the singles chart list for 1993?
9   In which country is the city of Tijuana?
10 Which ancient calculator used a frame and beads?
11 Which Richard starred in "Dr Kildare"?
12 The zodiac sign Libra covers which two calendar months?
13 In which decade of the 20th century was Jimmy Nail born?
14 Doug Mountjoy is associated with which sport?
15 N is the chemical symbol for which element?
16 The character ARP Warden Hodges appeared in which TV series?
17 In the 90s, who had a No. 1 with "Things Can Only Get Better"?
18 What is the administrative centre for the county of Humberside?
19 Which Dennis wrote "The Singing Detective"?
20 Who was the British monarch at the start of the 20th century?
21 In which country did the 1992 Olympics take place?
22 What does 1/4 x 1/4 equal?
23 How many players are there in a hockey team?
24 What is the only English anagram of TEACHING?
25 What kind of animal is Sooty's friend Soo?
26 Who won an Oscar for Best Actress in *Funny Girl*?
27 Who plays rugby union at the Recreation Ground, London Road?
28 If March 1 is a Saturday, what day is April 1?
29 In the Royal Navy which rank is higher - commander or commodore?
30 Cotton denotes which wedding anniversary?

1   Who was the first permanent female presenter of "Points of View"?
2   Which Team heroically helped those in trouble in the 80s?
3   Who replaced Leslie Crowther on "The Price is Right"?
4   In which country is "Prisoner Cell Block H" set?
5   Which quiz features a picture board and "what happens next"?
6   Which political programme is based on radio's "Any Questions"?
7   Which series focused on the King's Fusiliers Infantry Regiment?
8   What were the "Spitting Image" puppets made from?
9   Which racing driver was BBC Sports Personality of the Year twice in the 90s?
10 Which decade was the setting for "Tenko"?
11 Who was the main female presenter of "That's Life"?
12 Which "EastEnders" character died on his allotment?
13 Which country is Rab C. Nesbitt from?
14 Which former "Opportunity Knocks" presenter died in 1997?
15 Who is resident cook on "Food and Drink"?
16 Who always embarked on a long monologue in "The Two Ronnies"?
17 What did Denis Neville and Oz say to those they left behind in the North-East in the 80s?
18 In which series does Assumpta Fitzgerald appear?
19 In which decade did the action of "M*A*S*H" take place?
20 Which sort of containers are Yogi Bear's favourite?
21 In which sitcom did Private Secretary Bernard Woolley appear?
22 Which joker presents "You've Been Framed"?
23 On which day of the week is "The Antiques Roadshow" broadcast?
24 Which series features the firefighters of Blue Watch B25?
25 Who presents her programme "Through the Cakehole"?
26 Which cook presented a Winter and Summer Collection in the 90s?
27 Which former Olympic swimmer left "The Big Breakfast" in 1997?
28 What are the surname of Richard and Judy of "This Morning"?
29 Which Bob assists Cilla Black in "Surprise Surprise"?
30 Which comedy drama was dubbed "The Antiques Rogue Show"?

Quiz 113 Pot Luck 50

Answers - see page 122

LEVEL 1

1   Kelvedon Wonder and Little Marvel are types of what?
2   Which programme presented prizes on a conveyor belt?
3   In the 90s, who had a No. 1 with "I Believe"?
4   Arnold J. Rimmer BSc SSC appeared in which TV series?
5   On a Monopoly board, what colour is Pentonville Road?
6   Billy Liddell is associated with which sport?
7   Who wrote the novel *The Inimitable Jeeves*?
8   Which of Queen Elizabeth II's children was first to marry?
9   What is the administrative centre for the county of Suffolk?
10 In which decade of the 20th century was Joanna Lumley born?
11 Who went to sea with silver buckles on his knee?
12 How many fluid ounces in a pint?
13 The character David Hunter appeared in which TV soap?
14 What is 1/6 as a percentage to two decimal places?
15 How is the singer Concetta Franconero better known?
16 Who was England's manager for Gary Lineker's last international?
17 Which UK car manufacturer produced the Stag?
18 In music, what note is written on the bottom line of the treble clef?
19 On a dartboard what number is opposite 5?
20 RIBA is the Royal Institute of British what?
21 What is Lucinda Prior-Palmer's married name?
22 In which month is Independence Day in the USA?
23 Which Keith starred in "Duty Free"?
24 In which country is the city of Turin?
25 How are angles measured other than degrees?
26 The Battle of Waterloo was fought in which country?
27 The letter O is on which row of a typewriter or computer keyboard?
28 What colour is the centre of an archery target?
29 Pop and Ma Larkin appeared in which TV series?
30 Which kind of pear is usually served as a starter?

Answers

The Last Round (see Quiz 115)
1 The A-Team. 2 Pavarotti. 3 Gold. 4 Acid. 5 The man in the moon. 6 Toblerone. 7 Pudding Lane. 8 Snooty. 9 Cricket. 10 The Hanging Gardens. 11 Volkswagen Beetle. 12 A shilling (now 5p). 13 Pizza. 14 Green. 15 Everton. 16 Six. 17 Elgin Marbles. 18 Oliver Twist. 19 German. 20 Boston. 21 Six. 22 Nothing. 23 A fish. 24 Palindromes. 25 Kiwi fruit. 26 Poncho. 27 Six. 28 Insects. 29 Five. 30 Bird.

Quiz 114 Sporting Chance 3

LEVEL 1

Answers - see page 123

1 Which Nick won the US Masters in 1989?
2 Which England cricketer had the first names Ian Terrence?
3 What sport do the New York Yankees play?
4 Which Pete had a hat-trick of Wimbledon triumphs in the 90s?
5 What did Dionicio Ceron win in London in 1994, 95 and 96?
6 In which city did Linford Christie win Olympic 100-metres gold?
7 What sport does Michael Jordan play?
8 The businessman Samuel Ryder initiated a cup in which sport?
9 Which rugby league team are the Bulls?
10 What do the initials WBC stand for?
11 Gary Kasparov became world champion in which game?
12 Which major British racing event was postponed in 1997 after a bomb scare?
13 How often are showjumping World Championships held?
14 At which sport did Liz Hobbs find fame?
15 Which rugby union club moved to QPR's soccer ground in the 90s?
16 Which Lloyd was undisputed welterweight world champion in 1986?
17 What relation is the batsman Tom Graveney to the 90s England selector David Graveney?
18 What sport do the Dallas Cowboys play?
19 Horse racing's Belmont Stakes is run in which country?
20 In golf, what is a double bogey?
21 How many players a side are there in basketball?
22 A cricket umpire waves an arm from side to side to signal what?
23 Who was the Brown Bomber?
24 What did Emerson Fittipaldi break at Michigan in 1996?
25 Which team said goodbye to their home Baseball Ground in 1997?
26 Which Dan was the BBC's voice of tennis from the 50s to the 90s?
27 Anita Lonsbrough is associated with which sport?
28 In which decade was cricket's first World Cup Final played?
29 Where is the Horse of the Year show staged?
30 Which county cricket club has its home at Edgbaston?

Pot Luck 50 (see Quiz 113)

1 Pea. 2 "Generation Game". 3 Robson and Jerome. 4 "Red Dwarf".
5 Light blue. 6 Football. 7 P G Wodehouse. 8 Princess Anne. 9 Ipswich.
10 40s. 11 Bobby Shaftoe. 12 20. 13 "Crossroads". 14 16.66. 15 Connie
Francis. 16 Graham Taylor. 17 Triumph. 18 E. 19 17. 20 Architects.
21 Green. 22 July. 23 Barron. 24 Italy. 25 Radians. 26 Belgium.
27 Top letters row. 28 Gold. 29 "The Darling Buds Of May". 30 Avocado.

Quiz 115 The Last Round

Answers - see page 121

1 BA and Face were members of which alphabetically aware team?
2 Which opera singer gave a concert in Hyde Park in the pouring rain?
3 The discovery of what caused a rush to California in 1848?
4 What is the opposite of alkali?
5 In rhyme, who asked his way to Norwich when he came down too soon?
6 Which nutty chocolate is sold in triangular bars?
7 In which lane is the Great Fire of London said to have started?
8 Which lord was removed from the *Beano* in 1992?
9 In which game could an Australian's Chinaman beat an Englishman?
10 Which of the Wonders of the World was at Babylon?
11 In films, what kind of car is the "Love Bug"?
12 A bob was the popular name of which old English coin?
13 What was the Teenage Mutant Turtles' favourite food?
14 What comes after red, orange and yellow in the rainbow's colours?
15 Which soccer team does the DJ Ed Stewart support?
16 How many legs does a male insect have?
17 Which Greek Marbles are housed in the British Museum?
18 Which workhouse boy asked for more?
19 Which language does the word kitsch come from?
20 What is the state capital of Massachusetts?
21 How many strings does a Spanish guitar have?
22 What did Old Mother Hubbard keep in her cupboard?
23 What kind of creature is an anchovy?
24 Dad, kayak and rotavator are examples of what type of words?
25 Which juicy green fruit is named after a New Zealand bird?
26 What is the name for a blanket-like cloak with a slit for the head?
27 Most snow crystals have how many sides?
28 What does an entomologist study?
29 In Britain a general election must be held after how many years?
30 What sort of creature is a treecreeper?

Sporting Chance 3 (see Quiz 114)
1 Faldo. 2 Botham. 3 Baseball. 4 Sampras. 5 Marathon. 6 Barcelona.
7 Basketball. 8 Golf. 9 Bradford. 10 World Boxing Council. 11 Chess.
12 Grand National. 13 Every four years. 14 Water Skiing. 15 Wasps.
16 Honeyghan. 17 Uncle. 18 American football. 19 USA. 20 Two over
par for a hole. 21 Five. 22 Boundary for 4 runs. 23 Joe Louis. 24 His neck.
25 Derby. 26 Maskell. 27 Swimming. 28 1970s. 29 Wembley Arena.
30 Warwickshire.

Medium Questions

Welcome to the land of the bland, the grey area. Say hello to Mr Middle and Mickey Mean, who are all ruled by the law of averages and live in this the not-too-easy/not-too-hard world of the Medium section. Some of these questions will find your contestants sailing along, shrugging their shoulders and snubbing the opposition through a pall of thick smoke and nauseous self-confidence and others will leave them banging on the carpet (chance'd be a fine thing) and gurning like gargoyles.

The point is this: these questions should see the average contestant score about 50% to 80% and those they fail on will be subjects they happen to know absolutely nothing about. Still, a well-balanced team should have all the subjects covered by one member or another. And if they don't? Well, that's their lookout.

Sprinkle these questions liberally through your quizzes as you might sprinkle Parmesan on your spag boll.

Quiz 1 Pop: Who's Who?

Answers - see page 127

LEVEL 2

1　Who had a 70s hit with "Feelings"?

2　Who had a "Pretty Good Year" in the charts in 1994?

3　Which Irish singer has made records with Clannad and Sinatra?

4　"Don't Worry" was the first solo success for which female singer?

5　Who was lead singer with the Animals?

6　Who did Nick Berry play in "EastEnders" at the time of his first No. 1?

7　Who did Marc Almond sing with for his first No. 1?

8　Who - in song - lived high on a mountain in Mexico?

9　Which group introduced Dina Carroll to the charts?

10　Who has recorded with Cliff Richard, Steve Harley and Jose Carreras?

11　Who was the "Wichita Lineman"?

12　What word added to Bells, Mink and Pearl completes group names?

13　Who was lead singer with the Bay City Rollers?

14　Which country did Aneka - who sang "Japanese Boy" - come from?

15　Who sang "Private Number" with William Bell?

16　Who was responsible for the English lyrics of "My Way"?

17　Who were Bobby, Mike, Cheryl and Jay?

18　Who did Chubby Checker sing with on the 80s twist revival single?

19　Who is Pat Boone's singing daughter?

20　Which female singer starred in the 80s video for "Ant Rap"?

21　Who was the Geno referred to in Dexy's Midnight Runners' No. 1?

22　Which Spice Girl comes from Leeds?

23　Who wrote and sang the original "Spirit In The Sky"?

24　Who took "Wonderwall" into the charts for the second time in 1995?

25　Who was the first female artist to have a No. 1 and wear an eye patch?

26　Who wrote "All By Myself"?

27　Who sang "Never On A Sunday"?

28　Who sang with Peabo Bryson on "A Whole New World"?

29　Our Cilla's "Anyone Who Had A Heart" was a cover of which singer's song?

30　Who was the guitar virtuoso who wrote "Albatross"?

Answers

TV Soaps (see Quiz 3)

1 Annie. **2** "Emmerdale". **3** April. **4** Sam Mitchell. **5** "Coronation Street". **6** Lisa Riley (Mandy Dingle, "Emmerdale"). **7** Letitia Dean (Sharon). **8** Chris Collins. **9** The Queen Vic. **10** The Meal Machine. **11** Rosie, Sophie. **12** "Family Affairs". **13** Wellard. **14** "Brookside". **15** "The High Road". **16** Raymond. **17** Steph. **18** Helen Daniels. **19** Julia Brogan. **20** Fraser Henderson. **21** Shane. **22** Martin Platt. **23** "Pacific Blue". **24** Hills. **25** Nigel Bates. **26** Steven and Peter. **27** Audrey Roberts. **28** Gary and Judy Mallett. **29** Roy Evans. **30** In a fire.

Quiz 2 Pot Luck 1

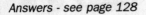

Answers - see page 128

LEVEL 2

1   Which moor is named after the county town of Cornwall?
2   Who laid the foundation stone at Coventry Cathedral?
3   In which city was Stephane Grappelli born?
4   Who had a No. 1 in the 60s with "Everlasting Love"?
5   Which tennis player was given the name "Ice Man" by the press?
6   Who cleaned at the Crossroads Motel?
7   Which does fibrin cause the blood to do?
8   What name links a former "EastEnders" actor and a radio DJ?
9   In which county are England's highest cliffs?
10 What is the Russian word for citadel?
11 In which century was George Frederick Handel born?
12 Which sportsman wrote the autobiography *Unleashed*?
13 What is John Gielgud's first name?
14 Who was the first female presenter of "Busman's Holiday"?
15 What is the Pentateuch?
16 In which sitcom did Sandra Hennessey appear?
17 What was the name of the first cloned sheep?
18 Which school did Billy Bunter go to?
19 Who wrote the books on which "The Jewel in the Crown" was based?
20 Who has advertised Brut, Patrick boots, Shredded Wheat and Sugar Puffs?
21 Allurophobia is a fear of what?
22 What do the letters P.S. stand for at the end of a letter?
23 Whose last words were "That was a great game of golf, fellas"?
24 In the Chinese calendar which year follows the year of the tiger?
25 Who was the first person to captain, coach and manage England at cricket?
26 Who was King of the Huns from 406 to 453?
27 What word can go after "tar" and before "gent"?
28 With which sport is Willie Wood connected?
29 In which decade of the 20th century was Eric Clapton born?
30 Which actor played the only Dirty Dozen member to survive?

Answers

Around the UK (see Quiz 4)

1 Four. 2 Portsmouth. 3 The Guild Hall. 4 Tobermory. 5 Sark.
6 Anglesey. 7 Cambridge. 8 Lloyd's of London. 9 Scillies. 10 Cheviots.
11 Glasgow. 12 Irish Sea. 13 Buckinghamshire. 14 York Minster.
15 Solway Firth. 16 Coventry. 17 Melton Mowbray. 18 The Backs.
19 Derbyshire. 20 Ermine Street. 21 Lytham St Annes. 22 Parkhurst.
23 Grosvenor Square. 24 The Great Fire of London. 25 The Solent.
26 Windsor. 27 Southend. 28 Downing Street. 29 Mermaid.
30 Northumberland.

Quiz 3 TV Soaps

Answers - see page 125

LEVEL 2

1   What is the name of "EastEnders" club owner George Palmer's daughter?
2   Which soap was made in Esholt until 1997?
3   In "EastEnders" what was Carol Jackson's sister called?
4   Who was Ricky Butcher's first wife?
5   Tony Blair was seen on which soap set prior to the '97 General Election?
6   Which soap star modelled Etam clothes for larger ladies?
7   Which ex-EastEnder starred in "The Hello Girls" on BBC1?
8   The actor who was Danny Weir in "Emmerdale" played which "Coronation Street" character?
9   Eddie Royle was the landlord of which soap pub?
10 What was Ian Beale's catering business called?
11 In "Coronation Street" what are Kevin and Sally's daughters called?
12 Which was the first major UK soap on Channel 5?
13 What was the name of Robbie Jackson's dog in "EastEnders"?
14 Which soap did Lily Savage appear in?
15 In which soap does Mrs Mack appear?
16 What is the surname of Tiffany's brother Simon in "EastEnders"?
17 Who was Mrs Des Barnes when they moved into the Street ?
18 Which of the original "Neighbours" characters lasted the longest?
19 Who is Doreen Corkhill's mum in "Brookside"?
20 In the Street, what was the name of the gangster who had an affair with Liz McDonald?
21 In "Home and Away" what was Shane and Angel's daughter called?
22 Which male "Coronation Street" character trained to be a nurse?
23 Which Sky 2 soap was dubbed "Baywatch" on bikes?
24 What was "EastEnders" Kathy Mitchell's maiden name?
25 Who is Clare Tyler's stepfather in Albert Square?
26 Which children did Cindy Beale take with her to France?
27 Who is Martin Platt's mother-in-law in "Coronation Street"?
28 Who bought Jack and Vera's house in "Coronation Street"?
29 Which "EastEnders" character shares his name with a famous football manager?
30 How did Dave Glover die in "Emmerdale"?

Answers

Pop: Who's Who?   (see Quiz 1)

1 Morris Albert. **2** Tori Amos. **3** Bono. **4** Kim Appleby. **5** Eric Burdon.
6 Simon Wicks. **7** Gene Pitney. **8** Angelo (Brotherhood of Man). **9** Quartz.
10 Sarah Brightman. **11** Glen Campbell. **12** Blue. **13** Les McKeown.
14 Scotland. **15** Judy Clay. **16** Paul Anka. **17** Bucks Fizz. **18** Fat Boys.
19 Debby. **20** Lulu. **21** Geno Washington. **22** Mel B (Scary). **23** Norman
Greenbaum. **24** Mike Flowers Pops. **25** Gabrielle. **26** Eric Carmen.
27 Lynn Cornel. **28** Regina Belle. **29** Dionne Warwick. **30** Peter Green.

Quiz 4 Around the UK

LEVEL 2

1   How many faces has the clock on Big Ben's tower?
2   In which port were Dickens and Brunel both born?
3   In which London building is the Lord Mayor's banquet held?
4   Which Womble was named after the town on the Isle of Mull?
5   Which Channel Island is famous for having no cars?
6   Where is Beaumaris Castle?
7   Girton and Newnham are colleges of which university?
8   Where in London is the Lutine Bell?
9   Bryher is part of which islands?
10 Which Hills divide England and Scotland?
11 Cumbernauld is near which British city?
12 Which Sea joins the St George's Channel and the North Channel?
13 In which county is Chequers, the Prime Minister's country residence?
14 What is England's second largest cathedral?
15 Which Firth lies between south west Scotland and north west England?
16 Where is The Cathedral Church of St Michael, consecrated in 1962?
17 Which Leicestershire town is famous for its pork pies?
18 What are the canals in Cambridge called?
19 In which county is the southern end of the Pennine Way?
20 Which Roman road shares its name with a type of fur?
21 What is ERNIE's home town?
22 What is the high security prison on the Isle of Wight called?
23 In which London Square is the US Embassy?
24 Which disaster does London's Monument commemorate?
25 Which waterway divides the Isle of Wight from the mainland?
26 Which castle has St George's Chapel?
27 What is the nearest seaside resort to London?
28 Where in London are there gates named after Margaret Thatcher?
29 Which theatre was founded in 1959 at Blackfriars in London?
30 Dogger Bank is off which English county?

Pot Luck 1 (see Quiz 2)
1 Bodmin Moor. 2 Queen Elizabeth II. 3 Paris. 4 Love Affair. 5 Bjorn Borg.
6 Amy Turtle. 7 Clot. 8 Mike Reid. 9 Devon. 10 Kremlin. 11 17th.
12 Jack Russell. 13 Arthur. 14 Sarah Kennedy. 15 First five books of the
Old Testament. 16 "The Liver Birds". 17 Dolly. 18 Greyfriars. 19 Paul
Scott. 20 Kevin Keegan. 21 Cats. 22 Postscript. 23 Bing Crosby.
24 Rabbit. 25 Ray Illingworth. 26 Attila. 27 "Tan". 28 Bowls. 29 40s.
30 Charles Bronson.

1 In medical terms, what are you if you are "DOA"?

2 In which crisis, in 1956, did England become involved?

3 What does Anno Domini mean?

4 Which Neil Diamond song was a No. 1 for UB40?

5 In which city is the area of Toxteth?

6 Who was the vocalist on Gary Moore's hit "Parisienne Walkways"?

7 In the farce, where did Charley's Aunt come from?

8 Over which sea was Glenn Miller lost?

9 Where is Britain's most southerly mainland point?

10 Which song title links Go West and Blondie?

11 What do W and S stand for in W.S. Gilbert's name?

12 Tony Doyle is connected with which sport?

13 In which century was Leonardo da Vinci born?

14 What was invented by Lewis E. Waterman?

15 Who wrote the novel *Emma*?

16 In which German town was "Auf Wiedersehen Pet" set?

17 Which birthstone is linked to January?

18 In which decade was the series "Agony" screened for the first time?

19 How is the General Purpose (GP) Vehicle commonly known?

20 Which poem begins, "Is there anybody there? said the Traveller"?

21 Who did George Bush defeat to become US President in 1988?

22 "The Town Of Titipu" is the subtitle of which light opera?

23 Which English cheese officially went on sale in 1982?

24 Which Japanese word means "divine wind"?

25 What did Fred Quimby produce so that his name is still seen today?

26 What was the live cargo on the *Mayflower* on its second trip to America?

27 Who played the title role in *Edward Scissorhands*?

28 What did both Johnny Haynes and Dennis Compton advertise?

29 Who had a 90s No. 1 with "Abba-Esque"?

30 In which county is Stonehenge?

Pot Luck 3 (see Quiz 7)

Answers

1 County of Swansea (was West Glamorgan till 1996). 2 Metal strips. 3 Brazil. 4 Abraham Lincoln. 5 Damascus. 6 Greater London. 7 A chef. 8 Eagle. 9 Olivia Newton-John. 10 Seville. 11 19th. 12 J.G. Ballard. 13 "Ring-a-ring-a Roses". 14 Benny Goodman. 15 Rocky Cassidy. 16 Hockey. 17 George Best. 18 Born same year (1935). 19 Died of syphilis. 20 Siamese. 21 *Prima facie*. 22 17. 23 Rick Parfitt. 24 Publishing (Writing). 25 Greek island of Kos. 26 Oldham. 27 30s. 28 Lady Chatterley. 29 Tropic of Cancer. 30 Tasmin Archer.

Quiz 6 Hobbies & Leisure 1

LEVEL 2

Answers - see page 132

1   Fountains Abbey is in which county?
2   In which museum would you see Constable's *Haywain*?
3   In what activity would you make a banjo cable or a leaf rib?
4   What moves when a chess player moves two pieces in one move?
5   Where would you go to see the Battle of the Flowers?
6   What would you have if you were a collector of Coalport?
7   How many tricks make up a grand slam in bridge?
8   What is the Viking Centre in York called?
9   What is the national game of the Basques?
10 In which seaside resort is Frontierland?
11 What is the value of the ace in baccarat?
12 What is the practice of creating replicas of animals from their dead skins called?
13 Which Cluedo weapon is nearest the beginning of the alphabet?
14 What is the minimum number of players in a game of bezique?
15 The aim is to knock down how many pins in a game of skittles?
16 What was the name of the first Rolls-Royce?
17 What is Brighton Pier called?
18 Which Essex town is famous for its Oyster Festival?
19 The Eurotunnel Exhibition Centre is nearest which port?
20 In pottery what is slip?
21 What is numismatics?
22 Alfred Wainwright wrote books on which leisure activity?
23 How many wheels are there normally on a skateboard?
24 In which month is the London-to-Brighton Veteran Car Run?
25 Where did bonsai gardens originate?
26 What would you be doing if you practised a strathspey and a pas de basque?
27 What is the practice of formal handwriting called?
28 In knitting what does psso mean?
29 In which city would you be if you went to the Fitzwilliam Museum?
30 What do British stamps not have on them which most other stamps do?

Quiz 7 Pot Luck 3

Answers - see page 129

LEVEL 2

1 In which Welsh county is the Gower Peninsula?
2 What was first put into £1 notes in 1940?
3 Who were defending champions at the 1966 football World Cup?
4 Who was the first American president to be assassinated?
5 Which city in the book of Genesis is still in existence?
6 What did the City of London and 32 metropolitan boroughs become in 1965?
7 What did Ian Beale train to be in the early "EastEnders" episodes?
8 What bird is depicted over the door of the US Embassy in London?
9 Who has had hits with ELO, Cliff Richard and John Travolta?
10 In which city is Bizet's *Carmen* set?
11 In which century was Abraham Lincoln born?
12 Who wrote *Empire Of The Sun*?
13 Which children's rhyme was associated with the Black Death?
14 Who was known as the King of Swing?
15 Which character did Neil Morrissey play in "Boon"?
16 Vera Chapman played 66 times for England at which sport?
17 Which footballer's biography is *Where Do I Go from Here?*?
18 What do Johnny Mathis, Elvis Presley and Little Richard all share?
19 How did Al Capone meet his death?
20 Blue and seal-points are types of which cat?
21 Which Latin term - usually applied to legal evidence - means at first sight?
22 What is the next highest prime number above 13?
23 Which veteran rock star had a quadruple coronary heart bypass in May 1997?
24 What is Victor Gollancz particularly associated with?
25 Where did young Ben Needham mysteriously vanish in 1991?
26 Where in England was a railway station called Mumps?
27 In which decade of the 20th century was Sean Connery born?
28 Who had a lover called Mellors?
29 Which Tropic line goes through Taiwan?
30 Who had a 90s No. 1 with "Sleeping Satellite"?

Pot Luck 2 (see Quiz 5)
1 Dead On Arrival. 2 The Suez Crisis. 3 In the year of our Lord. 4 "Red Red Wine". 5 Liverpool. 6 Phil Lynott. 7 Brazil. 8 English Channel. 9 Lizard Point. 10 "Call Me". 11 William Schwenck. 12 Cycling. 13 15th. 14 Fountain Pen. 15 Jane Austen. 16 Dusseldorf. 17 Garnet. 18 1970s. 19 Jeep. 20 "The Listeners". 21 Michael Dukakis. 22 *The Mikado*. 23 Lymeswold. 24 Kamikaze. 25 Tom and Jerry cartoons. 26 Slaves. 27 Johnny Depp. 28 Brylcreem. 29 Erasure. 30 Wiltshire.

Quiz 8 Living World

Answers - see page 130

1   What is the male honey bee known as?
2   Hermit and spider are types of what?
3   What is another name for an insect's feelers?
4   What name is given to the body a parasite feeds on?
5   How many eyes does a bee have?
6   Which beetle was sacred to the Egyptians?
7   What is the process of casting skin, hair or feathers called?
8   What is a gurnard?
9   Which bird is associated with Lundy Island?
10 What is a conch?
11 What sort of animal is a papillon?
12 What is the olfactory sense?
13 What does the term metamorphosis mean?
14 What is a hummingbird's hum caused by?
15 Which is the largest member of the crow family?
16 What and where is Minsmere?
17 What is another name for thunderflies or thunderbugs?
18 How many parts are there to an insect's body?
19 What do lugworms live in?
20 What is a dunnock?
21 Which system controls touch, sight and hearing?
22 From which language does the word budgerigar come?
23 What do the Americans call what the British call a ladybird?
24 How many wings does a flea have?
25 For whom is the Glorious Twelfth not glorious?
26 What is another name for cartilage?
27 How does a stoat's appearance change in the winter?
28 What is a mavis?
29 What is the smallest living unit called?
30 What do polled cattle not have?

Answers

Hobbies & Leisure 1 (see Quiz 6)
1 North Yorkshire. 2 National Gallery. 3 Knitting. 4 Castle, King. 5 Jersey.
6 China. 7 13. 8 Jorvik. 9 Pelota. 10 Morecambe. 11 One.
12 Taxidermy. 13 Candlestick. 14 Two. 15 Nine. 16 Silver Ghost.
17 Palace Pier. 18 Colchester. 19 Folkestone. 20 Liquid clay. 21 Study
and collection of coins. 22 Fell walking. 23 Four. 24 November. 25 China.
26 Scottish dancing. 27 Calligraphy. 28 Pass slipped stitch over.
29 Cambridge. 30 The name of the country.

Quiz 9 Pot Luck 4

Answers - see page 135

Answers - see page 135

LEVEL 2

1 Which London hospital took its first infant patient in 1852?
2 Which Cornish village claims to be the birthplace of King Arthur?
3 Which is the main river to flow through Hamburg?
4 Which band had a lead singer called Morrissey?
5 Who was jilted on her wedding day in *Great Expectations*?
6 What patent did Graham Bell file three hours before Elisha Gray?
7 What was the nickname given to V1 Flying bombs in World War II?
8 Which common British garden creature belongs to the locust family?
9 What damaged Alexandra Palace in both 1873 and 1980?
10 Which motel provides the setting in *Psycho*?
11 In which century was David Livingstone born?
12 Which character was the transvestite in "M*A*S*H"?
13 Who was the first female presenter of "Blue Peter"?
14 What does Genghis Khan mean?
15 Who wrote the book *Clayhanger*?
16 Which ocean liner, retired in 1967, became a hotel in Long Beach?
17 Paper sized 210mm x 297mm is known by which A number?
18 If it's 12 noon GMT what time is it in Berlin?
19 For Elton John's 50th birthday party who did Janet Street-Porter go dressed as?
20 Preston is on which river?
21 In which drama series did Frank Carver appear?
22 Which was the last Oxford University college to be made up of all female students?
23 Alan Minter was undisputed world boxing champion at which weight?
24 Who had a 90s No. 1 with "A Little Time"?
25 On a World War II battleship, what was called a Mae West ?
26 On record, who was the child with the talking magic piano?
27 Who had the only speaking part in Marcel Marceau's *Silent Movie*?
28 Charles Ross and Epicure are types of which fruit?
29 What time is it when Wee Willie Winkie runs through the town?
30 Who founded the Jesuits?

Answers

Pot Luck 5 (see Quiz 11)

1 Greater Manchester. **2** The Pope. **3** *The Pickwick Papers*. **4** Miami Beach.
5 Sinn Fein. **6** The Cresta Run. **7** Mandrills. **8** Richard Clayderman. **9** 12.
10 Richard Nixon. **11** William Ewart. **12** Pet Shop Boys. **13** Sir James
Goldsmith. **14** God. **15** London Marathon. **16** Malcolm Bradbury.
17 Cribbage. **18** Comma. **19** 15th. **20** *Dandy*. **21** Dog. **22** "Bar".
23 Androcles. **24** A contour line. **25** 20s. **26** Chigwell. **27** None.
28 Ruby. **29** Champagne Charlie. **30** Aardvark.

LEVEL 2

1   Who was the first boss to win the championship with separate English clubs?

2   How many FA Cup Finals did George Best play in?

3   Faustino Asprilla joined Newcastle from which club?

4   Which Scottish team are known as the Wee Roves?

5   Which club's ground has the Darwen End?

6   Which boss has won the League Cup for Sheffield Wednesday and Aston Villa?

7   Which country did Dennis Tuert play for?

8   John Collins made his debut at which Scottish club?

9   Where was John Barnes born?

10   Who was the first keeper to captain an FA Cup winning side?

11   Which Yorkshire club has its ground in Grove Street?

12   Which Spurs manager signed Ossie Ardiles?

13   Which Athletic side are known as the Wasps?

14   Which London team won the first Full Members' Cup in 1986?

15   Which footballing Danny refused to go on "This Is Your Life"?

16   Which Gary was crocked by Gazza's wild 1991 FA Cup Final tackle?

17   Who was the first black player/manager of an English league side?

18   To a year, how old was Karen Brady when she became managing director at Birmingham?

19   Which Scottish striker did Terry Venables take to Barcelona?

20   What did Bolton, Derby and Stoke all do in the summer of '97?

21   In which decade did Wales first reach the final stages of the World Cup?

22   Which was the first Belgian club to win a major European trophy?

23   Which England manager was born in Sacriston, Co. Durham?

24   Which country does the club Flamengo come from?

25   What was Stirling Albion's famous Scottish first for their ground?

26   In the 90s which player has played against and for Chelsea in FA Cup Finals?

27   Who were the only British team to win the UEFA Cup in the 80s?

28   Which team knocked the Republic out of the 1994 World Cup in USA?

29   David James joined Liverpool from which team?

30   Who play at Brockville Park?

Quiz 11 Pot Luck 5

1 In which county is Wigan?

2 Who sends encyclical letters?

3 Mr Wardle of Dingley Dell appeared in which Dickens book?

4 Where was the *Police Academy 5* movie set?

5 Which Party was introduced to Ireland in 1902 by Arthur Griffin?

6 Which world-famous European sporting track is rebuilt every year?

7 What name is given to the monkeys with red and blue bottoms?

8 What is French pianist Philippe Pages' stage name?

9 What is the highest number on the Richter scale?

10 Which US President had a wife called Thelma?

11 What do W and E stand for in W.E. Gladstone's name?

12 Who had a 80s No. 1 with "Heart"?

13 Who led the Referendum Party in 1997?

14 Theophobia is a fear of what?

15 Katrin Dorre had a hat-trick of wins in the 90s in which event?

16 Who wrote *The History Man*?

17 What card game can you peg out in?

18 Which punctuation mark has the same name as a butterfly?

19 In which century was Michelangelo born?

20 In which comic did Korky the Cat first appear?

21 1994 was the Chinese year of which creature?

22 What word can go before "gain", "row" and "tender"?

23 In legend, who removed the thorn from the lion's paw?

24 What line on a map connects points of the same height?

25 In which decade of the 20th century was Doris Day born?

26 In which suburb was "Birds of a Feather" set?

27 How many professional fights did Rocky Marciano lose?

28 Which birthstone is linked to July?

29 In song, who states that "Champagne drinking is my game"?

30 Alphabetically, which is the first creature in the dictionary?

Quiz 12 Action Movies

Answers - see page 134

LEVEL 2

1   Which Bond villain has been played by Telly Savalas and Donald Pleasence?
2   Who directed *Hustle* and *The Dirty Dozen*?
3   What was the second Bond film?
4   Which role did Jim Carrey play in *Batman Forever*?
5   In which 1997 film does Pierce Brosnan play a vulcanologist?
6   Whose film biography was called *Dragon*?
7   What does "Ice Cold" refer to in the John Mills film *Ice Cold in Alex*?
8   Which sport are *Kid's Return* and *Tokyo Fist* about?
9   What was the occupation of the Fugitive?
10 Which means of transport dominates in *Speed*?
11 Which 1997 Mafia film starred Al Pacino and Johnny Depp?
12 In which US city is *Metro* set?
13 What was Pierce Brosnan's second film as James Bond?
14 What was the third *Die Hard* film called?
15 Who played Bond girl Solitaire in *Live and Let Die*?
16 In which decade does the action of *Raiders of the Lost Ark* take place?
17 What was Oliver Stone's final Vietnam Trilogy film?
18 Which means of transport features in *The Hunt For Red October*?
19 Which country is the setting for Oliver Stone's *Platoon*?
20 Who plays the US captain escaping an Italian POW camp in *Von Ryan's Express*?
21 Who co-wrote and starred in *Cliffhanger* in 1993?
22 Which action movie is subtitled *Judgment Day*?
23 Who is the actress caught between an undercover cop and a drug dealer in *Tequila Sunrise*?
24 Which film critic's father produced *The Cruel Sea*?
25 Who directed the first three *Godfather* films?
26 Which 1995 film allegedly cost £1.3 million per minute screen time?
27 Which singer joined Mel Gibson for *Mad Max Beyond Thunderdome*?
28 Which city is the setting for *French Connection II*?
29 Which film's action begins with "Houston, we have a problem"?
30 Who played 007 in 1984 in *Never Say Never Again*?

Answers

Football   (see Quiz 10)
1 Herbert Chapman. 2 None. 3 Parma. 4 Albion Rovers. 5 Blackburn Rovers. 6 Ron Atkinson. 7 England. 8 Hibs. 9 Jamaica. 10 Dave Beasant. 11 Barnsley. 12 Keith Burkinshaw. 13 Alloa. 14 Chelsea. 15 Blanchflower. 16 Charles. 17 Viv Anderson. 18 25. 19 Steve Archibald. 20 Moved grounds. 21 50s. 22 Anderlecht. 23 Bobby Robson. 24 Brazil. 25 First artificial pitch. 26 Mark Hughes. 27 Ipswich. 28 Holland. 29 Watford. 30 Falkirk.

Quiz 13 Pot Luck 6

Answers - see page 139

LEVEL 2

1 What was a hit for Bobby "Boris" Pickett and the Crypt-Kickers?
2 What is the real name of the 90s road protestor Swampy?
3 Which former US president was born in Tampico, Illinois?
4 Which country signed the Waitangi Treaty with Britain?
5 What was the sequel to *Winnie the Pooh*?
6 What is the common name for inflamed sebaceous glands?
7 What kind of creature is a Queen Alexandra's Birdwing?
8 What returned to Piccadilly Circus in 1947 after being in hiding during the war?
9 What is the subject of Landseer's painting *The Monarch of the Glen*?
10 Which member of Queen wrote "Radio Ga Ga"?
11 What is the only English anagram of CROUTON?
12 Which English county was the home to the world's first iron bridge?
13 The Thomas Cup is awarded in which sport?
14 In woodwork, what does a tenon fit to form a joint?
15 Who was the hero of *The Camels Are Coming*, published in 1932?
16 What was Tonto's horse called?
17 What is the capital of Angola?
18 Who wrote the novel *The Tenant Of Wildfell Hall*?
19 What type of skate was invented in 1760 by Joseph Merlin?
20 Which Indian cricketer was nicknamed "Little Master"?
21 In fiction, where did Tom Brown graduate to?
22 In which century was Mozart born?
23 Which character did Laurence Olivier play in "Brideshead Revisited"?
24 What revolutionary fought with Castro and eventually died in Bolivia?
25 Who wrote the First World War poem "Anthem For Doomed Youth"?
26 In Scrabble, how many points is the letter R worth?
27 Who had an 80s No. 1 with "Doctorin' The Tardis"?
28 Who was Inspector Clouseau's manservant?
29 In which Dickens novel does John Jarndyce appear?
30 Which US city felt an earthquake for 47 seconds on April 18 1906?

Answers

Pop: Groups (see Quiz 15)
1 Bangles. 2 Norway. 3 Manfred Mann. 4 Oasis. 5 "Heart Of Glass".
6 Art Of Noise. 7 Applejacks. 8 Goss. 9 Bananarama. 10 Andy
Fairweather-Low. 11 "Yowsah Yowsah Yowsah". 12 The Bay City Rollers.
13 Pink Floyd. 14 The Byrds. 15 "With A Little Help From My Friends".
16 Aphrodite's Child. 17 Ireland. 18 The Small Faces. 19 Middle of the
Road. 20 Adam Faith. 21 The Jam. 22 The Band. 23 The Bluebells.
24 Hot Chocolate. 25 The Bachelors. 26 Jonathan King. 27 The Wombles.
28 Beautiful South. 29 Colchester. 30 Hull.

Quiz 14 TV Who's Who?

LEVEL 2

1 Who presented "Crimewatch UK" with Nick Ross prior to Jill Dando?
2 Who were the two regulars on Gary Lineker and David Gower's teams in "They Think It's All Over"?
3 Who is the priest played by Stephen Tomkinson in "Ballykissangel"?
4 Who replaced Botham and Beaumont on "A Question of Sport"?
5 Who had a late-night chat show when Channel 5 was launched?
6 Who left "Blue Peter" to join the "Clothes Show" team?
7 Who is known as "Mr Trick Shot"?
8 Who starred as Blanco in "Porridge"?
9 Which TV star's first record release was "Extremis"?
10 What is the "Baywatch" star Pamela Anderson's son called?
11 Who were the stars of "A Close Shave"?
12 Who wrote "The Singing Detective" and "Pennies From Heaven"?
13 Which actress is married to John Thaw?
14 Who co-starred with Adam Faith in "Love Hurts"?
15 Who is Anthea Turner's TV presenter sister?
16 Who left "Peak Practice" for "Bliss"?
17 Whose TV wife was played by Teri Hatcher?
18 Who was known as the Green Goddess?
19 Who first presented the weather on BBC's "Breakfast Time"?
20 Who was known as the Galloping Gourmet?
21 Who became resident cook on GMTV in spring 1997?
22 Who first presented "The Antiques Roadshow" in 1981?
23 Who are team captains in Bob Holness's "Call My Bluff"?
24 Who hosted the retrospective quiz show "Backdate"?
25 Which TV star was flown in from the US to introduce the Spice Girls' first live UK performance?
26 Who is dubbed the King of Swing during election campaigns?
27 Who replaced Anthea Turner on GMTV's breakfast couch?
28 Who is Beverley Callard's actress daughter?
29 Who first presented "Nine O'Clock Live" on GMTV?
30 Which actress is married to the playwright Jack Rosenthal?

Pot Luck 7 (see Quiz 16)

1 Light blue. 2 Four years. 3 Winchester. 4 Lake Superior. 5 Darts.
6 Ermine Street. 7 Japan. 8 Elton John. 9 King's Oak. 10 It turns to stone.
11 16th. 12 Prince Philip. 13 Small Faces. 14 Andante. 15 Atlantic.
16 Bob Monkhouse. 17 Anthony Burgess. 18 Kansas. 19 "On the Up".
20 "Birds Of A Feather". 21 Hooves. 22 An Oscar. 23 Moon River.
24 Benjamin Jonson. 25 40s. 26 Jimmy Young. 27 American Football.
28 Haile Selassie. 29 Ruth. 30 Bashful.

Answers

Quiz 15 Pop: Groups

Answers - see page 137

LEVEL 2

1   Which all-girl group included Michael Steele?
2   Which country did A-Ha come from?
3   Mike D'Abo and Paul Jones sang with which group?
4   Tony McCarroll was the only non-family member of which group?
5   What was Blondie's first No. 1?
6   Who has had hits featuring Duane Eddy, Max Headroom and Tom Jones?
7   Which 60s group charted with "Tell Me When"?
8   What was the surname of Luke and Matt of Bros?
9   Who were Sarah Dullin, Siobhan Fahey and Keren Woodward?
10 Who was lead singer with Amen Corner?
11 What was in brackets in the title of Chic's "Dance Dance Dance"?
12 Which group featured Stewart "Woody" Wood?
13 Which group made records about an Arnold and an Emily?
14 Roger McGuinn and David Crosby were in which 60s band?
15 What was Wet Wet Wet's first No. 1?
16 Which 60s group featured Demis Roussos and Vangelis?
17 Thin Lizzy came from which country?
18 Steve Marriott and Ronnie Lane were in which band?
19 Which group were responsible for "Chirpy Chirpy Cheep Cheep"?
20 In the 60s who did the Roulettes back?
21 Who were "Going Underground" in 1980?
22 Who backed Bob Dylan on his late 60s and 70s tour?
23 Which Scottish group hit No. 1 after splitting up thanks to airplay from a Volkswagen ad in 1993?
24 Errol Browne is lead singer with which long-standing group?
25 Which group first charted with the Paul Simon classic "The Sound Of Silence"?
26 Who links Sakkarin, Bubblerock and Weathermen?
27 Which furry group were put together by Mike Batt?
28 Jacqueline Abbott and Briana Corrigan have sung with which group?
29 What is Blur's hometown?
30 Where were the Housemartins based?

Answers

Pot Luck 6 (see Quiz 13)
1 "The Monster Mash". 2 Daniel Hooper. 3 Ronald Reagan. 4 New Zealand.
5 *The House at Pooh Corner*. 6 Acne. 7 A butterfly. 8 Eros. 9 A stag.
10 Roger Taylor. 11 Contour. 12 Shropshire. 13 Badminton. 14 Mortise.
15 Biggles. 16 Scout. 17 Luanda. 18 Anne Brontë. 19 Roller skate.
20 Sunil Gavaskar. 21 Oxford. 22 18th. 23 Lord Marchmain. 24 Che
Guevara. 25 Wilfred Owen. 26 1. 27 The Timelords. 28 Cato.
29 *Bleak House*. 30 San Francisco.

Quiz 16 Pot Luck 7

Answers - see page 138

1   What is the background colour of the United Nations flag?
2   How old is a horse when it changes to a mare from a filly?
3   Which city is home to Britain's longest cathedral?
4   Which of the Great Lakes is the largest freshwater lake in the world?
5   The BDO is the UK governing body of which sport?
6   Which Roman road linked London to York?
7   What country are chrysanthemums native to?
8   Which former Watford chairman married Renate?
9   What was the name of the suburb in which "Crossroads" was set?
10 What happens to something if it is - literally - petrified?
11 In which century was William Shakespeare born?
12 Which Royal celebrates his birthday on June 10?
13 Who had a 60s No. 1 with "All Or Nothing"?
14 Which musical term means at a walking pace?
15 What does the A stand for in NATO?
16 Who was the first presenter of "Celebrity Squares"?
17 Who wrote the novel *A Clockwork Orange*?
18 Which American state is home to Dodge City?
19 In which sitcom did Sam and Mrs Wembley appear?
20 Which programme pushed "Panorama" out of its traditional 9.30 p.m. Monday slot in 1997?
21 What does an ungulate animal have?
22 What is 10 inches tall, gold-plated and weighs seven pounds?
23 In song, what river is wider than a mile?
24 In 1616, who became the first Poet Laureate?
25 In which decade of the 20th century was Robert de Niro born?
26 Which Radio 2 DJ used to finish his show with "TTFN" or "BFN"?
27 Emmitt Smith is associated with which sport?
28 How was Ras Tafari Makonnen better known?
29 In the Old Testament, the book of which woman directly follows Judges?
30 Alphabetically, who is the first of Snow White's Seven Dwarfs?

Quiz 17 Food & Drink 1

Answers - see page 143

LEVEL 2

1　Which type of wheat is used in gnocchi?
2　What type of meat is used in osso bucco?
3　What is the flavour of kummel?
4　Which cream has more fat, clotted cream or double cream?
5　What are suntinas?
6　What is special about porcini mushrooms?
7　How is Parmigiano Reggiano usually known in the UK?
8　Burtonwood Ales were originally based near which town?
9　What sort of meat is silverside?
10　What is the Italian equivalent of a French vin de table?
11　Which spirit is used in a Manhattan?
12　Which fruit flavour is used in crêpes suzette?
13　What are the two main ingredients of a coulibiac?
14　What is sake wine made from?
15　Which flavoured liqueur is used to make Kir?
16　What are the two main ingredients of kedgeree?
17　Which breeds of cow produce so-called gold-top milk?
18　Which liqueur is used in a sidecar?
19　Which type of pastry is usually bought frozen in wafer-thin slices?
20　Which two cheeses are layered in a Huntsman cheese?
21　How many standard bottles of wine are equivalent to a methuselah?
22　What is pancetta?
23　What type of flour is traditionally used in blinis?
24　What are flageolet and cannellini?
25　Which country does chorizo sausage come from?
26　From which part of France does Calvados originate?
27　What is focaccia?
28　Which two main ingredients would you add to spaghetti to make spaghetti alla carbonara?
29　What type of milk has a bottle with a blue-and-silver-checked cap?
30　What is arborio?

1. What was Disney's second animated feature film?
2. What is a glow worm as it is not a worm?
3. Where are the world headquarters of the Mormon Church?
4. Which Motown group featured Lionel Richie before he went solo?
5. What was the nickname of boxer Dave Green?
6. Which animal's name is Aboriginal and means "No drink"?
7. Which role did Phil Collins play in a stage version of *Oliver!*?
8. Which flowering plant family includes asparagus?
9. Which Irish county would you be in if you were in Tipperary?
10. Who was Muhammad Ali's first professional opponent outside the US?
11. Who wrote the children's classic *The Secret Garden*?
12. What was the nickname of Sir Arthur Travers Harris?
13. What genus and species is man classified as?
14. Which imaginary island was created in 1516 by Sir Thomas More?
15. Who had a 50s No. 1 with "The Story Of My Life"?
16. In which state was "Dynasty" set?
17. Which British school did Kurt Hahn found in the 1930s?
18. In which decade was the series "'Allo 'Allo" screened for the first time?
19. What word can go after "port" and before "seaman"?
20. In which continent is Lake Titicaca?
21. Who was asked for the bolt in the original "The Golden Shot"?
22. Which American Football team did Gavin Hastings first play for?
23. In which century was Charles Perrault collecting his fairy stories?
24. If the weather is calm what is wind force on the Beaufort scale?
25. What is the capital of Libya?
26. What was the name of the chess-playing computer that beat Kasparov?
27. Concorde and Louise Bonne are types of which fruit?
28. Who was the first winner on Wimbledon's new 1997 No. 1 court?
29. Who did Wimbledon players describe as a jellyfish?
30. What type of quadrilateral has all sides the same length but contains no right angles?

World Leaders (see Quiz 20)

Answers

1 Spiro Agnew. **2** Milton Obote. **3** Hirohito. **4** Raisa. **5** Anwar Sadat.
6 Arkansas. **7** Sirimavo Bandaranike. **8** 1970s. **9** Zimbabwe. **10** Mary
Robinson. **11** Juan Peron. **12** Makarios. **13** Charles de Gaulle. **14** Haiti.
15 Menachem Begin. **16** The Red Brigade. **17** 1960s. **18** Firing squad.
19 Benazir Bhutto. **20** Dan Quayle. **21** Cardiff. **22** Gough Whitlam.
23 Leonid Brezhnev. **24** Zimbabwe. **25** Gerald Ford. **26** Pieter Botha.
27 Philippines. **28** Egypt. **29** General de Gaulle. **30** Albania.

Quiz 19 The Royals

Answers - see page 141

LEVEL 2

1 Who did Prince William invite to a parents' event at Eton in 1997?
2 Who is the first female in line to the throne?
3 Which King (name and number) was the subject of a 1995 film?
4 Who are the parents of Lady Helen Taylor?
5 Who played John Brown when Judi Dench was Victoria on TV?
6 Who interviewed Princess Diana for "Panorama" in 1995?
7 Princess Diana confessed to having had an affair with whom?
8 Who was Princess Anne's bridesmaid when she married Mark Phillips?
9 Who is Serena Linley's mother-in-law?
10 How many lots were there in the Christie's sale of Diana's dresses?
11 Who was Prince Charles's mother-in-law for 14 years?
12 Which Princess was married to the bodyguard Daniel Ducruet?
13 Emily Davison died under the hooves of which king's horse?
14 Which country did Princess Diana visit to publicize the dangers of landmines?
15 Who was Susan who accompanied Princess Elizabeth on her honeymoon?
16 Who was the first royal after Henry VIII to marry after a divorce?
17 Which letters did _Britannia_ have before its name?
18 Who are the oldest royal bodyguards?
19 Reputedly how much was the Princess of Wales's divorce settlement?
20 Who presented the trophy at the 1997 Grand National?
21 What colour are "Princess of Wales" roses?
22 Who was Queen Elizabeth II's first prime minister?
23 In which church did Princess Anne's second marriage take place?
24 Who was the last Empress of India?
25 Which gardener's name was linked with Princess Margaret in the 70s?
26 In which month of the year is the Garter Service?
27 Which two Princes have birthdays in June?
28 Which Royal was an exhibitor at the 1997 Chelsea Flower Show?
29 Princess Diana is patron of which ballet company?
30 What role does Sir Robert Fellowes have amongst the Queen's staff?

Answers

Food & Drink 1 (see Quiz 17)
1 Semolina. 2 Veal. 3 Caraway. 4 Clotted cream. 5 Citrus fruits. 6 Dried.
7 Parmesan cheese. 8 Warrington. 9 Beef. 10 Vino da tavola. 11 Whiskey
or Bourbon. 12 Orange. 13 Fish, pastry. 14 Rice. 15 Blackcurrant.
16 Smoked fish, rice. 17 Guernseys and Jerseys. 18 Cointreau. 19 Filo.
20 Double Gloucester and Stilton. 21 Eight. 22 Bacon. 23 Buckwheat.
24 Dried beans. 25 Spain. 26 Normandy. 27 An Italian bread. 28 Bacon
and eggs. 29 Skimmed. 30 Italian rice.

Quiz 20 World Leaders

Answers - see page 142

LEVEL 2

1 Who was Richard Nixon's first vice-president?
2 In the 70s who did Idi Amin oust from power in Uganda?
3 Which Emperor of Japan ruled for over 60 years in the 20th century?
4 What was the first name of Mrs Gorbachev?
5 Who succeeded President Nasser in Egypt?
6 Bill Clinton has been governor of which state?
7 Who was the world's first woman prime minister?
8 In which decade did Juan Carlos I become King of Spain?
9 Robert Mugabe was prime minister and president of which country?
10 Who became Ireland's first woman president?
11 Who was president of Argentina from 1946 to 1955?
12 Which archbishop became the first president of an independent Cyprus?
13 Who was French president during the Paris student riots of the 60s?
14 In which country did Baby succeed Papa?
15 Which Israeli leader won the Nobel Peace Prize in 1978?
16 Which terrorist group murdered Italy's Aldo Moro?
17 In which decade did Indira Gandhi first become Indian prime minister?
18 How was Romanian dictator Ceaucescu executed?
19 Who was the first prime minister to give birth while in office?
20 Who was George Bush's vice president?
21 The former British PM James Callaghan became Baron Callaghan of where?
22 Which Australian PM got the push by the Governor General in the 70s?
23 Who ousted Khruschev in the Kremlin coup of the 60s?
24 Canan Banana was the first president of which country?
25 Nelson Rockefeller was vice-president to which USA president?
26 Who was president of South Africa before F.W. de Klerk?
27 Corazon Aquino was president of which country?
28 In which country did King Farouk abdicate after a military coup?
29 Who was the first president of the Fifth French Republic?
30 The splendidly named King Zog ruled which East European country?

1   Which is the third film of the *Star Wars* trilogy?
2   What is the diameter in inches of a standard competition dartboard?
3   Which children's programme had the sci-fi strip "Bleep and Booster"?
4   A beluga is a type of what?
5   Lent always begins on which day of the week?
6   Which royal told the press to "naff off" at the Badminton Horse Trials?
7   David Wagstaffe was the first British footballer to be shown what?
8   Which language does the word "anorak" come from?
9   Why did the catfish get its name?
10 What title did Billy Connolly give to the Village People's "In The Navy"?
11 Who wrote the novel *The Woman In White*?
12 What was the nickname of Arthur Marx?
13 In which century was Richard the Lionheart born?
14 Which US state is renowned for its Black Hills?
15 What kind a school was run by Pussy Galore?
16 Photophobia is a fear of what?
17 What relation, if any, was Pitt the Elder to Pitt the Younger?
18 Who had a 80s No. 1 with "Never Gonna Give You Up"?
19 Which character did Emma Samms play in "Dynasty"?
20 Which countries share the world's longest frontier?
21 Bruce Woodcock was connected with which sport?
22 On what part of the body are mukluks worn?
23 Which film from 1970 tells of a relationship of a boy and a kestrel?
24 What is the first name of the girl who dies in *Love Story*?
25 In economics, who in the 90s was "Steady Eddie"?
26 What is the Royal Navy equivalent of the army rank of major general?
27 Which birthstone is linked to February?
28 Who is Welwyn Garden City's most famous golfer?
29 In which decade of the 20th century was Placido Domingo born?
30 What is the name of the Vatican's army?

Quiz 22 Technology & Industry

Answers - see page 148

1   Which country was the first to legalize trade unions?
2   In which decade was British Petroleum privatized?
3   Which revolutionary product did Proctor & Gamble launch in 1969?
4   Where did one of the worst industrial accidents take place in 1984?
5   Along with Corn Flakes which cereal did Kellogg's export to the UK in 1922?
6   What name is given to an alloy that joins surfaces together?
7   Which company's first computer, the 701, was produced in 1953?
8   Which company's red-triangle trademark was the first to be registered?
9   Which industrialist became first Lord Mayor of Dublin in 1851?
10 Who invented and marketed a vehicle powered by a washing-machine motor?
11 Which company did Israel Moses Sieff develop?
12 The jelly Vaseline was a bi-product from which industry?
13 Which convenience product was launched from its factory in St Andrews Road, Walthamstow, in 1945?
14 Which London retailer sold the first Heinz products in the UK 1895?
15 Who formed the Electric Suction Sweeper Co. in 1908?
16 How is a complex electronic circuit built on a small piece of silicon more commonly known?
17 Which two companies first developed the compact disc?
18 Who founded the British and North American Royal Mail Steam Packet Company which later bore his name?
19 Fred Dibnah was famous in which industry?
20 Which company introduced travellers' cheques?
21 Lord Nuffield was the first British mass producer of what?
22 Which of his names did Woolworth use as a brand name in stores?
23 Which business did Howard Hughes finance from his oil profits?
24 In which century was the first English patent granted?
25 Which Swiss company first developed waterproof watches?
26 How would polyvinyl chloride be relevant to a double-glazing salesman?
27 What was the first-ever household detergent?
28 What was founded as Fabbrica Italiana Automobili Torino in 1899?
29 Who gave his name to his invention the whirlpool bath?
30 Which company did Terence Conran found in 1971?

Answers

Movies: Superstars (see Quiz 24)

1 Jack Nicholson. 2 Harrison Ford. 3 Meg Ryan. 4 Clint Eastwood. 5 Sean Connery. 6 Clark Gable. 7 Katharine Hepburn. 8 Fletcher Christian. 9 Cary Grant. 10 Lawyer. 11 Tom Cruise. 12 Michael Douglas. 13 Michelle Pfeiffer. 14 Humphrey Bogart. 15 *Scent of a Woman*. 16 Spencer Tracy. 17 "Thanks For the Memory". 18 Fred Astaire and Ginger Rogers. 19 Joan Crawford. 20 Arnold Schwarzenegger. 21 *Waterworld*. 22 Anthony Hopkins. 23 Robert Redford. 24 Tony Curtis. 25 Demi Moore. 26 Dustin Hoffman. 27 Meryl Streep. 28 Bette Davis. 29 Sylvester Stallone. 30 Duke.

1 Which plant's scientific name is *Impatiens*?
2 Which Chinese city is home to the Terracotta Army?
3 What did the North West Mounted Police become in 1920?
4 Who were Roberta, Phyllis and Peter collectively known as?
5 Which drink is named after the Ethiopian city of Kaffa?
6 Who played Dot Cotton in "EastEnders"?
7 What coin was made compulsory in 1971 and illegal in 1985?
8 Which county is home to the Brecon Beacons?
9 Which King received the support of Robin Hood?
10 What is the highest UK peak south of the Scottish border?
11 In which century was Fred Astaire born?
12 Who wrote the novel *Crime and Punishment*?
13 How was Malcolm Little better known?
14 Who had a 90s No. 1 with "Pray"?
15 Which drink has "7X" as a secret formula?
16 How old was Brian Clough when he stopped playing soccer?
17 Who published *My Silent War* in the USSR in 1968?
18 In which series did Frank and Danny Kane appear?
19 Which country was the setting for *Carry On Up the Khyber*?
20 Who was the first presenter of "Give Us A Clue"?
21 What word can go after "rest" and before "hood"?
22 Which stone is used in snooker tables?
23 In song lyrics, you can bring Pearl or Rose but who can't you bring?
24 Who in 1997 became Britain's first Muslim MP?
25 In which decade did Minnie the Minx first appear in the *Beano*?
26 Alan Scotthorne was a 90s world champion in which sport?
27 Which well-known Frenchman designed Italy's flag?
28 Whose box was opened by Epimethius?
29 Which name derived from Greek means stone or rock?
30 Which team's football kit was designed by Bruce Oldfield in 1997?

Pot Luck 9 (see Quiz 21)
1 *Return of the Jedi*. 2 18. 3 "Blue Peter". 4 Whale. 5 Wednesday.
6 The Princess Royal. 7 A red card. 8 Eskimo. 9 It has whiskers.
10 "In the Brownies". 11 Wilkie Collins. 12 "Harpo". 13 12th. 14 South
Dakota. 15 A flying school. 16 Strong light. 17 Father. 18 Rick Astley.
19 Fallon Carrington-Colby. 20 Canada and USA. 21 Boxing. 22 Feet.
23 *Kes*. 24 Jenny. 25 Eddie George. 26 Rear admiral. 27 Amethyst.
28 Nick Faldo. 29 40s. 30 The Swiss Guard.

Answers

Quiz 24 Movies: Superstars

Answers - see page 146

LEVEL 2

1   Who played Garrett Breedlove in *Terms of Endearment*?
2   Who was the male co-star with Sigourney Weaver and Melanie Griffith in *Working Girl*?
3   How is Margaret Mary Emily Anne Hyra better known?
4   Which superstar was mayor of his home town Carmel, California?
5   Who was contestant No. 24 in the 1950 Mr Universe contest?
6   Whose most famous line was "Frankly, my dear, I don't give a damn"?
7   Who used Eleanor Roosevelt as her inspiration for her role in *The African Queen*?
8   Clark Gable, Marlon Brando and Mel Gibson have all played which sailor on film?
9   On film who did Mae West invite to "come up some time an' see me"?
10 What was Tom Hanks's profession in *Philadelphia*?
11 Who co-starred with Paul Newman in *The Color of Money*?
12 Which actor had the line "Greed is good" in *Wall Street* in 1987?
13 Who sang "Makin' Whoopee" on Jeff Bridges' piano in *The Fabulous Baker Boys*?
14 Who won an Oscar as Charlie Allnut in *The African Queen*?
15 For which film did Al Pacino win his first Oscar?
16 Who received an Oscar nomination for his last film *Guess Who's Coming to Dinner*?
17 What is Bob Hope's signature tune?
18 Who were first paired on screen in *Flying Down to Rio*?
19 Which actress was the subject of the film *Mommie Dearest*?
20 Who married the journalist Maria Shriver, a niece of President Kennedy?
21 Which Kevin Costner film was one of the most expensive flops ever?
22 Who played the doctor in *The Elephant Man*?
23 Who founded the the the Sundance Institute for new film-makers?
24 Who parodied his hero Cary Grant in *Some Like It Hot*?
25 How is Demetria Guynes better known?
26 Who played Carl Bernstein in *All the President's Men*?
27 Which actress sounded Polish in 1982, Danish in 1985 and Australian in 1988?
28 Who had six Best Actress Oscar nominations between 1938 and 1942?
29 Who wrote the script for *Rocky*?
30 What was John Wayne's nickname?

1 Which wartime hero had the same name as Hilda Ogden's cat?
2 What kind of plants is the name Harry Wheatcroft linked with?
3 Which ocean are the Seychelles in?
4 What expense became compulsory for cars in 1921?
5 Which university had Sir Robin Day as a former union president?
6 Which decade saw the first FA Cup Final at Wembley?
7 What kind of reference book was Bradshaw's?
8 What is a butterfly larva more commonly called?
9 Which actress appeared in Woody Allen's *The Purple Rose of Cairo*?
10 Which fictional doctor lived in Puddleby-on-Marsh?
11 In which decade of the 20th century was Mikhail Gorbachev born?
12 What was Bob Marley's middle name?
13 What is the only English anagram of TOENAIL?
14 If it's 12 noon GMT what time is it in Athens?
15 Who wrote *Journey To The Centre Of The Earth*?
16 Alan Hansen joined Liverpool from which club?
17 Who had a 90s No. 1 with "Rhythm Is A Dancer"?
18 Which is the only active volcano in mainland Europe?
19 In which century was Jane Austen born?
20 On which ranch was "Bonanza" set?
21 How many counters does backgammon have of each colour?
22 Who co-founded the Aldeburgh Festival in 1948?
23 What is the capital of Morocco?
24 Who authorized the authorized version of the Bible?
25 For how many years did David Coleman present "A Question of Sport"?
26 What is the next highest prime number above 23?
27 Who won the decathlon in the 1980 Olympics?
28 "The Lass That Loved A Sailor" is the subtitle of which light opera?
29 What is the name of Tony Blair's first-born son?
30 Careless and Invictor are types of which fruit?

1 Who fought Muhammad Ali in the Rumble in the Jungle?
2 Jennifer Susan Harvey is better known by what name?
3 Which Englishman scored the first 1997 Ashes century?
4 Which Italian said he could not "understand a word Dennis Wise is saying"?
5 Which Andy won rugby's Lance Todd Award in 1988 and 1990?
6 Who was skipper of Middlesbrough's 1997 FA Cup Final team?
7 Who was the female competitor excused a sex test at the 1976 Olympics?
8 Who was the first Swede to win Wimbledon's Men's Singles?
9 Who was Marvellous Marvin?
10 Who left Llanelli in 1989 to play rugby league for Widnes?
11 Who sponsored the 1997 one-day England v. Australia cricket?
12 Who won the 125th Open at Lytham?
13 Who was the first black athlete to captain Great Britain men's team?
14 Who retired in the 90s after 15 years as chairman of the FA?
15 Who is Michael Schumacher's younger racing driver brother?
16 Which Spanish player interrupted Graf's reign as women's singles champion at Wimbledon?
17 Who was the English captain of the 1980 British Lions tour?
18 Which boxer was born in Bellingham, London, on May 3 1934?
19 Which left-handed batsman has scored most test runs for England?
20 Who was Leeds's manager before George Graham?
21 Who is the first person to manage Everton three times?
22 Who was first to win the US Masters five times?
23 Who scored the last-minute play-off goal for Crystal Palace in 1997?
24 Who was first to ride seven Derby winners?
25 Who did Gazza flick the ball over for the Euro '96 goal against Scotland?
26 Who partnered Hingis to win Wimbledon's 1996 women's doubles?
27 Who won the US Tennis Open while her father was in a legal court?
28 Who had a set to with umpire Shakoor Rana at Faisalabad in 1987?
29 Who managed Frank Bruno?
30 Who scored Southampton's FA Cup Final winner in the 70s?

Quiz 27 Pot Luck 12

Answers - see page 149

LEVEL 2

1 Who said, "There's always something fishy about the French"?
2 What is thrown in the Olympics weighing 4lb 6oz?
3 Which house on the Isle of Wight was home to Queen Victoria?
4 Which Bob Marley song got to 22 in 1975 then the top ten in 1981?
5 Which Dickens character had a friend called Smike?
6 What name is given to a whale's breathing organs?
7 Alphabetically, who was last of the Twelve Apostles?
8 What is a devil's coachhorse?
9 Which actress became Sable Colby after appearing as Connie?
10 Which family built the town called Bourneville?
11 Who wrote the novel *Moll Flanders*?
12 Whose nickname was "Lord Haw Haw"?
13 What is the plural of mongoose?
14 Who had a 70s No. 1 with "Jealous Mind"?
15 In which century was Al Capone born?
16 What does the time abbreviation p.m. stand for?
17 Which character did Arnold Ridley play in "Dad's Army"?
18 In which language did St Patrick write his autobiography?
19 What is the only English anagram of ANTAGONIST?
20 What is the name of the dog in Peter Pan?
21 Pyrophobia is a fear of what?
22 What is the capital of Ecuador?
23 In Scrabble, how many points is the letter S worth?
24 Who were Booker T's backing group?
25 What was American Footballer Wiliam Perry's nickname?
26 What word can follow "cast", "pig" and "steam"?
27 How much was the Dracula stamp worth when first issued?
28 Which country is Mount Everest in?
29 1995 was the Chinese year of which creature?
30 Engelbert Humperdink is from which English city?

Answers

Pot Luck 11 (see Quiz 25)
1 Rommel. 2 Roses. 3 The Indian Ocean. 4 Tax discs. 5 Oxford.
6 1920s. 7 Railway timetable. 8 Caterpillar. 9 Mia Farrow. 10 Dr Doolittle.
11 30s. 12 Nesta. 13 Elation. 14 2 p.m. 15 Jules Verne.
16 Partick Thistle. 17 Snap. 18 Mount Vesuvius. 19 18th. 20 The
Ponderosa. 21 15. 22 Benjamin Britten, Peter Pears. 23 Rabat. 24 James I.
25 18. 26 29. 27 Daley Thompson. 28 *HMS Pinafore*. 29 Euan.
30 Gooseberry.

Quiz 28 TV Times 1

Answers - see page 150

LEVEL 2

1   What is the first name of Kavanagh QC?

2   What is the mascot for "The Great Antiques Hunt"?

3   Patrick Moore is famous for playing which musical instrument?

4   In which county was "Where the Heart Is" set?

5   What is Rab C. Nesbitt's wife called?

6   Henry Sandon became famous on which TV show?

7   Who did the Simpsons replace as TV's longest-running cartoon family in 1997?

8   What is the name of the infirmary in "Bramwell"?

9   Who is Jennifer Paterson's cooking partner?

10 Which female doctor succeeded Beth Glover in "Peak Practice"?

11 What is the fictional village where "Heartbeat" is set?

12 What is the profession of the chief characters in "This Life"?

13 Which actor is the son of Nigel Davenport and Maria Aitken?

14 Which role did Harry Enfield play in "Men Behaving Badly"?

15 What did the ARP warden call Mainwaring in "Dad's Army"?

16 Which children's TV character lives in Pontypandy?

17 Which detective has a dog called Snowy?

18 Who is the comedienne mother of the actress Suzy Aitchison?

19 In which decade was "Hi-De-Hi" first set?

20 Which comedian began his show with a shop-window illusion?

21 Where was Dot Cotton living before she returned to Walford in 1997?

22 Who was the blondest person on "Shooting Stars"?

23 Who was Reginald Perrin's boss?

24 Whose catchphrase in "Drop the Dead Donkey" was "I'm not here"?

25 Who plays the title role in "Dr Quinn: Medicine Woman"?

26 In which show would you find PC Goody?

27 Where would you find the Simpsons other than in "The Simpsons"?

28 In which series would you find Benton Fraser?

29 Which Geoff Hamilton series was first shown after his death?

30 Who left "Blue Peter" in 1996 and presented "Songs of Praise"?

Quiz 29 Pot Luck 13

Answers - see page 155

LEVEL 2

1   Which part of London is famous for its diamond trade?
2   What was first broadcast from Greenwich by the BBC in February 1924?
3   Who was the longest-reigning British king?
4   Which sport was the subject of the Popplewell Report in 1985?
5   Which building was Prime Minister Lloyd George the first to use?
6   Which group of islands includes Aran?
7   What is the Swiss author Johanna Spyri's best-known children's novel?
8   In sporting terms, what does the BBBC stand for?
9   On which river does New Orleans stand?
10 What was first published in *The Times* on February 1 1930?
11 In which century was Johan Sebastian Bach born?
12 Who wrote the novel *The Count of Monte Cristo*?
13 Who was the first presenter of "Grandstand"?
14 The "Cat And Mouse Act" was to counter activities of which movement?
15 Charles Ross and Epicure are types of which fruit?
16 What was Kojak's first name?
17 Which country has San Salvador as its capital?
18 Who had a 60s No. 1 with "I've Gotta Get A Message To You"?
19 Laurence Olivier took the title Baron Olivier of where?
20 In which drama series did Will Preston and Alice North appear?
21 How many laps are there in a single speedway race?
22 Which inflamed part of your body suffers from encephalitis?
23 In which decade of the 20th century was Che Guevara born?
24 What word can go after "race" and before "fly"?
25 How is the film director Sandor Kellner better known?
26 What is a Dorset Blue Vinney?
27 Where is the University of Strathclyde based?
28 Who is Melchester Rovers' most famous striker?
29 In April 1997 George Tenet became head of which US organization?
30 Which bird was on the old coin the farthing?

Answers

Pot Luck 14 (see Quiz 31)
1 Tower Bridge. 2 Idi Amin. 3 Personal best. 4 The ring. 5 Melbourne.
6 Cher. 7 Charlie Brown. 8 *Columbia*. 9 May Day. 10 London.
11 David Herbert. 12 David Soul. 13 Chronos. 14 Violin. 15 17th.
16 Bodies from graves. 17 E. 18 Sardonyx. 19 Skiing. 20 American
Independence. 21 Spain. 22 Piltdown Man. 23 The Goons. 24 Dublin.
25 Without an orchestra. 26 1970s. 27 Leskanich. 28 New York.
29 Daphne du Maurier. 30 Glasgow.

Quiz 30 Euro Tour

Answers - see page 156

LEVEL 2

1   In which city is the largest Christian church in the world?
2   What is the official home of the French President?
3   On which island is Ajaccio?
4   What is the French town of Limoges famous for?
5   Which part of Paris is famous as the artists' quarter?
6   Where is the European Court of Justice?
7   Ibiza and Majorca are part of which island group?
8   The Oise and the Marne are tributaries of which river?
9   Where is the Abbey Theatre?
10 What is Germany's highest mountain?
11 On which river does Florence stand?
12 Which Mediterranean island was the HQ of the Knights of St John?
13 Which country has most European neighbours?
14 The RER is part of which city's underground system?
15 The Azores belong to which European country?
16 How many Benelux countries are there?
17 Andorra is among which mountains?
18 Piraeus is the port of which city?
19 In which country is Lake Garda?
20 Where does the river Loire flow into the Atlantic?
21 In which central European country is Lake Balaton?
22 Which country do the Faeroe Islands belong to?
23 The Skagerrak links the Kattegat with which Sea?
24 Which country's official name is Konungariket Sverige?
25 The parliament of which country is called the Cortes?
26 Ljubljana is the capital of which country of the former Yugoslavia?
27 Which Republic lies between Poland and Hungary?
28 Utrecht is in which European country?
29 Where is Monegasque spoken?
30 Which is the southernmost and largest of Greece's many islands?

Pop: No 1s (see Quiz 32)

1 Partners In Kryme. 2 The Aces. 3 Chrissie Hynde. 4 Levi's jeans. 5 "Tiger Feet". 6 Robson & Jerome. 7 Los Lobos. 8 "Cabaret". 9 "Free." 10 90s. 11 "(Come Up And See Me)". 12 Blur. 13 "Dancing Queen". 14 David Soul. 15 "Saving All My Love For You". 16 Gary Brooker. 17 Eddie Calvert. 18 Jazzy Jeff. 19 "Day Tripper". 20 Reg Presley. 21 Kiki Dee. 22 Terry Jacks. 23 "Mr Blobby". 24 "The Legend Of Xanadu". 25 "Baby Come Back". 26 "Super Trouper". 27 Slim Whitman. 28 "Fairground". 29 "Let It Be". 30 "What's Another Year?".

Answers

Quiz 31 Pot Luck 14

Answers - see page 153

LEVEL 2

1   Which bridge on the Thames is closest to the Tower of London?
2   Who seized power in Uganda in 1971??
3   What does "PB" against a runner's name indicate?
4   What was made by Sauron in a J.R.R. Tolkien book?
5   On TV, in which city is Ramsay Street?
6   Who was the female voice on "Deadringer For Love"?
7   Which character loves the little red-haired girl in "Peanuts"?
8   Which US space shuttle was the first to gain orbit into space?
9   Which annual holiday did the 1992 government want to move?
10 Which city provides the setting for *1984*?
11 What do the D and H stand for in D.H. Lawrence's name?
12 Who had a 70s No. 1 with "Don't Give Up On Us"?
13 Who was the Greek god of time?
14 What musical instrument was played by Sherlock Holmes?
15 In which century was Sir Isaac Newton born?
16 If you were a resurrectionist, what would you steal?
17 In Morse code what letter is represented by one dot?
18 Which birthstone is linked to August?
19 Albert Tomba has been a world champion in which sport?
20 In which war was the Battle of Bunker Hill?
21 In which country did the fandango originate?
22 Which Man was discovered in East Sussex in 1912?
23 Which comic team included a Welshman, an Indian-born Anglo-Irishman and an Anglo-Peruvian?
24 Handel's *Messiah* was first put on for the public in which city?
25 What does karaoke mean?
26 In which decade was "The Antiques Roadshow" first screened?
27 What is the surname of the Eurovision Song Contest winner Katrina?
28 In which city was "Fame" set?
29 Who wrote the novel *Jamaica Inn*?
30 Which Scottish city has Saint Mungo as its patron saint?

Answers

Pot Luck 13 (see Quiz 29)
1 Hatton Garden. 2 The time signal. 3 George III. 4 Football. 5 Chequers. 6 The Hebrides. 7 *Heidi*. 8 The British Boxing Board of Control. 9 The Mississippi. 10 A crossword. 11 17th. 12 Alexandre Dumas. 13 Peter Dimmock 14 Suffragettes. 15 Apples. 16 Theo. 17 El Salvador. 18 Bee Gees. 19 Brighton. 20 "Peak Practice". 21 Four. 22 Brain. 23 20s. 24 "Horse". 25 Alexander Korda. 26 A cheese. 27 Glasgow. 28 Roy Race. 29 CIA. 30 The wren.

Quiz 32 Pop: No 1s

LEVEL 2

1   Who had a 90s No. 1 with "Turtle Power"?
2   Who backed Desmond Dekker on "The Israelites"?
3   Who had a No. 1 with Cher, Neneh Cherry and Eric Clapton?
4   Stiltskin's "Inside" was used to advertise which product?
5   What was Mud's first No. 1?
6   Who kept Oasis and "Wonderwall" off the top?
7   Who had a 80s No. 1 with "La Bamba"?
8   What was on the other side of Louis Armstrong's "What A Wonderful World"?
9   What was the title of Deniece Williams's 1977 No. 1?
10 In which decade did Lulu first top the UK charts?
11 What in brackets is added to the title "Make Me Smile"?
12 Who had the first No. 1 on the Food label?
13 Which No1 contains the words "hear the beat of the tambourine"?
14 Who had a 70s No. 1 with "Silver Lady"?
15 What was Whitney Houston's first UK No. 1?
16 Who was Procol Harum's "Whiter Shade Of Pale" vocalist?
17 Which trumpeter had two No. 1s in the 50s?
18 Who had a No. 1 with the Fresh Prince?
19 What was on the other side of the Beatles' "We Can Work It Out"?
20 Who wrote "Love Is All Around"?
21 Who partnered Elton John on his first UK No. 1?
22 Who had a 70s No. 1 with "Seasons In the Sun"?
23 In the 90s, which single bounced back to No. 1 a week after losing the top spot?
24 What was the only No. 1 for Dave Dee, Dozy, Beaky, Mick and Tich?
25 Which song gave a No. 1 for both the Equals and Pato Branton?
26 What was Abba's last No. 1?
27 Who had a 50s No. 1 with "Rose Marie"?
28 What was Simply Red's first No. 1?
29 The Zebrugge ferry disaster led to which song topping the charts?
30 Which Eurovision Song Contest winner gave Johnny Logan a No. 1?

Quiz 33 Pot Luck 15

Answers - see page 159

LEVEL 2

1 Which group of islands were the first discovery for Columbus in 1492?
2 Which actor from "The A-Team" appeared in *Rocky III*?
3 What is the inscription on the Victoria Cross?
4 Where is Frogmore?
5 What does an ice hockey match begin with?
6 Which family of birds includes the robin?
7 Who played Norman Bates in *Psycho*?
8 What did Steven Nice of Cockney Rebel change his name to?
9 What is Canada's largest port on the Pacific?
10 Which children's series featured the Soup Dragon?
11 Tony was the horse of which screen cowboy?
12 In which decade was Cadbury's Wispa bar launched?
13 Who had a 80s No. 1 with "The Edge Of Heaven"?
14 What is the capital of Latvia?
15 What colour was Moby Dick?
16 In which century was Walter Raleigh born?
17 What is another name for a natatorium?
18 Who wrote the novel *Silas Marner*?
19 Whose name is now used for a collaborator with the enemy?
20 In which country was Sir Alexander Fleming born?
21 Who introduced the "New Look" in 1947?
22 Tom Thumb, Tennis Ball and Winter Density are types of what?
23 What does "poly" mean as in "polygon" or "polyglot"?
24 In music, there must be at least how many flats if the D is played flat?
25 Which large bird is sacred in Peru?
26 In which decade of the 20th century was Prince Philip born?
27 Which type of course fishing uses a gag and gaff?
28 Which character did Catherine Zeta Jones play in "The Darling Buds of May"?
29 Euclid established the foundations of which branch of study?
30 How many were present at the Last Supper?

Pot Luck 16 (see Quiz 35)
1 Lily. 2 Spain. 3 3 points. 4 Meg. 5 Annie Walker. 6 Tear gas.
7 Berkshire. 8 Square. 9 Dr Zhivago. 10 The USA. 11 Henry Fielding.
12 Pol Pot. 13 "Bramwell". 14 Adamski. 15 Coagulate. 16 Polish.
17 Single. 18 13. 19 Cliff Michelmore. 20 Proverbs. 21 Macmillan (Lord
Stockton). 22 Fish. 23 Romania. 24 England. 25 16th. 26 Indianapolis.
27 C5. 28 Georgia. 29 Sylvia Plath. 30 Air marshal.

Quiz 34 Books

LEVEL 2

1 What was the first book in English to be printed in England?
2 Which books do castaways automatically receive on "Desert Island Discs"?
3 Who was responsible for *The Complete Hip and Thigh Diet*?
4 In which century was the *Oxford English Dictionary* started in earnest?
5 Which book had to be owned compulsorily by every member of his country's adult population?
6 Which religious sect published *The Truth That Leads to Eternal Life*?
7 Who wrote *The Hitch Hiker's Guide to the Galaxy*?
8 Which British publisher launched Penguin titles in 1935?
9 In which decade did Guinness start to publish their *Book of Records* annually?
10 Who began publishing Beatrix Potter's books in 1902?
11 Who wrote *The Thorn Birds*?
12 What was Jeffrey Archer's first successful novel?
13 Which MP's first novel went straight to No. 1 in the *Sunday Times* bestsellers list in 1994?
14 What was Jeffrey Archer's sequel to *Kane and Abel*?
15 Who wrote *The Downing Street Years*?
16 Who created the character Emma Harte?
17 Which French novelist wrote *Gigi*?
18 What was the difference between Delia Smith's 1986 *Complete Cookery Course* and her 1989 *Complete Cookery Course*?
19 Who wrote *The Female Eunuch*?
20 Which book title links Jules Verne and Michael Palin?
21 Which Roddy Doyle bestseller won the Booker Prize in 1993?
22 What was Audrey Eyton's bestselling book of the 1980s?
23 In which county was Jane Austen born?
24 What is a bibliophile?
25 What colour are the French Michelin guides?
26 Who wrote *The Godfather*?
27 Who wrote *Possession*?
28 What was the name of *Poirot's Last Case*?
29 Who also writes as Barbara Vine?
30 In which county was Catherine Cookson born?

1   Which family of plants does garlic belong to?
2   Which is the largest country on the Iberian peninsula?
3   What was the value of a rugby union try prior to 1971?
4   Who is the eldest of the March girls in *Little Women*?
5   Which character was played by Doris Speed in "Coronation Street"?
6   Which gas was first used by the Germans in 1915 against Russia?
7   Which county formerly had Abingdon as its county town?
8   What shape is the trunk of a cottonwood tree?
9   Which doctor was in love with Lara Antipova?
10 Which country is the largest producer of meat in the world?
11 Who wrote the novel *Tom Jones*?
12 Who has also been known as Saloth Sar and Kompong Thom?
13 In which drama series did Marsham and Nurse Carr appear?
14 Who had a 90s No. 1 with "Killer"?
15 What is the only English anagram of CATALOGUE?
16 What nationality was Marie Curie?
17 What does "mono" mean as in the words "monocle" or "monorail"?
18 How many people are portrayed in da Vinci's *The Last Supper*?
19 Who was the first presenter of "Holiday" ?
20 In the Old Testament which book directly follows Psalms?
21 Which member of the Lords denounced privatization as "selling the family silver"?
22 Ichthyophobia is a fear of what?
23 Which country was the birthplace of the tennis player Ilie Nastase?
24 In which country was the composer Gustav Holst born?
25 In which century was Elizabeth I born?
26 What is the state capital of Indiana, USA?
27 What name was given to Sinclair's electric, three-wheeled car?
28 In which American state was Ray Charles born?
29 Who wrote a semi-autobiographical novel called *The Bell Jar*?
30 What is the RAF equivalent of the Royal Navy rank of vice-admiral?

Answers - see page 158

1 Who starred in *The Towering Inferno* and *Naked Gun 2½*?

2 Who played Cruella de Vil in the "real" version of *101 Dalmatians*?

3 Which movie star played Shylock in London's West End in 1989?

4 Who played the aunts in *James and the Giant Peach*?

5 Who directed *Born on the Fourth of July* and *Natural Born Killers*?

6 Who played the Saint in the 90s movie?

7 Who was chosen to play Heathcliff in the 90s *Wuthering Heights*?

8 Who was the British star of *Fierce Creatures*?

9 Who starred as the Elephant Man?

10 Who married Mickey Rooney and Frank Sinatra?

11 Who insured whose legs for a million dollars with Lloyd's of London?

12 Who was the heroine in the 30s version of *King Kong*?

13 Who played the mother in *Mermaids*?

14 Who did Alan Rickman play in *Robin Hood, Prince of Thieves*?

15 Who was once known in Los Angeles as BK 4454813 OG 2795?

16 Whose film production company is called Jagged Films?

17 Who played Batman in the 1997 *Batman and Robin*?

18 Which blonde screen legend made only 11 films, three for Hitchcock?

19 Which rock star did Angela Bassett play in a 1993 biopic?

20 Who was Jack Somersby in *Somersby*?

21 Who wrote the screenplay of *The Crucible*?

22 How are Felix Ungar and Oscar Madison better known?

23 Who played Robin Williams's estranged wife in *Mrs Doubtfire*?

24 Who directed *Pulp Fiction* and *Reservoir Dogs*?

25 Who played Vince Vega in *Pulp Fiction*?

26 Which ex-007 appeared for two minutes at the end of *Robin Hood: Prince of Thieves*?

27 Who was never seen in his most successful pre-'93 film performance?

28 Which actress directed *Prince of Tides* and *Yentl*?

29 Which role did Dooley Wilson play in *Casablanca*?

30 Who produced the Hugh Grant movie *Extreme Measures*?

Answers

Books (see Quiz 34)
1 *The Canterbury Tales*. 2 The Bible and the complete works of Shakespeare.
3 Rosemary Conley. 4 19th. 5 *Chairman Mao's Little Red Book*. 6 Jehovah's
Witnesses. 7 Douglas Adams. 8 Allen Lane. 9 1960s. 10 Frederick Warne. 11
Colleen McCullough. 12 *Not a Penny More, Not a Penny Less*. 13 Edwina Currie.
14 *The Prodigal Daughter*. 15 Margaret Thatcher. 16 Barbara Taylor Bradford.
17 Colette. 18 The 1989 Course was *Illustrated*. 19 Germaine Greer.
20 *Around the World in Eighty Days*. 21 *Paddy Clarke Ha Ha Ha*. 22 *The F-Plan Diet*. 23 Hampshire. 24 A book lover. 25 Red. 26 Mario Puzo. 27 A.S.
Byatt. 28 *Curtain*. 29 Ruth Rendell. 30 County Durham.

Quiz 37 Pot Luck 17

Answers - see page 163

LEVEL 2

1 Who was Don Brennan's best man when he married Ivy Tilsley?
2 Which US president won a Nobel Prize in 1906?
3 Which national holiday was first celebrated in England in 1974?
4 What was Fletcher's first name in "Porridge"?
5 Which city is the capital of the Andalusia region of Spain?
6 What name is given to a coffin by Americans?
7 Who played Eddie in the musical movie *The Rocky Horror Picture Show*?
8 Which area of Spain did Don Quixote come from?
9 Which British birds are shot in braces and form a nye?
10 Who was England's 1980 rugby union Grand Slam winners captain?
11 Who wrote the novel *The Great Gatsby*?
12 In which decade of the 20th century was Paul Newman born?
13 What was the name of the chef in "Fawlty Towers"?
14 What was Margaret Thatcher's maiden name?
15 What word can go before "beans", "quartet" and "vest"?
16 Who succeeded Wordsworth as Poet Laureate?
17 What is the capital of Venezuela?
18 Who had a 70s No. 1 with "Don't Cry For Me, Argentina"?
19 Giles, Jak and Trog are all examples of what?
20 Which country has the football team Anderlecht?
21 What is dowsing?
22 Other than Austria, what other country do Tyroleans come from?
23 The artist Roy Lichtenstein comes from which country?
24 The song "Three Coins In A Fountain" came from which 50s film?
25 Who is the clown in Shakespeare's *Henry IV*?
26 Nitrous oxide is also known as what?
27 What was Richard Nixon's middle name?
28 If it's 12 noon GMT what time is it in Jerusalem?
29 In which century was Charles Dickens born?
30 In which county is Ambridge?

Answers

Cricket (see Quiz 39)
1 Durham. 2 Australia. 3 Northamptonshire. 4 "Tich". 5 Glamorgan.
6 Warwickshire. 7 Dragon. 8 Phil Edmonds, John Emburey. 9 New Zealand. 10 Yellow. 11 Derbyshire. 12 Ian Botham. 13 Surrey. 14 David Lloyd. 15 Mike Denness. 16 Jim Laker. 17 Worcestershire. 18 Left-handed. 19 South Africa. 20 Bob Willis. 21 25. 22 Dominic Cork. 23 Victoria. 24 Essex. 25 1981. 26 Hampshire. 27 1870s. 28 Graham Gooch. 29 Australia. 30 Yes.

1 Who presents "Fifteen To One"?

2 What was top prize on Anthea Turner's "Turner Round the World"?

3 Which Channel 4 show was devised and presented by Tim Vine?

4 What is the name of Channel 5's gardening quiz?

5 Who was host for the first series of "The Other Half"?

6 How many contestants were there on each show of "Blankety Blank"?

7 Which show handed out a bendy Bully?

8 Who was the first female presenter of "Busman's Holiday"?

9 Who hosted "Call My Bluff" in the late 90s?

10 Who was the first presenter of "Celebrity Squares"?

11 Which show has been hosted by Richard Madeley and Chris Tarrant?

12 Which show did Armand Jammot create?

13 Who did Ed Tudor-Pole replace in "The Crystal Maze"?

14 What was the top prize in "Double Your Money"?

15 Which quiz show had a dummy keyboard?

16 Which late afternoon quiz is hosted by Martyn Lewis?

17 Who was the second hostess on "The Generation Game"?

18 Who succeeded Bob Monkhouse as presenter of "Family Fortunes"?

19 Who originally recorded the theme song to "Whatever You Want"?

20 What shape are the letter blocks in "Blockbusters"?

21 Which mature team reached the finals of 1997's "University Challenge"?

22 Who succeeded Matthew Kelly as host of "You Bet!"?

23 Which show spawned the catchphrase "You get nothing for a pair - not in this show"?

24 Who first said, "Come on down" on "The Price is Right"?

25 Which word-puzzle show was hosted by Bradley Walsh and Jenny Powell?

26 Fred Housego was arguably the most famous winner on which show?

27 What are the two voting symbols in "Ready, Steady, Cook"?

28 Who introduced "Odd One Out" and "Wipeout"?

29 What was introduced as "The Quiz of the Week"?

30 What was the name of the game show on "Sunday Night at the London Palladium"?

Pot Luck 18 (see Quiz 40)

Answers

1 The Sun. 2 A butcher. 3 Severn. 4 Nigel Mansell. 5 The United Nations.
6 Telephone directory. 7 Gladioli. 8 Donald Campbell. 9 Arthur Fowler.
10 Raglan. 11 E.M. Forster. 12 Duarte. 13 16th. 14 3. 15 Minnehaha.
16 Eight. 17 Lily Savage. 18 Neville Chamberlain. 19 Tour de France.
20 18. 21 Cherry. 22 Edinburgh. 23 Lions. 24 Roger Hargreaves.
25 Seventh. 26 Rat. 27 Rose Petals. 28 Creedence Clearwater Revival.
29 Lucy. 30 Dr Toby Latimer.

Quiz 39 Cricket

Answers - see page 161

1　Which county were admitted to the County Championship in 1992?
2　Which country batted first in the1997 Ashes First Test in England?
3　Which county did Allan Lamb play for?
4　What was Alfred Freeman's nickname?
5　Which county has its HQ at Sophia Gardens?
6　Which county did Dermot Reeve take to the championship?
7　What creature is on the Somerset badge?
8　Which pair of spinners - both with surnames beginning with an E - dominated the 80s at Middlesex?
9　Which country did Martin Crowe play for?
10　What is the colour of the *Wisden Cricketers' Almanac*?
11　Which county has its headquarters in Nottingham Road?
12　Which cricketer has advertised Nike boots, Dansk low-alcohol lager and Shredded Wheat?
13　Which county took to an all-chocolate strip in the 90s?
14　Which cricket personality is known as Bumble?
15　Who was the first Scotsman to captain England?
16　Who became the first Test bowler to take 19 wickets in a game?
17　Which county did Ian Botham join on leaving Somerset?
18　Is Brian Lara a right- or left-handed batsman?
19　Which country does umpire Cyril Mitchley come from?
20　Which England fast bowler took Dylan as a middle name in honour of Bob Dylan?
21　How old was Mike Atherton when he was made England captain?
22　In 1995, which Englishman took a Test hat-trick against the West Indies?
23　Shane Warne first captained which Australian state side?
24　Which county does Nasser Hussain play for?
25　In what year was the series that became known as Botham's Ashes?
26　Which county did Malcolm Marshall and Gordon Greenidge play for?
27　In which decade did the first Australia v England Test take place?
28　Who has played most Tests for England?
29　Which country did Ian Redpath play for?
30　Did Geoff Boycott ever captain England?

Pot Luck 17 (see Quiz 37)

1 Jack Duckworth. 2 Theodore Roosevelt. 3 January 1. 4 Norman.
5 Seville. 6 A casket. 7 Meatloaf. 8 La Mancha. 9 Pheasants. 10 Bill Beaumont. 11 F. Scott Fitzgerald. 12 20s. 13 Terry. 14 Roberts.
15 "String". 16 Tennyson. 17 Caracas. 18 Julie Covington.
19 Newspaper cartoonists. 20 Belgium. 21 Water divining. 22 Italy.
23 America. 24 *Three Coins In A Fountain*. 25 Falstaff. 26 Laughing gas.
27 Milhous. 28 2 p.m. 29 19th. 30 Borsetshire.

Quiz 40 Pot Luck 18

Answers - see page 162

1   Which is the only star in our solar system?
2   What was Mr Jones's job other than a Corporal in "Dad's Army"?
3   Which river flows from the Cambrian Mountains to the Bristol Channel?
4   Which World Champion appeared on Isle of Man stamps in 1992?
5   Which organization replaced the League of Nations?
6   What was first produced listing 255 names in London in 1880?
7   What is the plural of gladiolus?
8   Who was the last person to hold both water- and land-speed records?
9   Which EastEnder had a screen affair with Michael Aspel's wife?
10 Which Welsh town gave its name to a style of sleeve?
11 Who wrote the novel *Howard's End*?
12 What was Eva Peron's maiden name?
13 In which century was Francis Drake born?
14 How many pedals does a grand piano have?
15 Who was Hiawatha's wife?
16 In Scrabble, how many points is the letter X worth?
17 How is Paul O'Grady better known?
18 Who was proved wrong when he said, "I believe it is peace for our time"?
19 Which sporting event did Bernard Hinault win three times in the 80s?
20 What is the diameter in inches of a basketball hoop?
21 Merton Glory and Napoleon Bigarreau are types of which fruit?
22 The Napier University is located in which city?
23 In American football which creatures come from Detroit?
24 Who wrote about the Mr Men?
25 Which of the Ten Commandments deals with adultery?
26 1996 was the Chinese year of which creature?
27 Which petals are used by the royal family as confetti?
28 Who had a 60s No. 1 with "Bad Moon Rising"?
29 What was the name of David Blunkett's dog at the 1997 election?
30 Which character did Tony Britton play in "Don't Wait Up"?

Answers

TV Game Shows (see Quiz 38)

1 William G. Stewart. 2 Two round-the-world air tickets. 3 "Fluke". 4 "The Great Garden Game". 5 Dale Winton. 6 Four. 7 "Bullseye". 8 Sarah Kennedy. 9 Bob Holness. 10 Bob Monkhouse. 11 "Cluedo".
12 "Countdown". 13 Richard O'Brien. 14 £1,000. 15 "Face the Music".
16 "Today's the Day". 17 Isla St Clair. 18 Max Bygraves. 19 Status Quo.
20 Hexagonal. 21 Open University. 22 Darren Day. 23 "Play Your Cards Right". 24 Leslie Crowther. 25 "Wheel of Fortune". 26 "Mastermind".
27 Green peppers, red tomatoes. 28 Paul Daniels. 29 "Sale of the Century".
30 "Beat the Clock".

Quiz 41 The 60s

Answers - see page 167

Answers - see page 167

LEVEL 2

1   What did widow Jackie K. become?
2   What was ITV's first live pop programme?
3   Where did the world-record-breaking runner Peter Snell come from?
4   Who was premier of Rhodesia when UDI was declared?
5   In what year was the death penalty abolished in Britain?
6   What did the L stand for in Mary Whitehouse's NVLA?
7   Who was best man at the wedding of David Bailey and Catherine Deneuve?
8   Which No. 1 started "The taxman's taken all my dough"?
9   Which group did away with the "magic circle" process of choosing a leader?
10 Which former boxing world champion was found shot dead in Soho?
11 Jan Palach set himself alight to protest against the Russian invasion of which country?
12 Who did Lulu marry on February 18 1969?
13 What was the nickname of the East End murder victim Jack McVitie?
14 What was the BBC's longest-running radio show which ended in 1969?
15 Which line on the Underground was opened in 1969?
16 In which city did John and Yoko hold their honeymoon bed-in?
17 Which senator was involved in the car crash at Chappaquiddick?
18 Who did Ann Jones beat in the 1969 Wimbledon women's singles?
19 Where did the Stones gave a free, open-air concert, after Brian Jones's death?
20 The Queen dedicated an acre of land in Runnymede to whom?
21 What did Dr Michael Ramsay become in June 1961?
22 Who phoned Neil Armstrong on his first moon walk?
23 Barbara Hulanicki founded which store?
24 How old was Prince Charles when he was invested as Prince of Wales?
25 On which course did Tony Jacklin win the British Open in 1969?
26 Where was the home town of round the world sailor Alec Rose?
27 Who designed the new cathedral at Coventry?
28 Who did Sharon Tate marry in 1968?
29 In which city did the first heart transplant operation take place?
30 Who was linked with the phrase "Turn on, tune in and drop out"?

Answers

Time & Space (see Quiz 43)

(see Quiz 43)

1 Venus. 2 Mice. 3 First human fatality. 4 Halley. 5 Hawaii. 6 Uranus.
7 Southern Crown and Northern Crown. 8 Six. 9 Eclipse. 10 Gemini.
11 Manchester. 12 Neptune. 13 Order of discovery. 14 Mr Spock.
15 Valentina Tereshkova. 16 Extra Vehicular Activity. 17 Earth. 18 One.
19 Aurora Borealis. 20 Jupiter. 21 27.3 days. 22 Pluto. 23 Saturn.
24 Big Bang Theory. 25 Light year. 26 Mars. 27 Away from it. 28 Venus.
29 Proxima Centauri. 30 The Sun.

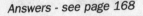
1 What is the capital of County Antrim in Ireland?
2 What was Roy Orbison's first UK No. 1 single?
3 What was banned by Napoleon which led to the development of sugar beet?
4 What was the fictional village in "All Creatures Great and Small"?
5 Which motorway goes across the Pennines west to east?
6 How many points win a game of badminton?
7 Who cut off Van Gogh's ear?
8 What musical invention was developed by David Rockola?
9 How many lines in a sonnet?
10 Which fruit is Spain's national symbol?
11 Who wrote stories about Kirrin Island?
12 What was the nickname of Milton Marx?
13 Who had a 90s No. 1 with "The One And Only"?
14 Which birthstone is linked to March?
15 In which series did Danny Wilde and Lord Brett Sinclair appear?
16 Which story was *West Side Story* based on?
17 In which century was John Constable born?
18 Who was the first presenter of "The Late Late Breakfast Show"?
19 What is special about the feet of a palmiped?
20 What was Lady Churchill's reaction to Graham Sutherland's portrait of her husband?
21 Which US general was nicknamed Old Blood and Guts?
22 What word can go after "leg" and before "ear"?
23 The Aldeburgh Festival is held in which county?
24 In which decade of the 20th century was Jack Nicklaus born?
25 Carnophobia is a fear of what?
26 What is the name of John Major's daughter?
27 Which "Dallas" actor also played the Man from Atlantis?
28 Bob Wyatt captained England in which sport?
29 Who was Ken Russell's film *A Song Of Summer* about?
30 What is the deepest land gorge in the world?

Pop: Superstars (see Quiz 44)

Answers

1 "Earth Song". 2 "Reason To Believe". 3 Barbra Streisand. 4 Pink Floyd.
5 Mississippi. 6 *Aladdin Sane*. 7 "Rocket Man". 8 Scotland. 9 Prince.
10 George Michael. 11 "Chain Reaction". 12 Breathless Mahoney. 13 Left.
14 Eric Clapton. 15 The Jordanaires. 16 Tina Turner. 17 Queen. 18 Bob
Marley. 19 *Off The Wall*. 20 Prince. 21 Jade. 22 Dolly Parton.
23 *Voulez-Vous*. 24 George Michael. 25 *Never A Dull Moment*.
26 Madonna. 27 Phil Collins. 28 Neil Diamond. 29 Elvis Presley.
30 Elton John.

Quiz 43 Time & Space

Answers - see page 165

1   Which planet appears brightest to the naked eye?
2   What creatures were Laska and Beny, who went into space in 1958?
3   Which space first was Vladimir Komarov in 1967?
4   Who first predicted correctly the intermittent return of a famous comet?
5   In which US state is the Keck Telescope?
6   Which planet's moons have names of Shakespearean characters?
7   How are Corona Australis and Corona Borealis also known?
8   How many Apollo missions resulted in successful moon landings?
9   When the Earth or the moon enters the other's shadow what is it called?
10 Which is the only sign of the zodiac named after two living things?
11 Jodrell Bank is the observatory of which university?
12 Which planet did Johann Galle discover in 1846?
13 What is the system of numbering asteroids?
14 Which "Star Trek" character is asteroid No. 2309 named after?
15 Whose spacecraft was called *Vostok VI*?
16 In moon exploration what was EVA?
17 Which planet lies between Venus and Mars?
18 How many orbits of the Earth did Gagarin make in *Vostok I*?
19 What are the Northern Lights also known as?
20 Ganymede and Io are moons of which planet?
21 How long does it take the moon to complete a revolution of Earth?
22 Which planet did Clyde Tombaugh discover in 1930?
23 Which planet's rings and moons were photographed by *Voyager 1* in 1980?
24 Which theory states that the universe came into being as a result of an explosion?
25 What does the abbreviation 'ly' stand for?
26 Which planet has two moons called Phobos and Demos?
27 In relation to the sun in which direction does a comet's tail point?
28 Which planet in our solar system is only slightly smaller than Earth?
29 What is the nearest star to our sun?
30 The sidereal period is the time it takes a planet to orbit what?

Answers

The 60s (see Quiz 41)

1 Jackie O. (Onassis). **2** "Ready, Steady, Go!". **3** New Zealand. **4** Ian Smith.
5 1965. **6** Listeners. **7** Mick Jagger. **8** "Sunny Afternoon" (The Kinks).
9 Conservatives. **10** Freddie Mills. **11** Czechoslovakia. **12** Maurice Gibb.
13 "The Hat". **14** "The Dales". **15** The Victoria Line. **16** Amsterdam.
17 Edward Kennedy. **18** Billie Jean King. **19** Hyde Park. **20** President
Kennedy. **21** Archbishop of Canterbury. **22** Richard Nixon. **23** Biba.
24 20. **25** Lytham St Annes. **26** Portsmouth. **27** Sir Basil Spence.
28 Roman Polanski. **29** Cape Town. **30** Timothy Leary.

Quiz 44 Pop: Superstars

Answers - see page 166

LEVEL 2

1   What was Michael Jackson's 1995 Christmas No. 1?
2   What was coupled with "Maggie May" on Rod Stewart's single?
3   Which singer co-wrote "Evergreen"?
4   Reclusive Syd Barrett was a founder of which supergroup?
5   In which state was Elvis Presley born?
6   Which album has Bowie with a red lightning flash design on his face?
7   Which Elton John song starts "She packed my bags last night pre-flight"?
8   In which country was Mark Knopfler born?
9   Whose albums include *Diamonds and Pearls* and *Symbol*?
10   In the 90s who got into legal battle with Sony over his contract?
11   Which Gibb brother's song gave Diana Ross a No. 1?
12   What role did Madonna portray in the film *Dick Tracy*?
13   On the cover of *Thriller* Jackson is leaning on which elbow?
14   Which guitarist was "Unplugged" in 1992?
15   Which vocal harmony group backed Elvis from the mid 50s?
16   Who appeared as the Acid Queen in the film *Tommy*?
17   Roger Taylor was a member of which supergroup?
18   Which reggae superstar was given a state funeral in Jamaica?
19   Which Michael Jackson album first included "Don't Stop 'Til You Get Enough"?
20   Which superstar produced music for the 1989 *Batman* film?
21   What is the name of Mick Jagger's daughter by Bianca?
22   Which female singer wrote "I Will Always Love You"?
23   Which Abba album had a French title?
24   Who was "In A Different Corner" in 1986?
25   Which album sleeve featured Rod Stewart sitting in an armchair?
26   A fly on the wall 90s documentary invited the public to be in bed with who?
27   Who recorded the album *Face Values*?
28   Who duetted with Streisand on "You Don't Bring Me Flowers"?
29   Who won a talent show, aged ten, singing "Old Shep"?
30   Who recorded the album *Sleeping With The Past*?

Answers

Pot Luck 19 (see Quiz 42)

1 Antrim. 2 "Only the Lonely". 3 Imported sugar. 4 Darrowby. 5 M62.
6 15. 7 Himself. 8 The jukebox. 9 14. 10 Pomegranate. 11 Enid Blyton.
12 Gummo. 13 Chesney Hawkes. 14 Aquamarine (bloodstone). 15 "The
Persuaders". 16 *Romeo & Juliet.* 17 18th. 18 Noel Edmonds 19 They're
webbed. 20 She destroyed it. 21 George Patton. 22 "End". 23 Suffolk.
24 40s. 25 Meat. 26 Elizabeth. 27 Patrick Duffy. 28 Cricket. 29 Delius.
30 The Grand Canyon.

Quiz 45 Pot Luck 20

Answers - see page 171

1   What is a compote?
2   Which of Boeing's jets were launched in 1958 seating 189?
3   Who sang the theme song to the Bond film *Octopussy*?
4   Which mining town is named Berneslai in the Domesday Book?
5   What is the main edible export of Argentina?
6   Who was assassinated by Satwant and Beant Singh?
7   What colour is a telephone kiosk which will take only phone cards?
8   Which family of fruit does the kumquat belong to?
9   Which Soviet football team was the first to make a European final?
10 Michael Henchard was the mayor of which fictional town?
11 Who had a 90s No. 1 with "Everything Changes"?
12 What is the only English anagram of FIENDISH?
13 Which desert spreads into South West Africa from Botswana?
14 "The King Of Barataria" is the subtitle of which light opera?
15 In which suburb was "The Good Life" set?
16 In which decade was "Baywatch" screened for the first time in the UK?
17 Which play by George Bernard Shaw inspired *My Fair Lady*?
18 Which letter and number follow Albert Square, Walford?
19 Which England soccer keeper had the first names Raymond Neal?
20 Who wrote the novel *The French Lieutenant's Woman*?
21 Who sits on the Woolsack?
22 Athene is the Greek goddess of wisdom. Who is the Roman?
23 Who wrote "Hark, the Herald Angels Sing"?
24 Which state became the 50th American state?
25 Who created Perry Mason?
26 Which former film star was US Ambassador to Ghana in the 70s?
27 Who got the sack from the Beatles before they hit the big time?
28 What do H and G stand for in H.G. Wells's name?
29 What was called the Pluto Platter when it was originally sold?
30 In which century was Captain James Cook born?

Quiz 46 Crime & Punishment

LEVEL 2

Answers - see page 172

1 In which sensational case was wireless telegraphy first used to apprehend a murderer?

2 At what number in Rillington Place did John Christie live?

3 In the 60s who did James Earl Ray assassinate?

4 What treasure trove did Colonel Thomas Blood try to steal in the 17th century?

5 To two years, when was the last hanging in Britain?

6 In 1981, which leading figure was wounded by John Hinckley?

7 Which parts of the body went into a pillory?

8 Albert de Salvo was better known as what?

9 In which city did Burke and Hare operate?

10 In light opera who wanted "to let the punishment fit the crime"?

11 To ten years each way, when was Dick Turpin hanged?

12 In which month was President Kennedy assassinated?

13 Mary Ann Nicholas and Mary Kelly were victims of who?

14 In which Gloucester street was the West's House of Horrors?

15 The Old Bailey figure of justice holds a sword and what else?

16 What was the the profession of Mary Ann Cotton, hanged in 1873?

17 Who was Britain's last chief hangman?

18 Alphonse Bertillon and Sir Francis Galton were concerned with which aid to criminal detection?

19 George Cornell was shot in which East End pub?

20 In the 70s who was accused of stealing a fur coat and passport from Miss World?

21 In the 17th century which judge sat for the so-called Bloody Assizes?

22 Hawley Harvey were the first names of which murderer?

23 On August 6 1890, Auburn Prison, New York, had the first what?

24 In what decade was flogging finally abolished in Britain?

25 What weapon was used to murder the Bulgarian defector Georgi Markov in London in the 70s?

26 In the 90s which Kray brother was found guilty of drug trafficking?

27 Who shot the person believed to have shot President Kennedy?

28 Who was the first British PM murdered while in office?

29 In the 70s who became the first convict executed in the US for ten years?

30 Which doctor was at the centre of the Profumo affair?

TV Gold   (see Quiz 48)

Answers

1 "The Army Game". 2 Ian Carmichael. 3 Audrey. 4 Jimmy Edwards. 5 Victoria. 6 Bob Symes. 7 Jim Davidson. 8 Sister. 9 "You dirty old man". 10 Sid James. 11 "Robin's Nest". 12 Hinge and Bracket. 13 "The Jewel in the Crown". 14 "Nearest and Dearest". 15 The Munsters. 16 Thora Hird. 17 "Porridge". 18 Privet. 19 Richard Briers, Prunella Scales. 20 Roper. 21 Mobile Army Surgical Hospital. 22 "The Liver Birds". 23 A talking horse. 24 "Brideshead Revisited". 25 Morris Minor. 26 "On the Buses". 27 Tom Baker. 28 Samantha. 29 "Only When I Laugh". 30 "The Rag Trade".

Quiz 47 Pot Luck 21

Answers - see page 169

LEVEL 2

1   What is the Caspian Sea, as it is not a sea?
2   What do Americans call braces?
3   Which Michelle played Betty, Frank Spencer's wife?
4   Who sang the Bond theme "From Russia With Love"?
5   Where is the tomb of King Henry VIII?
6   Who was James Gatz better known as?
7   What accounts for only 28 per cent of the Sahara Desert ?
8   Who was the youngest female Conservative candidate in the1951 General Election?
9   Which spice is the most produced in Zanzibar?
10 If April Fools' Day is a Tuesday what day is St George's Day?
11 Who wrote the novel *The Power and The Glory*?
12 What was the first name of the man known as the Desert Fox?
13 Todd Woodbridge was conected with which sport?
14 What is the capital of the People's Republic of Congo?
15 In Scrabble, how many points is the letter Q worth?
16 What do frogs have that toads do not in their mouths?
17 In which century was T.S. Eliot born?
18 In "The Man from UNCLE", what did the E stand for?
19 In 1971 Pakistan won the first World Cup in which sport?
20 Kirt Brandon brought a court case against which rock star?
21 Which direction does the Nile River flow?
22 Which character did Francesca Annis play in "Edward VII" in the 70s?
23 What is the next-highest prime number above 43?
24 Who pined for the love of his reflection?
25 In which decade of the 20th century was Bjorn Borg born?
26 Hawk's Champagne and Prince Albert are types of which fruit?
27 What colour was Starsky and Hutch's car?
28 What is the most common colour of amethyst?
29 Who had a 80s No. 1 with "First Time"?
30 What was Lech Walesa's job in the Gdansk shipyards?

Answers

Pot Luck 20 (see Quiz 45)
1 Stewed fruit. 2 The 707. 3 Rita Coolidge. 4 Barnsley. 5 Beef. 6 Mrs Indira Gandhi. 7 Green. 8 Citrus. 9 Moscow Dynamo. 10 Casterbridge. 11 Take That. 12 Finished. 13 Kalahari. 14 *The Gondoliers*. 15 Surbiton. 16 1990s. 17 *Pygmalion*. 18 E20. 19 Clemence. 20 John Fowles. 21 Lord Chancellor. 22 Minerva. 23 Charles Wesley. 24 Hawaii. 25 Erle Stanley Gardner. 26 Shirley Temple Black. 27 Pete Best. 28 Herbert George. 29 The Frisbee. 30 18th.

Quiz 48 TV Gold

Answers - see page 170

LEVEL 2

1 In which sitcom did Bootsie and Snudge first appear?

2 Who played Bertie Wooster in the 60s Wodehouse adaptation?

3 What was Terry's sister called in "The Likely Lads"?

4 Who played the blustering headmaster in "Whack-O!"?

5 Who was the third of "Take Three Girls" with Kate and Avril?

6 How was the "Tomorrow's World" presenter Robert Alexander Baron Symes-Schutzmann von Schutzmannstorf better known?

7 Who was Jim London in "Up the Elephant and Round the Castle"?

8 What relation was Hattie Jacques to Eric in their "Sykes and ..." series?

9 What did Harold Steptoe always call his father?

10 Who played Sid Stone in the UK sitcom "Taxi"?

11 What was the Richard O'Sullivan spin-off from "Man About the House"?

12 Who lived in the Suffolk village of Stackton Tressel?

13 Daphne Manners and Hari Kumar were characters in which series?

14 Jimmy Jewel and Hylda Baker were Eli and Nellie Pledge in which show?

15 Which TV family were headed by Herman and Lily?

16 Which veteran actress played the wife in "Meet the Wife"?

17 In which classic did you find Blanco, Lukewarm and Gay Gordon?

18 What was Bernard Hedges' nickname in "Please Sir"?

19 Who were the two stars of "Marriage Lines"?

20 What was the surname of George and Mildred?

21 What does M*A*S*H stand for?

22 Which flatmates originally lived in Huskisson Road, Liverpool?

23 Who or what was Mr Ed?

24 Which classic drama centred on the Marchmain family?

25 What make of car did Nurse Emmanuel drive in "Open All Hours"?

26 In which show did Reg Varney play Stan Butler?

27 Who was the fourth Doctor Who?

28 What was the name of the young blonde witch in "Bewitched"?

29 In which series were Figgis, Glover and Norman hospital patients?

30 Which sitcom was about Fenner Fashions and starred Miriam Karlin?

Quiz 49 Pot Luck 22

Answers - see page 175

LEVEL 2

1 Which James Bond actor covered his tattoos when filming?
2 What name is given to a hill in the centre of any Greek city?
3 What canal was closed from 1967 to 1975?
4 Which comedy series saw Oliver Smallbridge with Simon Peel?
5 Which Olympic sport needs a planting box?
6 Which popular tourist area is Northern Africa's smallest country?
7 Who was the leader of Cuba's rebel July 26 faction?
8 In which American TV show would you find the Cunningham family?
9 What animal was the first sent into space by the Americans?
10 Which city did the Cowardly Lion want to get to?
11 In which century was Charles Darwin born?
12 Who was the first female presenter of "Magpie"?
13 What did the D stand for in Franklin D. Roosevelt's name?
14 In which series did Phyllida Erskine-Brown appear?
15 Which radio and TV star used the phrase "in the best possible taste"?
16 What colour was the Trotter's Independent Trading van?
17 What is the capital of Costa Rica?
18 Which store group's slogan is "Never Knowingly Undersold"?
19 Scott Hamilton was a world champion in which sport?
20 Who wrote "Honeysuckle Rose" and "Ain't Misbehavin'"?
21 What do we call the place known by the Romans as Camulodunum?
22 In which place does Desperate Dan live?
23 What was the original meaning of the name Sarah in Hebrew?
24 Karl Landsteiner's work centred of discovering which groups?
25 Which rock star named his son Zowie?
26 Who wrote the novel *She*?
27 Where did the rumba originate?
28 Who had a 60s No. 1 with "Do It Again"?
29 If it's 12 noon GMT what time is it in Cairo?
30 What was the first issued decimal coin in Britain?

Answers

Pot Luck 23 (see Quiz 51)
1 Grace Kelly. 2 Victoria. 3 Peter Gabriel. 4 Moll Flanders. 5 A tidal wave.
6 Ervin Johnson. 7 Salzburg. 8 Felix. 9 Cancer. 10 Liberia. 11 Ernest
Hemingway. 12 S. 13 Spoonerism. 14 Coffee/Chocolate. 15 19th.
16 Berlin. 17 "A Ruby Murray". 18 Green. 19 Bach. 20 Duke of
Wellington. 21 26. 22 Rembrandt. 23 Lancashire. 24 Niece. 25 Mad dogs
and Englishmen. 26 Ronald Reagan. 27 Rooster. 28 *David Copperfield*.
29 TV. 30 30s.

Quiz 50 Movies: Westerns

LEVEL 2

Answers - see page 176

1. *The Magnificent Seven* was a remake of which 50s Japanese film?
2. In which film did John Wayne play his first leading role?
3. Which London-born actor played a boy adopted by Indians in *Last of the Mohicans*?
4. In which 1992 western with Gene Hackman did Clint Eastwood star and direct?
5. What was the sequel to *A Fistful of Dollars* called?
6. Who played the sheriff in *High Noon*?
7. Who was the female star of *Butch Cassidy and the Sundance Kid*?
8. Who played Bernardo in *The Magnificent Seven*?
9. Who co-starred with John Wayne in *The Man Who Shot Liberty Valance*?
10. Who played Wyatt Earp in the 1946 film *My Darling Clementine*?
11. Which musical western has the song "You Can't Get A Man with a Gun"?
12. Who was a singing "Calamity Jane"?
13. Which country singer starred in *True Grit*?
14. In which film did John Wayne play Davy Crockett?
15. Which then romantic partner of Clint Eastwood starred with him in *Bronco Billy* in 1980?
16. Who was the star of *Jeremiah Johnson* in 1972?
17. Which director was famous for his so-called "Cavalry Trilogy"?
18. Who was famous for playing the Man With No Name?
19. Which Indian tribe features in *Dances With Wolves*?
20. Who starred with Bob Hope in the comedy western *The Paleface*?
21. Which former child star starred in *Fort Apache* in 1948?
22. Which western star's theme song was "Back in the Saddle Again"?
23. Who starred in the musical western *Don't Fence Me In* in 1945?
24. Which 1994 western starred Mel Gibson and Jodie Foster?
25. In which 1969 musical western did Clint Eastwood sing?
26. Who was *Little Big Man*?
27. Who sang "Blaze of Glory" in *Young Guns II*?
28. Which director of westerns was born Sean Aloysius O'Fienne?
29. Which comedian did Roy Rogers star with in *Son of Paleface*?
30. Where was *A Fistful of Dollars* filmed?

Quiz 51 Pot Luck 23

Answers - see page 173

1 Which actress had her wedding televised in April 1956?

2 What is Africa's largest lake and Australia's smallest mainland state?

3 Who was vocalist in Genesis before Phil Collins?

4 Which character was born in Newgate Prison in the Defoe novel?

5 What hit the ship in *The Poseidon Adventure* causing it to turn over?

6 What is Magic Johnson's real name?

7 Which Austrian city was Mozart's birthplace?

8 Which famous cat was created by Otto Mesmer?

9 Who or what killed Eva Peron?

10 Which country boasts the world's largest registered shipping fleet?

11 Who wrote the novel *The Old Man and The Sea*?

12 In Morse code what letter is represented by three dots?

13 What describes inverting the initial letters of two words?

14 Which two flavours combined make mocha?

15 In which century was Charlotte Brontë born?

16 Who had an 80s No. 1 with "Take My Breath Away"?

17 How would Del Boy have ordered a curry?

18 What colour is the inside of a pistachio nut?

19 Which classical composer's *Air* has been used by Hamlet cigar ads?

20 Who was nicknamed the Iron Duke?

21 What was the percentage rise that MPs voted for themselves in 1996?

22 Who painted *The Night Watch*?

23 In which county was "Juliet Bravo" set?

24 What relation was Queen Victoria to her predecessor on the throne?

25 According to Noël Coward, who go out in the midday sun?

26 Who married the American actress Nancy Davis?

27 1993 was the Chinese year of which creature?

28 In which Dickens novel does Dora Spenlove appear?

29 What went from 405 lines to 625 lines?

30 In which decade of the 20th century was Melvyn Bragg born?

1 What does BAFTA stand for?
2 Jeremy Isaacs was the first chief executive of which channel?
3 Which title is given to the chief executive of the BBC?
4 Which London-based Sunday paper was founded in 1990?
5 In which town is Red Rose radio based?
6 What is the more common name for a teleprompt?
7 Who sets the rate for the television licence?
8 *Izvestia* was a Soviet newspaper. What does Izvestia mean?
9 Which channel has the slogan "Make the voyage"?
10 In a TV studio what is a dolly?
11 What is a studio's chief electrician called?
12 Which was the first British newspaper to issue a colour supplement?
13 In comics what was Black Bob?
14 What is the American Express magazine called?
15 Which daily publication is Britain's oldest?
16 Where is the *Western Mail* based?
17 In which country is *Yomiuri Shimbun* a daily newspaper?
18 How many Sky channels were there originally in 1989?
19 Which TV technician is responsible for hardware such as props, cranes etc.?
20 Which newspaper did the *Sun* replace in 1964?
21 Which newspaper group is David Sullivan associated with?
22 Which UK broadsheet has issues published in Frankfurt and New York?
23 Which publication, founded in 1868, consists wholly of adverts?
24 What is Liverpool's own regional daily paper called?
25 In 1997 Michael Barry stepped down in his post at which independent radio station?
26 What does ILR stand for in the media?
27 What has been published anually since 1697?
28 Which telext system was replaced on ITV by Teletext UK?
29 What was HTV originally called?
30 What did the ITC replace in 1991?

Quiz 53 Famous Names

Answers - see page 179

LEVEL 2

1 Who did the former model Victoria Lockwood marry?
2 How is the actress Estelle Skornik better known in the advertising world?
3 Who are Jane Fellowes and Sarah McCorquodale?
4 What is Lord Lloyd-Webber's wife's first name?
5 Which post was English-born Pamela Harriman given by President Clinton?
6 What are Steffi Graf's parents called?
7 Who is patron of the National Osteoporosis Society?
8 Helen O'Reilly is known on TV as who?
9 In which role is Marion Crawford best known?
10 Who was the first public-school-educated PM of the last third of the 20th century?
11 Who are the parents of Lady Gabriella Windsor?
12 Which TV personality is the wife of the editor Michael Wynn-Jones?
13 How is James Crossley better known?
14 How is the challenging former Mrs Nick Allott better known?
15 Who is sometimes known as TPT?
16 Whose file states she was Mrs Clyde Klotz?
17 Which two comedy actors have a daughter called Billie?
18 Whose name was Henriette Peace first linked with in 1997?
19 Who was Martin Bell's campaigning daughter in the 1997 General Election?
20 What is Earl Spencer's first name?
21 Who left "EastEnders" to have baby daughter Maia?
22 Which illness do cook Michael Barry and actress Mary Tyler Moore suffer from?
23 What is Carol Vorderman's university degree in?
24 Romantically, Dani Behr and Victoria Adams have been linked with which football club?
25 Charles Worthington is a famous name in which field?
26 Which actress was the first Mrs Mike Tyson?
27 Sue Barker and Penelope Keith's respective spouses have been members of which profession?
28 In whose garden was Alistair Coe found in 1997?
29 What would Claire Latimer provide for a society occasion?
30 Who did Renate Blauel marry in 1984?

Sporting Records (see Quiz 55)
1 Bobby Robson. 2 Squash. 3 Bob Taylor. 4 Salford. 5 Rand. 6 Ruud Gullit. 7 Sandwich. 8 First £1,000 soccer transfer. 9 David Campese. 10 Kapil Dev. 11 Pole vaulting. 12 Leyton Orient. 13 Smallwood. 14 Table tennis. 15 Notts County. 16 Tiger Woods. 17 60s. 18 Alan Shearer. 19 Angling. 20 Jim Clark. 21 Gipsy Moth IV. 22 Bonds. 23 Brian Bevan. 24 Imran Khan. 25 Emerson Fittipaldi. 26 Liz McColgan. 27 Gliding. 28 Allan Border. 29 Juventus. 30 Newbold.

1   Which Sinatra sang the Bond theme "You Only Live Twice"?

2   Which part of France would you come from if you were a Breton?

3   Huey Lewis had a hit with "The Power of Love" from which film?

4   Which South American country's name translates to "Rich Coast"?

5   How many inches wide should a wicket be?

6   What make of car was Lesley Crowther driving in his 1992 accident?

7   Who was seriously injured at the Nurburgring circuit in August 1976?

8   In which county is the Duke of Norfolk's castle at Arundel?

9   Which Chicago rock band was formed by Terry Kath in 1967?

10 Name Switzerland's largest city?

11 Who wrote the novel *Eyeless In Gaza*?

12 Which character did Ruby Wax play in "Girls on Top"?

13 How is Lev Davidovich Bronstein better known?

14 Who played Prue Manson in "Bouquet of Barbed Wire"?

15 What was the name of Darwin's survey ship?

16 Who had a 80s No. 1 with "Ghost Town"?

17 How many finger holes are there in a tenpin bowling ball?

18 What was the name of Gene Autry's horse?

19 What is the capital of Liechtenstein?

20 The gemstone Sapphire is linked to which month?

21 Who has a friend called Pie-Face?

22 Who redesigned the Girl Guide and Brownie uniforms in 1990?

23 Who captained the MCC in the "Bodyline" series of the 30s?

24 Whose 1977 autobiography was called *Dear Me*?

25 What is produced by the lacrymal glands?

26 In which century was Beethoven born?

27 Which sea contains four ounces of salt to every pint of water?

28 Apiphobia is a fear of what?

29 Which piece of music was used as the Monty Python theme?

30 Which liner made her maiden voyage in 1946?

Quiz 55 Sporting Records

Answers - see page 177

1 Who was Barcelona's boss for their record fourth European Cup Winner's Cup Final triumph in 1997?
2 In November '95 Jansher Khan won his seventh World Open title in which sport?
3 Which Derbyshire wicket-keeper set a career record number of dismissals from 1960 to 1988?
4 David Watkins scored 221 goals in a season for which rugby league club?
5 Which athlete Mary was BBC Sports Personality of 1964?
6 Who was the first overseas manager to win the FA Cup?
7 At which venue did Greg Norman set a lowest four-round Bittish Open total in 1993?
8 What record will Alf Common always hold?
9 Who was the first rugby union player to reach 50 international tries?
10 Who overtook Sunil Gavaskar's Test appearance record for India?
11 Sergei Bubka has broken a record over 30 times in which event?
12 Peter Shilton played his 1,000th league game with which club?
13 What was athlete Kathy Cook's maiden name?
14 Fred Perry was world champion in which sport before becoming a major tennis star?
15 Which soccer club is generally accepted to be the oldest in England?
16 Who is the youngest ever winner of the US Masters?
17 In which decade did Clive Lloyd first play Test cricket?
18 Who was the first player to hit 100 Premiership goals?
19 Bob Nudd had been a world champion in which sport?
20 Which British driver was first to have seven Grand Prix wins in a year?
21 Francis Chichester made his 60s solo round the world trip in which boat?
22 Which Billy set an appearance record for West Ham?
23 From the 40s to the 60s, who set a league record for tries in a career?
24 Who in the 80s and early 90s set a record for captaining Pakistan at cricket?
25 Who in 1972 became the youngest F1 Motor Racing world champ?
26 Which record beaker won the first major Marathon she entered?
27 George Lee has been three time world champ in which sport?
28 Which Australian holds the world record for most Test runs in cricket?
29 Gianlucca Vialli moved for a then record £12 million from Sampdoria to which club in 1992 ?
30 What is Seb Coe's middle name?

Quiz 56 Pot Luck 25

Answers - see page 178

1   What is the former colony of the Gold Coast now called?
2   Which marsupial's native home is North America?
3   What was discovered at Lascaux in 1940?
4   Which work by Blackmore has a hero called John Ridd?
5   Which place was a hit for Martha and the Muffins?
6   Which organization had its first troop formed in 1908 in Glasgow?
7   Which racing circuit has a bend called Paddock?
8   What became illegal in 1984 on the London Underground?
9   Where is the world's oldest rowing club, Leander, based?
10 What was Captain Mainwaring's occupation?
11 Who wrote the novel *Finnegans Wake*?
12 If A is alpha and B is bravo what is F?
13 What is exceeded to produce a sonic boom?
14 In which sitcom did Bill Macgregor and Faith Grayshot appear?
15 Which is the last book of the Old Testament ?
16 Which country is partly surrounded by the Coral and Tasman Seas?
17 Who was the first presenter of "One Man and his Dog"?
18 In which century was J.M. Barrie born?
19 What did America buy from Russia for a mere two cents an acre?
20 Who played Ria Parkinson in "Butterflies"?
21 Harold Wilson became Baron of where when he became a peer?
22 What word can go before "cup", "scotch" and "fly"?
23 What is the army equivalent of the Royal Navy rank of Admiral of the Fleet?
24 What is the capital of Haiti?
25 Which guitarist was the Marquis of Salobrena?
26 Which Kray twin enforcer gave East End gangland tours in the 90s?
27 Who had a 80s No. 1 with "Stand And Deliver"?
28 In which decade of the 20th century was Marlon Brando born?
29 Which famous Italian explorer is buried in the Dominican Republic?
30 Who was the first British prime minister to take office four times?

Quiz 57 The 70s

Answers - see page 183

LEVEL 2

1 Which veteran feline star of the Kattomeat adverts died in 1976?
2 Which outstanding female runner died of cancer at the age of 22?
3 What free item to schools did Education Secretary Thatcher cancel?
4 Who was Arsenal's double winning captain?
5 Who led the Madison Square Garden concert for Bangladesh?
6 Which team bought Bob Latchford from Birmingham making him Britain's costliest player?
7 Who was Randolph Hearst's kidnapped daughter?
8 Who did Ruby Flipper replace?
9 What was Lord Louis Moutbatten doing when murdered by the IRA?
10 What was Gail's last name before her marriage to Brian Tilsley?
11 What did Brighton Council agree to on a section of the beach?
12 In which month did Princess Anne marry Captain Mark Phillips?
13 Singers Lyn Paul and Eve Graham went solo to break up which group?
14 What did Rolls-Royce declare in February 1971?
15 Which northern town was advertised for the vodka it produced?
16 Who was British prime minister during the Winter of Discontent?
17 Who did Virginia Wade beat in the ladies singles final at Wimbledon?
18 Who wrote *Roots*, adapted as a TV blockbuster?
19 In 1978 Pope John Paul I died after roughly how long in office?
20 Who were Jilly, Kelly and Sabrina?
21 What was Saigon renamed after the North Vietnamese take over?
22 Percy Shaw passed away, but what had he passed on to road users?
23 Where was cricket's first World Cup Final held?
24 In which country was vanishing Labour MP John Stonehouse arrested?
25 What was the name of Edward Heath's Admiral's Cup yacht?
26 Where in Ireland did the Bloody Sunday shootings take place?
27 Who was leader of the Khmer Rouge in the Killing Fields?
28 In 1976, it was goodnight all for which copper after 20 years on TV?
29 Pele went on the dollar trail in 1975 with which team?
30 Who was Live At Treorchy?

Pop: Albums (see Quiz 59)
1 Ashton and Simpson. 2 "Wuthering Heights". 3 *Every Picture Tells A Story*.
4 *Music From Big Pink*. 5 Meat Loaf. 6 Max Bygraves. 7 Vivaldi. 8 Prince.
9 Virgin. 10 *Spice*. 11 Gilbert O Sullivan. 12 The Seekers. 13 Queen.
14 Peter Cook and Dudley Moore. 15 Chet Atkins. 16 4,000. 17 Beautiful
South. 18 Roxy Music. 19 Jose, Luciano, Placido. 20 Bowie. 21 Elton John.
22 Led Zeppelin. 23 *No Parlez*. 24 Madonna. 25 Abba. 26 Genesis.
27 Deep Purple. 28 Collins. 29 *Brothers In Arms*. 30 *Abbey Road*.

Quiz 58 Pot Luck 26

LEVEL 2

1   In which book would you find Magwitch?
2   Who opened the Manchester Ship Canal in 1894?
3   What did Anna Ford once throw over Jonathan Aitken?
4   Which paper was formerly called the *Daily Universal Register*?
5   Which brothers in the film industry were Jack, Sam, Harry & Albert?
6   Who sang the theme song for "Absolute Beginners"?
7   Which horse ran the 1973 Grand National in record time?
8   What was the nickname of the landscape gardener Lancelot Brown?
9   Which American-owned store opened in 1909 in Oxford Street?
10 Which country was formerly known as Southern Rhodesia?
11 Who wrote the novel *The Honourable Schoolboy*?
12 In which decade was "Birds of a Feather" screened for the first time?
13 What was Idi Amin's nickname?
14 In which decade was 80s TV series "The Charmer" set?
15 Who had a 90s No. 1 with "The Real Thing"?
16 In which century was Christopher Columbus born?
17 What runs every July in Pamplona?
18 What do the letters DPP stand for?
19 What is the only English anagram of GRAPHICALLY?
20 In Scrabble, how many points is the letter Z worth?
21 Who signs himself as Ebor?
22 Turnhouse Airport serves which city?
23 What letter goes before 100 to categorize Curcumin?
24 Which American actress was the first to appear on a postage stamp?
25 Who was the mother of John the Baptist?
26 How old was the boy named Sue when his daddy left home?
27 The 1997 London Proms featured "Yellow Shark" by which rock musician?
28 Blackburn's ground Ewood Park stands by which river?
29 What is the height, in feet, of a football goal?
30 In which city was "Albion Market" set?

Quiz 59 Pop: Albums

Answers - see page 181

1 Which duo were Solid?
2 Which track on Kate Bush's *The Kick Inside* was a No. 1 single?
3 What was Rod Stewart's first No. 1 album?
4 "The Weight" by the Band was on which album?
5 *Dead Ringer* was the first No. 1 album for who?
6 Who released a series of Singalonga songs?
7 Which composer gave Nigel Kennedy the chance to chart through the four seasons?
8 Who recorded *Graffiti Bridge*?
9 Mike Oldfield's *Tubular Bells* came out on which label?
10 What was the Spice Girls first album called?
11 In the 70s which singer/songwriter recorded *Back To Front*?
12 Which 60s group came back in the 90s producing a *Carnival Of Hits*?
13 Whose album was *Made In Heaven*?
14 Who were the voices behind Derek and Clive?
15 Who was on Neck and Neck with Mark Knopfler?
16 On *Sergeant Pepper,* how many holes were in Blackburn, Lancashire?
17 Which group's best-of album was called *Carry On Up The Charts*?
18 Which group had Jerry Hall as a siren on the rocks on an album cover?
19 What are the first names of the chart-topping Three Tenors?
20 Which David spent most weeks in the charts in 1973,1974 and 1983?
21 Who recorded *Captain Fantastic & The Brown Dirt Cowboy*?
22 Which group had eight No. 1 albums in a row from 1969 to 1979?
23 Which album did Paul Young record with an almost French title?
24 Who in 1987 became the first solo female to spend most weeks in the charts?
25 Which group produced their *Greatest Hits* before their *Arrival*?
26 Who had a mid-80s No. 1 with *Invisible Touch*?
27 Which heavy rock group recorded *Fireball* and *Machine Head*?
28 Which Phil spent most weeks in the charts in 1990?
29 "Money For Nothing" first appeared on which Dire Straits album?
30 Which Beatles album featured a zebra crossing on the cover?

The 70s (see Quiz 57)

1 Arthur. 2 Lillian Board. 3 Milk. 4 Frank McClintock. 5 George Harrison.
6 Everton. 7 Patricia Hearst. 8 Pan's People (on "Top of The Pops").
9 Fishing. 10 Potter. 11 Naturist bathing. 12 November. 13 New Seekers.
14 It was bankrupt. 15 Warrington. 16 Jim Callaghan. 17 Betty Stove.
18 Alex Haley. 19 One month (33 days). 20 Charlie's Angels. 21 Ho Chi
Minh City. 22 Invented cat's-eyes. 23 Lord's. 24 Australia. 25 *Morning
Cloud*. 26 Londonderry. 27 Pol Pot. 28 PC George Dixon. 29 New York
Cosmos. 30 Max Boyce.

1   Which range of hills has Cleeve Hill as its highest point?
2   Who painted a "Self Portrait with Bandaged Ear"?
3   Who co-wrote "We Are The World" with Michael Jackson?
4   Where, on the River Stort, was the birthplace of Cecil Rhodes?
5   Which year was the Hiroshima bombing?
6   Which lager is the name of Britain's second-most important men's tennis tournament?
7   Which toll bridge crosses the River Severn?
8   Which band joined Girlschool on the "St Valentine's Day Massacre"?
9   What is the first thing you should do if you have a motor accident?
10 What is Cape Kennedy now called?
11 What do P and G stand for in P.G. Wodehouse's name?
12 Who had a 90s No. 1 with "Everything Changes"?
13 What were the Harts first names in "Hart to Hart"?
14 Which character did Simon Cadell play in "Hi-De-Hi!"?
15 What word can go after "gall" and before "hem"?
16 What is the capital of Vietnam?
17 Which actor portrayed Rowdy Yates in "Rawhide"?
18 In which century was Chopin born?
19 Whose was the voice of Dangermouse in the cartoon series?
20 Which Sheffield theatre opened in 1972?
21 Where are British monarchs crowned?
22 Whose Organ Symphony was used for the theme of *Babe*?
23 Who made the first nonstop double flight across the English Channel?
24 In which Dickens novel does Alfred Jingle appear?
25 What colour caps do the Australians cricket team wear?
26 Which girl's name means grace and favour in Hebrew?
27 Who wrote *The Rainbow*?
28 In which decade of the 20th century was Ray Charles born?
29 Alfresco, Golden Boy and Shirley are types of what?
30 What is the capital of Sri Lanka?

Quiz 61 TV Sitcoms

Answers - see page 187

LEVEL 2

1   Who is Gary's wartime wife in "Goodnight Sweetheart"?
2   Which ministry did Jim Hacker run before he became PM?
3   What are the names of Father Ted's equally eccentric colleagues?
4   What is the name of the Vicar of Dibley?
5   Who had an incompetent personal assistant called Bubbles?
6   Which sitcom was set in the stately home of Lord Meldrum?
7   In which show did Brenda and Malcolm enjoy ornithology?
8   Who was the slave played by Frankie Howerd in "Up Pompeii"?
9   What are the Porter children called in "2 Point 4 Children"?
10 Which 80s series took its name from a 50s Little Richard song title?
11 Whose son-in-law was to him a "randy Scouse git"?
12 What was the name of the cab firm in the US sitcom "Taxi"?
13 In which show did Dr Sheila Sabatini appear?
14 What was Steptoe and Son's horse called?
15 Which character did Ronnie Corbett play in "Sorry!"?
16 Which US sitcom character was mother to Becky, Darlene and DJ?
17 David Jason won a BAFTA for the role of Skullion in which sitcom?
18 What were Fletcher's two first names in "Porridge"?
19 In "Birds of a Feather" what is Dorien's husband called?
20 What is the TV news company called in "Drop the Dead Donkey"?
21 Who, collectively, had a landlord called Jerzy Balowski?
22 Which show had Diana and Tom at the Bayview Retirement Home?
23 Who was the caretaker, played by Deryck Guyler, in "Please Sir"?
24 What was Henry Crabbe's restaurant called?
25 What type of shop was the setting for "Desmond's"?
26 Which spin-off about a couple followed "Man About the House"?
27 What was the occupation of Peter in "The Peter Principle"?
28 What was the profession of Victor Meldrew's neighbour Pippa?
29 In which sitcom did Charlie Burrows work for Caroline Wheatley?
30 Which sitcom had butler Brabinger and the Czech Mrs Polouvicka?

Answers

On The Map (see Quiz 63)
1 They are all new towns. 2 San Andreas Fault. 3 Andes. 4 California.
5 Iceland. 6 Romania. 7 Archipelago. 8 Brown. 9 Paris. 10 Hobart.
11 Mountain. 12 Edinburgh. 13 Winchester. 14 Belize. 15 Zambesi.
16 Channel Islands. 17 Venezuela. 18 Columbus. 19 Bury St Edmunds.
20 Romney. 21 Canada. 22 St Paul's. 23 Cemetery. 24 Sudan.
25 North. 26 Parliament Square. 27 Yorkshire Dales. 28 Scotland
(Highland Region). 29 Parishes. 30 Don.

Quiz 62 Pot Luck 28

LEVEL 2

Answers - see page 188

1 What name is given to dried and germinated barley?
2 Which TV rat had a hit with "Love Me Tender"?
3 Where was the original Capodimonte factory in Italy?
4 On which ship did Sir Francis Drake receive his knighthood?
5 Which chemical formula represents ice?
6 What day of the week did the 1984 Boat Race take place on?
7 Sutton Coldfield is a suburb of which city?
8 What fruit is grown by viticulturists?
9 On which day of the week are US elections always held?
10 Who joined the Pogues on "Fairytale of New York"?
11 Who wrote the novel *Coming Up For Air*?
12 What was the nickname of Herbert Marx?
13 In which police series did Captain Dobey and Huggy Bear appear?
14 What was the name of Labour's '97 General Election campaign bulldog?
15 Which actress played Sandra's mum in "The Liver Birds"?
16 With which sport do we associate the term "double axel"?
17 Who had a 50s No. 1 with "Dream Lover"?
18 To ten years, when was the storming of the Bastille?
19 Jonathan Edwards specialised in which athletics event?
20 Which birthstone is linked to April?
21 Bathophobia is a fear of what?
22 Corinthian, Doric and Ionian are all types of what?
23 In which century was Samuel Taylor Coleridge born?
24 How many points are there in a perfect hand of cribbage?
25 In which decade was the first Chelsea Flower Show?
26 What was Muhammad Ali's name when he was born?
27 In Morse code what letter is represented by two dots?
28 What is the name of Tony Blair's first-born daughter?
29 Who was the first presenter of "Points of View"?
30 Which is darker - muscovado or demerara sugar?

Answers

Movies: The Oscars (see Quiz 64)

1 *Casablanca.* 2 Clarice Starling. 3 *On Golden Pond.* 4 Forrest Gump.
5 *The Philadelphia Story.* 6 Muhammad Ali v. George Foreman in Zaire.
7 Chicago. 8 A roll of film. 9 *The Color Purple.* 10 *Gone With the Wind.*
11 Richard Burton. 12 Jessica Tandy. 13 Jeremy Irons. 14 Turned it down.
15 Kristin Scott Thomas. 16 *Cabaret.* 17 Fred Astaire and Ginger Rogers.
18 Best Director. 19 John Wayne. 20 *Schindler's List.* 21 Glenda Jackson.
22 Vanessa Redgrave. 23 Walt Disney. 24 Peter Finch. 25 Nun. 26 1920s.
27 Kathy Bates. 28 Three. 29 "Can You Feel the Love Tonight".
30 Anthony Minghella.

Quiz 63 On The Map

Answers - see page 185

LEVEL 2

1 What do Washington, Basildon and Cwmbran have in common?
2 What is the fault in San Francisco called?
3 What is the world's longest mountain range?
4 What is the third largest US state after Alaska and Texas?
5 Which country has IS as its international registration letters?
6 Where is Transylvania?
7 What is a sea containing many islands called?
8 What colour is the Bakerloo line on the London Underground map?
9 Orly airport is near which city?
10 What is the capital of Tasmania?
11 In Austria what is the Grossglockner?
12 Where are Waverley and Haymarket stations?
13 Where is the administrative HQ of Hampshire?
14 How was British Honduras subsequently known?
15 On which river is the Kariba Dam?
16 Herm is one of which group of islands?
17 Which South American country was named after Venice?
18 What is the capital of the US state of Ohio?
19 In which East Anglian town is the Greene King brewery based?
20 Which of the Cinque Ports has six letters in its name?
21 Which country has the longest coastline?
22 How is London Cathedral now known?
23 Which 77-acre site was founded at Kensal Green in London in 1832?
24 What is the largest country in Africa?
25 Which of the divisions of Yorkshire has the largest perimeter?
26 Which Square is in front of the Palace of Westminster?
27 After the Lake District which is England's largest National Park?
28 Which country of the British Isles has the largest county in terms of area?
29 What are the smallest units of local government in rural areas?
30 On which river does Sheffield stand?

TV Sitcoms (see Quiz 61)
Answers
1 Phoebe. 2 Administrative Affairs. 3 Dougal, Jack. 4 Geraldine Granger.
5 Edina Monsoon. 6 "You Rang, M'Lord". 7 "Watching". 8 Lurcio.
9 Jenny, David. 10 "Tutti Frutti". 11 Alf Garnett. 12 Sunshine Cab
Company. 13 "Surgical Spirit". 14 Hercules. 15 Timothy Lumsden.
16 "Roseanne". 17 "Porterhouse Blue". 18 Norman Stanley. 19 Marcus.
20 Globelink. 21 The Young Ones. 22 "Waiting For God". 23 Potter.
24 Pie in the Sky. 25 Barber's. 26 "George and Mildred". 27 Bank
manager. 28 Bus driver. 29 "The Upper Hand". 30 "To the Manor Born".

Quiz 64 Movies: The Oscars

LEVEL 2

1 Which film ends, "Louis, I think this is the beginning of a beautiful friendship"?

2 Who did Jodie Foster play in *The Silence of the Lambs*?

3 What was Henry Fonda's last film, for which he won an Oscar?

4 Who said, "Life is like a box of chocolates, you never know what you're going to get"?

5 James Stewart won his only Best Actor Oscar for which classic?

6 The film documentary *When We Were Kings* told of which sports clash?

7 In which city is *The Sting* set?

8 What does the male figure stand on, on the Oscar statuette?

9 Which Whoopi Goldberg film had 14 nominations and no win at all?

10 Which film was the first all-colour winner of the Best Picture award?

11 From 1952 to 1977, which Brit had 10 nominations and never won?

12 Who was the oldest Best Actress award recipient when she won in 1989?

13 Which British star was the first Best Actor award winner of the 1990s?

14 What did Marlon Brando do with his 1972 Oscar?

15 Who played Katharine Clifton in *The English Patient*?

16 Best Director Bob Fosse was the only 70s winner whose film was not Best Picture that year. Which picture was it?

17 Who danced together for the last time at the 1966 Oscar ceremony?

18 Kevin Costner was nominated for Best Director and Best Actor for *Dances With Wolves*, which did he win?

19 Which cancer sufferer's last public appearance was at the 1979 Oscar ceremony?

20 Which was the first black-and-white film to win Best Picture after *The Apartment* in 1960?

21 Which British actress won two Oscars in the 70s?

22 Who criticised "militant Zionist hoodlums" in her '77 Oscar speech?

23 Who was given one large Oscar and seven small ones in 1938?

24 Who was the first posthumous recipient of the Best Actor award?

25 What is Susan Sarandon's occupation in *Dead Man Walking*?

26 In which decade were the first Academy Awards given?

27 Who won the Oscar for Best Actress for her role in *Misery*?

28 How many Oscars did Katharine Hepburn win after her 60th birthday?

29 Of the three *The Lion King* songs nominated, which won the Oscar?

30 Who directed *The English Patient*?

Answers

Pot Luck 28 (see Quiz 62)

1 Malt. 2 Roland. 3 Naples. 4 The *Golden Hind*. 5 H2O. 6 Sunday. 7 Birmingham. 8 Grapes. 9 Tuesday. 10 Kirsty MacColl. 11 George Orwell. 12 Zeppo. 13 "Starsky and Hutch". 14 Fitz. 15 Mollie Sugden. 16 Figure skating. 17 Bobby Darin. 18 1789. 19 Triple jump. 20 Diamond. 21 Depth. 22 Orders (or styles) of architecture. 23 18th. 24 29. 25 1910s. 26 Casius Clay. 27 I. 28 Kathryn. 29 Robert Robinson. 30 Muscovado.

Quiz 65 Pot Luck 29

Answers - see page 191

LEVEL 2

1   How much did the wedding ring of the Owl and the Pussycat cost?
2   Which country was the first to retain the football World Cup?
3   Who sang about 99 red balloons?
4   What do the Mexicans make from the Agave cactus?
5   Which horse was kidnapped in February 1983?
6   What trade was abolished in 1807 in England?
7   Who did Maradona play for immediately before Napoli?
8   Who walked the length of the South Coast for charity in 1992?
9   Which doggy event was originally held in Newcastle?
10 Whose first UK top ten hit was "When Doves Cry"?
11 In which decade of the 20th century was Neil Armstrong born?
12 What was Al short for in Al Capone's name?
13 What is the only English anagram of GYRATED?
14 Where was soccer's Terry Butcher born?
15 Who wrote *Brideshead Revisited*?
16 Who was the narrator of "Paddington" on TV?
17 In World War II, what were Chindits?
18 Where was "Home and Away" set?
19 Which monarch reigned for only 325 days?
20 If A is alpha and B is bravo what is R?
21 Who first won the Embassy World Snooker Championship twice?
22 In which century was Geoffrey Chaucer born?
23 Are there more days in the first six months or the last six months of the year?
24 "The Merryman And His Maid" is the subtitle of which light opera?
25 How long in years is a French presidential term?
26 How many edges does a cube have?
27 What is the main colour of Biffo the Bea?
28 What is heraldic black called?
29 Clint Eastwood was born in which city?
30 Who had a 60s No. 1 with "I'm Alive"?

Pot Luck 30 (see Quiz 67)

1 Vanessa Paradis. 2 Black-and-white. 3 Books of stamps. 4 Someone's life. 5 The Turkey. 6 Batons. 7 "Hit" or "Miss". 8 Four. 9 Harry. 10 Green. 11 18th. 12 Jilly Cooper. 13 Manchester Airport new runway. 14 Barbie Batchelor. 15 David Essex. 16 *The Tempest*. 17 37. 18 Chicago. 19 Radio Luxembourg. 20 "Her". 21 El Greco. 22 Zagreb. 23 Maria. 24 2 pm. 25 Joseph Stalin. 26 One. 27 Johannesburg. 28 Greenland. 29 Hydrogen. 30 Dorothy Wordsworth.

189

Quiz 66 Hobbies & Leisure 2

LEVEL 2

Answers - see page 192

1   In which city is the National Railway Museum?
2   What is the maximum number of players in a game of poker?
3   Which game takes its name from the Chinese for sparrow?
4   How many pieces are on a chess board at the start of a game?
5   Which card game derives its name from the Spanish word for basket?
6   Which stately home is sometimes called the Palace of the Peak?
7   In which county would you visit Sissinghurst Gardens?
8   In which museum is the "Mona Lisa"?
9   How did Canterbury Cathedral announce it would emulate St Paul's in 1997?
10 In which city is Tropical World, Roundhay Park?
11 In which French château is there a Hall of Mirrors?
12 Which Suffolk Hall hosts days where Tudor life is re-created in great detail?
13 The Bluebell Railway straddles which two counties?
14 What does *son et lumiere* mean?
15 What do you use to play craps?
16 How many dominoes are there in a double-six set?
17 How many different topics are there in a game of Trivial Pursuits?
18 In which month would you go to watch Trooping the Colour?
19 Where in Paris would you go to see Napoleon's tomb?
20 In which county is Whipsnade Park Zoo?
21 *Chemin de fer* is a type of which game?
22 Which is England's most visited zoo after London?
23 What is Margarete Steiff famous for making?
24 Which phenomenon might you be interested in if you went to Drumnadrochit?
25 UK Legoland is near which town?
26 What sort of leisure attraction is Twycross?
27 In which country is the De Efteling theme park?
28 The National Trust adminsters properties in which three countries?
29 Which tourist attraction is next door to Madamme Tussaud's in London?
30 Which two Cluedo weapons begin with the same letter?

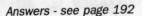

Answers

History Who's Who? (see Quiz 68)
1 Edward VII. 2 Bosworth Field. 3 Lord Louis Mountbatten. 4 Henry II.
5 Catherine Parr. 6 Spain. 7 George IV. 8 Robert Baden-Powell. 9 Henry.
10 Rasputin. 11 Farmer George. 12 Queen Anne. 13 Prussian.
14 Alexander the Great. 15 George V. 16 James I (James VI of Scotland).
17 Edward (later Edward II). 18 Anne Boleyn. 19 Philip II. 20 Edward II.
21 1936. 22 Robert Walpole. 23 Clarence. 24 Stephen. 25 He drowned.
26 Mrs Wallis Simpson. 27 Three. 28 Napoleon Bonaparte. 29 James I.
30 Jane Seymour.

1   Who had her first UK hit with "Joe Le Taxi"?
2   What two colours were five pound notes before 1961?
3   Which necessity was first sold in Post Offices in 1904?
4   What do you save in order to win an Albert Medal?
5   Who conducted the Owl and the Pussycat's wedding ceremony?
6   What were first used by relay racers in 1893?
7   Which choice of verdict could the Juke Box Jury make?
8   How many sides does a tetrahedron have?
9   What is songwriter/singer Nilsson's first name?
10 Which colour is the Libyan flag?
11 In which century was Robbie Burns born?
12 Who wrote the novel *Appassionata*?
13 At which site were the Jimi Hendrix camp and Zion Tree camp?
14 Which character did Peggy Ashcroft play in "The Jewel in the Crown"?
15 Who had a 70s No. 1 with "Hold Me Close"?
16 Which Shakespeare play begins with a storm at sea?
17 What is the next highest prime number above 31?
18 Where did Frank Sinatra say was his "kind of town"?
19 On which radio station did "Opportunity Knocks" begin?
20 What word can go after "heat" and before "on"?
21 Which Greek artist painted the "View of Toledo"?
22 What is the capital of Croatia?
23 What is Jose Carreras' middle name?
24 If it's 12 noon GMT what time is it in Helsinki?
25 Which Russian succeeded Lenin?
26 In Scrabble, how many points is the letter E worth?
27 The rugby ground Ellis Park is in which city?
28 Which is the largest island in the world?
29 Which element has the atomic number 1?
30 Who wrote *Grasmere Journal*?

Quiz 68 History Who's Who?

Answers - see page 190

1   Which British monarch succeeded Queen Victoria?
2   Richard III died at which battle?
3   Who was the last viceroy of India?
4   Which English monarch married Eleanor of Aquitaine?
5   Who was the last wife of Henry VIII?
6   Which country did Britain fight in the War of Jenkins' Ear?
7   Which King George did the Prince Regent become?
8   At the Siege of Mafeking who led the British forces?
9   The House of Lancaster kings were all called what?
10 Under what name is Gregor Efimovich better known?
11 Apart from Mad George which kinder nickname did George III have?
12 Which English queen married Prince George of Denmark?
13 Blucher commanded which country's troops at the Battle of Waterloo?
14 Who had a horse called Bucephalus?
15 Queen Elizabeth II's grandfather was which monarch?
16 Who was the Wisest Fool In Christendom?
17 Who was the first Prince of Wales?
18 Whose last words are reputed to be, "My neck is very slender"?
19 Which Spanish king sent his unsuccessful Armada?
20 Which monarch was murdered in Berkeley Castle?
21 In what year did Edward VIII abdicate?
22 In Britain, who first held the office that today is known as Prime Minister?
23 In the 15th century which Duke was drowned in Malmsey wine?
24 Who ruled England between Henry I and Henry II?
25 How did Lord Kitchener die?
26 Who with royal connections had the middle name Warfield?
27 In 1066 how many monarchs ruled England in the year?
28 Which ruler referred the English to a nation of shopkeepers?
29 Which monarch ordered the execution of Sir Walter Raleigh?
30 Which wife gave Henry VIII the male heir that he wanted?

Answers

1　What colour did the legendary keeper Lev Yashin play in?
2　Which striker was known as the Octopus in his own country?
3　Bobby Robson left which club to join Barcelona?
4　Oscar Ruggeri became the highest capped player for which country?
5　Who had the final kick of the 1994 World Cup Final?
6　In which decade did Bayern Munich first win the UEFA Cup?
7　Former Italian prime minister Silvio Berlusconi took over which club?
8　Thomas Ravelli became the most capped player for which country?
9　The stadium the Monumental is in which country?
10　Which Dutchman came with Arnold Muhren to Ipswich in the 80s?
11　Alfredo di Stefano played for Argentina, Spain and which other country?
12　Before 1994 when did Brazil last win the World Cup?
13　The club Feyenoord is based in which city?
14　Which club play at the Bernabeu Stadium?
15　Who scored England's last gasp winner against Belgium in Italia 90?
16　What colour are Germany's shorts?
17　How old was Maradona when he first played for Argentina?
18　Who captained Italy in the 1994 World Cup Final?
19　Gullit, Van Basten and Rijkaard lined up at which non-Dutch club?
20　Which country does Stefan Schwartz play for?
21　Who was first player from Ghana to play in the English league?
22　Which Arsenal manager signed Dennis Bergkamp?
23　Which French league club did Glenn Hoddle play for?
24　Who were the first African country to reach the World Cup quarter-finals?
25　Which Swede played for Arsenal, Everton and Birmingham?
26　Which club play at the Olympiastadion?
27　Ravanelli joined Middlesbrough from which club?
28　What colour are Portugal's shorts?
29　Which country did Mario Kempes play for?
30　Which Spanish side did John Aldridge play for?

Animal World (see Quiz 71)

Answers

1　Ants and termites. 2　Yellow with black markings. 3　Okapi. 4　Omnivore.
5　Orang-utan. 6　Bones. 7　Mammals. 8　Caribou. 9　Grey. 10　Amphibian.
11　Cold-blooded. 12　Dog. 13　Fangs. 14　Camel. 15　Bat. 16　Deer.
17　Backbone. 18　Dodo. 19　Borzoi. 20　Blue. 21　Tasmania.
22　Underground. 23　Gorilla. 24　Barbary apes. 25　Milk. 26　Grizzly.
27　Otter. 28　Racoon. 29　America. 30　A monkey.

1   What is the official currency of Liechtenstein?
2   Who was the longest reigning British monarch before Victoria?
3   Which ponies were originally used in coal mines?
4   Who was the first post war British winner of a British Grand Prix?
5   At which London tourist attraction would you find a Chinese pagoda?
6   What do Americans call the silencer on the car?
7   Which bird-shooting season runs from October 1 to February 1?
8   What is the name of Andy Capp's wife?
9   Who was the original owner of *Today* newspaper?
10 What name is given to America's most westerly time zone?
11 Who wrote the novel *Sharpe's Tiger*?
12 In which decade of the 20th century was George Harrison born?
13 What word can go before "beer", "bread" and "nut"?
14 Who lit the Eternal Flame on the grave of John F. Kennedy?
15 What is the capital of Colombia?
16 What do G and K stand for in G.K. Chesterton's name?
17 What specialist line of trade did Tom Keating follow?
18 What would a Mexican submerge into a beer to make a "Submarino"?
19 What night is Burns Night?
20 Abbas Gokal got the Old Bailey's longest fraud sentence for scams centred on which company?
21 Who was the first TV newsreader to be knighted?
22 Which monarch was murdered at Pontefract Castle?
23 Which actress's real surname is Anistonopoulos?
24 Who was the first presenter of "A Question of Sport"?
25 Which club has members called Barkers?
26 Who are the landlords of the Bull, Ambridge?
27 Glen Cova and Joy are types of which fruit?
28 Who had a 80s No. 1 with "Jealous Guy"?
29 In which century was Lewis Carroll born?
30 Which car company has the Corolla range?

Answers

Pot Luck 32 (see Quiz 72)

1 David Jason. **2** Pepperland. **3** Blood cells. **4** Anne of Cleves. **5** Scarlet. **6** Emily Davison. **7** Austria. **8** Paul Daniels. **9** Umbrellas. **10** Chest. **11** 1900. **12** Agatha Christie. **13** "Snap". **14** Othello. **15** Spike. **16** Boyz II Men. **17** Joseph Conrad. **18** Eight. **19** Red rose. **20** Manhattan. **21** Camelot. **22** Opal. **23** 1970s. **24** London. **25** Peter Mandelson. **26** Roses. **27** House of Commons. **28** Clouds. **29** Ladywood. **30** Melbourne.

1 What does the aardvark feed on?
2 What colour is an ocelot?
3 What is the only member of the giraffe family other than the giraffe itself?
4 What sort of animal feeds on plants and other animals?
5 Which ape's natural habitat is restricted to Sumatra and Borneo?
6 What are ossicles?
7 Which group has more teeth - mammals or reptiles?
8 What is the North American equivalent of the reindeer?
9 What colour is a coyote's coat?
10 What name is given to a creature equally at home on land and in water?
11 What term describes an animal which cannot control its body temperature and has to rely on its environment?
12 What was the first animal to be domesticated?
13 Which special mouth parts inject poison into prey?
14 The llama is a relative of which African animal?
15 Which is the only vertebrate capable of sustained flight?
16 The wapiti is a member of which family of animals?
17 What protects a vertebrate's nerve cord?
18 Which extinct animal's name is the Portuguese for "stupid"?
19 What is another name for the Russian wolfhound?
20 What colour tongue does a chow chow have?
21 Other than the Australian mainland the platypus is native to where?
22 Where does a gopher make its home?
23 What is the most intelligent of land animals after man?
24 What type of apes were imported into Gibraltar in the 18th century?
25 What do mammary glands produce?
26 The brown bear is also known by what name?
27 What is the only true amphibious member of the weasel family?
28 Which American native has a black masked face and a distinctive ringed tail?
29 The anteater is native to which continent?
30 What is a marmoset?

World Soccer (see Quiz 69)
1 Black. 2 Faustino Asprilla. 3 Porto. 4 Argentina. 5 Roberto Baggio.
6 1990s. 7 AC Milan. 8 Sweden. 9 Argentina. 10 Frans Thijssen.
11 Colombia. 12 1970. 13 Rotterdam. 14 Real Madrid. 15 David Platt.
16 Black. 17 16. 18 Franco Baresi. 19 AC Milan. 20 Sweden. 21 Tony
Yeboah. 22 Bruce Rioch. 23 Monaco. 24 Cameroon. 25 Anders Limpar.
26 Bayern Munich. 27 Juventus. 28 Green. 29 Argentina. 30 Real
Sociedad.

1   Which actor used the word "perfick" in "The Darling Buds of May"?
2   Which kingdom was the setting for "Yellow Submarine"?
3   What do most humans lose 15 million of every second?
4   Who was the second wife that Henry VIII divorced?
5   What colour, traditionally, is an Indian wedding sari?
6   Who was the first suffragette martyr?
7   In which country is the Spanish Riding School?
8   Who hosted "Every Second Counts"?
9   What is the subject of Renoir's painting "Les Parapluies"?
10 Which part of the body is known as the thorax?
11 To five years, when was Louis Armstrong born?
12 Who wrote the novel originally titled *Ten Little Niggers*?
13 What word can go after "brandy" and before "dragon"?
14 In Shakespeare, who kills Desdemona?
15 What is Snoopy's brother's name?
16 Who had a 90s No. 1 with "End Of The Road"?
17 How is Teodor Josef Korzeniowsky better known?
18 How many records is a castaway allowed on "Desert Island Discs"?
19 What flower is on the shirts of the English Rugby Union team?
20 In which part of New York was "Kojak" set?
21 Tim Holley and David Rigg found their pay rises in the news while at which company?
22 Which birthstone is linked to October?
23 In which decade was "Blankety Blank" first screened in the UK?
24 In which city did Phileas Fogg begin his trip around the world?
25 Which grandson of 50s Labour home secretary Herbert Morrison played a leading part in the 1997 election?
26 Bourbon, Gallica and Rugosa are types of what?
27 Which House in England may not be entered by the Queen?
28 Nephophobia is a fear of what?
29 Clare Short has represented which Birmingham constituency?
30 What was the first Australian city to have hosted the Olympics?

1   All Cilla Black's 60s hits were on which record label?
2   What was the Beach Boys' first British No. 1?
3   Which same-surname artists both charted with "Memphis Tennessee"?
4   Which No. 1 starts "I'm in heaven when I see you smile"?
5   The Byrds' first two British hits were written by who?
6   Which was the first No. 1 for the Shadows?
7   Who was backed by the Stingers?
8   Who had No. 1s that had the colours red and black in the titles?
9   Which group featured drummer Anne Lantree?
10 Which US group sang "Rhythm Of The Rain"?
11 What was the surname of Desmond and Molly in "Ob-La-Di-Ob-La-Da"?
12 Which Tom wrote and produced for the Seekers?
13 In the Ricky Valance song, who loves Laura?
14 "5-4-3-2-1" was the signature tune of which TV pop show?
15 Who sang "I'll Never Fall In Love Again"?
16 Which ex-Shadows hit No. 1 with "Diamonds"?
17 Who backed Tomy Bruce?
18 Jim Capaldi and Steve Winwood came together in which group?
19 Which animal did Cat Stevens first sing about in the charts?
20 Which husband-and-wife team wrote a string of Pet-Clark hits?
21 Who were the first to have a No. 1 - the Beatles or the Stones?
22 In "A Whiter Shade Of Pale" where were the vestal virgins leaving for?
23 On which label did Mary Hopkin record "Those Were The Days"?
24 Gladys Knight and Marvin Gaye had separate hits with which song?
25 "Yeh Yeh" was a No. 1 for who?
26 Which city did the Dave Clark Five come from?
27 Who became the first female singer to have three No. 1s?
28 Who wrote Chris Farlowe's "Out of Time"?
29 Which classic starts "Dirty old river"?
30 Whose last Top Ten hit of the 60s was "San Franciscan Nights"?

Quiz 74 Pot Luck 33

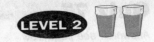

Answers - see page 200

1 What would you measure on the cephalic index?
2 Which name links Gwent, Rhode Island, USA, and the Isle of Wight?
3 When was VAT introduced in Britain?
4 What are the surnames of the TV presenters Judy and Richard?
5 Which breakfast dish was originally a hangover cure?
6 Which girls' name gave the Damned their only UK Top 10 hit?
7 Where would you find the Doge's Palace?
8 What is the minimum number of points to win on a tennis tie-break?
9 What colour hair did Churchill have before he went bald?
10 What is the main range of hills in gloucestershire?
11 Who wrote the novel *The Children Of Men*?
12 What is the only English anagram of PIMENTOS?
13 What is studied by a heliologist?
14 In which century was Thomas à Becket born?
15 In Morse code what letter is represented by one dash?
16 Which golfer first won the US amateur title three years in a row?
17 Which London street is famous for men's tailoring?
18 Which was the frequency of Radio Luxembourg?
19 Which famous chair was kidnapped by students from the Cranfield Institute of Technology in 1978?
20 Which character did Bonnie Langford play in "Just William"?
21 What was Spain's General Franco's first name?
22 In the Chinese calendar which year follows the year of the dragon?
23 What is the RAF equivalent to the army rank of Major?
24 What was Jacques Cousteau's research ship called?
25 Which city does the Halle Orchestra come from?
26 The fox-hunting season covers which months in Britain?
27 What is the Archbishop of Canterbury's official residence?
28 Who had a 50s No. 1 with "Young Love"?
29 In which decade of the 20th century was Jack Nicholson born?
30 What is the main flavour of aioli?

Quiz 75 TV Times 2

Answers - see page 197

LEVEL 2

1 Who was dubbed TV's Mr Sex?

2 Which drama/comedy was set in St Elgius Hospital?

3 What was Zoë's job in "May to December"?

4 In "Lovejoy" what was Tinker's surname?

5 Which ex-breakfast TV presenter has had a nightly show on Sky 1?

6 Where were the first three series of "Animal Hospital" based?

7 Who drew the animated titles sequence for "Yes Minister"?

8 What was the job of the heroes of "Common as Muck"?

9 Who was the most successful act on "The Big Time"?

10 Which city is "Casualty"'s Holby said to be?

11 What was the nickname of Sam Malone of "Cheers"?

12 In which month does the "Children in Need" appeal normally take place?

13 Who was the undertaker in "Dad's Army"?

14 Whose children included Primrose, Petunia, Zinnia and Montgomery?

15 Who was the sports commentator on "The Day Today"?

16 Who was Detective Sergeant Andy Crawford's father-in-law?

17 Which House was the surgery for Drs Finlay and Cameron?

18 Who was the third Doctor Who?

19 In the early 60s what was Radio 2 known as?

20 Which TV marriage began with "Happy Ever After" in 1969?

21 Which adolescent did Gian Sammarco play?

22 What was the sequel to "Are You Being Served"?

23 Where did Tom Good work before he began the Good Life?

24 In which series did Dawn French as Amanda work for *Spare Cheeks* magazine?

25 Which was the first UK TV listings magazine to join the Internet?

26 Who played Rocky in "Boon"?

27 Whose boss was Dr Gillespie?

28 Where does Marc Freden report from on GMTV?

29 Who played Frank Stubbs in "Frank Stubbs Promotes"?

30 How many episodes of "Fawlty Towers" were made?

Pop: 60s (see Quiz 73)

Answers

1 Parlophone. 2 "Good Vibrations". 3 Chuck and Dave Berry. 4 "Diane" (The Bachelors). 5 Bob Dylan. 6 "Apache". 7 B Bumble. 8 The Rolling Stones. 9 The Honeycombs. 10 The Cascades. 11 Jones. 12 Springfields. 13 Tommy. 14 "Ready Steady Go". 15 Bobbie Gentry. 16 Jet Harris and Tony Meehan. 17 The Bruisers. 18 Traffic. 19 Dog. 20 hatch and trent. 21 The Beatles. 22 The coast. 23 Apple. 24 "I Heard It Through The Grapevine". 25 Georgie Fame. 26 London. 27 Sandie Shaw. 28 Mick Jagger, Keith Richards. 29 "Waterloo Sunset". 30 The Animals.

Quiz 76 Performing Arts

LEVEL 2

Answers - see page 198

1   Which is London's oldest theatre?
2   The Royal Opera House in London is home to which branch of the arts other than opera?
3   How is Mozart's *Die Zauberflöte* known in English?
4   Who wrote *Tosca*?
5   Including intervals, approximately how long does Wagner's *Götterdämmerung* last?
6   Where is the Ballet Rambert based?
7   In which city is Europe's largest opera house?
8   Which theatre was the National's temporary home from 1963?
9   Who wrote the ballet *The Nutcracker*?
10 Which cornetist/pianist was considered to be the first great white jazz musician?
11 Which Duke's first names were Edward Kennedy?
12 Which London theatre was gutted by fire in 1990?
13 Which US clarinettist's real name was Arthur Jacob Arshawsky?
14 In 1984 The Society of West End Theatre Awards were renamed in honour of whom?
15 In which town is the largest stage in the UK?
16 How is *The Marriage of Figaro* known in Italian?
17 What is Shakespeare's longest play?
18 Which former prime minister's wife shares her name with a Bellini opera?
19 What nationality are two of the Three Tenors?
20 Which US director was the impetus behind the new Globe Theatre in London?
21 How is the Ballets Russes of Sergei Diaghelev now known?
22 What was *The Madness of King George* called as a play?
23 Which British playwright wrote the trilogy *The Norman Conquests*?
24 Which Czech-born playwright wrote *Jumpers and Arcadia*?
25 Who laid the foundation stone for the National Theatre on the South Bank?
26 Which newspaper presents awards for excellence in the London theatre?
27 Which of the three theatres within the National was named after the theatre's first Lord?
28 Who first produced *Les Miserables* in London?
29 In which street is London's Savoy Theatre?
30 In which city is the world's largest opera house?

Quiz 77 Pot Luck 34

Answers - see page 203

1   Who had a hit with "The Oldest Swinger in Town"?
2   Which Danish statue is a memorial to Hans Christian Andersen?
3   Where are rods and cones found in your body?
4   Which classic golf course is referred to as the Old Lady of golf?
5   What were the Boston Tea Party protesters unhappy about?
6   Which well-known trench was devised by Ferdinand De Lesseps?
7   Which royal owns the Castle of Mey?
8   Which short-lived soap saw Polly Perkins as Trish?
9   Which state in America is the Gambling State?
10 Which band included Martin Fry and Mark White?
11 On which island did Nelson Mandela serve most of his sentence?
12 What is the only English anagram of HEDONIST?
13 Who won the Australian Open as a Yugoslavian in 1993 and as American citizen in 1996?
14 Who was found guilty of the Oklahoma City bombing?
15 Who wrote the novel *Rob Roy*?
16 Which musical instrument does Tasmin Little play?
17 Who had a 60s No. 1 with "Mighty Quinn"?
18 How was Domenikos Theotocopolous better known?
19 Who shared the 1993 Nobel Peace prize with F.W. de Klerk?
20 Cecil Parkinson's affair with whom caused a scandal in 1983?
21 If A is alpha and B is bravo what is V?
22 What was the sport of Emerson's brother Wilson Fittipaldi?
23 In which series did Marion Jefferson and Beatrice Mason appear?
24 What name is given to the positive electrode of a battery?
25 Who was the first presenter of "Question Time"?
26 Who wrote "Love Shine A Light"?
27 What ship was Sir Francis Drake in when he circled the world?
28 In Norse mythology, who was god of thunder and war?
29 Gennifer Flowers claimed to have had a 12-year affair with whom?
30 In the Old Testament which book directly follows Numbers?

Quiz 78 Musical Movies

Answers - see page 204

1 What was Barbra Streisand character called in *Funny Girl*?

2 In which musical do Tracy Lord and CK Dexter Haven appear?

3 In which musical is *The Duelling Cavalier* a film in the making?

4 Who sings "As Long as He Needs Me" in *Oliver!*?

5 Who directed *A Chorus Line*?

6 Which singer - famous for dubbing other actresses' voices - played Sister Sophia in *The Sound of Music*?

7 What was the follow-up to *Saturday Night Fever* called?

8 Who did Betty Hutton replace as Annie in *Annie Get Your Gun*?

9 What was the job of Joel Grey's character in *Cabaret*?

10 Which musical was based on a Harold Gray comic strip?

11 What instrument does Robert de Niro play in in *New York New York*?

12 Which musical does "The Ugly Duckling" come from?

13 Who sang "Moon River" in *Breakfast at Tiffany's*?

14 Which song in *Evita* was composed specially for the film?

15 How many Von Trapp children are there in *The Sound of Music*?

16 "Hopelessly Devoted to You" is sung in which movie?

17 Who are the two gangs in *West Side Story*?

18 Which character did Liza Minnelli play in *Cabaret*?

19 Which movie musical has the song "Feed the Birds"?

20 Who played Mama Rose in the 1993 movie *Gypsy*?

21 Which two musical legends starred in *Easter Parade*?

22 "Shall We Dance" features in which movie?

23 What was Stanley Holloway's role in *My Fair Lady*?

24 In which film does Fat Sam fight it out with Dandy Dan?

25 "The Bare Necessities" comes from which film?

26 In which film did Gordon Macrae play Billy Bigelow after Frank Sinatra dropped out?

27 Which daughter of Judy Garland appeared in *Grease II*?

28 Which actress was I in *The King and I*?

29 In which musical would you see Lina Lamont?

30 Who directed *Everyone Says I Love You*?

Celebs (see Quiz 80)

Answers

1 Ireland. 2 Michael Jackson and Debbie Rowe. 3 Sulaiman. 4 Jackie Kennedy-Onassis. 5 Clothes design. 6 David Frost. 7 Madonna. 8 Scarlet. 9 Larry Fortensky. 10 Underwear. 11 Linley. 12 Hairdressing. 13 Chanel. 14 Raine. 15 Julia and Will Carling. 16 Costner. 17 Michael Heseltine. 18 Sylvester Stallone. 19 Joan Collins. 20 Fergie's Argentinian polo-playing step father. 21 Simpson's of Piccadilly. 22 Hawaii. 23 Barbara Hulanicki. 24 Marmaduke Hussey. 25 Frances Edmonds. 26 Britt Ekland. 27 Lady Diana Spencer. 28 Mark McCormack. 29 Norman Hartnell. 30 Sharon Maughan.

Quiz 79 Pot Luck 35

Answers - see page 201

1 Whose state visit was featured on the TV documentary "EIIR"?
2 Which hit for the Shadows is also a balsa raft?
3 In which county is Silbury Hill, Europe's biggest manmade mound?
4 Which film featuring David Bowie is also an organ of balance?
5 Which country does Martina Hingis represent in tennis?
6 Who founded the Communist newspaper *Pravda* in 1912?
7 What do we call the heating process which destroys enzymes in milk?
8 Who is the unproven author of the *Iliad*?
9 Which associate member of the EC is also a Commonwealth island?
10 In which century was Hans Christian Andersen born?
11 What word can follow "but", "car" and "bat"?
12 Who had a heart attack on his Never Ending Tour?
13 Which element has the atomic number 2?
14 In music, how many sharps in the key of A?
15 What are substitutes in cricket not normally allowed to do?
16 The College of Brasenose is part of which university?
17 Who had a 70s No. 1 with "Baby Jump"?
18 What was Captain Bligh's most famous ship?
19 What disaster did Kenny Morgan and Albert Scanlon survive?
20 In which county was HMP Slade from "Porridge"?
21 In Scrabble, how many points is the letter O worth?
22 In 1997 who stood for Tory leader but dropped out before the first ballot?
23 Which European city was the first home of the Statue of Liberty?
24 The composer Percy Grainger came from which country?
25 What is the profession of radio's Anthony Clare?
26 In which Dickens novel does Joe Gargery appear?
27 In the 60s who did hairdresser Maureen Cox marry?
28 Which John Wayne movie won him his only Oscar?
29 What is the capital of Chile?
30 In measuring a horse, how many inches in a hand?

Pot Luck 34 (see Quiz 77)
1 Fred Wedlock. 2 Little Mermaid. 3 Eyes. 4 St Andrew's. 5 Tea taxes.
6 The Suez Canal. 7 The Queen Mother. 8 "Eldorado". 9 Nevada.
10 ABC. 11 Robben Island. 12 Dishonest. 13 Monica Seles. 14 Timothy
McVeigh. 15 Sir Walter Scott. 16 Violin. 17 Manfred Mann. 18 El Greco.
19 Nelson Mandela. 20 Sara Keays. 21 Victor. 22 Motor racing.
23 "Tenko". 24 Anode. 25 Robin Day. 26 Kimberley Rew. 27 *The Golden Hind*. 28 Thor. 29 Bill Clinton. 30 Deuteronomy.

Quiz 80 Celebs

Answers - see page 202

1   Which country shares its name with Kim Basinger's daughter?
2   Who are the parents of Prince Michael Jr?
3   What is the son of Jemima and Imran Khan called?
4   Who was the famous sister of Lee Radziwill Ross?
5   In what field is Tommy Hilfiger a famous name?
6   Who is the son-in-law of the 17th Duke of Norfolk?
7   Carlos Leon has a famous daughter; who is the child's mother?
8   What colour dress did Paula Yates wear to marry Bob Geldof?
9   Who was Liz Taylor's eighth husband?
10 What type of clothes would you buy from Janet Reger?
11 Which Viscount attended Elton John's 50th birthday dressed as a lion?
12 In which field is Patrick Cameron famous?
13 Which fashion house does Stella Tennant model for?
14 What was Princess Diana's stepmother's first name?
15 Which couple advertised Quorn before their much-publicised split?
16 Which Cindy's divorce settlement from her actor/director husband was reputedly in the region of £50 million?
17 Which MP's children are called Annabel, Alexandra and Rupert?
18 Who married Jennifer Flavin as his third wife?
19 Who is Tara Newley's famous mother?
20 Who was the late Hector Barrantes?
21 Mrs Anthony Andrews' family own which London store?
22 On which island was model Marie Helvin brought up?
23 Which Polish-born designer founded Biba?
24 Which ex-BBC Chairman's wife was Lady-in-Waiting to the Queen?
25 Whose first book was *Another Bloody Tour* in 1986?
26 Who has been married to Peter Sellers and Jim McDonnell?
27 Who used the pseudonym Deborah Smithson Wells when arranging fittings for her wedding dress?
28 Which agent married tennis star Betsy Nagelson?
29 Who made the wedding dresses of Princesses Elizabeth and Margaret?
30 Which actress was known as the lady in the Gold Blend commercials?

Answers

Musical Movies (see Quiz 78)
1 Fanny Brice. 2 *High Society*. 3 *Singing in the Rain*. 4 Nancy. 5 Richard Attenborough. 6 Marni Nixon. 7 *Staying Alive*. 8 Judy Garland. 9 Master of Ceremonies. 10 *Annie*. 11 Saxophonist. 12 *Hans Christian Andersen*. 13 Audrey Hepburn. 14 "You Must Love Me". 15 Seven. 16 *Grease*. 17 Jets, Sharks. 18 Sally Bowles. 19 *Mary Poppins*. 20 Bette Midler. 21 Fred Astaire, Judy Garland. 22 *The King and I*. 23 Alfred P. Doolittle. 24 *Bugsy Malone*. 25 *Jungle Book*. 26 *Carousel*. 27 Lorna Luft. 28 Deborah Kerr. 29 *Singing in the Rain*. 30 Woody Allen.

1 Which organ in the body produces bile?

2 Which county first won cricket's Benson & Hedges Cup twice?

3 Who are the main characters in Milton's *Paradise Lost*?

4 Which continent is wider in the south than in the north?

5 Which game is played to the Harvard rules?

6 Which Pennsylvanian power station had a nuclear accident in 1979?

7 Who was Lord Vestey's dessert-loving, opera-singing, grandmother?

8 How many cards does each player start with in gin rummy?

9 If you have herpes labialis, what are you suffering from?

10 Where would you find the Dogger Bank?

11 In which century was Lord Byron born?

12 Who wrote the novel *East Of Eden*?

13 Which golfer declared that racially he was a "Cablinasian"?

14 What opened when Ali Baba said "Open sesame"?

15 Which character did Sean Blowers play in "London's Burning"?

16 Which birthstone is linked to May?

17 What word can go after "machine" and before "dog"?

18 Who was called the Serpent of the Nile?

19 In the New Testament which book directly follows Romans?

20 Who was head of Polly Peck International when it crashed in 1991?

21 Which sport includes sculls, strokes and slides?

22 Godfrey Evans played cricket for which county?

23 Which former prison chief wrote the book *Hidden Agendas*?

24 Cynophobia is a fear of what?

25 "The Slave Of Duty" is the subtitle of which light opera?

26 In which county do Bulls battle against Rhinos?

27 In Morse code what letter is represented by two dots?

28 Who had an 80s No. 1 with "Nothing's Gonna Change My Love For You"?

29 What was the nickname of Julius Marx?

30 In 1997 Jonathan Aitken dropped a court case against which TV company?

1 In 1990 Mr Frisk set a record time in which major race?

2 Which Earl of Derby gave his name to the race?

3 To a year each way, when was Red Rum's third Grand National win?

4 Where is the Lincoln Handicap held?

5 Which three races make up the English Triple Crown?

6 How did 19th century jockey Fred Archer die?

7 Which Irish rider won the Prix de L'Arc de Triomphe four times?

8 To two years each way, when did Lester Piggott first win the Derby?

9 Which classic race was sponsored by Gold Seal from 1984-92?

10 Who rode Devon Loch in the sensational 1956 Grand National?

11 What colour was Arkle?

12 How long is the Derby?

13 Sceptre managed to win how many classics outright in a season?

14 Shergar won the 1981 Derby by a record of how many lengths?

15 Which National Hunt jockey retired in 1993 with most ever wins?

16 What was the nickname of Corbiere?

17 Who rode Nijinsky to victory in the Derby?

18 In which decade was the Prix de L'Arc de Triomphe first run?

19 Who triumphed in the Oaks on Ballanchine and Moonshell?

20 Which horse was National Hunt Champion of the Year four times in a row from 1987 on?

21 Which horse stopped Red Rum getting three in a row Grand National wins?

22 How many times did the great Sir Gordon Richards win the Epsom Derby?

23 The Preakness Stakes, Belmont Stakes plus which other race make up the American Triple Crown?

24 Which Frank established a record nine victories in The Oaks?

25 Which jockey was the first ever winner of The Derby?

26 What actually is Frankie Detorri's first name?

27 Who holds the world record of riding 8,833 winners?

28 Riding Erhaab in 1994 which jockey won his fourth Epsom Derby?

29 What colour was Red Rum?

30 How old was Lester Piggott when he returned to racing in 1990?

Quiz 83 Pot Luck 37

Answers - see page 205

LEVEL 2

1 Which war did Charles Bronson return from in *Mr Majestyk*?
2 What name is given to a student of the alphabet?
3 Which illness killed Oliver Cromwell?
4 Who commissioned Holbein's painting of Anne of Cleves?
5 What is the metric word for one million?
6 What was tennis star Ann Haydon's married name?
7 Which company developed the pottery called Jasper Ware?
8 What did Monkee Mike Nesmith's mother invent?
9 Which travellers met at the Tabard Inn, Southwar?
10 What colour blood cells do lymph glands produce?
11 Who had a 90s No. 1 with "Oh Carolina"?
12 What are the colours of Humphrey the Downing Street cat?
13 Who wrote the novel *The Silmarillion*?
14 On which Canadian island is the city of Victoria?
15 In which century was Isambard Kingdom Brunel born?
16 What is the only English anagram of IMPRESSIVE?
17 In which country was Joe Bugner born?
18 In Scrabble, how many points is the letter A worth?
19 Which creature lives in a formicary?
20 What make of car was Jim Clark driving when he died?
21 In which drama did Father Ralph de Bricassart and Meggie Cleary appear?
22 If A is alpha and B is bravo what is T?
23 Which monster hit the British headlines in 1933?
24 Who were "overpaid, oversexed and over here"?
25 Which name means bringer of joys in Latin?
26 What was the nickname of the giant sperm whale grounded in the Firth of Forth in 1997?
27 What drug is obtained from foxgloves?
28 Ben Lomond and Baldwin are types of which fruit?
29 Which element has the atomic number 50 and the symbol Sn?
30 In which decade of the 20th century was Alan Ayckbourn born?

Answers

Pot Luck 36 (see Quiz 81)

1 Liver. 2 Leicestershire. 3 Adam & Eve. 4 Antarctica. 5 American Football. 6 Three Mile Island. 7 Dame Nellie Melba. 8 10. 9 Cold sores. 10 The North Sea. 11 18th. 12 John Steinbeck. 13 Tiger Woods. 14 His cave. 15 John Hallam. 16 Emerald. 17 "Gun". 18 Cleopatra. 19 First Corinthians. 20 Asil Nadir. 21 Rowing. 22 Kent. 23 Derek Lewis. 24 Dogs. 25 *The Pirates Of Penzance*. 26 West Yorkshire. 27 M. 28 Clive Medeiros. 29 Groucho. 30 Granada.

Quiz 84 The 80s

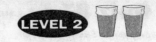

Answers - see page 206

LEVEL 2

1 Which controversial BBC Falklands film was broadcast in May 1988?
2 In which month was the marriage of Prince Charles and Lady Diana?
3 The SAS stormed which embassy in Knightsbridge?
4 Where did the 1980 Olympics take place?
5 Where did the Polish Solidarity movement start its strikes?
6 In August 1980 unemployment in Britain reached what figure?
7 Which US President ordered the aborted rescue of US hostages in Tehran?
8 Which Lord prepared a report following the Brixton riots?
9 Who did Pat Cash beat in the final when he won Wimbledon?
10 Who became the first Pope to visit Britain in 400 years?
11 Which charity record was the last to reach No.1 in the 80s?
12 Who were Liverpool's opponents in the FA Cup semi-final Hillsborough disaster?
13 Who "got on his bike and looked for work"?
14 What did Prince Edward resign?
15 How did Princess Grace of Monaco die?
16 Which Tory MP Keith was involved in dodgy applications for shares?
17 In which month of 1982 did Argentine forces invade the Falkland Islands?
18 Nuclear protests were based at Greenham Common in which county?
19 Which police officer was shot outside the Libyan embassy?
20 To a year, how old was Bjorn Borg when he retired from tennis?
21 What did Reagan's Strategic Defence Initative become known as?
22 What did Monday, October 19th, 1987 become known as?
23 Which North Sea oil rig exploded with the loss of over 150 lives?
24 Which former M15 man wrote *Spycatcher*?
25 Which American politician made the famous "watch my lips" speech?
26 In which books were golliwogs replaced by gnomes?
27 Which crazed gunman committed the Hungerford atrocities?
28 In which month was Michael Fish embarrassed by the gales of '87?
29 Where was the jumbo travelling to when it crashed at Lockerbie?
30 Who was Neil Kinnock's deputy when he became Labour leader?

Answers

Horse Racing (see Quiz 82)

1 Grand National. 2 12th. 3 1977. 4 Doncaster. 5 2,000 Guineas, Derby, St Leger. 6 Committed suicide. 7 Pat Eddery. 8 1954. 9 The Oaks. 10 Dick Francis. 11 Bay. 12 1 mile 4 furlongs. 13 Four. 14 Ten. 15 Peter Scudamore. 16 Corky. 17 Lester Piggott. 18 1920s. 19 Frankie Dettori. 20 Desert Orchid. 21 L'Escargot. 22 Once. 23 Kentucky Derby. 24 Buckle. 25 Sam Arnull. 26 Lanfranco. 27 Billie Lee Shoemaker. 28 Willie Carson. 29 Bay. 30 54.

Quiz 85 Easy Listening

Answers - see page 211

LEVEL 2

1 Who wrote "For The Good Times"?

2 Who charted in the 70s with "A Little Love And Understanding"?

3 Who made the Top Ten in 1952, had a 1968 No. 1 and was back in 1994?

4 Who had an album cryptically called *Last The Whole Night Long*?

5 After 60s success, which single charted for Mr Acker Bilk in the 70s?

6 Which close harmony Sisters were Connee, Martha and Helvetia?

7 Who had a No. 1 with the title in brackets of "Voler A Empezar"?

8 Which Nat King Cole song was re-issued and charted 30 years after the original?

9 In Sinatra's "High Hopes" what can't move a rubber-tree plant?

10 What was Lena Martell's only No. 1?

11 What was Perry Como's job before he became a singer?

12 Which 70s duo took the standard "Whispering Grass" to No. 1?

13 To two years, when did Johnny Mathis first have a Top Ten single?

14 Who did Gerry Dorsey become to sell thousands of 60s singles?

15 Who sang "I Just Want To Dance With You"?

16 Which Dickie had a 50s No. 1 with "Christmas Alphabet"?

17 Which singer/songwriter David fronted Bread?

18 What was Glenn Miller's main instrument?

19 Who wrote "Annie's Song"?

20 Where did Pat Boone write love letters?

21 Which city does James Galway come from?

22 How many were there in the Ink Spots?

23 Who had a British hit with "Guantanamera"?

24 Under what name did Brenda Gail Webb find fame?

25 Who wrote "This Guy's In Love With You"?

26 Whose singers invite radio listeners to "Sing Something Simple"?

27 Who had a 50s No. 1 with "Mary's Boy Child"?

28 What was Ken Dodd's huge 60s No. 1?

29 Which group used to accompany Herb Alpert?

30 In which decade of the 20th century was Mantovani born?

Answers

TV Cops & Robbers (see Quiz 87)

1 "Crime Traveller". 2 Cadfael. 3 Jonathan Creek. 4 "Crimewatch UK".
5 "Wokenwell". 6 The Saint. 7 "Cagney and Lacey". 8 David.
9 "Bodyguards". 10 The Baron. 11 Peter Cushing. 12 Sun Hill. 13 Three.
14 "The Chief". 15 Bergerac. 16 Los Angeles. 17 Criminal psychologist.
18 Afternoon. 19 Tony Curtis. 20 Danger Man. 21 Miss Marple.
22 Lynda LaPlante. 23 Jasper Carrott. 24 "Gideon's Way". 25 The Chinese
Detective. 26 Poirot. 27 Lochdubh. 28 Pathologists. 29 New York.
30 Campion.

Quiz 86 Pot Luck 38

Answers - see page 212

LEVEL 2

1 Which river is nearest to Balmoral Castle?
2 Which country and western singer appeared in *Gunfight*?
3 Which US probe was sent to land on Mars in 1997?
4 Which London park would you be in to ride along Rotten Row?
5 Which Swiss resort awards the Golden Rose TV awards?
6 How did Jane Austen's character Mr Woodhouse like his boiled egg?
7 Who was the first non-Englishman to play James Bond?
8 Which British airport was the first with its own railway station?
9 What did the 17 people in the dock at the Mike Tyson trial all ask for?
10 How many wives are allowed at one time under Islamic Law?
11 In which century was religious reformer John Calvin born?
12 Who had a 50s No. 1 with "Who's Sorry Now"?
13 If it's 12 noon GMT what time is it in Oslo?
14 Who is Jemima Khan's father?
15 Who wrote the novel *Anna Karenina*?
16 Which bridge joins a palace and a prison in Venice?
17 What word can follow "band", "mass" and "pass"?
18 Which battle came first - Agincourt or Bosworth Field?
19 What is the next highest prime number above 53?
20 In which American state are the Everglades?
21 What position in the House of Commons did George Thomas hold?
22 How did cabinet maker David Ashcroft become a multi-millionaire?
23 Which banned insecticide was the first to be manmade?
24 Which Marx Brother played the piano?
25 What is the capital of Georgia of the former USSR?
26 Whose motto is *Ich Dien*?
27 Who was the first presenter of "Tomorrow's World"?
28 Where was the Bayview Retirement Home in "Waiting for God"?
29 In which decade was "Blue Peter" screened for the first time?
30 Which river was Jesus Christ baptized in?

Answers

Pot Luck 39   (see Quiz 88)

1 Sean Connery. 2 "Mastermind". 3 Blue. 4 12. 5 19th. 6 Eat it. 7 O.
8 *The Old Curiosity Shop*. 9 Edward Heath. 10 Jack and Annie Walker.
11 American football. 12 Johnny Preston. 13 Refraction. 14 Oxford.
15 Horses. 16 France. 17 His ear. 18 Women being members. 19 Bishop
of Salisbury. 20 30s. 21 Keir Hardie. 22 Mark Knopfler. 23 Tessa Piggott
(later Carver). 24 Sheena Easton. 25 Greece. 26 In the sea. 27 Queen
Victoria. 28 H.G. Wells. 29 Cabbage. 30 A pancake.

Quiz 87 TV Cops & Robbers

Answers - see page 209

LEVEL 2

1. Which 1997 series featured detectives Slade and Holly?
2. Which TV detective is based in Shrewsbury?
3. Maddy Magellan assisted which offbeat TV detective?
4. In which show would you see Superintendent Hatcher and DC Hames?
5. Which series set in a northern town featured Sergeant Bonney?
6. Who had a business card which included a matchstick-man logo?
7. In which series did Detective Isbecki appear?
8. What was Callan's first name?
9. In which series did Louise Lombard star as Liz Shaw?
10. How was John Mannering better known?
11. Which horror actor played Sherlock Holmes in the 60s?
12. Chief Superintendent Charles Brownlow was in charge of which police station?
13. How many Angels did Charlie have?
14. Which drama featured Assistant Chief Constable Anne Stewart?
15. Who worked for the Bureau des Etrangers?
16. Where was "Columbo" set?
17. What is Cracker's job?
18. At what time of day was "Crown Court" first broadcast?
19. Who was the American half of "The Persuaders"?
20. How was 60s secret agent John Drake better known?
21. Which detective often embarrassed Inspector Slack?
22. Which writer created Superintendent Jane Tennison?
23. Who played the detective Bob Louis?
24. Which 60s series based on John Creasey's novels starred John Gregson?
25. How was Detective Sergeant Johnny Ho known?
26. Who had a secretary called Miss Lemon?
27. In which fictional town was "Hamish Macbeth" set?
28. In "Inspector Morse" what were the professions of Max and Dr Russell?
29. In "Dempsey and Makepeace" where was Dempsey from?
30. Who did Magersfontein Lugg assist?

Easy Listening (see Quiz 85)

1 Don McLean. **2** Gilbert Becaud. **3** Louis Armstrong. **4** James Last.
5 "Aria". **6** Boswell Sisters. **7** Julio Iglesias. **8** "When I Fall In Love". **9** An ant. **10** "One Day At A Time". **11** Barber. **12** Windsor Davies and Don Estelle. **13** 1958. **14** Engelbert Humperdinck. **15** Daniel O'Donnell.
16 Valentine. **17** Gates. **18** Trombone. **19** John Denver. **20** In the sand.
21 Belfast. **22** Four. **23** The Sandpipers. **24** Crystal Gayle. **25** Bacharach and David. **26** Cliff Adams. **27** Harry Belafonte. **28** "Tears". **29** Tijuana Brass. **30** First decade.

Quiz 88 Pot Luck 39

Answers - see page 210

LEVEL 2

1 Which actor was James Bond in the *Thunderball* movie?
2 Which TV show's format was based on the producer's experience at the hands of the Gestapo?
3 What colour is Scooby Doo's collar in the cartoons?
4 How many pairs of ribs does a human adult have normally?
5 In which century was Paul Cezanne born?
6 What do you do with a wonton?
7 In Morse code what letter is represented by three dashes?
8 In which Dickens novel does Kit Nubbles appear?
9 Which politician sailed the yacht *Morning Cloud*?
10 Who were the first married couple to be landlords of the Rovers in "Coronation Street"?
11 Which sport featured in the film *Semi Tough* starring Burt Reynolds?
12 Who had a 60s No. 1 with "Running Bear"?
13 What describes the bending of light as it passes from one medium to another?
14 Which university athletics team had Jeffrey Archer as a member?
15 What was the favourite subject of the artist George Stubbs?
16 Which European country is split by the Canal Du Midi?
17 What part of his anatomy did Carl Wells nail to a tree in the Manchester Runway protests?
18 In April 1997, Leander Rowing Club overturned a 179-year ban on what?
19 Who signs with the name Sarum?
20 In which decade of the 20th century was Brigitte Bardot born?
21 Who was the first Labour leader?
22 Which mega pop star formed the Notting Hillbillies?
23 Which character did Zoë Wanamaker play in "Love Hurts"?
24 Who performed the title song in the Bond film *For Your Eyes Only*?
25 Which country includes the Peloponnese?
26 Where were Olympic swimming events held prior to 1908?
27 Who laid the foundation stone at the Victoria and Albert Museum?
28 Who wrote the novel *The History Of Mr Polly*?
29 What variety of vegetable does kale belong to?
30 What is stuffed to make a blini or a blintz?

Pot Luck 38 (see Quiz 86)

1 The Dee. 2 Johnny Cash. 3 Pathfinder. 4 Hyde Park. 5 Montreux.
6 Very soft. 7 Sean Connery. 8 Gatwick. 9 His autograph. 10 Four.
11 16th. 12 Connie Francis. 13 1 p.m. 14 Sir James Goldsmith. 15 Leo Tolstoy. 16 The Bridge of Sighs. 17 "Age". 18 Agincourt. 19 59.
20 Florida. 21 Speaker. 22 He won the National Lottery. 23 DDT.
24 Chico. 25 Tbilisi. 26 The Prince Of Wales. 27 Raymond Baxter.
28 Bournemouth. 29 1950s. 30 The Jordan.

Answers

Quiz 89 Food & Drink 2

Answers - see page 215

LEVEL 2

1 What is ciabatta?
2 What is the predominant flavour of fennel?
3 What type of pulses are used in hummus?
4 What flavour is the drink Kahlua?
5 What is added to butter in a *beurre manié* ?
6 What type of wine is traditionally used in zabaglione?
7 What is radicchio?
8 What do the Spanish call a medium dry sherry?
9 What is panettone?
10 What are the three main ingredients of an Hollandaise sauce?
11 In the kitchen, what would a mandolin be used for?
12 What is harissa?
13 Which liqueur is used in a White Lady?
14 What sweet substance is added to whisky to make Drambuie?
15 From which continent does couscous originate?
16 What is the dish of stuffed vine leaves called?
17 In wine bottle sizes what is another name for a double magnum?
18 In the food world what is rocket?
19 From which country does balsamic vinegar originate?
20 Which spirit is used in a Daiquiri?
21 In which century was chocolate introduced into the UK?
22 Everards beers were originally based near which town?
23 What type of meat is used in moussaka?
24 What is the main ingredient of rosti?
25 Which traditional pudding ingredient comes from the cassava plant?
26 What is ghee?
27 Slivovitz is made from which fruit?
28 From what is angostura obtained?
29 What type of milk is a basic ingredient of Thai cookery?
30 What is a bruschetta?

Quiz 90 Politics

Answers - see page 216

LEVEL 2

1 Who was the first Tory leader to have gone to a grammar school?
2 In the 70s who was the Minister for Drought?
3 In 1997 David Blunket won which constituency?
4 What was the name of Harold Wilson's wife?
5 Who published the white paper "In Place Of Strife"?
6 Mrs Thatcher became Baroness Thatcher of where?
7 Which Tory Scottish Secretary lost his seat in 1997?
8 Who was deputy prime minister when Harold Macmillan resigned?
9 Who threw herself under the king's horse at the 1913 Derby?
10 What was the Tory slogan on posters of a queue of the unemployed?
11 Who first became prime minister - Gladstone or Disraeli?
12 To two years, when did John Major first win Huntingdon?
13 Who was beaten to the Labour leadership by Michael Foot in 1980?
14 What was the name of the male model in the Jeremy Thorpe affair?
15 Prime Minister Arthur James Balfour belonged to which party?
16 Dennis Skinner is known as the Beast of where?
17 Who followed Anthony Crossland as Labour's Foreign Secretary?
18 Who said that Gorbachev was "a man we can do business with"?
19 Who was Labour leader when the party adopted the red rose symbol?
20 Which politician was responsible for the creation of the police force?
21 How may rounds were there in the Tory leadership election of 1997?
22 Who was acting Labour leader on the sudden death of John Smith?
23 Who is Kingston-upon-Hull's most famous MP?
24 John Redwood and William Hague have held which cabinet post?
25 Who was Britain's first Socialist MP?
26 Who courted disaster with a weekend at the Paris Ritz in September 1993?
27 Roy Jenkins, David Owen, Shirley Williams and who else were the Gang Of Four?
28 Prime Minister Andrew Bonar Law belonged to which party?
29 How many general elections did Mrs Thatcher win for the Tories?
30 What constituency has Sir Edward Heath represented for many years?

Answers

Animation Movies (see Quiz 92)
1 Bashful. 2 Nick Park. 3 Mortimer. 4 *Snow White and the Seven Dwarfs.*
5 *Yellow Submarine.* 6 Tim Rice. 7 Jessica. 8 *Pinocchio.* 9 Scar.
10 Arthur. 11 *One Hundred and One Dalmatians.* 12 Mickey Mouse.
13 "Whole New World". 14 *Fantasia.* 15 Orang-utan. 16 Jasmine.
17 Pongo and Perdita. 18 Rabbit. 19 *Jungle Book.* 20 Basil. 21 15.
22 *Cinderella.* 23 Donald Duck. 24 *Pocahontas.* 25 *The Hunchback of Notre Dame.* 26 *The Return of Jafar.* 27 *Space Jam.* 28 1930s. 29 Ostriches.
30 Spaniel.

1 Which country includes the Isle of Tiree ?
2 Which British songwriter/actor wrote the first *Tarzan* movie script?
3 In which year did John Major become Prime Minister?
4 What is the only English anagram of KITCHENS?
5 Brontophobia is a fear of what?
6 Who wrote the novel *The Prince And The Pauper*?
7 What is the gas nitrous oxide also called?
8 Which Welsh town became a city in 1969?
9 In which century was Venetian painter Canaletto born?
10 What name describes a crack in a glacier?
11 Which leader of the Apache tribe died in 1909?
12 Which element has the atomic number 18 and the symbol Ar?
13 Which cuddly Hollywood sex symbol was born in 1935 in Dagenham?
14 Which fruit provides the basis for Cumberland Sauce?
15 Which birthstone is linked to November?
16 Which boxer was allegedly in an affray with Ray Sullivan in Legends nightclub?
17 In which series did Suzie Kettles and Eddie Clockerty appear?
18 Which Arthur Miller play is about witchcraft?
19 What is Scully's first name in "The X Files"?
20 Which bird's cry is known as a boom?
21 Which fish are turned into rollmops?
22 Who opened the recreated Globe Theatre in 1997?
23 Which Briton has been F1 World Champion on the most occasions?
24 Which country was the nearest to where *The Titanic* was found?
25 Which counties does Thames Valley FM serve?
26 The 400th edition of which radio comedy went out in May 1997?
27 How many hours in April?
28 Who had a 60s No. 1 with "Blue Moon"?
29 Which Florida national park is split by a road called Alligator Alley?
30 What bird was banned from fighting in Britain after 1848?

Food & Drink 2   (see Quiz 89)
1 An Italian bread. 2 Aniseed. 3 Chick peas. 4 Coffee. 5 Flour.
6 Marsala. 7 Red-leaved lettuce. 8 Amontillado. 9 Fruit bread. 10 Butter, egg yolk, wine vinegar. 11 Slicing. 12 Hot spicy paste. 13 Cointreau.
14 Heather honey. 15 Africa. 16 Dolmas. 17 Jeroboam. 18 Salad leaf.
19 Italy. 20 Dark rum. 21 17th. 22 Leicester. 23 Lamb. 24 Potatoes.
25 Tapioca. 26 Clarified butter. 27 Plums. 28 Tree bark. 29 Coconut milk.
30 Fried or toasted bread.

1 Which of the Seven Dwarfs had the longest name?
2 Who created Wallace and Gromit?
3 What was Mickey Mouse originally called?
4 What was Disney's first full-length cartoon called?
5 Which film takes place in Pepperland?
6 Who wrote the song lyrics for Aladdin?
7 Who is the *femme fatale* with Kathleen Turner's voice in *Who Framed Roger Rabbit?*?
8 "When You Wish Upon A Star" is from which Disney film?
9 What is Simba's uncle called in *The Lion King*?
10 *The Sword in the Stone* centres on the legend of which King?
11 Which film has the signal of the "twilight bark"?
12 Which character was the star of Disney's *Steamboat Willie*?
13 Which song from *Aladdin* in 1992 won an Oscar?
14 In which Disney film are Leopold Stokowski and the Philadelphia Orchestra seen?
15 What sort of animal is King Louie in *The Jungle Book*?
16 What is the Princess called in *Aladdin*?
17 Who were the original two Dalmatians in the 1961 classic?
18 What sort of creature was Thumper in *Bambi*?
19 Which was the first major Disney cartoon film released after Walt Disney's death in 1966?
20 What was the name of Disney's Great Mouse Detective?
21 How many puppies does Perdita produce in her first Dalmatian litter?
22 In which film is magic summoned by "Bibbidi-Bobbidi-Boo"?
23 Who had nephews called Dewey, Huey and Louie?
24 In which 90s film did "Colors of the Wind" appear?
25 Which 90s Disney film was based on a Victor Hugo story?
26 Which Disney film was the sequel to *Aladdin*?
27 Which 90s film starred Bugs Bunny and Michael Jordan?
28 In which decade was *Snow White and the Seven Dwarfs* released?
29 Which birds take part in the ballet in *Fantasia*?
30 What breed of dog is Lady in Lady and the Tramp?

1 Who is the Queen's only nephew?
2 In cricket, which county were Ireland's first victims?
3 Which country do Hyundai cars originate from?
4 Which boxer trained at St Thomas's Boys and Girls Club, Sheffield?
5 Which future Tory MP was told he could not run in the Moscow Olympics?
6 In which century was Catherine the Great born?
7 Which famous guitarist played for Casey Jones & the Engineers?
8 Who had a 70s No. 1 with "Ring My Bell"?
9 Which area of London first installed parking meters?
10 Who wrote the novel *Busman's Honeymoon*?
11 Which cocktail was dedicated to Tom Harvey, the surfing star?
12 What is the naval equivalent of the army rank of General?
13 Which modern instrument was developed from the sackbut?
14 If A is alpha and B is bravo what is J?
15 What was Gandhi's profession before politics?
16 What is the capital of the Canadian province Alberta?
17 Which band produced an album called *London Calling*?
18 In which decade of the 20th century was Idi Amin born?
19 What is the largest bay in the world?
20 Who was the first male presenter of "Treasure Hunt"?
21 Which world-renowned writer lived at Bateman's in Sussex?
22 In which suburb was "2 Point 4 Children" set?
23 Which radio star / *Sun* columnist was sued by the Pet Shop Boys?
24 In the story, who fell asleep on the Catskill Mountains?
25 What is the American equivalent of the British bilberry?
26 Vivian Stanshall was in which band?
27 In music, if a piece is in three flats which notes will be flat?
28 Who had the 50s original hit with "This Ole House"?
29 What organisation was set up by Agnes, Baden-Powell's sister?
30 In the Chinese calendar which year follows the year of the goat?

Quiz 94 Plant World

Answers - see page 220

LEVEL 2

1 What can follow "milk" and "rag" in the plant world?
2 What sort of fruit is a mirabelle?
3 Which Princess had a rose named after her at the 1997 Chelsea Flower Show?
4 Which grain is used to make semolina?
5 Which term is used for plants which store moisture in their thick fleshy leaves or stems?
6 Which part of a plant protects it as a bud?
7 What shape is a campanulate flower?
8 What is a morel?
9 What does lamina mean when referring to a leaf?
10 Which part of the tree is cinnamon obtained from?
11 Which parts of the potato are poisonous?
12 If a leaf is dentate what does it mean?
13 What colour are the flowers of a St John's Wort?
14 What is a prickly pear?
15 What is the main vegetation of the South African veld?
16 Why is the grapefruit so called?
17 What colour are borage flowers?
18 What is kelp?
19 Which plant's name means lion's tooth?
20 What is another name for the lime tree?
21 What is to be found in a plant's anther?
22 How long is the life cycle of a biennial plant?
23 The sycamore is native to which continent?
24 How many leaves does the twayblade orchid have?
25 What colour are the fruits on the deadly nightshade?
26 What type of plants are traditionally seen in a herbarium?
27 Which tree did archers need to cultivate to make bows?
28 Which King reputedly sought refuge in an oak tree?
29 The loganberry is a cross between which fruits?
30 What colour is the blossom of the blackthorn?

Quiz 95 Pot Luck 42

LEVEL 2

1 Who did David Soul campaign for in the 1997 General Election?
2 What do you do to mashed potatoes to make them Duchesse?
3 What sport do the Cardiff Devils play?
4 Which charity ceased in 1989 after 5 years and raising £90 million?
5 What word can go before "tress", "tune" and "ward"?
6 How often is a modern national census held in the UK?
7 Which England sports captain was born 12 December 1965, in Bradford-on-Avon?
8 Which famous Russian writer died on Astapova railway station?
9 What was the BBC theme for Euro 96?
10 Which creatures give birth to the world's biggest babies?
11 In which century was the astronomer Copernicus born?
12 Who earned $15 million on the tenth anniversary of his death in '88?
13 Height times breadth times 6 gives the surface area of which shape?
14 What is the main herb in pesto sauce?
15 Who wrote the novel *Simisola*?
16 In the BT TV commercials, what was the name of Beatie's son?
17 In the Old Testament which gloomy sounding book directly follows Jeremiah?
18 Which Philippino was accused of smuggling $225 million out of her country?
19 Who had a 80s No. 1 with "Japanese Boy"?
20 Which Government department is the second biggest UK landowner?
21 Which character did Paula Wilcox play in "Man About the House"?
22 Bruce Grobbelaar kept goal for which country?
23 Who was the first US president to visit China?
24 How old did women have to be to vote in 1918?
25 In music, how many sharps in the key of D?
26 What language is the Magna Carta written in?
27 What is halitosis?
28 Which royal-linked writer is renowned for her false eye lashes?
29 Who was Hitler's propaganda minister between 1933-45?
30 Which vegetable gives the flavour to a Bruxelloise sauce?

1   What does CNN stand for?

2   Who was the first director general of the BBC?

3   What must not be shown during religious broadcasts?

4   What is a squarial?

5   Which organisation's magazine is called *En Route*?

6   What is Manchester's own regional daily paper called?

7   BSkyB was an amalgam of which two companies?

8   Who was chief executive of Channel 4 from 1989 to 1997?

9   What was played at the end of daily transmission before the arrival of 24-hour TV?

10 In which decade was the *Beano* first issued?

11 What is the RSPB's own magazine called?

12 Which girls' magazine did *Mandy and Judy* amalgamate with in 1997?

13 Where is the *Eastern Daily* Press based?

14 Which subscription-bought periodical was founded in 1922 in the US?

15 Which channel had the slogan "From viewing to doing"?

16 What caused a change in licence fee funding in 1967?

17 What replaces Channel 4 in Wales?

18 What does CBS stand for?

19 How was the London Television Consortium better known?

20 Which women's weekly owned by H. Bauer was in the bestsellers list during the 90s?

21 Which magazine about the royals has had Ingrid Seward as Editor-in-Chief?

22 Which TV company launched its own magazine in May 1997?

23 In which town is Radio Orwell based?

24 Which TV company is based in Carlisle?

25 Sue Robinson became the first woman editor of which long-running magazine in 1996?

26 Which broadsheet newspaper has a tabloid-format Media section every Monday?

27 What was the first children's programme broadcast on BBC2?

28 How many colours were there in the original Channel 4 logo?

29 Which radio programme, begun in 1946 is still broadcast each weekday morning?

30 *Pravda* was a Soviet newspaper. What does Pravda mean?

Quiz 97 Speed Stars

Answers - see page 223

LEVEL 2

1. Which country did motor racing's Juan Manuel Fangio come from?
2. Who set a world record for the fastest ever maximum snooker break at the Crucible in April 1997?
3. Which England fast bowler received damages from *Wisden Cricket Monthly* over the article "Is It In The Blood?"?
4. What was the nost notable thing about Julio McCaw who raced against Jesse Owens?
5. In which event did Redgrave and Pinsent win Olympic gold?
6. Who was the first driver to register 50 Grand Prix victories?
7. Which horse won the 1996 Grand National?
8. In motor cycling, at what cc level was Barry Sheene world champ?
9. What was Mary Slaney's surname before her marriage?
10. Which Australian quick bowler is known as Pigeon?
11. To a year each way, when was James Hunt Formula 1 world champ?
12. Graeme Obree is connected with which sport?
13. Who holds the record for most Olympic swimming medals?
14. To a year each way, how old was Nigel Mansell when he was F1 world champion?
15. What famous first will Diomed always hold?
16. Where did the 93 Linford Christie v Carl Lewis challenge take place?
17. In April 1997 what did younger brother Florian give to Niki Lauda?
18. Colin Jackson's 60m hurdle record was set in Sindelfingen – in which country?
19. Who did Frank Williams recruit from IndyCar for the 1996 GP season?
20. Who succeeded Linford Christie as England's athletics team captain?
21. Which country does Donovan Bailey run for?
22. What nationality was Keke Rosberg?
23. Where in 1996 did Oliver Panis have his debut Grand Prix victory?
24. Who was the first man to swim 100 metres in less than a minute?
25. Who was Man Utd's left winger in the 60s European Cup triumph?
26. What are Daley Thompson's first two names?
27. Which Grand Prix did Damon Hill win first win when he became 1996 world champion?
28. Which England fast bowler was nicknamed George?
29. Which horse was Lester Piggott's first Derby winner?
30. Who in 1996 completed his hat-trick of titles as 500cc motor cycle world champ?

Soul & Motown (see Quiz 99)

1 Supremes. **2** James Brown. **3** Whitney Houston. **4** 1980s. **5** Georgia. **6** Billie Holliday. **7** Aretha Franklin. **8** Berry Gordy. **9** Organ. **10** Shot (by his father). **11** Aretha Franklin. **12** Gladys Knight. **13** "I Want You Back". **14** Michael Bolton. **15** Stevie Wonder. **16** Jimmy Ruffin. **17** The Wicked Pickett. **18** Four Tops. **19** 1966. **20** The Commodores. **21** The Four Tops. **22** Michael Jackson. **23** James Brown. **24** Rose. **25** Smokey Robinson. **26** 1960s. **27** "I Was Made To Love Her". **28** Stax. **29** Lionel Richie. **30** Floyd.

Answers

Quiz 98 Pot Luck 43

LEVEL 2

Answers - see page 224

1 Which film featured the single "Vogue" by Madonna?
2 In medical terms, what does an ECG stand for?
3 What was the occupation of Stephanie Slater who was kidnapped by Michael Sams?
4 With which two surnames did Aussie Evonne win Wimbledon?
5 Who had a 80s No. 1 with "Move Closer"?
6 Which canal linked Liverpool to London?
7 Which piece of attire took its name from a Pacific nuclear test site?
8 Who wrote the novel *Nostromo*?
9 Who was lost for six days in 1982's Paris-Dakar desert rally?
10 Which dessert is named after a ballerina?
11 Who invented the magnetic telegraph?
12 What word can go after "tea" and before "fast"?
13 Which word links a TV quiz show with space launches?
14 In which century was Boticelli born?
15 Who was Miss California in 1978?
16 What is the capital of Albania?
17 Which heroine was awarded Freedom of the City of London in 1908?
18 In Scrabble, how many points is the letter J worth?
19 In which country would you find the Great Sandy Desert?
20 In Morse code what letter is represented by four dots?
21 Alphabetically what is the last of the chemical elements?
22 What name is given to the larva of a fly?
23 Who became a Saint in 1909, nearly 500 years after she was killed?
24 In which Dickens novel does Jerry Cruncher appear?
25 What fruit can be made from the letters in TRANSCIENCE?
26 In which sitcom did Caroline Wheatley and Laura West appear?
27 In which decade of the 20th century was Warren Beatty born?
28 Which pop star ran for Mayor of Detroit in 1989?
29 What name describes the loose rocks on the side of a mountain?
30 Which hat took its name from a novel by George Du Maurier?

Answers

Pot Luck 44 (see Quiz 100)
1 Nicholas. 2 Sunderland. 3 Monopoly. 4 The Samaritans. 5 Agate.
6 Pink. 7 1970s. 8 Knesset. 9 Pennines. 10 Mrs Doubtfire. 11 A dotted line. 12 *Iolanthe*. 13 Ian Rush. 14 *Home Alone*. 15 Boeing.
16 Rosamunde Pilcher. 17 3 p.m.. 18 Housemartins. 19 Orange juice.
20 1958. 21 Clay. 22 16th. 23 Turkey. 24 Little Lord Fauntleroy.
25 Lynn Faulds Wood. 26 Marge & Homer. 27 Newcastle Upon Tyne.
28 India. 29 Michael Jackson. 30 St Mark.

LEVEL 2

1   "Nathan Jones" was a 70s hit for which group?

2   The Famous Flames backed which classic soul performer?

3   Which pop star did Bobby Brown marry in 1992?

4   In which decade did Stevie Wonder have his first British No. 1?

5   In "Dock Of The Bay" Otis Redding left his home in where when he headed for the Frisco Bay?

6   Who did Diana Ross play in *Lady Sings The Blues*?

7   Who duetted with George Michael on "I Knew You Were Waiting"?

8   Who founded Motown records?

9   What instrument did Booker T. play?

10 How did Marvin Gaye die?

11 Which female soul singer has recorded with the Eurythmics and George Benson?

12 In 1972, who recorded "Help Me Make It Through The Night"?

13 Which Jackson 5 hit of 1970 was remixed and back in 1988?

14 Who recorded the 90s album *Soul Provider*?

15 The song from the film *The Woman In Red* gave which star his first solo No. 1?

16 Who recorded the original "What Becomes Of The Broken Hearted"?

17 What nickname was applied to Wilson Pickett?

18 "Reach Out I'll Be There" was the first British No. 1 for which group?

19 To two years each way, when did Percy Sledge first chart with "When A Man Loves A Woman"?

20 Lionel Richie first charted with which group?

21 Levi Stubbs was lead singer with which group?

22 "One Day In Your Life" was a No. 1 for which superstar?

23 Who declared "Get Up I Feel Like Being A Sex Machine"?

24 What flower did Marv Johnson pick for his Rose?

25 Who wrote "Tracks Of My Tears" and "My Guy"?

26 In which decade did Sam Cooke die?

27 What was Stevie Wonder's first British top ten hit?

28 Otis Redding recorded on the Atlantic and which other label?

29 Who did Diana Ross duet with on "Endless Love"?

30 Which Eddie recorded the classic "Knock On Wood"?

Speed Stars (see Quiz 97)

1 Argentina. **2** Ronnie O'Sullivan. **3** Devon Malcolm. **4** Julio was a horse.
5 Coxless Pairs (Rowing). **6** Alain Prost. **7** Rough Quest. **8** 500 cc.
9 Decker. **10** Glenn McGrath. **11** 1976. **12** Cycling. **13** Mark Spitz.
14 37. **15** First Derby winner. **16** Gateshead. **17** Kidney in a transplant.
18 Germany. **19** Jacques Villeneuve. **20** Roger Black. **21** Canada.
22 Finnish. **23** Monaco. **24** Johnny Weismuller. **25** John Aston.
26 Francis Morgan. **27** Australia. **28** Brian Statham. **29** Never Say Die.
30 Michael Doohan.

Quiz 100 Pot Luck 44

1   What is the name of Tony Blair's second-born son?
2   Which English town became a city in 1992?
3   Which game features a top hat, a boot and a racing car?
4   "Love Shine A Light" was written for the 30th anniversary of which organisation?
5   What birthstone is linked to June?
6   What colour is the 39p postage stamp?
7   In which decade was "Emmerdale Farm" screened for the first time?
8   What is the Israeli parliament called?
9   Which range of Cumbrian hills has the highest point at Cross Fell?
10 How is the Robin Williams character Daniel Hillard better known?
11 How is a footpath indicated on a map?
12 "The Peer And The Peri" is the subtitle of which light opera?
13 Who returned to Liverpool in 1988 for £2.8 million from Juventus?
14 Which 1990 film featured a clip from the film *It's a Wonderful World*?
15 Who built the aircraft which dropped the bomb on Hiroshima?
16 Who wrote the novel *The Shell Seekers*?
17 If it's 12 noon GMT what time is it in Moscow?
18 Who had a 80s No. 1 with "Caravan Of Love"?
19 What is added to champagne to make a Bucks Fizz cocktail?
20 In what year was "Blue Peter" first broadcast?
21 What material is used to make a sumo wrestling ring?
22 In which century was Oliver Cromwell born?
23 What is the modern name for the country Asia Minor?
24 In literature, what title was inherited by Cedric Errol?
25 Who was the first female presenter of "Watchdog"?
26 Who are Bart Simpson's parents?
27 In which city was "Spender" set?
28 Which country has 845 languages with English and Hindu the main?
29 For Elton John's 50th birthday party who did Lenny Henry go dressed as?
30 Who is the patron saint of Venice?

Quiz 101 Children's TV

Answers - see page 227

LEVEL 2

1. How many programmes had "Blue Peter" notched up on their anniversary programme in May 1997?
2. Which pre-school characters live in Home Hill?
3. Who presented the first series of "Live and Kicking"?
4. What were the Teenage Mutant Hero Turtles called?
5. What was the name of the alien discovered, by Mike, in a wardrobe?
6. Who is the postmistress of Greendale?
7. What sort of creature is Children's BBC's Otis?
8. In which US state is "Sweet Valley High" set?
9. Which spacecraft was flown by Steve Zodiac?
10. Which character did Susan Tully play in "Grange Hill"?
11. Which comedian wrote the theme music for "Supergran"?
12. Where would you find Hugh, Pugh, Barney McGrew, Cuthbert, Dibble and Grubb?
13. Who numbered Barnabas, Willy and Master Bate in his crew?
14. Who did Captains White, Blue, Grey and Magenta deal with?
15. Which "historical" series included Barrington, Rabies and Little Ron?
16. What sort of creature is Dilly?
17. How many legs did the Famous Five have on TV?
18. Where is the teenage drama series "Sweat" set?
19. In which show would you find Dump-Pea?
20. In "Rag, Tag and Bobtail" what was Tag?
21. What is "Fablon" called on "Blue Peter"?
22. What did every contestant win on "Crackerjack"?
23. Who was the longest-lasting presenter of "Rainbow"?
24. The cartoon series about Willy Fogg was based on which book?
25. What sort of animal said, "I'm just a big silly old Hector"?
26. What day of the week was "The Woodentops" originally broadcast?
27. In "The Herbs" what were schoolteacher Mr Onion's pupils called?
28. Which characters live in Springfield?
29. Who has presented "How" and "How 2"?
30. What was Huckleberry Hound's favourite song?

Quiz 102 Pot Luck 45

LEVEL 2

1 Which harbour is the most famous on the island of Oahu?
2 What, in March 1988, ceased to be legal tender in England?
3 Who had the first-ever million-selling CD with *The Joshua Tree*?
4 What kind of vehicle was Charles Rolls of Rolls-Royce in when he died?
5 Which tree family is the basket-making osier a member of?
6 On which ground in England is the last cricket Test in a series held?
7 Which Italian ingredient helps to make a Harvey Wallbanger?
8 Who co-wrote with Bob Geldof the hit "Do They Know It's Christmas"?
9 Which sea did the Romans call *Mare Nostrum*?
10 Where is the largest gulf in the world?
11 Which royal resigned from the Royal Marines in January 1987?
12 What type of material was used by Rene Lalique for ornaments?
13 Who wrote the book *Aunts Aren't Gentlemen*?
14 Whose 100th single was called "The Best of Me"?
15 What do Australian's call a budgerigar?
16 What name is athlete Florence Griffith-Joyner better known as?
17 Which Liberal is known for the 1909 People's Budget?
18 Which No. 1 hit links Prince with Sinead O'Connor?
19 Which country had Queen Wilhelmina as Queen until she died in 1962?
20 What is the official language of Haiti?
21 Which actor co-starred with Sandra Bullock in the film *Speed*?
22 Which country has Jakarta as its capital?
23 What are the Southern Lights also called?
24 If June 1 is a Sunday what day is July 1?
25 Which US state has the largest share of Yellowstone National Park?
26 What is craved by phagomanicas?
27 Which Spanish region is so named because of its many castles?
28 Which comic-strip photographer used the alias Peter Parker?
29 Which character did Philip Michael Thomas play in "Miami Vice"?
30 Which country hosted Expo '88 and celebrated its bicentenary?

Answers

World Tour (see Quiz 104)
1 The Pentagon. 2 Sirocco. 3 Vancouver. 4 USA. 5 Indian. 6 Texas.
7 Ecuador. 8 Las Malvinas. 9 Harvard. 10 States with and without slavery.
11 China (16). 12 Florida. 13 Northern Territory. 14 The Zambesi.
15 Tanganyika, Zanzibar. 16 St Lawrence. 17 Fort Knox. 18 Vietnam.
19 Moscow. 20 Rio Grande. 21 New York. 22 Bechuanaland.
23 Venezuela. 24 Ellis Island. 25 K2. 26 Istanbul. 27 Texas.
28 Argentina. 29 Canaries. 30 McKinley.

Quiz 103 The 90s

LEVEL 2

1 How old was Tony Blair when he became Prime Minister?

2 Who first won the US Amateur Championship in 1994?

3 The invasion of which country sparked off the Gulf War?

4 Who was third in the 1997 Tory leadership election?

5 Which 25-year-old recording was 1990's best-selling single?

6 What is Bill Clinton's middle name?

7 Anthea Turner became the first female presenter of which live weekly event?

8 Who shared the 1993 Nobel Peace Prize with Nelson Mandela?

9 Paul Stewart scored an FA Cup Final goal for which team?

10 On TV, who were the Long Johns?

11 Which English fast bowler took the first wicket in the 1997 Ashes?

12 Jonathan Aitken withdrew from his court case against which paper?

13 Which royal financial advisor used toes for more than counting on?

14 In the 90s, who was Education Secretary, Home Secretary and Chancellor?

15 Which city hosted the 1992 Olympic Games?

16 Who succeeded Robert Runcie as Archbishop of Canterbury?

17 Andy Thomson became world indoor champion at what?

18 Which journalist helped write *Diana: Her True Story*?

19 Who made his last trip on the yacht *Lady Ghislaine*?

20 Who was the first man to win two Oscars in the 90s?

21 What does the S stand for in BSE?

22 Which sport's world series was cancelled due to the players' strike in 1994?

23 Who was No. 1 when Michael Jackson was No. 2 for five weeks with "Heal the World"?

24 Who stood against Margaret Thatcher for Tory leadership in 1990?

25 Who did 22-year-old model Rachel Hunter marry in 1990?

26 According to Queen Elizabeth what was 1992?

27 How many teams were in the Premier League's first season?

28 What tragic British first was the death of Stephen Cameron in 1996?

29 Who was US President at the time of the Gulf War?

30 In 1990 which England soccer player was jailed for drink driving?

Answers

Children's TV (see Quiz 101)

1 3000. **2** The Teletubbies. **3** Andi Peters, Emma Forbes. **4** Leonardo, Michaelangelo, Raphael, Donatello. **5** Angelo. **6** Mrs Goggins. **7** Aardvark. **8** California. **9** *Fireball XL5*. **10** Suzanne Ross. **11** Billy Connolly. **12** Trumpton. **13** Captain Pugwash. **14** The Mysterons. **15** Maid Marian and her Merry Men. **16** Dinosaur. **17** 12. **18** Australia. **19** "Poddington Peas". **20** Mouse. **21** Sticky back plastic. **22** Crackerjack pencil. **23** Geoffrey Hayes. **24** *Around the World in Eighty Days*. **25** Dog. **26** Friday. **27** The Chives. **28** The Simpsons. **29** Fred Dinenage. **30** Clementine.

Quiz 104 World Tour

Answers - see page 226

LEVEL 2

1　What is the largest office building in the USA?
2　Which wind blows from the Sahara to southern Italy?
3　Which Canadian island has Victoria as its capital?
4　Which country has the time zones Eastern, Central, Mountain and Pacific?
5　In which ocean are the Maldives?
6　Which US state is known as the Lone Star State?
7　In which country is Cotopaxi, the world's highest volcano?
8　How do the Argentinians refer to the Falkland Islands?
9　What is the USA's oldest educational institution called?
10　What did the Mason Dixon Line divide in the USA?
11　Which country has most neighbouring countries?
12　The Keys are islands off which US state?
13　Darwin is the capital of which Australian state?
14　Which river flows over the Victoria Falls?
15　Which two territories joined together to form Tanzania?
16　On which river are Quebec and Montreal?
17　Where are the US gold reserves?
18　In which country is the Mekong Delta?
19　Which capital is on the Moskva river?
20　Which river divides the USA and Mexico?
21　Where is Madison Square Garden?
22　How was Botswana known immediately prior to independence?
23　In which country is the world's highest waterfall?
24　Which US island was a registration point for immigrants until 1954?
25　Which of the world's highest mountains between India and China is not in the Himalayas?
26　How is Byzantium and Constantinople now known?
27　What is the second largest state of the US?
28　Tierra del Fuego is off which country?
29　Fuerteventura is in which island group?
30　Which is the highest mountain in North America?

LEVEL 2

1 Which leader of Bronski Beat also had solo hits?

2 Which British wild animal is quicker going uphill than downhill?

3 In which forest does the River Danube rise?

4 Who was the first person to score 100 runs and take 10 wickets in the same Test Match?

5 What was the nickname of Leonard Marx?

6 How many legs has a crane fly?

7 Which part of your body could suffer from astigmatism?

8 Which City is the capital of the US state of Nevada?

9 What nationality is Leonard Cohen?

10 Which star has Marilyn Monroe's signature tattooed on her bottom?

11 What was the first thing to leave the Ark when the rain stopped?

12 Which Irish singer was a schoolgirl in the *Hush A Bye Baby* film?

13 What is the opposite of aestivation?

14 Which tonic water flavour is taken from the cinchona tree?

15 What is the official language of Chile?

16 Who made the famous 70s album *Harvest*?

17 What is the longest river in France?

18 Who beat Kevin Curren in the '85 Wimbledon men's singles final?

19 Which Rochdale singer turned on the 1992 Blackpool Illuminations?

20 What comprises the diet of a pangolin?

21 Which country invented the duffel coat and bag?

22 Which British artist was greatly promoted by Delacroix in France?

23 Who beat President Marcos in the 1986 Philippines election?

24 What name are the Funchal Islands usually called?

25 Who wrote the book *Porterhouse Blue*?

26 What is the modern name for Hangman's Corner in London?

27 What are morels and chanterelles?

28 Who recorded the *Commoner's Crown* album featuring Peter Sellers?

29 Which channel separates Norway and Denmark?

30 In a title of a Bizet opera what were the people fishing for?

Answers

Pot Luck 47 (see Quiz 107)

1 Paisley Park. 2 Catalonia. 3 Townsend Thoresen. 4 Isle of Wight. 5 Holland. 6 Queen Nefertiti. 7 12. 8 Big Ben. 9 "Food Glorious Food". 10 M25. 11 Director General of the BBC. 12 Madrid. 13 Clowder. 14 India. 15 Solicitor. 16 I. 17 Liz McColgan. 18 Smell. 19 *Rainbow Warrior*. 20 Jason Donovan. 21 Jeremy Beadle. 22 Vanilla. 23 Great Maple. 24 Venice. 25 Hendersons. 26 Black, green, red. 27 "A Year in Provence". 28 Liza Goddard. 29 Fergal Sharkey. 30 Frederick Forsyth.

1 What was the first Lassie film called?
2 What was the most successful "creature" film of the 1970s ?
3 What was Clint Eastwood's co-star in *Every Which Way But Loose*?
4 What breed of dog was Beethoven?
5 Which country is the setting for *Born Free*?
6 Which animal adopts the piglet in *Babe*?
7 How many movie versions of *Black Beauty* had been made up to 1997?
8 In which decade was the first Lassie film made?
9 White Fang is a cross between which two animals?
10 What is Dorothy's dog called in *The Wizard of Oz*?
11 What was the sequel to *The Incredible Journey* called?
12 Which animals starred with Sigourney Weaver in a biopic of Dian Fossey?
13 Which film about rats had a theme song with lyrics by Don Black?
14 Which horse eventually had co star billing with Gene Autry?
15 Which film was described as "Eight legs. Two fangs. And an attitude"?
16 What was the Lone Ranger's horse called?
17 What sort of creature is Flicka in *My Friend Flicka*?
18 Which two types of animal feature in *Oliver and Company*?
19 Which nation's army dog was Rin Tin Tin?
20 What is the principal lioness called in *Born Free*?
21 In which decade was one of the first successful animal films *Rescued By Rover* released?
22 Which studio made the seven official Lassie films?
23 Which fictional whale did Keiko play in a 1993 movie?
24 Who wrote the book on which *Babe* was based?
25 Which film was directed by Hitchcock from a Daphne Du Maurier novel, other than *Rebecca*?
26 What was the sequel to *Beethoven* called?
27 What breed of dog features in *K-9*?
28 Which 1971 film was the predecessor of Ben a year later?
29 Which creatures contributed to the most successful film of 1993?
30 "Bright Eyes" was used as the music for a film about which animals?

1 What is the name of the artist formerly known as Prince's house and record label?
2 Barcelona is the capital of which region in Spain?
3 Who owned the capsized ferry *Herald of Free Enterprise*?
4 Which English county is completely surrounded by water?
5 The sport of speed skating originates from which country ?
6 Who was the wife of the Egyptian king, Ahkenaton?
7 How many yards is the penalty spot from a soccer goal line?
8 What stopped at 3.45 on 5 August 1975 in London?
9 Which musical song starts, "Is it worth the waiting for"?
10 Where did Chris Rea get held up which led to the hit "Road to Hell"?
11 Which job links Milne, Trethowan and Checkland?
12 What is the highest capital city in Europe?
13 Which term describes cats collecting together?
14 Which country invented snooker?
15 What was Bob Mortimer's job before joining up with Vic Reeves?
16 What is the chemical symbol for Iodine?
17 Which well-known athlete's maiden name was Elizabeth Lynch?
18 Which is the most sensitive of the human senses?
19 Which Greenpeace ship was sunk by the French in New Zealand?
20 Which Australian singer/soap star has a fear of boomerangs?
21 Who was the first presenter of "You've Been Framed"?
22 In music, which flavour ice was chosen by Bob van Winkle?
23 Which tree is the American version of the British Sycamore?
24 Which city is affectionately called the "Mistress of the Adriatic"?
25 Which TV family were friendly with Big Foot?
26 What three colours are on a roulette wheel?
27 Which 90s TV series was set in Luberon?
28 Which actress has been married to Alvin Stardust and Colin Baker?
29 Who had a 80s No. 1 with "A Good Heart"?
30 Who wrote the novel *The Devil's Alternative*?

1 What is the national game of Japan?
2 Which card game is based on dealing on the stock market?
3 Who is the only known unmarried person in Cluedo?
4 What is painted on to fabric in batik?
5 Carillon is a popular branch of what?
6 At which stately home would you see trees laid out in the form of troops at a famous battle?
7 In which month would you go to a Burns Night celebration?
8 Where is the National Museum of Geography?
9 The YOC is the junior branch of which society?
10 In bungee-jumping, what is a bungee?
11 Which type of wax is most commonly used in candle-making?
12 What is the traditional women's outfit in Scottish country dancing?
13 In which county would you visit St Michael's Mount?
14 What would you be making if you were following the bobbin or pillow method?
15 What order are trumps normally played at a whist drive?
16 How many counters does each player have at the start of a game of backgammon?
17 Which two Cluedo weapons are traditional weapons?
18 What are the two main activities in macrame?
19 Which manufacturer produces Sonic the Hedgehog computer games?
20 Which French theme park is named after a cartoon character?
21 Metroland is near which town?
22 In which city would you be if you went to the Ashmolean Museum?
23 In which resort is the golfing area of Birkdale?
24 How is the former Museum of Ornamental Art in London now known?
25 Which cathedral has ceiling decorations designed by "Blue Peter" viewers?
26 Which shopping centre in north-west London is near the foot of the M1?
27 Which world heritage site is near Amesbury in southern England?
28 Which is England's largest castle?
29 Which Safari Park is near Liverpool?
30 What is Edinburgh's main shopping street?

Movies: Animal Stars (see Quiz 106)

1 *Lassie Come Home*. 2 *Jaws*. 3 Orang-utan. 4 St Bernard. 5 Kenya. 6 Sheepdog. 7 Three. 8 1940s. 9 Dog and wolf. 10 Toto. 11 *Homeward Bound*. 12 Gorillas. 13 *Ben*. 14 Champion. 15 *Arachnophobia*. 16 Silver. 17 Horse. 18 Cats and dogs. 19 German. 20 Elsa. 21 1900s. 22 MGM. 23 Willy. 24 Dick King-Smith. 25 *The Birds*. 26 *Beethoven's 2nd*. 27 Alsatian. 28 *Willard*. 29 Dinosaurs (*Jurassic Park*). 30 Rabbits.

Quiz 109 Pot Luck 48

Answers - see page 235

1 Who had a 80s No. 1 with "Eye Of The Tiger"?
2 Which officer gives the results of a by-election?
3 Which gas was discovered in 1774 by Joseph Priestley?
4 What is the official language of Chad?
5 Which fruit has a variety called Ellison's Orange?
6 Which Disney film is based on a book by Dodie Smith?
7 Which country borders the Dead Sea together with Israel?
8 Bogota is the capital of which country?
9 Which sister group comprised Patty, Maxine and Laverne?
10 What event took place at Sears Crossing, Bedfordshire in August '63?
11 In which film did Michael Caine say, "Not a lot of people know that"?
12 Which former F1 champion has played golf in the Australian Open?
13 Who refused to appear on Virgin Island stamps with Michael Jackson?
14 Which England football manager was given the sack in 1974?
15 In which country was the Battle of Arnhem?
16 Whose best friend in the Movies was a boy called Elliot?
17 Kimberley, South Africa is famous for producing which gem?
18 Which everyday steel was invented by Harry Brearley in 1913?
19 Which character did Bruce Willis play in "Moonlighting"?
20 What word can go before "pet", "ton" and "mine"?
21 At which major English tourist attraction are the Aubrey Holes?
22 Which TV programme included Lisa Stansfield as a presenter?
23 Who invented 0 and 100 as freezing and boiling points of water?
24 The Harvard University is in which US state?
25 Which radio DJ featured a social worker called Damien in his show?
26 Who wrote the novel *Wild Swans*?
27 Which swimmer hit gold for Britain in the 1980 Olympics?
28 Which European country owns the island of Elba?
29 Which artist painted his garden's water lillies and bridges?
30 What is an appaloosa?

Pot Luck 49 (see Quiz 111)

Answers

1 Parking meter. 2 France. 3 Belize (formerly British Honduras). 4 Eagles.
5 Rudyard Kipling. 6 Bow Street. 7 Jokers. 8 Phil Collins. 9 The Menai.
10 Carbon monoxide. 11 Roman. 12 Saxophone. 13 Canada. 14 George
Bush. 15 Czechoslovakia. 16 *Spycatcher*. 17 Commonwealth. 18 Beach
Boys. 19 Translation (the Bible). 20 Max Bygraves. 21 Smallville.
22 Green. 23 A peacock. 24 Tungsten. 25 Starship Enterprise. 26 Ted
Dexter. 27 Flying Pickets. 28 People's car. 29 The nose. 30 Finnish.

1 How would you orally address an Archbishop?
2 Which seaside resort has Squires Gate airport?
3 Which charity can you phone on 0345 90 90 90 from anywhere in the country?
4 Which is a Freephone prefix other than 0800?
5 What is the emergency phone number in the US?
6 In Braille which letter consists of a single dot?
7 What does CompuServe provide access to?
8 What is a TAM ?
9 In telecommunications what is polling?
10 Which number can be used as an alternative to 999?
11 How often is *Reader's Digest* published?
12 What number do you dial for BT UK Directory Enquiries?
13 What do you dial if you do not want the person you are calling to know your phone number?
14 What would an Italian call a motorway?
15 What colour are telephone boxes in France?
16 What is the maximum weight you can send letters at the basic rate?
17 Which three cities are termini for the Eurostar service?
18 What is a local rate number other than 0345?
19 What colour is a 1p postage stamp?
20 What colour is an airmail sticker?
21 Which two cities are the termini for the Anglia rail region?
22 Which underground line goes to Heathrow Terminals?
23 In which US city is O'Hare airport?
24 Between which hours are BT's evening and night time phone rates?
25 What is the UK's oldest Sunday newspaper?
26 What do you dial for International Directory Enquiries?
27 Which newspaper cartoon strip is translated into Latin with characters Snupius and Carolius Niger?
28 Before 1991 which periodical had the highest circulation?
29 What colour is the logo for Virgin trains?
30 What is the most expensive denomination of UK postage stamp?

Answers

TV Times 3 (see Quiz 112)

1 Motorbike and sidecar. 2 Grand Prix racing. 3 Helen Mirren. 4 Eleanor, Robert. 5 "Have I Got News For You?". 6 Kenny Everett. 7 "Red Dwarf". 8 David Soul. 9 Kate. 10 Holland Park. 11 Anthony Jay. 12 "ER". 13 Joanna Lumley. 14 Alaska. 15 MP. 16 Alan B'Stard. 17 Cissie and Ada. 18 Ork. 19 "Minder". 20 "Happy Days". 21 Sport. 22 Pauline Quirke. 23 Compo and Clegg. 24 Elizabeth and Emmet. 25 Five. 26 "Solo". 27 Kenny Dalglish. 28 1940s. 29 Vince and Penny ("Just Good Friends"). 30 Alf Garnett .

Quiz 111 Pot Luck 49

Answers - see page 233

LEVEL 2

1   Which meter was invented in 1935 by C.C. Magee?
2   In which country is the port of St. Malo?
3   Which territory was Britain's last in Latin America?
4   What is the USA's rugby union team called?
5   Who was the author of *Gunga Din*?
6   Which London police station, 230 years old, closed in 1992?
7   What was not included in a pack of cards until 1857?
8   Who recorded an album called *Hello, I Must Be Going*?
9   Which bridge links the mainland to Anglesey?
10 Which fatal gas does burning coke emit?
11 Which civilization invented the arch?
12 Which musical instrument is played by Bart Simpson's sister?
13 Which country has the most coastline in the world?
14 Who beat Michael Dukakis in the US Presidential election in 1988?
15 Where was tennis star Ivan Lendl born?
16 Which book had Peter Wright as a co-author?
17 In 1949, what did Eire leave?
18 Which Californian band was joined in 1965 by Glen Campbell?
19 Miles Coverdale's greatest work was in which field?
20 Who released an autobiography titled *I Wanna Tell You a Story*?
21 Which town in Illinois was Superman's childhood home?
22 What colour are wild budgerigars?
23 Whose feathers according to superstition should not be in a house?
24 The letter W is the chemical symbol for what?
25 Which ship has the ID number NCC 1701?
26 Who followed Peter May as chairman of the Test Selectors?
27 Who had a 80s No. 1 with "Only You"?
28 What does Volkswagen actually mean?
29 Where are the sweat glands of a cow?
30 What nationality was the composer Sibelius?

Quiz 112 TV Times 3

Answers - see page 234

1   What is the favoured transport of the Two Fat Ladies TV cooks?
2   Jamiroquai's Jay Kay composed the theme music for coverage of which sport new to ITV in 1997?
3   In '97 who was voted sexiest woman on TV by *Radio Times* readers?
4   What are the first names of the Doctors Bramwell in the TV series?
5   Which show pits Merton v. Hislop with Deayton as referee?
6   Whose characters included Marcel Wave and Sid Snot?
7   In which sci-fi series did the red-suited Kochanski appear?
8   Which US actor accompanied Martin Bell on his election campaign?
9   What was the name of Nick's first wife in "Heartbeat"?
10 In which area of London was the "Ab Fab" Monsoon household?
11 Who co-wrote "Yes Minister" with Jonathan Lynn?
12 Which series featured the Carol Hathaway/Doug Ross saga?
13 Who was on a desert island as a "Girl Friday" in the mid-90s?
14 In which American state is "Northern Exposure" set?
15 What was the Job in "No Job For A Lady"?
16 Who was Conservative MP for Haltemprice?
17 What were Les Dawson and Roy Barraclough's old gossips called?
18 Which planet was Mork from?
19 In which series was business conducted at the Winchester?
20 "Laverne and Shirley" was a spin-off from which 70s US series?
21 What type of features would Eleanor Oldroyd present on TV?
22 Which Bird starred as 22-stone Olive in "The Sculptress"?
23 Who were Blamire's two companions in 1973?
24 Who are Hyacinth Bucket's most frequently seen neighbours?
25 How many children were there in the Partridge family?
26 In which series did Felicity Kendal play Gemma Palmer?
27 Which football star appeared as himself in Alan Bleasdale's "Scully"?
28 In which decade was "Shine On Harvey Moon" set?
29 Whose parents were Les and Rita, and Daphne and Norman?
30 Who was looked after by Mrs Hollingberry when his wife died?

Answers

Communications (see Quiz 110)
1 Your Grace. 2 Blackpool. 3 The Samaritans. 4 0500. 5 911. 6 A.
7 The Internet. 8 Telephone Answering Machine. 9 The ability to receive information from another fax machine. 10 112. 11 Monthly. 12 192. 13 141.
14 Autostrada. 15 Yellow. 16 60g. 17 London, Paris, Brussels. 18 0645.
19 Dark red. 20 Blue. 21 London, Norwich. 22 Piccadilly. 23 Chicago.
24 6 p.m. to 8 a.m.. 25 The *Observer*. 26 153. 27 Peanuts. 28 *Radio Times*.
29 Red-and-grey. 30 £10.

1   In which country is the town of Waterloo?
2   If you perform a rim shot, what instrument are you playing?
3   In the Chinese calendar which year follows the year of the rat?
4   What are you in if you are caught in a Haboob?
5   What is wrestler Big Daddy's real name?
6   What trade did a webster follow?
7   Who wrote the book *The Prodigal Daughter*?
8   Where does the River Seine empty?
9   What is the fourth letter of the Greek alphabet?
10 What day of the week did Solomon Grundy get married?
11 Which bone is the hardest in the human body?
12 Who was the last Chancellor of West Germany prior to reunification?
13 What was the pen name of Eric Blair?
14 In which decade was "Jim'll Fix It" screened for the first time?
15 Who solved the crime in *Death on the Nile*?
16 Who was the first presenter of "Wheel of Fortune" in the UK?
17 Who was John Major's last Party Chairman?
18 Which breed of dog does not have a pink tongue?
19 Who portrayed Jesus in the TV adaptation "Jesus of Nazareth"?
20 Which novel by Louisa May Alcott sold millions of copies?
21 Which city in India has an airport called Dum Dum?
22 What links a group of whales to a group of peas?
23 If a Vietnamese was depositing a dong, where would he be?
24 Which hat originates from Ecuador?
25 What medical procedure was Iceland the first country to legalise?
26 What was crossed on a tightrope by Charles Blondin in 1855?
27 Who had a 80s No. 1 with "Start"?
28 What colour smoke announces the election of a new Pope?
29 Which birthstone is linked to December?
30 Which Canadian province has Halifax as its capital?

Answers

Rugby (see Quiz 114)

1 Australia. 2 Gavin Hastings. 3 22. 4 Diana Ross. 5 Papua New Guinea. 6 Davies. 7 England. 8 Bath. 9 Heineken. 10 Wembley. 11 New Zealand. 12 England. 13 1970s. 14 Castleford. 15 Lynagh. 16 Salford Reds. 17 Paris St Germain. 18 Harlequins. 19 Australia, New Zealand. 20 Ivory Coast. 21 Maine Road (Man City's ground). 22 1940s. 23 New Zealand. 24 Leicester. 25 Widnes. 26 Phillippe Sella. 27 Mike Gibson. 28 Farr-Jones. 29 Nigel Melville. 30 Knowsley Road.

Quiz 114 Rugby

LEVEL 2

1 Which country won league's World Cup from 1975 to 1995?
2 Which Scot was British Lions captain for the '93 New Zealand tour?
3 How old was Will Carling when he first captained England?
4 Which superstar singer opened the 1995 World Cup?
5 The league Lions tour of 1996 visited Fiji and New Zealand and where else?
6 On his return to union which Jonathan said, "It's a challenge I don't particularly need"?
7 Which nation has won the Grand Slam most times?
8 Where was Jeremy Guscott born?
9 Which sponsor called last orders on its sponsorship of the Welsh League?
10 Which stadium hosted the League's 1995 World Cup Final?
11 The Ranfurly Shield is contested in which country?
12 Over half of the 1997 Lions squad came from which country?
13 In which decade was the John Player/Pilkington Cup begun?
14 Which English club did Franco Botica join when he left Wigan?
15 Which Michael has scored most points for Australia?
16 Which team ended Wigan's Challenge Cup record run in the 90s?
17 Which team won the first match in the Super League?
18 Which was the first team in the 90s other than Bath to win the Pilkington Cup?
19 Which two countries contest the Bledisloe Cup?
20 In the 1995 World Cup who were on the wrong end of an 89-0 score to Scotland?
21 Which ground staged the Wigan v Bath cross code game of 1996?
22 In which decade was Fran Cotton born?
23 Which country did Grant Fox play for?
24 Who did Bath beat 16-15 in the 95-96 Pilkington Cup?
25 What was Martin Offiah's first league side?
26 Which player – a Frenchman – became the first to win 100 caps?
27 Which Belfast born solicitor went on five British Lions tours?
28 Which Nick captained Australia from 1984 to 1992?
29 Who was director of rugby as Wasps won the 96-97 championship?
30 Where do St Helens play?

Quiz 115 The Last Round

Answers - see page 238

LEVEL 2

1. Who was the first British astronaut on the space station *Mir*?
2. Who was the second wife Henry VIII beheaded?
3. How many Popes were there in 1978?
4. What game is being played on the back of a £10 note?
5. David Mellor's affair with whom caused a scandal in the 90s?
6. What is Jennifer Aniston's character's full name in "Friends"?
7. What colour are the seats in the House of Lords?
8. What numbers do Barclaycards begin with?
9. Which ex sports minister won a Court action to have the family title?
10. In which county did Britain's first lifeguard training centre open?
11. In which career is Jodie Kidd famous?
12. Who was the first Mrs Warren Beatty?
13. Who presented "Desert Island Discs" immediately before Sue Lawley?
14. Which TV programme moved to radio in 1997?
15. Which drink was Lucky Vanous famous for advertising?
16. In the early 60s what was Radio 4 known as?
17. Who was the GP in Ambridge who lived with Usha Gupta?
18. What is the regulator of the National Lottery called?
19. Who played Ripley in the *Alien* movies?
20. A frittata is an Italian version of what?
21. Who unexpectedly won the 1997 Men's French Open?
22. Which childhood disease has the same virus as shingles?
23. Who was England ladies athletics team captain at the '96 Olympics?
24. What is Mulder's first name in "The X Files"?
25. What is the official language of Morocco?
26. Who was the British producer of *The Killing Fields*?
27. How many hours were there in February 1997?
28. Who wrote *The Partner*?
29. What was Ronald Reagan's most senior political role before he became president?
30. If you buy pamplemousses in France what do you buy?

Answers

Pot Luck 50 (see Quiz 113)

1 Belgium. 2 Drums. 3 Ox. 4 A sandstorm. 5 Shirley Crabtree.
6 Weaving. 7 Jeffrey Archer. 8 The English Channel. 9 Delta.
10 Wednesday. 11 The jawbone. 12 Helmut Kohl. 13 George Orwell.
14 1970s. 15 Hercule Poirot. 16 Nicky Campbell. 17 Brian Mawhinney.
18 Chow. 19 Robert Powell. 20 *Little Women*. 21 Calcutta. 22 They both
collect in pods. 23 A Bank. 24 Panama. 25 Abortion. 26 Niagara Falls.
27 Jam. 28 White. 29 Turquoise. 30 Nova Scotia.

Hard Questions

Are you bristling with intelligence? Do your pores seep clever stuff? Does knowledge flow through you like the mighty Nile, silting up your mind with facts? If not then get your head down because here's the HARD section. As difficult as plaiting fog, as tricky as puppy-juggling and yes, as taxing as a very hard question posed by the Inland Revenue in order to determine the amount of your income they can take away from you.

The Hard section; a quick scan through the pages will illustrate the point exactly: your forehead will crease, your memory will strain and your patience will stretch. Just two of the questions rejected by quiz setters were: 'Who?' and the immensely complex 'Why?'

Use these questions like heavy artillery. Revel in the percussive resonance as you go about pounding down the teams' defences, leaving their minds racked and their knowledge plundered. Wield them wisely, though, for a quiz set entirely with the Hard questions would make you as welcome as a polecat at a foxes's Ball.

Quiz 1 Pot luck 1

Answers - see page 243

1   What were the names of the three tunnels dug by POWs in *The Great Escape*?
2   Who had an 80s No. 1 with "Star Trekkin'"?
3   In which country is the city of Abu Dhabi?
4   Which shipping forecast area is due north of Shannon?
5   What is the only English anagram of GRANDIOSE?
6   In which country are the Shakta Pantjukhina caves?
7   What was William Atheling's real name?
8   In Monopoly how much does it cost to buy the Angel Islington?
9   If it's noon at GMT, what time is it in Addis Ababa?
10 Who was the first player to be disqualified from Wimbledon?
11 Who wrote the novel *The Sea, The Sea*?
12 Which English county provided the setting for "The Farming Week"?
13 Who founded the Newman Haas Racing Indy Car Team?
14 In which decade were postal orders first issued in Britain?
15 Mick Harford scored in a League Cup Final for which team?
16 What is Mystic Meg's surname?
17 In which fictitious town was "'Allo 'Allo" set?
18 Which ex-champ did Doug Flach beat in round 1 of Wimbledon '96?
19 What was Frederick John Robinson's title when he was UK prime minister?
20 In which round did Tyson lose in his '96 clash with Evander Holyfield?
21 Who is the patron saint of wine merchants?
22 What was the first British Top Ten hit for Argent?
23 Lipari and Salina are in which island group?
24 On which river does St Petersburg stand?
25 Which magazine did Cherie Booth (Blair) guest-edit in 1996?
26 What was the computer called in the TV series "The Tomorrow People"?
27 From which language does the word "limousine" originate?
28 Who did Norma Major write her first book about?
29 The airline Sansa is based in which country?
30 Which character was played by Prunella Scales in "After Henry"?

Answers

Pot Luck 2 (see Quiz 3)

1 1940s. 2 Ghana. 3 Kingsley Amis. 4 Jack Ruskin. 5 Chord. 6 Spanish.
7 The moon. 8 Algeria. 9 Free Parking. 10 Truffle. 11 T'Pau.
12 A meteorite. 13 J.C. Morton. 14 Smiles. 15 Kriss Akabusi. 16 Simian
Films. 17 Abdel Benazzi. 18 1500. 19 Rock Hudson. 20 Shot. 21 Over
300. 22 1440. 23 *Patience*. 24 Clement Ader. 25 Alan Mills. 26 Bolton
Wanderers. 27 Playboy. 28 Moonee Ponds. 29 A lighthouse. 30 Dog Eat
Dog.

1　Which girlfriend of Ken Barlow was played by Joanna Lumley?
2　What was Maureen Holdsworth's name before she married Reg?
3　Other than the Duckworths, who are Tommy's grandparents?
4　In the 80s which soap character was voted Britiain's most popular person after the Queen, Queen Mother and Princess Diana?
5　What was Susan Tully's first documentary series called after she left "EastEnders"?
6　Which future Oscar winner played Irma Ogden's boyfriend Ron Jenkins?
7　Who was killed in the first episode of "EastEnders"?
8　Which number Albert Square did Pauline and Arthur Fowler live at?
9　What was the name of Len Fairclough's son, played by Peter Noone?
10　What was the name of the programme that looked back at the Albert Square of 1942?
11　What had the original working title of "Meadowcroft"?
12　What were Deirdre's first two surnames in "Coronation Street"?
13　Brookside Close was a real estate but what was its first fake addition?
14　On which days of the week was "Albion Market" first broadcast?
15　Which husband-and-wife team produced "The Colbys"?
16　In "Dallas" what was the name of the baby Kristin had by JR?
17　In "Dynasty" which character was Rock Hudson's final role?
18　At what times of day was "Neighbours" first screened in the UK?
19　Which character did ex-EastEnder Letitia Dean play in "The Hello Girls"?
20　What did *Private Eye* ridicule "Brookside" as when it first started?
21　Which "Dynasty" character wrote *Sister Dearest* about Alexis?
22　Who sang the "Neighbours" theme song?
23　In "Emmerdale" what was Annie Sugden's first husband called?
24　Which soap star was Charlie's voice in "Charlie's Angels"?
25　In "Dallas" how did Jock die?
26　Who were Madge Mitchell's children in "Neighbours"?
27　Which beers did the Woolpack first sell in "Emmerdale"?
28　What is the link between Ian McShane's role in "Dallas" and Gene Kelly's in "Singin' in the Rain"?
29　Who played Peggy Mitchell before Barbara Windsor?
30　Who was the first owner of the Albert Square launderette?

Quiz 3 Pot Luck 2

Answers - see page 241

1 In which decade was Gerard Depardieu born?

2 In which country is the city of Accra?

3 Who wrote *Jake's Thing*?

4 Which character was played by Roy Marsden in "Airline"?

5 What name is given to a straight line that joins any two points on the circumference of a circle?

6 From which language does the word "bravado" originate?

7 Louis Daguerre took the first photograph of what?

8 The international car registration DZ applies to which country?

9 On a Monopoly board what is between Vine Street and the Strand?

10 What is the only English anagram of FRETFUL?

11 Who had an 80s No. 1 with "China In Your Hand"?

12 What is known to the Eskimos as Abnighito and is in Cape York Greenland?

13 What was Beachcomber's real name?

14 Which series of stamps featured Dennis the Menace and Mona Lisa?

15 Whose middle names are Kezie Uche Chukwu?

16 Which film company was founded by Liz Hurley and Hugh Grant?

17 Who captained France v. the Springboks in rugby in 1996?

18 What is the approximate distance of Athens airport from London in miles?

19 Which famous actor played Sammy Jo's father in "Dynasty"?

20 In which sport did Suzanne Allday achieve fame?

21 How many islands are in the Andaman group?

22 What is the sum total of the internal angles in a decagon in degrees?

23 How is Gilbert and Sullivan's *Bunthorne's Bride* better known?

24 Who invented the steam-powered aeroplane?

25 Who became Wimbledon referee in 1982?

26 Which football team does the Dewsbury MP Ann Taylor support?

27 Which organization financed Roman Polanski's Macbeth?

28 In which Melbourne suburb was Dame Edna Everage brought up?

29 What type of building did Mary live in, in "The Life and Loves of a She-Devil"?

30 What was the first British Top Ten hit for Adam and the Ants?

Answers

Pot Luck 1 (see Quiz 1)

1 Tom, Dick & Harry. 2 Firm. 3 United Arab Emirates. 4 Rockall.
5 Organized. 6 Russia. 7 Ezra Pound. 8 £100. 9 3 p.m. 10 Tim Henman.
11 Iris Murdoch. 12 Northamptonshire. 13 Carl Haas. 14 1880s.
15 Luton. 16 Lake. 17 Nouvion. 18 Andre Agassi. 19 Viscount Goderich of Nocton. 20 11th. 21 St Nicholas. 22 Hold Your Head Up. 23 Aeolian.
24 Neva. 25 *Prima*. 26 Tim. 27 French. 28 Dame Joan Sutherland.
29 Costa Rica. 30 Sarah France.

Quiz 4 Pop: Singers

LEVEL 3

1 Whose first solo single had the catalogue reference Virgin BOY 100?

2 Which 60s singer was backed by the Cruisers on his first recordings?

3 What is the middle name of Kenny Rogers?

4 What was Clarence Carter's one and only hit?

5 On what label did Buddy Holly record?

6 Where in America was Diana Ross born?

7 Rod Stewart's "Sailing" was used for a BBC series about which ship?

8 Which unlikely singer had a 50s hit with "Shifting Whispering Sands"?

9 Who was Marc of Marc and the Mambas?

10 Which country did Morris Albert come from?

11 "We Don't Talk Anymore" was Cliff's first No. 1 for how many years?

12 Which former singer became Leo Sayer's manager?

13 Who did Van Morrison record the *Irish Heartbeat* album with?

14 Under what name did David Spencer record?

15 What was Jennifer Rush's follow up to "The Power Of Love"?

16 What are Madonna's two middle names?

17 In the 50s who was accompanying Dion on his first single?

18 Peter Cunnah sang his way to No. 1 with who?

19 Which singer was backed by the Drells?

20 Both Carole King and Don McLean made an album called what?

21 Who was the most famous vocalist to sing with the Tourists?

22 Who is lead singer with UB40?

23 Who had a No. 1 with "Mambo Italiano"?

24 What was the first posthumous hit single for Jim Reeves?

25 Which Everly Brother sang the higher notes?

26 Who is the most successful singer to come from Douglas, Isle of Man?

27 Who played a character called Rachel Marron on film?

28 What was Joe Cocker's job before he became a singer?

29 What was Dionne Warwick's first Top Five hit in Britain?

30 What was Johnnie Ray's nickname?

Quiz 5 Pot luck 3

Answers - see page 247

LEVEL 3

1 Who wrote the novel *A Bend in the River*?
2 What was the first British Top Ten hit for Kenny Ball?
3 Who was the first host of "Wogan" other than Terry Wogan?
4 The airline Augusta Airways is based in which country?
5 Who led the British forces at the Battle of Princeton in 1777?
6 What number in Old Drum Lane was home to "Steptoe and Son"?
7 In which decade was Albert Finney born?
8 What was Acton Bell's real name?
9 What is the only English anagram of TRAGEDY?
10 On which river does Rangoon stand?
11 Who invented the swing-wing aeroplane?
12 If it's noon at GMT, what time is it in Casablanca?
13 From which language does the word "verandah" originate?
14 In Monopoly, what is the prize for winning a crossword competition?
15 Moluccas and Irian Jaya are in which island group?
16 Which character was played by Helen Shapiro in "Albion Market"?
17 Where was Nelson Piquet's last Formula 1 Grand Prix race in 1991?
18 In which country was J.R.R. Tolkien born?
19 If something is "fluviatile" what is it?
20 Alaska became what number state of America?
21 Bonny Lad and White Windsor are types of what?
22 In which country is the city of Dakar?
23 Who did Sharon Gless marry in 1991?
24 In which Dickens novel does Susan Nipper appear?
25 Which Frenchman became Armenia's representative at UNESCO?
26 If A is Alpha and B is Bravo what is H?
27 Who wrote the novel *The English Patient*?
28 When is Lammas Day?
29 What was the name of Elsie Tanner's nephew in "Coronation Street" played by Gorden Kaye?
30 Who had an 80s No. 1 with "Don't Turn Around"?

Pot Luck 4 (see Quiz 7)

1 Adverts. 2 Ken Boothe. 3 Svetlana Savitskaya. 4 Avenue Foch. 5 Italian.
6 Thames estuary. 7 167. 8 Erik Rotheim. 9 Rev Mervyn Noote.
10 Alessandro Filipepi. 11 6000. 12 Michael Moorcroft. 13 Stamford Brook.
14 Alex Stepney. 15 5-1. 16 1920s. 17 Tara Palmer-Tomkinson.
18 Golding. 19 Second cousin. 20 Between left thumb and forefinger.
21 "Manic Monday". 22 Marty McFly. 23 Edward Heath (1973). 24 Month
of the grape harvest. 25 Nigel Mansell. 26. Dolly Parton economics. 27
Diana Rigg. 28 John Leslie. 29 Cobbold. 30 USA.

1 In which two films did Paul Newman play "Fast Eddie" Felson?

2 Who did Tom Cruise play in *Born on the Fourth of July*?

3 Whose first film, for Disney, was called *Napoleon and Samantha*?

4 Who played Sherman McCoy in *Bonfire of the Vanities*?

5 Which two superstars collaborated on the massive flop *Ishtar*?

6 Which film gave Michelle Pfeiffer her first Oscar nomination?

7 Who has been married to Judy Carne and Loni Anderson?

8 For which film did Meryl Streep win her second Oscar?

9 Which role did Kim Basinger play in *Batman* in 1989?

10 Who co-wrote the screenplay for *Yentl* with Barbra Streisand?

11 Which role did Elizabeth Taylor play in *The Flintstones*?

12 What was Disney's first PG movie, which starred Michael J. Fox?

13 Who was the star and executive director of the remake of *The Return of Martin Guerre*?

14 Who won the Best Supporting Actress award for *Cactus Flower*?

15 Who starred with Natalie Wood in *Splendor* in the Grass in 1961?

16 In which film did Jack Lemmon first direct Walter Matthau?

17 Who was Jimmy Bond in *Casino Royale*?

18 Aged 21, who wrote his autobiography *Absolutely Mahvelous*?

19 Who has played the Boston Strangler and Houdini on screen?

20 Who won an Oscar for playing an Irish cop in *The Untouchables*?

21 Who won an Oscar nomination for her first feature-film role as Robin Williams's mother?

22 Who played Sean Connery's son and Matthew Broderick's father in the same film?

23 Who posed nude covered in paint which looked like a man's suit?

24 Who was the attorney played by Kevin Costner in *JFK*?

25 Who did Jack Nicholson play in *One Flew Over The Cuckoo's Nest*?

26 Whose 1991 autobiography was called *Me*?

27 Which actor won Australia's equivalent of an Oscar for *Tim*?

28 Who played Horace Vandergelder in *Hello Dolly!*?

29 Who was the Penguin in *Batman Returns*?

30 Who did Cher play in Robert Altman's *The Player*?

Quiz 7 Pot luck 4

Answers - see page 245

LEVEL 3

1   What is the only English anagram of STARVED?
2   Who had a 70s No. 1 with "Everything I Own"?
3   Who was the first woman to walk in space?
4   On a French Monopoly board, what is the equivalent to Oxford Street?
5   From which language does the word "piano" originate?
6   Where did the world-travelling aviator Amy Johnson vanish in flight?
7   To ten, how many islands are in the Zemlya Frantsa-Iosifa group?
8   Who invented the aerosol?
9   Who did Derek Nimmo play in *All Gas and Gaiters*?
10 What was Botticelli's real name?
11 What is the approximate distance of Bangkok airport from London in miles?
12 Who wrote the book *A Cure for Cancer*?
13 Which was the first London Underground station to have an automatic ticket barrier?
14 Which Manchester United keeper was a mid-season joint top-scorer in the 70s?
15 What are the odds of rolling any combination totalling seven in dice-throwing?
16 In which decade was Dirk Bogarde born?
17 Which *Sunday Times* columnist has a sister called Santa?
18 Which William won the Nobel Prize for Literature in 1983?
19 What relation is the actor Ralph Fiennes to the explorer Ranulph Fiennes?
20 Where does the actress Helen Mirren have a tattoo?
21 What was the first British Top Ten hit for the Bangles?
22 What was Michael J. Fox's character in the *Back to the Future* films?
23 Which prime minister introduced a 10.30 p.m. TV curfew?
24 In the French Republican calendar what did Vendemiare mean?
25 Who celebrated a Formula 1 win a lap too soon at Montreal in '91, losing to Nelson Piquet?
26 What did Kenneth Clarke call Gordon Brown's policy of "an unbelievable figure, blown out of all proportion with no visible means of support"?
27 Who played Vincent Price's daughter in *Theatre of Blood*?
28 Who did Tim Vincent replace on "Blue Peter"?
29 Knebworth has been the home of which family for over 500 years?
30 In which country is the city of El Paso?

Pot Luck 3   (see Quiz 5)
1 V.S. Naipaul. 2 "Midnight in Moscow". 3 Selina Scott. 4 Australia.
5 Lord Cornwallis. 6 24. 7 1930s. 8 Anne Brontë. 9 Gyrated.
10 Irrawaddy. 11 Grumman Co. 12 12 noon. 13 Portuguese. 14 £100.
15 Indonesia. 16 Viv Harker. 17 Montreal. 18 South Africa. 19 Belonging to or formed by rivers. 20 49th. 21 Broad Bean. 22 Senegal. 23 Barney Rosenzweig. 24 *Dombey and Son*. 25 Charles Aznavour. 26 Hotel.
27 Michael Ondaatje. 28 August 1st. 29 Bernard Butler. 30 Aswad.

Quiz 8 Living World

Answers - see page 246

LEVEL 3

1   RSPB founders campaigned specifically against the slaughter of birds for what purpose?
2   Which faunal region covers South/Central America and the Caribbean?
3   What is the largest class of sponges called?
4   Sea fans and sea whips are types of what?
5   What colour is the underside of the pipesnake's tail?
6   What is the world's largest eagle?
7   Which sense does the New World vulture have which the Old World vulture doesn't?
8   How many eyes does a tuatara have?
9   A sunstar is a type of what?
10 How is the early bird from Australasia, the butcherbird also known?
11 How does the flamingo get its colour?
12 Where does a blenny live?
13 What is a ratite?
14 Which bird can walk up to 20 miles a day?
15 What do oystercatchers eat?
16 Which seabird is also called the shag?
17 Which continent is the home of the electric eel?
18 What has the largest wingspan of any living bird?
19 The Puerto Rican boa is endangered due to which predator?
20 What does a white bait grow into?
21 Where does the axolotl come from?
22 Which part of a turtle is its carapace?
23 How is the goat fish also known?
24 Which flightless bird in addition to the emu is native to Australia?
25 What is a skink?
26 Which bone of birds is also called the furcula?
27 Which Australian male bird incubates the eggs and raises the young?
28 Where is the mesite native to?
29 Which fish is known as rock salmon when sold for food?
30 How does the monitor lizard consume its prey?

Answers

Movie Superstars (see Quiz 6)

1 *The Hustler, The Color of Money*. 2 Ron Kovic. 3 Jodie Foster. 4 Tom Hanks.
5 Warren Beatty, Dustin Hoffman. 6 *Dangerous Liaisons*. 7 Burt Reynolds.
8 *Sophie's Choice*. 9 Vicki Vale. 10 Jack Rosenthal. 11 Pearl Slaghoople.
12 *Midnight Madness*. 13 Richard Gere. 14 Goldie Hawn. 15 Warren Beatty.
16 *Kotch*. 17 Woody Allen. 18 Billy Crystal. 19 Tony Curtis. 20 Sean
Connery. 21 Glenn Close. 22 Dustin Hoffman. 23 Demi Moore. 24 Jim
Garrison. 25 Randall Patrick McMurphy. 26 Katherine Hepburn. 27 Mel
Gibson. 28 Walter Matthau. 29 Danny De Vito. 30 Herself.

Quiz 9 Pot Luck 5

Answers - see page 251

LEVEL 3

1   Which shipping forecast area is south of Sole?
2   Which fictional village was the TV series "Dear Ladies" set in?
3   Who was David Coulthard's teammate with the '97 Formula 1 McLaren team?
4   What was the lowest value on a Charles and Diana Royal Wedding stamp?
5   Who joined Michael Jackson on the 80s No. 1 "I Just Can't Stop Loving You"?
6   What is the northern boundary of South America?
7   To whom did Clive Anderson say, "Is there no beginning to your talents?"?
8   Whose autobiography was called *Crying With Laughter*?
9   Who wrote the novel *Nightmare Abbey*?
10   In which country is the city of Caracas?
11   What was Charlie Chaplin's first film?
12   How many islands are in the Azores group?
13   Who was President of the British Olympic Association from 1983?
14   Who won a Tony for his Broadway debut as Che in *Evita*?
15   Which soap had the characters Spanner and Craven and a drug dealer called Gibson?
16   Which character was played by Tim Healy in "Auf Wiedersehen Pet"?
17   If it's noon at GMT, what time is it in Mexico City?
18   What was the first British Top Ten hit for Shirley Bassey?
19   In which decade was Geoff Boycott born?
20   What is the only English anagram of GRIEVED?
21   What was Boz's real name?
22   The airline Tower Air is based in which country?
23   Who invented the non-rigid airship?
24   In Monopoly, what dividend does the Bank pay you in Chance?
25   Who followed Arthur Balfour as prime minister of the UK?
26   Which ex-Miss Black Tennessee was Oscar-nominated for *The Color Purple*?
27   In which sport did Chris Baillieu achieve fame?
28   What is the capital of the Canadian province New Brunswick?
29   From which language does the word "steppe" originate?
30   Which performer undertook the Serious Moonlight Tour?

Answers

Pot Luck 6 (see Quiz 11)

1 James Baldwin. **2** Electric Company. **3** Elizabeth II. **4** Brussels Sprout.
5 Switzerland. **6** Bangladesh. **7** Battersea. **8** Diana Ross, Ryan O'Neal.
9 Reims. **10** 1260. **11** Debbie Moore. **12** Jean Dominique Larrey.
13 Dutch. **14** New Edition. **15** Cranberry juice. **16** Mel Martin, John Bowe.
17 CQD. **18** Philippa Vale. **19** Hawaiian. **20** Cricket. **21** 1920s.
22 Ferns. **23** Friday. **24** Giovanni Antonio Canale. **25** Liz Hobbs.
26 Annika Reeder. **27** Kimbolton. **28** "Keep On Dancing". **29** 7000.
30 Gifted.

Quiz 10 UK Football

LEVEL 3

Answers - see page 252

1 How many different French clubs did Eric Cantona play for before joining Leeds?
2 Which club has its ground in Bumpers Lane?
3 To three each way, how many England caps did Alan Ball win?
4 What was the last English league club that George Best played for?
5 The world's first artificial pitch was built in which stadium in Texas?
6 How old was John Aldridge when he first played international soccer?
7 Which city does the striker Chris Armstrong come from?
8 Who was the first manager to record six FA Cup Final wins?
9 Cec Podd created an appearance record for which club?
10 Which England player was born in Southampton on March 3 1972?
11 Which ground was featured in L.S. Lowry's painting *Going To the Match*?
12 Andy Cole scored his first League goal for which club?
13 Which team used to be called Shaddongate United?
14 Who scored for Manchester United in Cantona's "Kung-Fu" game v. Palace?
15 Which City play at home at Glebe Park?
16 To three, how many England clean sheets did Gordon Banks keep?
17 Colombia's Rene Higuita made an amazing scorpion kick save from which England player at Wembley in 1995?
18 Ray Graydon scored in a League Cup Final for which club?
19 Which two teams were involved in Scotland's first ground share?
20 Steve D'Eath set an English clean sheet record while at which club?
21 At which club did Brian Horton follow Mark Lawrenson as manager?
22 Who scored the winning goal in the 1953 Matthews Final?
23 Which future international failed to impress Ipswich in trials in 1982?
24 Which teams played in the first international on an artificial pitch?
25 What were Barnet FC previously known as?
26 Which sponsors name was on '94-'95 Premiership winners' Blackburn shirts?
27 Who did Hereford replace in the Football League in the 70s?
28 Who scored England's Italia '90 goal against Egypt?
29 Which team was the first to retain the FA Cup in the 20th century?
30 Who was the boss for Alan Shearer's league debut?

Answers

Around The UK (see Quiz 12)
1 Ben Macdui. 2 Manchester. 3 Nith. 4 Edinburgh. 5 Bournemouth.
6 Aberdeen. 7 Neagh. 8 Aberystwyth. 9 Carlisle. 10 Hull. 11 Coventry.
12 Fenner's. 13 Jennie Lee. 14 Nottingham. 15 Perth. 16 Wakefield.
17 Towy. 18 Itchen. 19 Northern. 20 Leeds. 21 Douglas, Isle of Man.
22 Bangor. 23 Brighton. 24 The Octagon. 25 Dumfries. 26 Edinburgh,
Heriot-Watt. 27 York. 28 The Parks. 29 St Andrews. 30 Colne.

Quiz 11 Pot Luck 6

Answers - see page 249

LEVEL 3

1 Which woman was world water-skiing champion from 1981-5?
2 In Monopoly, where would you land with a double six from Go ?
3 Who was the first reigning sovereign to visit a television studio?
4 Widgen and Welland are types of what?
5 In which country did the Scottish writer A.J. Cronin die?
6 In which country is the city of Dhaka?
7 In which London suburb was the hospital drama "Angels" set?
8 Who were originally suggested for the two main roles in *The Bodyguard* back in the 70s?
9 Where was the first French Formula 1 Grand Prix held which counted toward the World Championship?
10 What is the sum total of the internal angles in a nonagon in degrees?
11 Who founded the Pineapple Dance Studios in London?
12 Who developed the ambulance?
13 From which language does the word "yacht" originate?
14 Who had an 80s No. 1 with "Candy Girl"?
15 In early '97, which drink did the Duchess of York advertise in the US?
16 Who played Demelza and Ross in the 90s "Poldark"?
17 What distress call did SOS replace?
18 Which character was played by Liza Goddard in "Bergerac"?
19 Niihau and Kahoolawe are in which island group?
20 In which sport did Enid Bakewell excel?
21 In which decade was Yassar Arafat born?
22 What does a pteridologist breed?
23 If Epiphany is on a Monday what day is Valentine's Day?
24 What was Canaletto's real name?
25 Which hit song refers to Guitar George?
26 Who was England's youngest Commonwealth Games gold medallist in 1994?
27 At which palace did Catherine of Aragon die?
28 What was the first British Top Ten hit for the Bay City Rollers?
29 What is the approximate distance of Buenos Aires airport from London in miles?
30 What is the only English anagram of FIDGET?

Pot Luck 5 (see Quiz 9)

1 Finisterre. 2 Stackton Tressle. 3 Mika Hakkinen. 4 14p. 5 Siedah Garrett. 6 The Panama Columbia boundary. 7 Jeffrey Archer. 8 Bob Monkhouse. 9 Thomas Love Peacock. 10 Venezuela. 11 *Making A Living.* 12 Nine. 13 Princess Anne. 14 Mandy Patinkin. 15 "The Archers". 16 Dennis Patterson. 17 6 a.m. 18 Banana Boat Song. 19 1940s. 20 Diverge. 21 Charles Dickens. 22 USA. 23 Henri Giffard. 24 £50. 25 Henry Campbell-Bannerman. 26 Oprah Winfrey. 27 Rowing. 28 Fredericton. 29 Russian. 30 Dave Bowie.

Quiz 12 Around the UK

LEVEL 3

1   What is the highest peak in Scotland after Ben Nevis?
2   Where is the Whitworth Art Gallery?
3   On which river does Dumfries stand?
4   Where is the James Clerk Maxwell Telescope?
5   Which town has the car index mark AA?
6   Where is Dyce Airport?
7   Which Lough is in the centre of the Sperrin, Antrim and Mourne ranges?
8   Where is the National Library of Wales?
9   Which town's football ground is farthest away from any other?
10 Which UK town has its own telephone system?
11 Where is Warwick University?
12 What is Cambridge's county-class cricket ground called?
13 Which Milton Keynes theatre is named after a politician who was also a famous politician's wife?
14 Where is the East of England Orchestra based?
15 What was Scotland's capital in the 11th-15th centuries?
16 Where is Pontefract racecourse?
17 What is the longest river in Wales?
18 On which river does Winchester stand?
19 On which tube line is London's longest tunnel?
20 Which is farther north, Leeds or Halifax?
21 Where is Jurby Ronaldsway airport?
22 Where is the University College of North Wales?
23 Which town has a Theatre Royal and a Gardner Centre?
24 What is Bolton's theatre called?
25 Where is Queen of the South Football Club?
26 What are Edinburgh's two oldest universities called?
27 Which is farther east, Middlesbrough or York?
28 What is Oxford's county-class cricket ground called?
29 Where is the Royal and Ancient Golf Club?
30 On which river does Colchester stand?

Answers

UK Football (see Quiz 10)

1 Five. 2 Chester. 3 72. 4 Bournemouth. 5 Houston Astrodrome. 6 28.
7 Newcastle. 8 George Ramsay (all with Aston Villa). 9 Bradford City.
10 Darren Anderton. 11 Burnden Park. 12 Fulham (on loan). 13 Carlisle.
14 David May. 15 Brechin. 16 35. 17 Jamie Redknapp. 18 Aston Villa.
19 Clyde, Partick Thistle. 20 Reading. 21 Oxford. 22 Bill Perry. 23 Paul Gascoigne. 24 Canada v USA. 25 Barnet Alston. 26 McEwan's Lager.
27 Barrow. 28 Mark Wright. 29 Newcastle Utd. 30 Chris Nicholl (Southampton).

Quiz 13 Pot Luck 7

Answers - see page 255

LEVEL 3

1 If it's noon at GMT, what time is it in Wellington?
2 Which soap was originally going to be called "One Way Street"?
3 Who wrote *The Pit and the Pendulum*?
4 What is the only English anagram of ORGANIST?
5 Since Christianity began when was the first visit by a Pope to the Holy Land?
6 The Bahamas is made up of approximately how many islands?
7 Which character was played by Luke Perry in "Beverley Hills 90210"?
8 Who invented the balloon?
9 Charles Eric are the middle names of which England soccer keeper?
10 What was the colour of the first decimal British 1/2p stamp?
11 Who had an 80s No. 1 with "Don't Leave Me This Way"?
12 In which decade was David Attenborough born?
13 Who became Mrs Jon Bigg in 1992?
14 In which country are the Sistema del Trave caves?
15 Which secretary to Oliver North admitted shredding certain documents?
16 Which actor's wife owns a horse called Hobb's Choice?
17 Caroline and Donald own which company in "Executive Stress"?
18 What was the first British Top Ten hit for the Beach Boys?
19 Where is the Circuit de Nevers, host of the French Formula 1 Grand Prix?
20 Who did George Thomas succeed as Speaker in the Commons?
21 What was Lewis Carroll's real middle name?
22 Who was Jennifer Aniston's most famous godfather?
23 Which was the first film to be released simultaneously in cinemas and on video?
24 Which Olympic finalist won the Nobel Peace Prize in 1959?
25 On which river does Tauton stand?
26 Which cars won Le Mans consecutively from 1928 to 1930?
27 What was the name of the character killed in the shower in Psycho?
28 From which language does the word "plunder" originate?
29 The airline Gronlandsfly is based in which country?
30 In Monopoly, what do you receive when your Building Loan matures?

Answers

Pot Luck 8 (see Quiz 15)
1 William Connor. 2 "Give Me The Night". 3 1930s. 4 £200. 5 Motor racing. 6 Maori. 7 Jackie "Kid" Berg. 8 Aland. 9 It threatened the practice of archery. 10 Somerset Maugham. 11 Lamenting. 12 Brazil. 13 Malcolm X. 14 Richard Mabey. 15 Thimphu. 16 Jerry Keller. 17 Yorkshire, Leicestershire. 18 Ned and Charles. 19 "The Archers". 20 Lucien B. Smith. 21 May. 22 4,000. 23 Dijon. 24 Four. 25 Duke of Grafton. 26 Speedway. 27 Robert Maxwell. 28 Ed McBain. 29 Argentina. 30 Jaime Sommers.

Quiz 14 TV Who's Who

LEVEL 3

Answers - see page 256

1 Who was the housekeeper in "All Creatures Great and Small"?
2 Who narrated "Roobarb and Custard"?
3 Who replaced Anneka Rice on "Treasure Hunt"?
4 Which pseudonym did Ronnie Barker use when writing for "The Two Ronnies"?
5 Who sang the theme song for "Absolutely Fabulous"?
6 Which doctors presented "Where There's Life"?
7 Who was "concert chairman" at the "Wheeltappers and Shunters"?
8 Who played Princess Vicky in the drama "Edward VII"?
9 Who created the characters Mikki the Martian and Tich and Quackers?
10 Who was the first presenter of ITV's "World of Sport"?
11 Who played Shane O'Neill in TV's adaptation of "A Woman of Substance"?
12 Which job did Terry Wogan have before going into broadcasting?
13 Which TV presenter managed Dewsbury and Leeds rugby clubs?
14 Who played Mrs Bridges in "Upstairs Downstairs"?
15 Which MD of BBC Radio sacked Kenny Everett for insulting a politician's wife?
16 Which character did Timothy Spall play in "Outside Edge"?
17 Who created "Soldier Soldier"?
18 Who was the first female presenter of "New Faces"?
19 Who is the mother of the actress Gaynor Faye aka Judy Mallett in "Coronation Street"?
20 What relation, if any, are the TV news journalists Jon and Peter Snow?
21 Who was known as the "godmother of soap"?
22 Who starred with Cilla Black in the first series of "Surprise Surprise"?
23 In which country was the actress Carmen Silvera born?
24 Who wrote the first series of "Black Adder"?
25 Who succeeded Robin Day as regular presenter of "Question Time"?
26 Which sitcom star sang the theme music for the fly-on-the-wall documentary series "Starting Together"?
27 Who wrote "The Phantom Raspberry Blower of Old London Town" for "The Two Ronnies?
28 Which two MPs, unseated in 1997, were contestants on "University Challenge"?
29 Who achieved notoriety as the first person to use the F-word on British TV?
30 Which role did Robbie Coltrane play in "Tutti Frutti"?

Answers

Books (see Quiz 16)

1 Pocket books. **2** *The Common Sense Book of Baby and Child Care*. **3** Shelton's sytsem. **4** 49 (excluding covers). **5** Bentley Drummell. **6** 1884. **7** Richard Bach. **8** Galsworthy. **9** René Goscinny. **10** Enid Blyton. **11** *The Mysterious Affair at Styles*. **12** Kazuo Ishiguro. **13** Ruth Rendell. **14** Lord Peter Wimsey, Harriet Vane. **15** John Mortimer. **16** 1907. **17** Evelyn Waugh's *Decline and Fall*. **18** Queen's Bench Courtroom No. 7. **19** Alan Clark. **20** Isaac Bashevis Singer. **21** Philippa Carr, Jean Plaidy, Victoria Holt. **22** Ruth Prawer Jhabvala. **23** Endeavour. **24** Vera Brittain. **25** Elinor, Marianne. **26** *A Kestrel For a Knave*. **27** The Balkan Trilogy. **28** 56. **29** White. **30** Marilyn French.

1   What was Cassandra's real name?
2   What was the first British Top Ten hit for George Benson?
3   In which decade was David Bailey born?
4   In Monopoly how much does it cost to buy Vine Street?
5   In which sport did Tim Birkin excel early in the 20th century?
6   From which language does the word "kiwi" originate?
7   How was the East End boxer Judah Bergman better known?
8   Vardo and Lemland are in which island group?
9   Why did Edward III ban bowls?
10 Who wrote the novel *The Razor's Edge*?
11 What is the only English anagram of ALIGNMENT?
12 In which country is the city of Jaboatoa?
13 Betty Shabazz was whose widow?
14 Who wrote Food For Free about edible wild plants?
15 What is the capital of Bhutan?
16 Who had an 50s No. 1 with "Here Comes Summer"?
17 Which two counties did Dickie Bird play for?
18 Who were the two Cherryble Brothers in *Nicholas Nickleby*?
19 What is Godfrey Baseley's most durable creation?
20 Who first patented barbed wire?
21 In what month did Mrs Thatcher first become prime minister?
22 What is the approximate distance of Chicago airport from London in miles?
23 Where did the Formula 1 racing driver Alain Prost obtain his maiden triumph?
24 How many successive years did Britain win the Davis Cup in the 30s?
25 What was Augustus Henry Fitzroy's title when he was UK prime minister?
26 In which sport did Nigel Boocock excel?
27 Who was elected Labour MP for North Bucks in 1964?
28 How is Salvatore Lombino better known?
29 The international car registration RA applies to which country?
30 Which character was played by Lindsay Wagner in "The Bionic Woman"?

Pot Luck 7 (see Quiz 13)

1 12 midnight. **2** "Neighbours". **3** Edgar Allan Poe. **4** Roasting. **5** 1960s.
6 700. **7** Dylan McKay. **8** Jacques and Joseph Montgolfier. **9** Chris Woods
80. **10** Blue. **11** Communards. **12** 1920s. **13** Sally Gunnell. **14** Spain.
15 Fawn Hall. **16** Frazer Hines. **17** Oasis Publishing. **18** "I Get Around".
19 Magny Cours. **20** Selwyn Lloyd. **21** Lutwidge. **22** Telly Savalas.
23 *The Bitch*, starring Joan Collins. **24** Philip Noel Baker. **25** Tone.
26 Bentleys. **27** Marion Crane. **28** German. **29** Greenland. **30** £150.

Quiz 16 Books

LEVEL 3

1   What were the first US equivalent of Penguin paperbacks?
2   What is the title of Dr Benjamin Spock's top bestseller?
3   In which shorthand system did Samuel Pepys write his diary?
4   How many pages did a book have to have to be termed a book according to UNESCO in 1950?
5   Who marries Estella in *Great Expectations*?
6   To ten years, when was the *Oxford English Dictionary* first published?
7   Who wrote *Jonathan Livingstone Seagull*?
8   Which John won the Nobel Prize for Literature in 1932?
9   Who wrote the Asterix books?
10 Which British author has written over 700 books and has sold over 60 million copies about one particular character?
11 What was the first Agatha Christie book in Penguin paperback?
12 Who won the Booker Prize for Remains of the Day?
13 In whose novels are Myfleet, Stowerton and Cheriton Forest found?
14 In *Busman's Honeymoon*, who is on honeymoon?
15 Whose autobiography was called *Clinging to the Wreckage*?
16 To five years when did Rudyard Kipling win the Nobel Prize for Literature?
17 In which book would you find Captain Grimes, Mr Prendergast and Egdon Heath Prison?
18 In Leon Uris's *QBVII* what is QBVII?
19 Whose diaries tell of events at Saltwood and in government?
20 Who wrote the novel on which the Barbra Streisand film *Yentl* was based?
21 Which three pseudonyms did Eleanor Alice Burford Hibbert use?
22 Who wrote *Heat and Dust* later filmed by Merchant Ivory?
23 What did Colin Dexter eventually reveal to be Morse's first name?
24 Who followed up her first success with *Testament of Experience*?
25 Who are the two sisters in *Sense and Sensibility*?
26 Which novel was the film *Kes* based on?
27 How are the novels *The Great Fortune*, *The Spoilt City* and *Friends and Heroes* known collectively?
28 To five, how many novels did Georgette Heyer write?
29 Which Patrick won the Nobel Prize for Literature in 1973?
30 Who wrote *The Women's Room* in 1977?

Answers

TV Who's Who (see Quiz 14)

1 Mrs Hall. 2 Richard Briers. 3 Annabel Croft. 4 Gerald Wiley. 5 Adrian Edmondson, Julie Driscoll. 6 Miriam Stoppard, Rob Buckman. 7 Colin Crompton. 8 Felicity Kendal. 9 Ray Alan. 10 Eamonn Andrews. 11 Liam Neeson. 12 Bank clerk. 13 Eddie Waring. 14 Angela Baddeley. 15 Ian Trethowan. 16 Kevin Costello. 17 Lucy Gannon. 18 Marti Caine. 19 Kay Mellor. 20 Cousins. 21 Julia Smith. 22 Christopher Biggins. 23 Canada. 24 Rowan Atkinson, Richard Curtis. 25 Peter Sissons. 26 Su Pollard. 27 Spike Milligan. 28 Malcolm Rifkind, David Mellor. 29 Kenneth Tynan. 30 Danny McGlone.

Quiz 17 Pot Luck 9

Answers - see page 259

LEVEL 3

1 What were the names of Harold Wilson's two sons?
2 Which character was played by Julie Walters in "The Boys from the Black Stuff"?
3 The airline Air Littoral is based in which country?
4 Who had a 70s No. 1 with "Yes Sir, I Can Boogie"?
5 From which language does the word "paddy" originate?
6 Who invented artificial blood?
7 Utila in the Caribbean is part of which island group?
8 In 1968 who became the first Briton to win Olympic Gold at shooting for 44 years?
9 Whose wives include Dorothy Squires and Luisa Mattioli?
10 Who wrote *One-Upmanship*?
11 Which shipping forecast area is east of Finisterre?
12 Who played Bob Champion in "Champions"?
13 Hispy and Quickstep are types of what?
14 Which Formula 1 racing circuit has bends called Estoril, Lycée and Adelaide?
15 How old was Mae West when she died?
16 Who was the first host of "Crackerjack"?
17 What is the only English anagram of ALSATIANS?
18 What was Leslie Charteris's real name?
19 What are the odds of rolling any combination totalling nine in dice-throwing?
20 How many islands are in the Virgin group?
21 Which John won the Nobel Prize for Literature in 1962?
22 In Monopoly, what is the amount of the speeding fine?
23 Which racehorse trainer was the first to win over £1 million?
24 Which hospital ward was "The Singing Detective" in?
25 Who guided Oxford to ten successive boat race victories from 1976?
26 What was the first British Top Ten hit for the Beverley Sisters?
27 If it's noon at GMT, what time is it in Yokohama?
28 Helen Liddell entered Parliament after winning the by-election caused by which MP's death?
29 Which two jockeys' injuries brought about the setting up of the Injured Jockeys Fund in 1964?
30 Which Nazi was played by Ian Holm in *Holocaust*?

Pot Luck 10 (see Quiz 19)
1 L.S. Lowry. 2 Ancestral. 3 Ross Davidson. 4 Brooklands. 5 "Love Shack". 6 VisiCalc. 7 Pentonville. 8 Alfred Hitchcock. 9 Ian Stark. 10 Saul Bellow. 11 Chinese. 12 Mohammed Al Fayed. 13 Chance. 14 Lord Sebastian Flyte. 15 Gilbert. 16 Windmill. 17 White sari with a blue border. 18 900. 19 Cullinan II. 20 Yvon Petra. 21 Tower of London. 22 Evanglelista Torricelli. 23 The Tremoles. 24 Michael and Margaret. 25 David Steele. 26 Dining car on a train. 27 Badminton. 28 1080. 29 Ohio. 30 Willie Carson.

Quiz 18 Pop: Charts

Answers - see page 260

LEVEL 3

1   What took the Les Baxter Orchestra, Al Hibbler and Liberace into the charts?
2   Frank Infante and Chris Stein first made No. 1 in which group?
3   Which record gave the 70s hearthrob David Cassidy a mid-80s hit?
4   Who wrote the Rolling Stones' first No. 1?
5   Which Beatle made it first to No. 1 with a solo single?
6   What was Peter Sarstedt's follow up to "Where Do You Go To My Lovely?"?
7   What finally knocked Wet Wet Wet's "Love Is All Around" off No. 1?
8   Who charted with "Britannia Rag" and "Coronation Rag"?
9   What was A-Ha's first British Top Ten hit?
10 "Don't Cry For Me Argentina" was a big flop for whom after a previous No. 1 single?
11 What word links a door and a tambourine in No. 1 titles?
12 Who had a 70s hit with "Oh Babe What Would You Say"?
13 Who first charted with "Cowpuncher's Cantata"?
14 Camp Grenada provided the setting for whose hit?
15 Kevin Parrot and Michael Coleman made No. 1 under what name?
16 What was Tracey Ullman's first UK Top Ten hit?
17 Which magazine produced the first record chart?
18 On which label did George Michael have his first solo No. 1s?
19 How many hits did Russ Conway have in 1959 and 1960?
20 Eddie Reader had her first No. 1 with which group?
21 Which hit's title had the words "And That's The Truth" in brackets?
22 Who had his first UK hit in the 50s with "Young At Heart"?
23 First charting in 1971, when did Elton John have a solo No. 1?
24 How many Top Ten singles did New Kids On the Block have in 1990?
25 On what label did Oasis first make the charts?
26 Which artist has spent most weeks at No1 in a calendar year?
27 What was New Order's first UK Top Ten single?
28 What was Elvis's folow up to "It's Now Or Never"?
29 Who did Annie Lennox duet with on "Why"?
30 Who had their only UK hit with "Let Me Try Again"?

Answers

Movie Tough Guys (see Quiz 20)
1 Ringo Kid. 2 Lee Van Cleef. 3 Edward G. Robinson. 4 Gert Frobe.
5 Medicine. 6 Steve Guttenberg. 7 Harvey Keitel. 8 Richard Gere. 9 *The Blob.* 10 Max Cady. 11 Gene Hackman. 12 *Sands of Iwo Jima.* 13 Charles Bronson. 14 James Cagney. 15 Clint Eastwood. 16 *Patriot Games, Clear and Present Danger.* 17 Ronald Reagan. 18 The Austrian Oak. 19 Duke Mantee.
20 *Mean Streets.* 21 James Cameron. 22 *In the Heat of the Night.*
23 *Bananas.* 24 *Drum Beat.* 25 Britt. 26 *The Public Enemy.*
27 A pregnant man. 28 Terry Molloy. 29 Kirk Douglas. 30 *First Blood.*

1 Which artist said, "I draw like a child … entirely out of my head"?
2 What is the only English anagram of LANCASTER?
3 Which actor went from "EastEnders" to present "Daytime Live"?
4 Where was Britain's first motor-racing course, opening in 1909?
5 What was the first British Top Ten hit for the B-52s?
6 What was the name of the first spreadsheet program developed by Apple in 1979?
7 In which prison was Dr Crippen executed?
8 Who featured on the 34p - the highest-priced - of the 1985 British Film Year stamps?
9 Who won double gold for three-day eventing at the European Championships in 1991?
10 Who wrote the novel *Herzog*?
11 From which language does the word "tea" originate?
12 Who bought Fulham FC in May 1997?
13 On a Monopoly board what is between Park Lane and Liverpool Street Station?
14 Who did Anthony Andrews play in "Brideshead Revisited"?
15 Beru and Nonouti are in which island group?
16 What do the Americans mean by a pinwheel?
17 What is the dress of the order of the Missionaries of Charity founded by Mother Teresa?
18 What is the approximate distance of Rome airport from London in miles?
19 What is the diamond the Second Star of Africa also called?
20 Before Cedric Pioline who was the last Frenchman to contest a Wimbledon singles final?
21 Josef Jakobs was the last man to be hanged where?
22 Who invented the barometer?
23 Who had an 60s No. 1 with "Silence Is Golden"?
24 What were the names of James Callaghan's two children?
25 Which BBC Sports Personality of the Year shares his name with a one-time political party leader?
26 In Germany what is a *speisewagen*?
27 In which sport did Ray Stevens excel?
28 What is the sum total of the internal angles in an octagon in degrees?
29 On which river does Cincinnati stand?
30 Who was the first Scot to be champion jockey?

Pot Luck 9 (see Quiz 17)
1 Robin and Giles. 2 Angie Todd. 3 France. 4 Baccara. 5 Malay. 6 Clark and Gollan. 7 Bay Islands. 8 Bob Braithwaite. 9 Roger Moore. 10 Stephen Potter. 11 Biscay. 12 John Hurt. 13 Cabbage. 14 Magny Cours. 15 88. 16 Eamonn Andrews. 17 Assailant. 18 Leslie Boyer Yin. 19 8-1. 20 Over 50. 21 Steinbeck. 22 £15. 23 Henry Cecil. 24 Sherpa Tensing Ward. 25 Daniel Topolski. 26 "I Saw Mommy Kissing Santa Claus". 27 9 p.m. 28 John Smith (Monklands East). 29 Tim Brookshaw, Paddy Farrell. 30 Himmler.

Answers

1. Which character did John Wayne play in *Stagecoach*?
2. Who was lead villain to Clint Eastwood in *For a Few Dollars More*?
3. Who played the boxing manager in *Kid Galahad* in 1937?
4. Who played Goldfinger in 1964?
5. What did Humphrey Bogart study before entering the navy in the World War One?
6. Who was the star of the first four *Police Academy* films?
7. Which tough guy was Judas in Martin Scorsese's *The Last Temptation of Christ*?
8. Who was the violent hustler in *Looking For Mr Goodbar*?
9. Which film gave the real-life tough guy Steve McQueen his first lead role?
10. What was Robert De Niro's role in Scorsese's *Cape Fear* in 1991?
11. Who played Buck Barrow in *Bonnie and Clyde*?
12. Which film gave John Wayne his first Oscar nomination?
13. Who once said, "I look like a quarry that someone has dynamited"?
14. Which movie tough guy started out as a female impersonator?
15. Whose production company was called Malpaso?
16. What were Harrison Ford's first two films as the ex-CIA agent Jack Ryan?
17. Who played the crime boss to Lee Marvin's contract killer in *The Killers*?
18. What was Schwarzenegger's nickname after he won a record seven Mr Olympia titles?
19. Who did Bogart play in one of his first movies *The Petrified Forest*?
20. What was the first Martin Scorsese film Robert De Niro appeared in?
21. Who directed Schwarzenegger in the *Terminator* films?
22. For which movie did Rod Steiger win his first Oscar?
23. In which film was Sylvester Stallone a thug threatening Woody Allen?
24. In which 1954 film was Charles Bronson first credited as Charles Bronson?
25. Who was the tough knife-thrower James Coburn played in *The Magnificent Seven*?
26. In which 30s movie did James Cagney push half a grapefruit into Mae West's face?
27. What unusual character did Schwarzenegger play in *Junior*?
28. What was the name of Brando's character in *On The Waterfront*?
29. Whose autobiography was called *The Ragman's Son*?
30. In which film did Stallone first play Rambo?

Quiz 21 Pot Luck 11

Answers - see page 263

LEVEL 3

1　Which character was played by Nicholas Lyndhurst in "Butterflies"?
2　What was Joseph Conrad's real name?
3　What did Dr Henry Durant first carry out in Britain in the 30s?
4　Which country has a top-selling newspaper called *Esto*?
5　What is another name for the scaly anteater?
6　To a hundred, how many names were in the first British telephone directory, published 1880?
7　Which shipping forecast area is north of Lundy?
8　Who was WBA's FA Cup Final keeper of the 60s?
9　What is the only English anagram of ANTIDOTES?
10　Who had an 50s No. 1 with "I See The Moon"?
11　What was Colonel Thomas Blood disguised as when trying to steal the Crown Jewels?
12　The Caroline Islands belong to which country?
13　What did Bill Clinton call "the most powerful song I have ever heard"?
14　How many islands are in the Tristan da Cunha group?
15　Which TV series featured the Western Stagecoach Service?
16　If it's noon at GMT, what time is it in Vancouver?
17　In Monopoly, what is the fine for being drunk in charge?
18　Who invented the bicycle?
19　What is Michael Crawford's real name?
20　Which MP died a week after the 1997 General Election?
21　From which language does the word "tycoon" originate?
22　The Lugano Cup is awarded in which sport?
23　In which city was Cary Grant born?
24　What was the first British Top Ten hit for Big Country?
25　What was William Lamb's title when he was UK prime minister?
26　Which boxing champ shares his birth day and year with Glenda Jackson?
27　The airline Dragonair is based in which country?
28　Where was Britain's first road-race circuit, opening in 1933?
29　Who was the main figure in a Michael Browne painting unveiled in April 1997?
30　Which writer produced the work *Gargantua*?

Pot Luck 12 (see Quiz 23)
1 Authoress. **2** Voltaire. **3** Hugo Montenegro. **4** Blue. **5** Bristol. **6** Charles Edouard Jeanneret. **7** Sir Joseph Whitworth. **8** London. **9** The King's Singers (1997). **10** Putney. **11** 4800. **12** *La Cage Aux Folles*. **13** Avenue Matignon. **14** Silverstone. **15** Poland. **16** Frederica "Fred" Smith. **17** Sixth. **18** D.H. Lawrence. **19** Sri Lanka. **20** Two points. **21** Benjamin Franklin. **22** Dateline. **23** Captain Marryat. **24** Fiddler's Dram. **25** Alexander. **26** Punch Tavern. **27** Carrot. **28** Magyar (Hungarian). **29** Nautilus. **30** "Summer Set".

Quiz 22 World Leaders

Answers - see page 264

1   In which city was Spain's King Juan Carlos born?
2   Who followed Lloyd George as prime minister of the UK?
3   Who did Sanni Abacha overthrow in Nigeria in 1994?
4   How is Emperor Akihito known in Japan?
5   Who became president of Georgia in 1992?
6   What was the name of Mrs Ceausescu who was executed with her husband?
7   Who became King of Sweden in 1973?
8   What was the nationality of the former UN Secretary General, Boutros Boutros Ghali?
9   Who won the 1990 elections in Burma while under house arrest?
10 Who went from vice-president to president of Ghana in 1967?
11 Archibald Philip Primrose was prime minister of where?
12 Who established Bloc Quebecois in 1990 in Canada ?
13 Other than politics, what is the profession of Jean-Bertrand Aristide of Haiti?
14 Who was the first science graduate to become British prime minister?
15 What post was Chief Buthelezi given in Mandela's cabinet in 1994?
16 Which faction did Robert Mugabe head before becoming prime minister of Zimbabwe?
17 Who was Bill Clinton's first Secretary of State?
18 In 1997 who was the only monarch who had been reigning longer than Elizabeth II?
19 Which Spanish prime minister took Spain into the EC?
20 Who became leader of Italy's Forza Italia Party in 1993?
21 Al Gore was senator of which state before becoming vice-president?
22 Who became the German president in 1994?
23 Who was the next non-Italian Pope after Adrian VI in 1522?
24 Who did Lionel Jospin succeed as French prime minister in 1997?
25 Who did T.N.I. Suharto overthrow to become president in 1967?
26 Who became Helmut Kohl's deputy in 1993?
27 Who is heir to the throne of Monaco?
28 Flight Lieutenant Jerry Rawlings first took power where in 1979?
29 What is the nationality of Jacques Santer?
30 Who became Portugal's first civilian president for 60 years in 1986?

Answers

The Royals (see Quiz 24)

1 Lady Diana Spencer. **2** Princess Margaret. **3** Balmoral. **4** University Labour Club. **5** Prince and Princess Michael of Kent. **6** Fabergé. **7** Les Jolies Eaux. **8** British Lung Foundation. **9** Four. **10** George Cross. **11** The Hon. Lady Ogilvy. **12** Bryan Organ's. **13** Before her father's coffin at his funeral. **14** Princess Diana. **15** Shand. **16** Princess Diana's flatmates before her marriage. **17** 17 Bruton St, London W1. **18** George VI. **19** Architect. **20** Kanga. **21** The Duchess of Kent. **22** Prince Philip. **23** *The Heart Has Its Reasons*. **24** Wednesday. **25** Queen Sonja. **26** Prince Philip. **27** Queen Victoria. **28** Dan Maskell. **29** *War and Peace*. **30** Duchess of Kent.

Quiz 23 Pot Luck 12

LEVEL 3

1 What is the only English anagram (minus its hyphen) of SHARE-OUTS?
2 How is François Marie Arouet better known?
3 Who had a 60s No. 1 with "The Good, The Bad and The Ugly"?
4 What colour was *Monty Python's Big Red Book* cover?
5 At which city did Concorde make its first supersonic test flight?
6 What was Le Corbusier's real name?
7 Which mechanical engineer standardized screw threads?
8 Where were the first Olympics after the World War Two held?
9 Who first brought Lennon and McCartney music to the Proms?
10 In which London suburb was the TV series "Bless This House" set?
11 What is the approximate distance of Vancouver airport from London in miles?
12 Which musical contains "A Little More Mascara" and "Masculinity"?
13 On a French Monopoly board, what is the equivalent to the Strand?
14 Which Formula 1 circuit includes Maggotts Curve, Abbey Curve and Priory?
15 In which country is the city of Katowice?
16 Which character was played by Leslie Ash in "C.A.T.S. Eyes"?
17 In the Bible which commandment says, "Thou shalt not kill"?
18 Which writer was born at 8a Victoria Street, Eastwood?
19 The international car registration CL applies to which country?
20 In Scrabble, how much is a letter D worth?
21 Who invented the bifocal lens?
22 Which agency was launched by John Patterson in 1966?
23 Who wrote *Mr Midshipman Easy*?
24 Which group went on a Day Trip To Bangor?
25 Baranof and Prince of Wales are in which island group?
26 What is the 20th-century name of Fleet Street's pub, the Crown and Sugarloaf?
27 Favourite and Figaro are types of what?
28 From which language does the word "goulash" originate?
29 What was the name of the first US nuclear submarine?
30 What was the first British Top Ten hit for Mr Acker Bilk?

Quiz 24 The Royals

Answers - see page 262

1 Who was the first new royal to include her family's motto on her marital coat of arms?
2 Who said, "I have as much privacy as a goldfish in a bowl"?
3 Which royal residence did George V not visit during World War One?
4 Which club was Prince Charles not allowed to join by the master of his Cambridge college?
5 Which royals were not allowed to marry where they wished in 1978?
6 In 1907 who was commissioned to make models of Sandringham farm animals?
7 What is the name of Princess Margaret's house on Mustique?
8 Thirty per cent of the proceeds of Princess of Wales roses went to which charity at the Chelsea Flower Show?
9 How many British kings were emperors of India?
10 Which medal did Inspector Beaton receive after Princess Anne was attacked in the Mall in 1974?
11 Which title does Princess Alexander now have through her husband?
12 Whose portrait of Diana was damaged in the National Portrait Gallery in 1981?
13 When did Queen Elizabeth II last curtsey officially?
14 Who switched on the Christmas lights in Regent Street in November '81?
15 What was Camilla's surname before marrying Andrew Parker-Bowles?
16 Who were Virginia Pitman and Carolyn Pride?
17 Where was Queen Elizabeth II born?
18 Which 20th-century monarch is or was left-handed?
19 What was the Duke of Gloucester's profession before he became a duke?
20 What is the Prince of Wales's nickname for his friend Lady Tryon?
21 Sir William Worsley was the father of which royal?
22 Who said, "Constitutionally, I don't exist"?
23 What was the autobiography of the Duchess of Windsor called?
24 On what day of the week was Queen Elizabeth II born?
25 Who is the wife of King Harald of Norway?
26 Who is taller, Prince Philip or Prince Charles?
27 Which royal wrote *Our Life in the Highlands*?
28 Who taught Princess Anne to play tennis?
29 Which book did Princess Margaret choose for her desert island on "Desert Island Discs"?
30 Which royal performed with the Bach Choir at the Albert Hall?

Answers

World Leaders (see Quiz 22)
1 Rome. 2 Andrew Bonar Law. 3 General Babangida. 4 The Heisei Emperor. 5 Edvard Shevardnadze. 6 Elena. 7 Carl Gustaf XVI. 8 Egyptian. 9 Aung San Suu Kyi. 10 Omar Bongo. 11 UK. He was the Earl of Rosebery. 12 Lucien Bouchard. 13 Clergyman. 14 Margaret Thatcher. 15 Minister of the Interior. 16 ZANU - Zimbabwe African National Union. 17 Warren Christopher. 18 King Bhumipol of Thailand. 19 Felipe Gonzalez. 20 Silvio Berlusconi. 21 Tennessee. 22 Roman Herzog. 23 John Paul II. 24 Alain Juppé. 25 Achmed Sukarno. 26 Klaus Klinkel. 27 Prince Albert. 28 Ghana. 29 Luxembourgeois. 30 Mario Soares.

1 Where did Jacques Villeneuve take his first Formula 1 victory?
2 In Monopoly, how much is payed for school fees?
3 Which character was played by Cheryl Ladd in "Charlie's Angels"?
4 Which shipping forecast area is north of Rockall?
5 From which language does the word "bungalow" originate?
6 How many cricket caps did Alan Butcher - Mark's dad - win?
7 What cabinet post did Michael Heseltine resign from over the Westland affair?
8 Transavia Airlines is based in which country?
9 In which Dickens novel does Thomas Traddles appear?
10 Who had an 60s No. 1 with "Do You Mind"?
11 How old was King George III when he died?
12 Who wrote *All Quiet on the Western Front*?
13 The first Boy Scouts to be registered were based in which city?
14 If A is Alpha and B is Bravo what is N?
15 What is the American equivalent to "University Challenge"?
16 How was novelist Henri Beyle better known?
17 If it's noon at GMT, what time is it in Tehran?
18 How many islands are in the Bismarck Archipelago group?
19 What was Robin Leigh-Pemberton's job between 1983 and 1993?
20 Who invented the burglar alarm?
21 What is the only English anagram of BARGAINED?
22 What was the first British Top Ten hit for Black Sabbath?
23 Who was George Oldfield determined to catch?
24 Who created Dan Dare?
25 What does ALGOL stand for?
26 Who did Martina Navratilova beat to win her ninth Wimbledon?
27 In which churchyard was Sir Winston Churchill buried?
28 Which Mel became the Manchester City soccer boss in 1987?
29 When did Britain first occupy Hong Kong?
30 What was Colin Cowdrey born?

Pot Luck 14 (see Quiz 27)
Answers

1 W. Ritter. 2 "The Yeomen Of the Guard". 3 Versatile. 4 Boris Yeltsin.
5 "Living On The Ceiling". 6 John Stalker. 7 British Racing Drivers' Club.
8 Richmal Lambourn. 9 Sudan. 10 John McEnroe. 11 Sow. 12 Flight
Lieutenant Simon Carter. 13 Arabic. 14 Robert Louis Stevenson.
15 Thunderclap Newman. 16 Newcastle. 17 Marengo. 18 Marlborough St.
19 900. 20 1910s. 21 Jim Dale. 22 August. 23 *Gloriana*. 24 Halifax
Building Society turning into a bank. 25 Willie Whitelaw. 26 Arnold Ridley.
27 8-1. 28 4000. 29 John Braine. 30 Galapagos.

1 Who scored 11 goals for QPR in their first season in Europe?
2 Who delighted in the nickname Ambling Alp?
3 The first university boat race was contested from where to where?
4 Which brothers asked to wear England shirts while playing at Wimbledon during Euro '96?
5 Which great soccer manager was boss at Grimsby and Workington?
6 Who died during a bout with Drew Docherty in October 1995?
7 Who was Rob Andrew's first signing at Newcastle RFC?
8 Who were the only team not to score in soccer's Euro '96?
9 Who won cricket's Gillette Cup in 1970, '71 and '72?
10 Who took 5-67 on his first class debut, for Hants, in August 1996?
11 Which horse was Carson riding when he sustained serious injuries arguably hastening his retirement?
12 Who scored twice for Villa in the 50s FA Cup Final win over Manchester United?
13 Who did Steven Redgrave win Olympic Gold with in 1988?
14 Who was the first woman to be elected to the Wimbledon Championships Committee?
15 Who did Monica Seles beat to win her first Grand Slam after her attack?
16 Which soccer keeper was known as the Flying Pig?
17 What did Robbie Paul win for scoring a hat trick in the 1996 Challenge Cup Final?
18 In the 1990s who first won the World ProSnooker Championship after Stephen Hendry?
19 Mike Tyson pulled out of a fight with Buster Mathis Jnr in 1995 due to an injured what?
20 Who followed Geoff Hurst as manager of Chelsea?
21 Who coached Torvill and Dean to Olympic success?
22 Who rode Red Rum for the third Grand National triumph?
23 Who was the first footballer to marry a managing director of football?
24 Who was the manager who brought Dwight Yorke to Aston Villa?
25 Who in 1995 became the first favourite to win the Grand National for 14 years?
26 Which breaking of the law was revealed about Jack Charlton in '95?
27 Who kept goal for Spurs in the 1981 FA Cup Final?
28 Who was the first woman to ride in the Derby?
29 What were the odds on Dettori's seven-race card win in 1996?
30 Who was Manchester United manager when they were last relegated?

Answers

1 Who invented the cable car?

2 The 18p stamp - the cheapest in the 1992 set - showed which Gilbert and Sullivan opera?

3 What is the only English anagram of RELATIVES?

4 Which Russian wrote *Against the Grain*?

5 What was the first British Top Ten hit for Blancmange?

6 Which former policeman presented "Beat the Cheat"?

7 Who owns Silverstone Motor Racing Circuit?

8 What was Richmal Crompton's real name?

9 In which country is the city of Khartoum North?

10 Which Wimbledon winner was born the day Castro took over in Cuba?

11 On which river does Stafford stand?

12 Which character was played by David McCallum in "Colditz"?

13 From which language does the word "algebra" originate?

14 Whose nickname was Tusitala the Samoan for *The Storyteller*?

15 Who had a 60s No. 1 with "Something In The Air"?

16 Chris Waddle first played for England while with which club?

17 What was the name of Napoleon Bonaparte's favourite horse?

18 In Monopoly, where would a throw of seven from Pall Mall land you?

19 What is the sum total of the internal angles in a heptagon in degrees?

20 In which decade were photographs first required on British passports?

21 Which *Carry On* film actor had a hit with "Be My Girl"?

22 In which month does the oyster season open?

23 Which Benjamin Britten opera was commisioned for the Coronation of Queen Elizabeth II?

24 What made Mike Blackburn send out millions of letters in 1997?

25 Which Home Secretary talked about a "short, sharp shock"?

26 Who wrote the classic play *The Ghost Train*?

27 With two dice, what are the odds of rolling any combination totalling five?

28 What is the approximate distance of Karachi airport from London in miles?

29 Who wrote the novel *Room at the Top*?

30 Fernandina and Floreana are in which island group?

Quiz 28 TV Game Shows

LEVEL 3

1　Who asked the questions in "Ask the Family"?

2　What was the prize in the early series of "What's My Line?"?

3　Who created "Winner Takes All" and co-presented it unseen?

4　In which decade did "A Question of Sport" begin?

5　In TV's "Cluedo" where does the mystery take place?

6　Which show was a 70s forerunner of "Cluedo"?

7　Which show was based on the Spanish programme "Uno, Dos Tres"?

8　Which "Archers" character read out the scores in "Telly Addicts"?

9　Who announced the prizes in the original "Take Your Pick"?

10　What indicated you were doing well in "Blockbusters" but cancelled success in "Strike It Lucky"?

11　In 70s/80s "Sale of the Century" how much were the questions worth?

12　Which contestant on "Double Your Money" became a permanent hostess on the show?

13　Who succeeded Barry Davies as presenter of "Quiz Ball"?

14　Which sportswoman was on Emlyn Hughes's team when "A Question of Sport" celebrated its 200th edition?

15　Which quizmaster first produced "The Price Is Right" in the UK?

16　How long did you have to answer the questions in "Mastermind"?

17　Which quiz shared its name with a Beatles hit?

18　Who was the first regular female captain on "Call My Bluff"?

19　What was special about the contestants in "Bob's Your Uncle"?

20　Who was the female team captain opposing Kenny Everett in "That's Showbusiness"?

21　Which radio DJ was on the very first "Celebrity Squares"?

22　How long do the chefs have to cook a meal in "Ready Steady Cook"?

23　Who first presented "The Golden Shot"?

24　Which show was originally called "Een Van De Aacht"?

25　Which show featured Mr Babbage?

26　What was the top prize when "Double Your Money" came from Communist Moscow in 1966?

27　Under what title was "Double Your Money" revived in the 70s?

28　Who was the regular innumerate blonde on "The Golden Shot"?

29　What is the prize for the ultimate champion of the series on "Countdown"?

30　Which programme had a mechanical caged bird over the opening and closing credits?

Sport: Who's Who (see Quiz 26)

1　Stan Bowles. **2**　Primo Carnera (boxer). **3**　Hambledon Lock to Henley Bridge. **4**　Luke and Murphy Jensen. **5**　Bill Shankly. **6**　James Murray. **7**　Dean Ryan. **8**　Turkey. **9**　Lancashire. **10**　Liam Botham. **11**　Meshhed. **12**　Peter McParland. **13**　Andrew Holmes. **14**　Virginia Wade. **15**　Anke Huber. **16**　Tommy Lawrence. **17**　Lance Todd Trophy + £10,000. **18**　John Parrot. **19**　Thumb. **20**　John Neale. **21**　Betty Callaway. **22**　Tommy Stack. **23**　Paul Peschisolido. **24**　Graham Taylor. **25**　Rough Quest. **26**　Fishing without a licence. **27**　Milija Aleksic. **28**　Alex Greaves. **29**　25,095/1. **30**　Tommy Docherty.

Quiz 29 Pot Luck 15

1 In which country are the San Agustin caves?
2 What was Sir Robin Day's profession before he turned to TV?
3 From which language does the word "divan" originate?
4 Who had an 60s No. 1 with "Michael"?
5 How was the Birmingham Royal Ballet previously known?
6 What is the capital of the Canadian province Saskatchewan?
7 How many islands are in the Shetland group?
8 When did Swansea become a city?
9 In which city was Felix Mendelssohn born?
10 If it's noon at GMT, what time is it in Sydney?
11 What is the only English anagram of LACRYMOSE?
12 Alpha and Snow Cap are types of what?
13 In which city did Harold MacMillan deliver his "Wind of Change" speech?
14 John Arlott was a fan of which soccer club?
15 How is Tiziano Vecelli better known?
16 Where did Gina G finish in the 1996 Eurovision Song Contest?
17 Which Robert discovered the law of elasticity that is now known by his name?
18 On television, in which fictitious road was Shelley's flat set?
19 In which country is the city of Kigali?
20 Which character was played by Lewis Collins in "The Cuckoo Waltz"?
21 What was Daniel Defoe's real name?
22 Where was the first German Formula 1 Grand Prix staged in 1926?
23 Which England soccer captain was born in Ironbridge, Shropshire?
24 Who wrote *The Raj Quartet*?
25 How long after Jock Stein's death in 1985 was there another Wales v. Scotland game?
26 What was the first British Top Ten hit for Blondie?
27 In Monopoly, how much do you receive on 7% preference shares?
28 Who did Ramsay MacDonald follow when he first became prime minister of the UK?
29 How old was Buddy Holly when he died?
30 The airline Kyrnair is based in which country?

LEVEL 3

1 Who was the first young man to win the Junior Grand Slam?
2 Before Henman and Rusedski who were the last two Brits to be in the men's last eight together at Wimbledon?
3 Whose match had been interrupted by rain when Cliff Richard did an impromptu concert on Centre Court?
4 Where was Martina Hingis born?
5 How many times did Navratilova win the Wimbledon singles as a Czech?
6 Who holds the record for the most Wimbledon titles?
7 What was Chris Evert's second married name?
8 Who is Vera Puzejova's daughter?
9 Who won the women's singles at the 1992 Olympics?
10 Who took over sponsorship of the Virginia Slims Tournament in '79?
11 Where was the US Open played before Flushing Meadow?
12 What is Boris Becker's eldest son called?
13 What did Major Wingfield call lawn tennis when he first showed off his new game?
14 Who were known as the Three Musketeers?
15 Who was the first European to win the women's singles at Roland Garros in the 70s?
16 Who did Billie Jean Moffitt win her first women's doubles with?
17 With whom did Ann Jones win the Wimbledon mixed doubles in '69?
18 Who was the first male Brit to win a Wimbledon title after Fred Perry?
19 Where did Fred Perry die?
20 Who did Chris Evert beat to win her first Wimbledon title?
21 Who was known as the Rockhampton Rocket?
22 Who was the first Swede to win the Australian men's singles?
23 Who contested Wimbledon's longest-ever match?
24 Which tennis trophy did Hazel Hotchkiss donate?
25 Who was the first man to hold all four Grand Slam titles at once?
26 Which two countries has Hana Mandlikova played for?
27 Where were the very first US Championships held?
28 Who was the last men's singles champion at Wimbledon before it became open?
29 Who was the first person to lose in the opening round in the defence of his championship?
30 Where were the Australian Championships held in 1906 and 1912?

Pop: No. 1s (see Quiz 32)

Answers

1 Pussycat. **2** Scott McKenzie. **3** Celine Dion. **4** Seal. **5** Jane Morgan.
6 "Two Little Boys" (Rolf Harris). **7** "The Fly" (U2). **8** Tony Visconti.
9 Rotherham. **10** October. **11** Joe Dolce Music Theatre. **12** Victoria Wood.
13 "His Latest Flame". **14** 1957. **15** None. **16** "Sailor". **17** The Buggles.
18 Kriss Kristofferson. **19** "Temptation". **20** David Gates. **21** Johnny Kidd.
22 St Winifred's School Choir. **23** "Goody Two Shoes". **24** San Pedro.
25 "Vincent". **26** Aneka. **27** Mitch Miller. **28** "Oh Boy". **29** Shirley
Bassey. **30** "You Spin Me Round (Like A Record)".

1   Who had an 70s No. 1 with "Hey Girl Don't Bother Me"?
2   Which title is the Irish prime minister also known by?
3   Who wrote *The Sea-Wolf*?
4   Waitangi Day, the national day of New Zealand, is in which month?
5   Brian McClair made his soccer league debut with which club?
6   Haiti and Puerto Rico are in which island group?
7   Which character was played by Lee Majors in *The Fall Guy*?
8   In the 1990s Richard Roberts discovered what to win a Nobel prize?
9   From which language does the word "kiosk" originate?
10   What was the Hockenheimring circuit originally built to test?
11   Which cast from a TV series had a hit with "Hi-Fidelity"?
12   What do the initials JRR stand for in J.R.R. Tolkien's name?
13   In the 70s, where did Mick Burke, a cameraman, lose his life?
14   Canada was ceded to Britain by which treaty in 1763?
15   What is the approximate distance of Lima airport from London in miles?
16   What was the first British Top Ten hit for the Boomtown Rats?
17   In which country is the city of Kitchener?
18   In Monopoly how much does it cost to buy Coventry Street?
19   In ITV's "The Dustbinmen", which soccer team did Winston support?
20   Who invented canning?
21   "Um" appears how many times in the title of a Major Lance hit?
22   Who did Bolton Wanderers play in their last league game at Burnden Park?
23   Anne Hyde was the mother of which British monarch?
24   At which university did Steve Heighway get his BA degree?
25   Who was the first Russian to win the Nobel Peace Prize?
26   Who played Sergeant Major Bullimore in "The Army Game"?
27   Gerald Carr, Edward Gibson and William Pogue returned from what in 1974?
28   What is the only English anagram of SECTIONAL?
29   What was the trade of Abraham Lincoln's father?
30   What was an MP's basic pay in 1975?

Quiz 32 Pop: No. 1s

Answers - see page 270

1 Who were the first Dutch group to top the British charts?

2 Philip Blondheim had a 60s No. 1 under what name?

3 Which female spent 13 weeks on the chart before making No. 1 in February 1995?

4 Who was the uncredited vocalist of Adamski's "Killer"?

5 Who had a 50s No. 1 with "The Day The Rains Came"?

6 What was the final No. 1 of the hippy decade the 60s?

7 Which record ended Bryan Adams's 16-week record run at No. 1?

8 Who produced all the T. Rex No. 1s?

9 Where in England was the Music Factory Studios that mixed the Jive Bunny discs?

10 In which month did "Here Comes Summer" top the charts in 1959?

11 Who had a No. 1 with "Shaddap Your Face"?

12 Who was on the other side of Hale and Pace and the Stonkers' No. 1?

13 Which song was coupled with Elvis's "Little Sister"?

14 Jackie Wilson's "Reet Petite" made No. 1 in 1986, but in what year did it first chart?

15 How many instrumentals topped the charts in the 80s?

16 What was Petula Clark's first No. 1?

17 Under what name did Trevor Horn and Geoff Downes make No. 1?

18 Who wrote Lena Martell's chart-topper "One Day At A Time"?

19 What was the fourth and last No. 1 for the Everly Brothers?

20 Who wrote "Everything I Own"?

21 Who was the first artist at No. 1 to wear an eye patch?

22 Who were the last all-girl group to reach No. 1 before Eternal in 1989?

23 Which was the first No. 1 for Adam Ant as opposed to Adam and the Ants?

24 Which island is lamented in "La Isla Bonita"?

25 Which No. 1 begins, "Starry, starry night"?

26 Under what name did Mary Sandeman reach No. 1?

27 Who produced No. 1s for Guy Mitchell, Frankie Lane and Johnnie Ray?

28 What was Mud's last No. 1?

29 Who had a 50s No. 1 with "As I Love You"?

30 What was the first Stock, Aitken and Waterman-produced No. 1?

1   What was the first solo British Top Ten hit for Cher?
2   If it's noon at GMT, what time is it in Tangier?
3   In which school was "Whack-O" set?
4   What was George Eliot's real name?
5   Which shipping forecast area is west of forecast area Plymouth?
6   What plants were featured on a set of 1993 British stamps?
7   On which river does Calcutta stand?
8   How many islands are in the Bissagos group?
9   Who was widowed by the death of Stefano Casiraghi in 1990?
10 Who had a 70s No. 1 with "You To Me Are Everything"?
11 The airline Flitestar is based in which country?
12 In the 1850s what did the discovery by Edward Hargreaves lead to?
13 Who won the Formula 1 German Grand Prix in three successive years, 1988/89/90?
14 In Monopoly, how much do you collect following a bank error?
15 What is the only English anagram of CONTINUED?
16 Matilda Alice Victoria Wood was known for what type of entertainment?
17 Which Road in Drumcree was the centre of unrest in July 1997?
18 Who did Danniella Westbrook play in "Frank Stubbs Promotes"?
19 Who was the youngest MP after the 1997 general election?
20 In Bob Dylan's view what "don't work 'cos the vandals took the handles"?
21 Where did the 1997 Tour de France start?
22 Autumn Jackson claimed to be whose illegitimate daughter?
23 Which valley gives the setting for the TV soap "A Country Practice"?
24 In which month was John Lennon murdered?
25 Which beaten finalist said, "Pete [Sampras] doesn't let you breathe"?
26 Who invented the cannon?
27 The writer John Buchan became Governor General of where?
28 From which language does the word "floe" originate?
29 How was the actress Beatrice Stella Tanner better known?
30 Mary Shelley's novel was called *Frankenstein; or the...* what?

Quiz 34 Euro Tour

Answers - see page 276

LEVEL 3

1 The Croatian currency kuna is divided into 100 what?
2 On which river does Berlin stand?
3 Which three major Spanish international airports begin with "V"?
4 In which city is Interpol's HQ?
5 Where was the World Council of Churches established in 1948?
6 Which country's official name is Republika e Shqipërisë?
7 What is Europe's lowest point below sea level?
8 Where is the UN's Food and Agriculture agency - FAO - based?
9 Who are the two heads of state of Andorra?
10 What is the capital of Saxony?
11 Which country has Letzeburgish as its most widely used language?
12 What is Europe's highest waterfall called?
13 Where is the European Investment Bank?
14 Where is the petroleum company ENI based?
15 What are the only armed forces in Monaco?
16 The Aland Islands belong to which country?
17 Where is the HQ of the World Meteorological Organization?
18 The Glomma is one of the principal rivers of which country?
19 Which three French regions begin with A?
20 Which country's highest point is Rysys?
21 Which has the greater area, Iceland or Ireland?
22 What is San Marino's second-largest town?
23 Where is Ulemiste Airport?
24 Which is farther north, Moscow or Copenhagen?
25 Where was the UN peacekeeping mission UNPROFOR in force?
26 What is Belgium's highest point?
27 On which river does Amsterdam stand?
28 Other than Denmark where is Danish currency used?
29 Where is Italy's principal stock exchange?
30 Gozo and Comino are to the north west of which island?

Movies: Who's Who? (see Quiz 36)

Answers

1 Louis Malle. 2 Simone Signoret. 3 Anne Fine. 4 Kiefer Sutherland.
5 Tilda Swinton. 6 Patrick Swayze, Lisa Niemi. 7 Catherine Deneuve.
8 Gerard Depardieu. 9 Bo Derek's. 10 Divine. 11 Whoopi Goldberg.
12 Michael Gough. 13 Richard E. Grant. 14 Melanie Griffith. 15 Bernard
Herrmann. 16 Charlton Heston. 17 Glenn Close. 18 John Malkovitch.
19 Steve Martin. 20 Melina Mercouri. 21 Liza Minnelli. 22 Carmen
Miranda. 23 Val Kilmer. 24 Joanne Woodward. 25 Michael Douglas.
26 Pee-Wee Herman. 27 Henry Mancini. 28 Joanne Whalley-Kilmer.
29 Natalie Wood. 30 Dr Kellogg.

Quiz 35 Pot Luck 18

Answers - see page 273

LEVEL 3

1   Which character was played by Julie Walters in "GBH"?
2   Which literary figure was born at Somersby rectory in Lincolnshire?
3   On a Monopoly board what is between Marylebone Station and Community Chest?
4   At which circuit did Damon Hill achieve his first GP victory in 1993?
5   Who was massacred on Valentine's Day in 1779 at Kealakekua Bay?
6   Which Dickens novel was set in Cloisterham?
7   What is John Cleese's middle name?
8   Who had a 70s No. 1 with "Son Of My Father"?
9   Who said William Hague had "no ideas, no experience and no hope"?
10 In the 1984 charts, who felt like Buddy Holly?
11 What is the only English anagram of MADDENING?
12 Amrum and Nordstrand are in which island group?
13 What was William Henry Cavendish's title when he was UK prime minister?
14 What is the sum total of the internal angles in a hexagon in degrees?
15 In which county was Southfork Ranch in "Dallas"?
16 Which writer used the assumed name Peter Goldsmith?
17 Who protected her nursery school class from a machete wielding attacker in 1996?
18 Philippa Roberts was a world champion in which sport?
19 From which language does the word "gauntlet" originate?
20 Who wrote the book *Greenmantle*?
21 What was the first British Top Ten hit for Chicago?
22 Who designed Queen Elizabeth II's coronation gown?
23 The international car registration ET applies to which country?
24 Tokyo Slicer and Pepita are types of what?
25 Who founded the Creation record label?
26 In what decade did Malta become independent after British rule?
27 Who did the US *Entertainment Weekly* magazine's Jim Mullen say was "the only known antidote to 'Baywatch'"?
28 Which soccer club did the ex-PM Harold Wilson support?
29 Who was the first black person on "The Black and White Minstrel Show"?
30 What is the approximate distance of Manila airport from London in miles?

Pot Luck 17 (see Quiz 33)

Answers

1 "All I Really Want To Do". 2 12 noon. 3 Chislebury. 4 Mary Ann Evans.
5 Sole. 6 Orchids. 7 Hooghy. 8 15. 9 Princess Caroline of Monaco.
10 The Real Thing. 11 South Africa. 12 Australian Gold Rush. 13 Ayrton
Senna. 14 £200. 15 Unnoticed. 16 Music hall (Marie Lloyd). 17 Garvaghy.
18 Dawn Dillon. 19 Christopher Leslie. 20 The pump. 21 Rouen. 22 Bill
Cosby. 23 Wandin Valley. 24 December. 25 Cedric Pioline. 26 Archimedes.
27 Canada. 28 Norse. 29 Mrs Patrick Campbell. 30 *Modern Prometheus*.

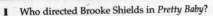
1 Who directed Brooke Shields in *Pretty Baby*?

2 Who was born in Germany as Simone Kaminker?

3 Who wrote the book that *Interview with the Vampire* was based on?

4 Whose first screen role was in *Max Dugan Returns* with his father?

5 Who played Queen Isabella in Derek Jarman's *Edward II*?

6 Which husband-and-wife team starred in *Steel Dawn* in 1987?

7 Who earned her first Oscar nomination in 1992 for *Indochine*?

8 Whose film US debut was opposite Andie MacDowell in *Green Card*?

9 David Letterman once introduced a plank of wood as whose acting coach?

10 How was Harris Glenn Milstead better known?

11 Who was the voice of Shenzi in *The Lion King*?

12 Who played Alfred in the 1989, 1992 and 1995 *Batman* films?

13 Who played the harrassed executive in *How to Get Ahead in Advertising*?

14 Which 18-year-old divorcee made her screen debut in *Night Moves*?

15 Who died the night after conducting his score for *Taxi Driver* in '75?

16 Whose diary, *The Actor's Life* was published in 1978?

17 Andie MacDowell starred in the Tarzan film *Greystoke*, but who was later asked to dub her voice?

18 Who played the Vicomte de Valmont in *Dangerous Liaisons*?

19 Whose first film role saw him enacting "Maxwell's Silver Hammer" in the *Sgt Pepper* movie?

20 Which actress and political activist was married to the director Jules Dassin?

21 Whose movie debut was in a film starring her mother, *In the Good Old Summertime*, in 1949?

22 Who died of a heart attack after a dance routine on Jimmy Durante's TV show?

23 Who played Elvis's spirit in *True Romance*?

24 Who narrated Martin Scorsese's *The Age of Innocence*?

25 Who appeared in and co-produced *The China Syndrome*?

26 Who played the Penguin's father in *Batman Returns*?

27 Who published his life story, *Did They Mention the Music?* in 1989?

28 Who has played Christine Keeler on film and Vivien Leigh on TV?

29 Who was the little girl who did not believe in Santa Claus in the 1947 film *Miracle on 34th Street*?

30 Who was the hero of *The Road to Welville*, played by Anthony Hopkins?

Euro Tour (see Quiz 34)

1 Para. 2 Spree. 3 Valencia, Vigo, Vitoria. 4 Lyon. 5 Amsterdam.
6 Albania. 7 Caspian Sea. 8 Rome. 9 President of France, Spanish Bishop of Urgel. 10 Dresden. 11 Luxembourg. 12 Ormeli. 13 Luxembourg City.
14 Italy. 15 Palace guard. 16 Finland. 17 Geneva. 18 Norway.
19 Alsace, Aquitaine, Auvergne. 20 Poland. 21 Iceland. 22 Serraville.
23 Tallinn, Estonia. 24 Moscow. 25 Bosnia-Herzegovina and Macedonia.
26 Mount Botrange. 27 Amstel. 28 Greenland and the Faeroe Islands.
29 Milan. 30 Malta.

1. What was the first British Top Ten Hit for Clannad?
2. What was Richard Gordon's real name?
3. What are the odds of rolling double six in dice-throwing?
4. How many islands are in the Seychelles group?
5. Who invented air conditioning for cars?
6. Which Radio 2 presenter's first novel was called *Charlotte's Friends*?
7. What is the only English anagram of DIAMETRIC?
8. What was the title of the "Coronation Street" creator Tony Warren's autobiography?
9. Which rock star had been a grave digger and a Brentford footballer?
10. In which country is the city of La Paz?
11. Who wrote the novel *Saturday Night and Sunday Morning*?
12. Liverpool signed Ian St John from which club?
13. Which Kirsty MacColl record did Gordon Brown choose on "Desert Island Discs"?
14. Which 19th-century trainer won the St Leger 16 times?
15. Who had the first British No. 1 with a song titled "Tears On My Pillow"?
16. Which song did Aled Jones forget the words of during a Royal Variety Show?
17. Which character was played by Tony Adams in "General Hospital"?
18. From which language does the word "tattoo" originate?
19. Who won the 1989 Hungaroring Formula 1 Grand Prix, giving Ferrari their only success at the track?
20. If it's noon at GMT, what time is it in Cape Town?
21. How much is the doctor's fee in Monopoly?
22. Which British newspaper was founded in 1843?
23. The Rowe sisters were world champions in which sport?
24. What was co-founded by Denise O'Donoghue in 1985?
25. What was Sir Allan Green, then Director of Public Prosecutions, cautioned for in 1992 ?
26. What do the initials AJ stand for in A.J. Cronin's name?
27. In which century was Nostradamus born?
28. What was the codename for the 1941 German plan to invade the Soviet Union?
29. The airline NFD is based in which country?
30. Who was given a mess of pottage in return for his birthright in the Book of Genesis?

Pot Luck 20 (see Quiz 39)

Answers

1 Byron. 2 Hedonists. 3 Spa-Francorchamps. 4 "Manimal". 5 Carrickfergus Castle. 6 December. 7 Psephologist. 8 Mexico. 9 Franz Kafka. 10 Snap. 11 George Best. 12 *The Times*. 13 Andrew. 14 Guy Lofthouse. 15 Rumen. 16 25th October. 17 Frankie Laine. 18 St. Ogg's. 19 Latin. 20 Lesser Antilles. 21 Rosie Barnes. 22 Frederick W Lanchester. 23 Chesterfield. 24 Sir Adrian Boult. 25 6,000. 26 "The Little Shoemaker". 27 Freddie Starr. 28 Delaware. 29 Pineapple Face. 30 Boulevard de La Villette.

Quiz 38 TV Gold

Answers - see page 280

LEVEL 3

1 What was Billy Cotton's theme tune?
2 In the Street what were Ken Barlow's parents called?
3 Who was the leader of the Daleks?
4 Who had his own series "Do It Yourself" in 1957?
5 Which adventurer battled against "The Face"?
6 Which future TV prime minister was one of Robin Hood's Merry Men?
7 Who first presented "Sunday Night at the London Palladium"?
8 Which programme replaced "Tonight"?
9 "Watchdog" was originally part of which programme?
10 Who succeeded Robert Wilson as host of "The White Heather Club"?
11 Who owned the corner shop in "Coronation Street" until 1974?
12 Which role did Gabrielle Drake play in "The Brothers"?
13 Who played Governor Faye Bowell in "Within These Walls"?
14 What was the name of the pub in "Albion Market"?
15 Who succeeded Keith Fordyce as presenter of "Thank Your Lucky Stars"?
16 Which star of "Jason King" was born Cyril Louis Goldbert?
17 Which role did Jane Wyman play in "Falcon Crest"?
18 Who were the first two teams on "University Challenge"?
19 Which three ports featured in "Triangle"?
20 Who was the host on "Stars and Garters"?
21 Who was the first Sports Personality of the Year in 1954?
22 In "Coronation Street" who was Linda Cheveski's mother?
23 Who were the first presenters of "Top Gear"?
24 Who played Dr Richard Moone in "Emergency Ward 10"?
25 Which arts programme did "The South Bank Show" replace?
26 Who played Emma Callon in "The Onedin Line"?
27 What was the first series to feature John Wilder and Scott Furlong?
28 Which bandleader introduced "Television Dancing Club"?
29 Who created "Come Dancing"?
30 Who was the original choreographer of Pan's People?

Answers

Sporting Speed Stars (see Quiz 40)
1 Jean-Pierre Jabouille. 2 Gay Lord. 3 Jesse Owens. 4 1926. 5 100 metre sprint. 6 Bruce McLaren. 7 Joyce Smith. 8 Nelson Piquet. 9 Ron Hutchinson (one win). 10 Lammtarra. 11 Roller skating. 12 Hungary. 13 Drum Taps. 14 Stephen Roche. 15 Heinz-Harald Frentzen. 16 Scobie Breasley. 17 Alan Morton. 18 Nelson Piquet. 19 Cecil Sandford. 20 Rallying. 21 Johnny Herbert. 22 Paul Seaton. 23 Sherry's Prince. 24 9 for 57 (v. SA, Oval 1994). 25 Mill Reef. 26 Carlos Pace. 27 John Surtees. 28 Leroy Burrell. 29 1,000 Guineas. 30 Eddie Irvine.

Quiz 39 Pot Luck 20

Answers - see page 277

LEVEL 3

1   What was James Dean's middle name?
2   What is the only English anagram of DISHONEST?
3   Where is the Formula 1 motor racing circuit in Belgium?
4   What series saw Simon MacCorkindale changing into animals?
5   The 80s British castle stamps showed Caernarfon, Edinburgh, Windsor and where?
6   In which month in 1960 was "Coronation Street" first screened?
7   What word is given to someone who studies elections and voting?
8   In which country is the city of Leon?
9   Who wrote the book *The Castle*?
10 Who had a 90s No. 1 with "The Power"?
11 Who owned the nightclubs Blinkers and Slack Alice?
12 Which was the first paper to publish a daily weather chart?
13 Which name comes from the Greek and means manly?
14 Which character was played by Keith Barron in "The Good Guys"?
15 What is the first stomach of a cow called?
16 When is St Crispin's Day
17 Under what name did Frank Paul Lo Vecchio become a singing star?
18 What was the name of the Cathedral in "All Gas and Gaiters"?
19 From which language does the word "premium" originate?
20 Leeward and Windward are in which island group?
21 Who was the only female Social Democrat MP when the party was wound up?
22 Who invented car disc brakes?
23 Morris, Dyche and Hewitt were FA Cup semi-final scorers for whom?
24 Who founded the BBC Symphony Orchestra in 1930?
25 What is the approximate distance of Hong Kong airport from London in miles?
26 What was the first British Top Ten hit for Petula Clark?
27 What is Freddie Starr's real name?
28 On which river does Philadelphia stand?
29 What nickname was given to the dictator President Noriega?
30 On a French Monopoly board, what is the equivalent to Pall Mall?

Answers

Pot Luck 19 (see Quiz 37)

1 "Theme from *Harry's Game*". **2** Gordon Ostlere. **3** 35-1. **4** 115. **5** J. Wilkinson. **6** Sarah Kennedy. **7** Matricide. **8** *I was Ena Sharples' Father*. **9** Rod Stewart. **10** Bolivia. **11** Alan Sillitoe. **12** Motherwell. **13** "Days". **14** John Scott. **15** Johnny Nash. **16** "Memory". **17** Dr Neville Bywaters. **18** Polynesian. **19** Nigel Mansell. **20** 2 p.m. **21** £50. **22** *News Of the World*. **23** Table tennis. **24** Hat Trick Productions. **25** Kerb crawling. **26** Archibald Joseph. **27** 16th. **28** Operation Barbarossa. **29** Germany. **30** Esau.

Quiz 40 Sporting Speed Stars

1 Which Formula 1 racing driver secured Renault their first victory at Dijon in 1979?

2 What was the name of Gordon Richards's first winning horse?

3 Which great athlete died at Tuscon, Arizona, in 1980?

4 In which year did Brooklands stage its first Formula1 Grand Prix?

5 Armin Harry and Harry Jerome set world records in what?

6 Who was driving for McLaren when they won their first Fomula 1 race?

7 Which UK woman won the first two London Marathons?

8 Who won the first Formula 1 Grand Prix at Hungaroring in 1986, 38 seconds in front of Senna?

9 Who won the St Leger from 1967 to 1972 appart from Lester Piggott?

10 In 1995 on which horse did Walter Swinburn set a Derby record time?

11 Chloe Ronaldson was a speed star of the 60s, 70s and 80s at what?

12 At which 1992 race did Nigel Mansell secure enough points to win the Formula 1 World Championship?

13 Frankie Dettori won the Ascot Gold Cup in 1992 and 1993 on which horse?

14 Who was the first Irishmam to win the Tour de France?

15 Who partnered Jacques Villeneuve at the Williams team in 1997?

16 Who won the Derby on the unseasonably named Santa Claus?

17 Which Rangers speedy left winger made goals for Gallagher and James in the 1920s?

18 Who won the first Formula 1 world championship San Marino Grand Prix in 1981?

19 Who was the first British motorcycle rider to be world 125cc champ?

20 What was the sport of Stirling Moss's sister Pat?

21 Who, surprisingly, won the 1995 Formula 1 British Grand Prix at Silverstone?

22 Who was the first UK man to be European water sking champ?

23 Which greyhound first won a hat trick of Grand National races?

24 What is Devon Malcolm's best return in a Test innings?

25 In the 70s, which horse gave Geoff Lewis his only Derby triumph?

26 Who gave his name to the Brazilian Formula 1 Grand Prix circuit?

27 Who was the first man to have been world champ on two wheels as well as four?

28 Who was the first person to officially run 100 metres in 9.9 seconds?

29 Which of the five Classics has Lester Piggott won least times?

30 Who partnered Michael Schumacher at Ferrari in 1997?

1   Which character was played by Susan Tully in "Grange Hill"?
2   Remus and Sprite are types of what?
3   What is a paronomasia?
4   Who had an 70s No. 1 with "So You Win Again"?
5   If it's noon at GMT, what time is it in Ho Chi Minh City?
6   In whose fictitious fashion workshop was "The Rag Trade" set?
7   How much is received in Monopoly from the sale of stock?
8   Who invented the carpet sweeper?
9   Which UK paper size is 52 x 74 mm?
10 Which shipping forecast area is north of Malin?
11 What was O. Henry's real name?
12 What did John Mason Neale write?
13 Roger Palmer is all-time top league scorer for which soccer club?
14 What was founded in 1844 by George Williams?
15 Achluophobia is the fear of what?
16 Who was the first woman to win the tennis French Open two years running on more than one occassion?
17 What is the only English anagram of FOUNDLING?
18 What was the name of the first custom-built oil tanker?
19 What was the first British Top Ten hit for Russ Conway?
20 From which US state would a Nutmegger come from?
21 The airline Norontair is based in which country?
22 Who wrote *The Adventures of Peregrine Pickle*?
23 Which South African played in Ireland's first-ever victory over a county cricket side?
24 The Indy car racer Bobby Unser was born on the same day as which fashion designer?
25 What was Edward George Stanley's title when he was UK prime minister?
26 What is Joan Collins's middle name?
27 In which country is the city of Medellin?
28 Which soap had a building with three white feathers as its logo?
29 From which language does the word "robot" originate?
30 How many islands are in the Cape Verde group?

Pot Luck 22 (see Quiz 43)
1 Coventry Street. **2** 540. **3** "Chain Gang". **4** "Pot Black". **5** James Wight.
6 Eskimo. **7** Cycling. **8** Citroën. **9** Finland. **10** Anthony Burgess.
11 Surtees. **12** The Delrons. **13** Alabama. **14** Cartoonist Vicky (Victor Weisz). **15** Metal strips were added. **16** Names used by crossword compilers.
17 Wonder Woman. **18** Argentina. **19** Cyborg. **20** Fiji. **21** John W. Hyatt.
22 15th. **23** 3,200. **24** Mountaineer (died on Everest). **25** Robin Beck.
26 Gradients. **27** Jim Clark. **28** Piltdown Man. **29** Perón. **30** Austria.

Quiz 42 Pop: 60s

Answers - see page 284

1   Which one-hit wonders sang "Gimme Gimme Good Lovin'"?
2   What was the first No. 1 single on the Apple label?
3   Which hit came from James Garner's film *A Man Could Get Killed*?
4   Which group backed Mike Berry?
5   Who had a hit with "Gin House Blues"?
6   Which label did the Bee Gees record on in the 60s?
7   What's the only 60s No. 1 to mention a soft fruit in the title?
8   Denny Doherty and Michelle Gillam were part of which group?
9   Who co-wrote "Sugar Sugar" with Jeff Barry?
10 Who sang about "Ramona", "Marie" and "Marta"?
11 Under what name did John Henry Deighton have his only No. 1?
12 Tony Hatch was an in-house producer for which company?
13 "A Whiter Shade of Pale" was released on which label?
14 Which No. 1 had the backing vocals "ook-a-chunka, ook-a-chunka"?
15 What was on the other side of Roy Orbison's "Blue Bayou"?
16 Freddie Heath and the Nutters became who for a 1960 No. 1?
17 What was the Stones' last No. 1 of the 60s (and 70s, 80s and 90s!)?
18 What was the Beatles' next album after *A Hard Day's Night*?
19 What was the number of the flight on which Ebony Eyes was killed?
20 What were the real surnames of the one-hit wonders Zager and Evans?
21 What was Billy J. Kramer's last chart success of the 60s?
22 What was Sinatra's follow-up to "Strangers in the Night"?
23 Clem Curtis was lead vocalist with which chart-topping group?
24 Who produced the Kinks' No. 1 hits?
25 Which group were first to get a cover of a Beatles album track to No. 1?
26 Who wrote the hippy anthem "San Francisco"?
27 Which No. 1 mentioned "a friend of Sacha Distel"?
28 What was Elvis's last hit of the 60s?
29 Who wrote "MacArthur Park"?
30 Who produced Cilla's No. 1 hits?

Food & Drink (see Quiz 44)

1 Lettuce. 2 Calves' stomachs. 3 Auvergne. 4 Buffalo milk. 5 Thiamin.
6 Ram's horn. 7 Chicken Marengo. 8 Pine nuts. 9 Parmigiano-Reggiano.
10 Wormwood. 11 Tomato purée. 12 In foil or paper. 13 USA. 14 A type of cider. 15 Angel hair. 16 Still water. 17 Japan. 18 President Thomas Jefferson. 19 Preservative. 20 Moulin Rouge. 21 Eggs. 22 Perrier water.
23 Wimpy. 24 Chopsticks. 25 Whey. 26 Haagen-Dazs ice cream.
27 Two legs and saddle. 28 Hass. 29 Bows - means butterflies. 30 Cake.

Answers

Quiz 43 Pot Luck 22

Answers - see page 281

1   In Monopoly, where would a double four from Vine Street land you?
2   What is the sum total of the internal angles in a pentagon in degrees?
3   What was the first British Top Ten hit for Sam Cooke?
4   Which sports programme had a theme tune called "Ivory Rag"?
5   What was James Herriot's real name?
6   From which language does the word "kayak" originate?
7   Eileen Sheridan was a record-breaker at which sport?
8   Which car manufacturer made the first front-wheel-drive vehicle?
9   The international car registration SF applies to which country?
10 Who wrote the novel *Time for a Tiger*?
11 Which John was BBC Sports Personality of the Year in 1959?
12 Who sang with Reparata on "Captain Of Your Ship"?
13 Which US state is known as the Camellia State?
14 Who first dubbed Harold Macmillan "Supermac"?
15 What happened to Bank of England £1 notes in 1940?
16 Who or what are Chifonie, Orlando and Paul?
17 What was the other name for Princess Diana of Paradise Island?
18 In which country is the city of Mendoza?
19 The TV series "Six Million Dollar Man" was based on which book?
20 Viti Levu and Vanua Levu are in which island group?
21 Who invented celluloid?
22 In which century was Martin Luther born?
23 What is the approximate distance of Montreal airport from London in miles?
24 What was the profession of Malcolm Duff, who died in April 1997?
25 Who had an 80s No. 1 with "First Time"?
26 What is the only English anagram of ASTRINGED?
27 Who won the Belgian Formula 1 Grand Prix each year from 1962 to 1965?
28 Charles Dawson was involved in which discovery?
29 Which president gave backing to the Argentine Formula 1 Grand Prix circuit which opened in 1952?
30 In which country are the Schwersystem caves?

Pot Luck 21 (see Quiz 41)

1 Suzanne Ross. **2** French Bean. **3** A play upon words. **4** Hot Chocolate.
5 7 p.m. **6** Fenner. **7** £50. **8** Melville Bissell. **9** A8. **10** Hebrides.
11 William Sydney Porter. **12** Hymns. **13** Oldham Athletic. **14** Y.M.C.A.
15 Darkness or the night. **16** Chris Evert (Lloyd). **17** Unfolding.
18 Gluckauf. **19** "The Party Pops". **20** Connecticut. **21** Canada. **22**
Tobias Smollett. **23** Hansie Cronje. **24** Gloria Vanderbilt. **25** Earl Of Derby.
26 Henrietta. **27** Colombia. **28** "Crossroads". **29** Czech. **30** 10.

Quiz 44 Food & Drink

LEVEL 3

Answers - see page 282

1 A batavia is a variety of what?
2 From where is rennet normally obtained?
3 Which part of France does Cantal cheese come from?
4 What was mozzarella cheese originally made from?
5 What is the chemical name of vitamin B1?
6 A rhyton was a drinking vessel in the shape of what?
7 Which chicken dish was named after a Napoleonic battle of June 1800?
8 What sort of nuts are used to make a pesto sauce?
9 What does authentic Parmesan cheese have stamped on its rind?
10 The leaves of which plant are the main ingredient of absinthe?
11 What do you add to a white sauce to make an aurore sauce?
12 How do you cook food *en papillote*?
13 Where is the home of the Anheuser-Busch Inc. brewery?
14 What is Ameleon?
15 What does the name of the pasta *capelli d'angelo* mean?
16 What sort of drink is Volvic?
17 Where is the Kirin Brewery based?
18 Who had signed the wine bottle sold for £105,000 at Christie's in 1985?
19 What are the ingredients with E numbers 200-29 used for in foods?
20 In which restaurant did Escoffier begin his career?
21 What is the main ingredient of a piperade?
22 Which drink is Les Bouillens famous for?
23 Which fast-food chain opened its first UK outlet in London in 1954?
24 What do the Chinese call "lively fellows"?
25 What is ricotta cheese made from?
26 What was Reuben Mattus's most famous creation of 1961?
27 What does a baron of lamb consist of?
28 Which type of avocado has a knobbly skin?
29 What shape is farfalle pasta?
30 What is a *kugelhopf*?

Answers

Pop: 60s (see Quiz 42)

1 Crazy Elephant. **2** "Hey Jude". **3** "Strangers In the Night". **4** The Outlaws. **5** Amen Corner. **6** Polydor. **7** "Blackberry Way". **8** Mamas and the Papas. **9** Andy Kim. **10** The Bachelors. **11** Chris Farlowe. **12** Pye. **13** Deram. **14** "Running Bear" (Johny Preston). **15** "Mean Woman Blues". **16** Johnny Kidd and The Pirates. **17** "Honky Tonk Women". **18** *Beatles For Sale*. **19** 1203. **20** Zager and Evans. **21** "Trains and Boats and Planes". **22** "Summer Wind". **23** The Foundations. **24** Shel Talmy. **25** The Overlanders ("Michelle"). **26** John Phillips. **27** "Where Do You Go To, My Lovely". **28** "Suspicious Minds". **29** Jim Webb. **30** George Martin.

Quiz 45 Pot Luck 23

Answers - see page 287

1 Under what name did William White open the door to stardom?
2 In Monopoly, how much do you inherit in Community Chest?
3 Which British TV personality was Australia's first female newsreader?
4 Who was Damon Hill's teammate with the 1997 Formula 1 Arrows Team?
5 Who played Chingachgook in the old TV series "Hawkeye and the Last of the Mohicans"?
6 Who had an 80s No. 1 with "Seven Tears"?
7 How did Ivan Owen's voice become widely heard on TV?
8 Who invented Portland cement?
9 Where in England was Mystic Meg born?
10 Androphobia is the fear of what?
11 In which country is the city of Mogadishu?
12 What is the only English anagram of SIGNATORY?
13 Which character was played by David McCallum in "The Invisible Man"?
14 If A is Alpha and B is Bravo what is P?
15 How was Mikhail Khristodoulou Mouskos better known?
16 Who wrote *Corridors of Power*?
17 Who was the voice of Buzby in the BT adverts?
18 Who was Nigel Mansell's teammate in the year he won the Formula 1 World Championship?
19 How many islands are in the Scilly group?
20 On which river does Kilmarnock stand?
21 The adjective hircine refers to which creatures?
22 Who replaced Aldershot in the Football League?
23 What is the capital of the US State of Kansas?
24 What was the name of the dog in the TV series "Hart to Hart"?
25 Who was painted by both Antony Williams and Susan Ryder?
26 If it's noon at GMT, what time is it in Panama City?
27 What was the first British Top Ten hit for Rita Coolidge?
28 In which Dickens novel does Dolly Varden appear?
29 What was Harry Lauder's real name?
30 From which language does the word "lemming" originate?

Pot Luck 24 (see Quiz 47)

1 4,200. 2 Inferiors. 3 Charles Blondin (Tightrope walker). 4 11-1. 5 Andy Williams. 6 Rolihlahla. 7 Gliding. 8 New Hampshire. 9 Geneva. 10 Leek. 11 Wilfred Owen. 12 Queen Elizabeth II & Queen Victoria. 13 Azores. 14 Wore a leg iron. 15 Stirling Moss. 16 Billy Fisher (Billy Liar). 17 Arabic. 18 Osnabruck (Hanover). 19 £320. 20 Connie Booth. 21 Original FA Cup entrants. 22 Barry Bucknell. 23 Insomnia. 24 Liberia. 25 "One Day I'll Fly Away". 26 Issey Miyake. 27 Willie Carson. 28 Storting. 29 St Swithin's. 30 Marble.

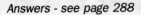

Quiz 46 History: Turning Points

LEVEL 3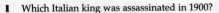

Answers - see page 288

1 Which Italian king was assassinated in 1900?
2 In 1903 Panama was seceded from which country?
3 What was nationalized first in Britain, the railway or coal industry?
4 Where did the 1929 Hunger March to London begin?
5 The Chaco War broke out in 1928 between which two countries?
6 Which US Acts of the 1930s prevented involvement in non-American wars?
7 Who annexed Bosnia and Herzegovina in 1908?
8 Who first reached the North Pole in 1909?
9 Who was emperor of Japan during World War One?
10 What did the 1948 Marshall Plan provide?
11 In World War One who made up the Triple Entente?
12 What did the British Citizenship Act of 1948 guarantee?
13 Where in Europe did women gain the vote in 1971?
14 What did the Balfour Declaration of 1917 support?
15 How many independent republics was the USSR divided into in 1991?
16 Who clashed at the Battle of Midway Island in 1942?
17 Which dynasty was overthrown in China in 1912?
18 Who established a Nationalist Chinese Government in 1923?
19 Who left the Commonwealth in 1949?
20 Who was deposed from the Spanish throne in 1931?
21 In World War One how was the third battle of Ypres also known?
22 Where did a military coup bring about the first Marxist state in Africa?
23 Who seized power in Iran in 1921?
24 Where was there a war against Portuguese rulers from 1962-74?
25 In which country was the Mau Mau uprising?
26 In which war was the Battle of Ebro River?
27 Who was head of the Turkish republic formed in 1923?
28 Immediately after which war was the PLO formed?
29 Whose murder took place at Birla House?
30 Contrary to tradition, whose presence was not required at the birth of Prince Charles?

TV: Sitcoms (see Quiz 48)
1 Aristotle. 2 Neville Hope. 3 1-2-1 Club. 4 George. 5 Bob Monkhouse.
6 Lady Falkender. 7 Dick Van Dyke. 8 Miss Flood. 9 Erotica. 10 Bette.
11 Vince Pinner. 12 Medford. 13 Phyllis and Sidney. 14 Mr Lewis.
15 Geraldine. 16 Footballer. 17 Yetta Feldman. 18 "Sitting Pretty".
19 Mrs Edna Hawkins. 20 George and Pauline. 21 Restaurant in Fulham.
22 "Rising Damp". 23 *Person*. 24 Paddy. 25 Peter Cook. 26 Gash and
Burney. 27 Chumley-on-the-Water. 28 Bygone Books. 29 Shirley Temple.
30 Greengrocer.

286

1   What is the approximate distance of Nairobi airport from London in miles?
2   What is the only English anagram of FIREIRONS?
3   Under what name did Jean Garvelet ply his high-risk trade?
4   What are the odds of rolling any combination totalling four in dice-throwing?
5   Who had a 50s No. 1 with "Butterfly"?
6   What is Nelson Mandela's middle name?
7   George Lee was three times world champion in which sport?
8   Concord is the capital of which US state?
9   Which city was the TV series "The Champions" set in?
10 Musselburgh and Early Market are types of what?
11 Who wrote the poems "Mental Cases" and "Futility"?
12 Who appeared on stamps for the Penny Black's 150th anniversary?
13 Formigar and Terceira are in which island group?
14 What handicap did Sydney Smith overcome to win Wimbledon doubles?
15 Who was the first Englishman to win the British Grand Prix?
16 Who worked at an undertaker's with the motto "Taste, Tact, Economy"?
17 From which language does the word "assassin" originate?
18 George I was born at which castle?
19 In Monopoly how much does it cost to buy Bond Street?
20 Who co-wrote "Fawlty Towers" with John Cleese?
21 What links Hampstead Heathens, Reigate Priory and Maidenhead?
22 Whose first DIY programme was broadcast in 1957?
23 What plagued Mark Twain, Groucho Marx and Franz Kafka?
24 In which country is the city of Monrovia?
25 What was the first British Top Ten hit for Randy Crawford?
26 Who designed the 1992 Barcelona Olympics team outfit for Lithuania?
27 Who rode Troy and Henbit to Derby triumphs?
28 What is the Norwegian parliament called?
29 In which teaching hospital was "Doctor in the House" set?
30 What is formed by the metamorphosis of limestone?

1   What was the name of Gomez Addams's pet octopus?

2   Which character did Kevin Whatley play in "Auf Wiedersehen Pet"?

3   What was the name of the club in the 80s sitcom "Dear John"?

4   What was Captain Mainwaring's first name in "Dad's Army"?

5   Who sang the theme to "You Rang M'Lord" with its star Paul Shane?

6   Which former secretary was consultant on the first two series of "Yes Minister"?

7   Who starred in his own sitcom as Rob Petrie?

8   Who was the older secretary in "May to December"?

9   In "Up Pompeii" who was the daughter of Ludicrus and Ammonia?

10   In "2 Point 4 Children" what was Bill's mum called?

11   Who was assistant manager at Eddie Brown's turf accountant?

12   What was the surname of Terry and June in the sitcom?

13   Who were Timothy Lumsden's parents in "Sorry"?

14   Who was the Spencers' neighbour in the last series of "Some Mothers Do 'Ave 'Em"?

15   What was the goat called in "The Good Life"?

16   In "The Upper Hand" what did Charlie do before he was a housekeeper?

17   What was the name of the ghost in "So Haunt Me"?

18   Which 90s sitcom featured the "Jackie Onassis of Bethnal Green"?

19   Who was Shelley's landlady in Pangloss Road?

20   What was the name of Adrian Mole's parents?

21   What and where was "Robin's Nest"?

22   Which sitcom resulted from a one-off play called "The Banana Box"?

23   In "Agony", of which magazine was Jane Lucas problems-page editor?

24   What was Miriam Karlin's militant character in "The Rag Trade"?

25   In "Blackadder" who played Richard III?

26   What were Rab C. Nesbitt's children called?

27   What was the fictitious setting for "The River" with David Essex?

28   Which company did Sarah first work for in "After Henry"?

29   By which film star's name did Alf Garnett refer to his son-in-law?

30   What is the "day job" of ARP Warden Hodges in "Dad's Army"?

Quiz 49 Pot Luck 25

Answers - see page 291

LEVEL 3

1   Which celebrity fell over on the first of his own UK television chat shows?
2   Charlottetown is the capital of which Canadian province?
3   Who invented the chronometer?
4   Gilles Villeneuve was killed during testing at which 1982 Formula 1 Grand Prix race?
5   What is the only English anagram of INTRODUCE?
6   Who wrote *The Gulag Archipelago*?
7   Who had an 80s No. 1 with "The Model"?
8   How was Ferdinand Joseph Lemott better known?
9   If it's noon at GMT, what time is it in Brasilia?
10 Who is the villain in the Wilkie Collins novel *The Woman In White*?
11 Who followed Lord North as prime minister of the UK?
12 In Monopoly, how much do you receive when your annuity matures?
13 In which country is the city of Monterrey?
14 Which shipping forecast area is east of Shannon?
15 The author Tom Wolfe was born on the same day as which Soviet leader?
16 Against which team did Alan Shearer hit his first Newcastle hat-trick?
17 How many islands are in the Caroline group?
18 What do the letters WG stand for in W.G. Grace's name?
19 What was the first British Top Ten hit for Bing Crosby?
20 Which TV play was based on the football-pools winner Viv Nicholson?
21 Anthophobia is the fear of what?
22 Who made the album *Bad Penny Blues*?
23 From which language does the word "census" originate?
24 Parson Lot was an assumed name of which writer?
25 Who was Foreign Secretary before John Major replaced him in 1989?
26 Which US state is known as the Badger State?
27 The picosecond is the smallest unit of what?
28 Whose three-volume autobiography was called *Diary of a Genius*?
29 The airline Malev is based in which country?
30 Which character was played by Charles Dance in "The Jewel in the Crown"?

Answers

Pot Luck 26   (see Quiz 51)
1 Simpson. 2 G.K. Chesterton. 3 200. 4 "The Love Cats". 5 150. 6 Violet Elizabeth Bott. 7 Turkish. 8 Buster Mottram Ronay. 9 Ellice. 10 Stan Laurel (born Arthur Jefferson). 11 Langley, Virginia. 12 Christie. 13 A portrait of Queen Victoria. 14 Steve Collins. 15 Trenton. 16 Della Street. 17 Piccadilly. 18 A7. 19 Wide-screen cinema. 20 The Post Office. 21 Cecil Day-Lewis. 22 Jerez. 23 Books (binding and selling). 24 Noiseless. 25 John F. Kennedy. 26 Five. 27 Frank Buckle. 28 Duke of Plaza Toro (*Gondoliers*). 29 Portugal. 30 Mike Hawthorn (champ) & Stirling Moss.

1　For what did *Four Weddings and a Funeral* win Oscar nominations?
2　Who was Juliet to Gielgud's Romeo in 1935?
3　How many roles did Alec Guinness play in *Kind Hearts and Coronets*?
4　Who was Jane Seymour's first father-in-law?
5　What was Anthony Hopkins's role in *Bram Stoker's Dracula*?
6　Who played Stephen Ward in *Scandal*?
7　In which film did Emma Thompson play a 1940s European and a present-day Californian?
8　Which actor won a BAFTA for *Chariots of Fire*?
9　Which was Julie Andrews's first film with her husband Blake Edwards?
10　Who appeared with Robert Redford, when just six, in *The Great Gatsby*?
11　Who played Schindler's Jewish accountant in *Schindler's List*?
12　What was Roger Moore's second movie as James Bond?
13　Who starred in and composed the score for *Bedazzled*?
14　Which actor has been co-owner of London's Langan's Brasserie?
15　Who played General Allenby in *Lawrence of Arabia*?
16　The reciting of whose poem in *Four Weddings and a Funeral* resulted in a book of his poetry becoming a bestseller?
17　Who won an Oscar for Best Picture in 1968, which his nephew also starred in?
18　Who played Anne Boleyn in *A Man For All Seasons*?
19　What was Glenda Jackson's film debut?
20　What was Cilla Black's first feature film?
21　Who wrote an autobiography *Beginning* in 1989, aged 28?
22　What was Robert Donat's final film?
23　Who said she was "the only sex symbol England produced since Lady Godiva"?
24　Who played opposite Hayley Mills in *The Family Way*?
25　Who played Poirot in *Murder on the Orient Express*?
26　Which character did Alec Guinness play in *Dr Zhivago*?
27　Which *Carry On* film was called *Carry On Venus* in the US?
28　Who directed *Whistle Down the Wind* in 1961?
29　Who wrote of his relationship with his actress wife in *Meeting Mrs Jenkins*?
30　Who played Noël Coward in *Star!*?

Answers

Plant World (see Quiz 52)
1 Meilland. 2 Wild cherry. 3 Borlotti beans. 4 Egypt. 5 Sap. 6 Poisonous mushroom. 7 Hydroponics. 8 Red. 9 Starch. 10 Latex. 11 Gold/orange. 12 Calcifuge. 13 Insects. 14 *Weigelas*. 15 Brambles. 16 Lichens. 17 Salt. 18 Pappus. 19 Tomatoes. 20 Figs. 21 Carrot. 22 Its cap. 23 The stems of plants. 24 Old tree or log. 25 Study of plant diseases. 26 Tea. 27 Coconut palm. 28 Pertaining to the soil. 29 Giant cactus. 30 Unopened flower buds.

1 What does S stand for in Ulysses S. Grant's name?
2 Who wrote the book *The Napoleon of Notting Hill*?
3 What is the approximate distance of Paris airport from London in miles?
4 What was the first British Top Ten hit for the Cure?
5 How many degrees are there in each internal angle of a dodecagon?
6 Which character was played by Bonnie Langford in "Just William"?
7 From which language does the word "horde" originate?
8 The 50s tennis player Joy Gannon became mother of which tennis player?
9 Nanumea and Nukulailai are in which island group?
10 Who was the most famous comedian to be born in Ulverston, north-west England?
11 Where is the HQ of the CIA?
12 Who had a 70s No. 1 with "Yellow River"?
13 What is buried under Cleopatra's Needle with a razor and cigars?
14 Who inflicted Chris Eubank's first defeat as a professional fighter?
15 What is the capital of the US State of New Jersey?
16 What was the name of Perry Mason's secretary?
17 On a Monopoly board what is between Water Works and Go To Jail?
18 Which UK paper size is 74 x 105 mm?
19 Raoul Grimoin-Sanson devloped what for the entertainment world?
20 Who did Keith Richards work for before becoming a Rolling Stone?
21 Which Irish poet wrote detective novels under the pseudonym Nicholas Blake?
22 Where was the Spanish Formula 1 Grand Prix held prior to 1991?
23 What did the physicist and chemist Michael Faraday train to work with?
24 What is the only English anagram of LIONESSES?
25 Who was US president when racial discrimination was made illegal?
26 Before the 20th century how many moons of Jupiter had been discovered?
27 Lestor Piggott overtook whose record for English classic wins?
28 In light opera, who "led his regiment from behind"?
29 When Elsie Tanner left the Street, which country did she move to?
30 Who were the first UK pairing of world champion and runner-up in Formula 1 Grand Prix racing?

Quiz 52 Plant World

Answers - see page 290

LEVEL 3

1   Who bred the first Peace rose?
2   What sort of tree is a gean?
3   How are Boston or pinto beans also known?
4   Where did liquorice originate?
5   Which part of asafoetida is used as a spice?
6   What is a clouded agaric?
7   What is the practice of growing plants in liquid nutrients instead of soil called?
8   What colour is the pigment leghaemoglobin found in legumes?
9   The breakdown of what produces malic acid?
10 What is the milky juice of the dandelion called?
11 What colour is a cloudberry?
12 What term applies to a plant which is lime-hating?
13 What does the bladderwort live on?
14 Which shrubs are also known as bush honeysuckles?
15 What does a batologist study?
16 What is litmus obtained from?
17 A halophyte tolerates soil or water containing what?
18 What is the ring of fine down on a dandelion called?
19 What would you grow if you grew Peruvian apples?
20 What fruit is produced on a banyan tree?
21 Which common vegetable family does chervil belong to?
22 What is a toadstool's pileus?
23 Cauliflowers are vegetables but technically what are caulis?
24 Where would you normally find a bracket fungus?
25 What is phytopathology?
26 What is *Camellia sinensis* more commonly called?
27 From what is the oil copra obtained?
28 What does edaphic mean?
29 What is a saguaro?
30 Which part of the plants are the cloves you buy as a spice?

Quiz 53 Pot Luck 27

Answers - see page 295

LEVEL 3

1   What was Alicia Markova's real name?
2   Who did Stacy Dorning play in "Keep It In The Family"?
3   What was the number of the London bus involved in the bomb explosion of February '96?
4   Who invented the mechanical clock?
5   Astraphobia is the fear of what?
6   What is the only English anagram of MEANS TEST?
7   Who played McHeath in the TV adaptation of *The Beggar's Opera*?
8   Springfield is the capital of which US state?
9   How many sets of tyres can an Indy Car use in a race weekend?
10 Who had an 80s No. 1 with "Give It Up"?
11 If it's noon at GMT, what time is it in Halifax, Nova Scotia?
12 When was the first race meeting at Royal Ascot?
13 Whose recording of which piece was the first classical record to sell over a million copies?
14 How many islands are in the Queen Charlotte group?
15 In which century was John Bunyan born?
16 Which instrument brought fame to Shirley Abicair?
17 From which language does the word "ombudsman" originate?
18 In Scrabble what is the letter T worth?
19 What was the number of the Trotter's flat in Nelson Mandela House?
20 A set of British stamps was issued in 1990 for which charity's 150th anniversary?
21 On which river does Milan stand?
22 What word is given to the fear of bees?
23 Whose autobiography was called *Child of Change*?
24 In how many test matches did Ian Botham captain England?
25 What was the first British solo Top Ten hit for Roger Daltrey?
26 In which country is the city of Murcia?
27 In Monopoly, how much do you receive for your birthday if there are four players?
28 Longleat is the stately home of whom?
29 The airline Crossair is based in which country?
30 Sabine and Saladin are types of what?

Pot Luck 28 (see Quiz 55)
1 Richard Thorpe. **2** Boulevard de Belleville. **3** The Simon Park Orchestra. **4** Henry James. **5** Italian. **6** Bahamas. **7** Fred Noonan. **8** Keith Chegwin. **9** Wrestling. **10** Leslie Poles. **11** Samuel de Champlain. **12** *The Pickwick Papers*. **13** Leicester. **14** The name Winston. **15** "Eloise". **16** Oscar Wilde. **17** 1954. **18** Christiaan Huygens. **19** Olivier Panis. **20** No place (Greek). **21** 5800. **22** Violet Robinson. **23** Carnation. **24** On the moon. **25** Lord Grenville. **26** Monte Marmolada. **27** Derby-winning horses. **28** Delaware. **29** Mobilises. **30** Royal Opera House.

1. Who was Tiger Woods's caddie for his first Masters win?
2. When did Great Britain first win the Walker Cup?
3. Where did Nick Faldo win his first British Open?
4. What was Jack Nicklaus's nickname in his first Walker Cup in the 50s?
5. What is the name of Hole 8 at Troon?
6. In the 1996 US Masters, how many strokes did Norman lead Faldo before the final round?
7. Who won the British Open the year after Lee Trevino's first triumph?
8. Henry Cotton won the British Open at Sandwich, Muirfield and where?
9. Who was the first South African to win the British Open?
10. Which champion's father was a pro at Hawkstone Park golf course?
11. Where in England was Tony Jacklin born?
12. Where in America did Great Britain and Ireland first win the Walker Cup?
13. Who got the nickname the Walrus?
14. Who is Jack Nicklaus's personal clubmaker?
15. After World War Two, who got the first three-in-a-row hat-trick of British Opens?
16. Who set the course record of 64 at Troon in the Open of 1989?
17. Horton Smith was the first winner of which major event?
18. Which management group did Tiger Woods sign up to on turning pro?
19. What was the original prize for winning the British Open?
20. In what year did Nick Faldo turn professional?
21. Who was the first New Zealander to win the British Open?
22. In which decade was the Walker Cup staged at an English course?
23. Who got the nickname Dough Boy?
24. In what capacity did Devereux Emmet leave his mark on golf?
25. Who was the last golfer before Faldo to be BBC Sports Personality of the Year?
26. What first did Peter Butler manage in the 1973 Ryder Cup?
27. Which golfer's first tour victory was the 1982 Swiss Open?
28. Which course contains the Rabbit and the Seal?
29. Tom Lehman became the first American since who to win an Open at Royal Lytham?
30. Where was the great Harry Vardon born?

Quiz 55 Pot Luck 28

Answers - see page 293

LEVEL 3

1　Which "Emmerdale" actor was Dr Rennie on "Emergency Ward 10"?
2　On a French Monopoly board, what is the equivalent to Old Kent Road?
3　Who had an 80s No. 1 with "Eye Level"?
4　Who wrote *The Turn of the Screw*?
5　From which language does the word "parasol" originate?
6　Cat Crooked and Acklins are in which island group?
7　Who died with Amelia Earhart on her round-the-world attempt?
8　Who is the brother of the former Radio 1 DJ Janice Long?
9　Which sport was dropped from our screens by ITV in 1988?
10　What do the letters LP stand for in L.P. Hartley's name?
11　Which explorer founded Quebec?
12　In which Dickens novel does Job Trotter appear?
13　Where in Britain did the first women traffic wardens go on duty?
14　What did John Lennon share with Gary Lineker?
15　What was the first British Top Ten hit for the Damned?
16　What was Sebastian Melmoth's real name?
17　In which year did food rationing end in Britain?
18　Who invented the pendulum clock?
19　Who broke both legs in a Montreal 1997 Formula 1 Grand Prix crash ?
20　What does the word "Utopia" mean?
21　What is the approximate distance of Rio de Janeiro airport from London in miles?
22　Who did Pat Coombs play in *Lollipop Loves Mr Mole*?
23　What is the national flower of Spain?
24　Where is the Marsh of Sleep located?
25　What was William Wyndham's title when he was UK prime minister?
26　What is the highest peak of the Dolomites called?
27　What's the link between Blue Peter, Pearl Diver and Sir Peter Teazle?
28　Which US state is known as the Diamond State?
29　What is the only English anagram of OMNISSIBLE?
30　Genista McIntosh resigned as chief executive of what in May 1997?

Pot Luck 27　(see Quiz 53)

Answers

1　Lillian Marks. **2**　Susan Rush. **3**　117 (In the Aldwych). **4**　I-Hsing.
5　Lightning. **6**　Statesman. **7**　Roger Daltrey. **8**　Illinois. **9**　Seven. **10**　K.C. and the Sunshine Band. **11**　8 a.m. **12**　1711. **13**　Dame Joan Hammond - *Puccini's Turandot*. **14**　150. **15**　17th. **16**　A zither. **17**　Swedish. **18**　One. **19**　368. **20**　RSPCA. **21**　Olono. **22**　Apiphobia. **23**　Chess player Gary Kasparov. **24**　12. **25**　"Giving It All Away". **26**　Spain. **27**　£30 (£10 each from the three other players). **28**　Marquess of Bath. **29**　Switzerland. **30**　Lettuce.

1 Tania Evans and Jay Supreme are part of which group?
2 Who was the first person to write a British No. 1 both for himself and for someone else?
3 Who produced "House Of The Rising Sun" for the Animals?
4 With what did the ex-Housemartin Norman Cook next hit No. 1?
5 Who sang lead on "Sausalito (Is the Place to Go)" as Ohio Express?
6 Which ex-Siouxsie and the Banshees guitarist penned the Adam Ant No. 1s?
7 Whose first Top Ten hit was "Hit and Miss"?
8 Who were the next Irish group to top the British charts after the Bachelors?
9 Who was Hilary Lefter when she hit the top of the charts in 1982?
10 Who was the synthesizer player in Soft Cell?
11 Who wasn't one of the brothers in Bros?
12 Acapulco, Casablanca and Moscow feature in whose record titles?
13 Who left the Go Gos in '85 and had her first UK No. 1 in 1988?
14 Whose last single, in 1975, was called "Pandora's Box"?
15 The fifties "Pickin' A Chicken" singer, Eve Boswell, came from which country?
16 Who led the Ram Jam Band in the 60s?
17 In which band did Bobby Brown make No. 1 in 1983?
18 In Praise of Lemmings wisely changed their name but kept which name-change singer?
19 Who made up Scaffold with Roger McGough and Mike McGear?
20 Who was the first British female to have two consecutive No. 1s?
21 Who wrote the hits for ELO?
22 Who provided backing vocals on Elvis's "It's Now or Never"?
23 Whose first hit song started out with the title "Mr Jellybun"?
24 Whose first No. 1 was originally called "Io Che No Vivo Senza Te"?
25 The percussionist of which band duetted with Phil Collins on "Easy Lover" in 1985?
26 Who had the second posthumous No. 1 in the British charts?
27 Who were Anita Dels and Ray Slijngaard?
28 Who was born Orville Richard Burrell in Jamaica in 1968?
29 Who had the original hit with "A Rockin' Good Way" in 1960?
30 Who directed Duran Duran's video of "Girls on Film"?

Quiz 57 Pot Luck 29

Answers - see page 299

LEVEL 3

1   What did George Shillibeer introduce in London in 1829?
2   Who won the first Australian Formula 1 Grand Prix in Adelaide in 1985?
3   Who is credited with having conceived the first automatic digital computer.
4   Who had a 70s No. 1 with "Up Town Top Ranking"?
5   What is the only English anagram of SCHEMATIC?
6   What did Lovejoy affectionately call his Morris Minor?
7   Which Samuel won the Nobel Prize for Literature in 1969?
8   The comic actor Eric Idle was born on the same day as which British prime minister?
9   What is Denis Healey's middle name?
10 How many islands are in the Cyclades group?
11 Which shipping forecast area is east of Fastnet?
12 Which poet referred to himself as Merlin in a summing-up of his poetical career?
13 What is the capital of the US State of Florida?
14 Who replaced Darlington when they dropped out of the Football League?
15 In 1973 Mrs Susan Shaw became the first woman to set foot where?
16 Batrachophobia is the fear of what?
17 In which country are the Abisso Olivifer caves?
18 What was the first ventriloquist's dummy to have a TV series?
19 Who wrote "Keep the Home Fires Burning"?
20 What was the first British solo Top Ten hit for Doris Day?
21 In the Monopoly Community Chest, how much is the insurance premium?
22 The airline Linjeflyg is based in which country?
23 Which character was played by Tom Baker in "Medics"?
24 Which Royal has Albert Christian Edward as his three other names?
25 What are the odds of rolling any combination totalling eleven in dice-throwing?
26 What is the opposite of occidental?
27 From which language does the word "bazaar" originate?
28 What was the title of the theme tune from the TV series "Top Secret"?
29 Which country's secret police is called Savak?
30 If it's noon at GMT, what time is it in Managua?

Answers

Pot Luck 30 (see Quiz 59)
1 Blair General Hospital. 2 Enigma. 3 David Coleman. 4 Morocco.
5 144. 6 Italian. 7 Onion. 8 Peritonitis. 9 Arthur C. Clarke. 10 Surfers
Paradise, Australia. 11 Peter Sellers. 12 Claire Bloom (Blume). 13 Maine.
14 Spottable. 15 Hockey. 16 Dodecanese. 17 14th February. 18 Phyllis
Dorothy. 19 Damon Hill. 20 "Candida". 21 François Hennebique. 22 Go
To Jail. 23 Leeches. 24 6,800. 25 Caitlin Davies. 26 Milkman. 27 *Sunday
Post*. 28 Poker World Series. 29 Neckar. 30 Fort Sill (Oklahoma).

1. Which company marketed the first diesel-engined private car?
2. Which north-west town has Central and Bank Quay stations?
3. What was the first vehicle-registration plate in Britain?
4. How many London Underground lines begin with letters in the second half of the alphabet?
5. Where, near Calais, is the French terminus of the Channel Tunnel?
6. Who was with Jean Pierre Blanchard in the first balloon crossing of the English Channel?
7. Which two Great Lakes does the Welland Canal link?
8. Who was the first person to walk in space without a safety line?
9. What did TML stand for in Channel Tunnel construction?
10. In which American state was the first railway station opened?
11. Which airline did British Airways acquire in 1988?
12. Where is Baltasound Airport?
13. What did Enrico Forlanini develop in 1898?
14. The first section of the London Underground ran from Paddington to where?
15. Which was Thor Heyerdahl's third raft after *Kontiki* and *Ra*?
16. Lord King, ex-chairman of British Airways, was Lord King of where?
17. Where was the flight from London going to when Concorde entered supersonic service in 1976?
18. Which aircraft from which company crashed on the motorway near Kegworth in 1989?
19. What was the first turbine-driven steamship called?
20. Where were the *Apollo 1* astronauts when they perished in the 60s?
21. Who were the first two countries to offer flags of convenience?
22. Which two rivers does the Albert Canal link?
23. How many major private rail companies were nationalized in 1947?
24. What does the Seikan Tunnel link?
25. Which international airport company was the first to be floated on the Stock Exchange?
26. What was the *Queen Elizabeth* called when it was destroyed by fire in Hong Kong?
27. Who was the first person to fly over both Poles and the Atlantic?
28. Which report recommended changes after the 1987 King's Cross fire?
29. Where is the deepwater port of Tuticorin?
30. What did the Soviets call their first nuclear-powered ship?

TV Detectives (see Quiz 60)

1 Charley Farley and Piggy Malone. **2** "Johnny Todd". **3** Auguste Dupin.
4 Piet. **5** George Cross. **6** "Target". **7** Inspector Tsientsin. **8** Manchester.
9 Starsky and Hutch. **10** Taggart. **11** Denise Welch. **12** Special Branch.
13 Wyvern. **14** Kelly Garrett. **15** Radio West. **16** Bill Owen alias Compo.
17 Sexton Blake. **18** "The Racing Game". **19** LA Coroner's Office.
20 Suzanne "Pepper" Anderson. **21** Whitehaven Mansions. **22** Barstock CID.
23 1960 Mark 2. **24** Through the Del Floria tailor's shop. **25** Inspector Claude Eustace Teal. **26** Inspector Wexford. **27** Seven. **28** Answerphone message.
29 Laura Holt. **30** Granada.

Quiz 59 Pot Luck 30

Answers - see page 297

LEVEL 3

1 In which hospital was "Dr Kildare" set?
2 Who had a 90s No. 1 with "Sadness Part 1"?
3 Which sports commentator was a champion mile runner for Cheshire?
4 In which country is the city of Oujda?
5 How many degrees are there in each internal angle of a decagon?
6 From which language does the word "scenario" originate?
7 Turbo and Stuttgarter Giant are types of what?
8 What was Rudolph Valentino's cause of death?
9 Who wrote *The City and the Stars*?
10 Where did Nigel Mansell achieve his first pole position and win in an Indy car race?
11 Who featured on the 17p - the cheapest - of the 1985 British Film Year stamps?
12 Which 30s-born actress Claire changed two vowels for her stage name?
13 Augusta is the capital of which US state?
14 What is the only English anagram of TABLETOPS?
15 In which sport was Mary Russell-Vick famous?
16 Tilos and Astipalaia are in which island group?
17 What special birthday links Kevin Keegan and P.G. Wodehouse?
18 What do the letters PD stand for in P.D. James's name?
19 Who won the inaugural Melbourne Formula 1 Grand Prix in 1996?
20 What was the first British Top Ten hit for Dawn?
21 Who invented reinforced concrete?
22 In Monopoly, where would double one from Water Works land you?
23 The adjective hirudinal refers to which creatures?
24 What is the approximate distance of Singapore airport from London in miles?
25 Which character was played by Sheena Easton in "Miami Vice"?
26 What was Benny Hill's trade before he became a comic?
27 Which Dundee-based paper first appeared in 1920?
28 Huckleberry Seed won which World Series in 1996?
29 On which river does Stuttgart stand?
30 Geronimo died at which US Fort?

Answers

Pot Luck 29 (see Quiz 57)
1 First regular bus service. 2 Keke Rosberg. 3 Charles Babbage. 4 Althia and Donna. 5 Catechism. 6 Miriam. 7 Beckett. 8 John Major. 9 Winston. 10 About 220. 11 Lundy. 12 Alfred, Lord Tennyson. 13 Tallahassee. 14 Maidstone. 15 Floor of the London Stock Exchange. 16 Reptiles. 17 Italy. 18 Archie Andrews. 19 Ivor Novello. 20 "My Love and Devotion". 21 £50. 22 Sweden. 23 Professor Geoffrey Hoyt. 24 Prince Andrew. 25 17.5-1. 26 Oriental. 27 Persian. 28 "Sucu Sucu". 29 Iran. 30 6 a.m.

Quiz 60 TV Detectives

Answers - see page 298

1   Who were the private investigators played by the Two Ronnies?
2   Which folk song was the "Z Cars" theme based on?
3   Which Edgar Allen Poe detective did Edward Woodward play in the "Detective" series?
4   What was Van de Valk's first name?
5   Which medal had Detective Inspector Frost won?
6   Which TV drama featured Detective Steve Hackett?
7   Which character did David Suchet play in "Reilly - Ace of Spies"?
8   Where was "Strangers" first set?
9   Who had a street contact called Huggy Bear?
10 Who was assisted by Detective Sergeant Peter Livingstone?
11 Which future "Coronation Street" actress played Jimmy Nail's wife in "Spender"?
12 Craven and Haggerty starred in which series?
13 Where did the action of "Softly Softly" take place?
14 Which agent was played by Jaclyn Smith in "Charlie's Angels"?
15 Who did Eddie Shoestring work for?
16 Who played Inspector Lestrade in the 60s Sherlock Holmes series?
17 Which detective on children's TV had a bloodhound called Pedro and a Rolls-Royce called the Grey Panther?
18 Which 70s/80s series was based on the books of Dick Francis?
19 Where did Quincy work?
20 Which role did Angie Dickinson play in "Police Woman"?
21 In the TV series what was Hercule Poirot's London address?
22 Which police force was Henry Crabbe retired from?
23 What year and model were Morse's most famous red Jaguar?
24 What was the secret entrance to the headquarters of U.N.C.L.E.?
25 Which police officer was a regular adversary of Simon Templar?
26 Who did Inspector Mike Burden assist?
27 How many Babies did Rockliffe have in the 80s series?
28 What did each episode of "The Rockford Files" begin with?
29 Who owned Remington Steele Investigations?
30 Which TV company made the "Prime Suspect" series in the UK?

Travel & Transport (see Quiz 58)

1 Mercedes Benz. 2 Warrington. 3 A1. 4 Three (Northern, Piccadilly, Victoria). 5 Coquelles. 6 John Jeffries. 7 Ontario to Erie. 8 Bruce McCandless. 9 TransManche Link. 10 Baltimore. 11 British Caledonian. 12 Unst, Shetland. 13 Hydrofoil. 14 Farringdon Street. 15 *Tigris*. 16 Wartnaby. 17 Bahrain. 18 British Midland Boeing 737. 19 Turbinia. 20 Cape Kennedy (fire at a ground test). 21 Liberia and Panama. 22 Meuse, Scheld. 23 Four. 24 Islands of Honshu and Hokkaido. 25 BAA. 26 *Seawise University*. 27 Richard Evelyn Byrd. 28 Fennel Report. 29 India. 30 Lenin.

LEVEL 3

1   In which month is Venezuela's national day?
2   How was Angelo Giuseppe Roncalli better known?
3   What was the nickname of the Locomotives and Highway Act of 1865?
4   Who wrote *Tortilla Flat*?
5   Which mountain range gave the setting for most of TV's "William Tell" series?
6   Where was the first Formula 1 World Championship race held outside Europe in 1953?
7   Which newspaper first introduced box numbers in the UK?
8   What was Moliere's real name?
9   If it's noon at GMT, what time is it in Montevideo?
10   Which character was played by Hattie Jacques in "Miss Adventure"?
11   In Scrabble what is the letter L worth?
12   Which film was based on Sir Laurence Van Der Post's novel *The Seed and the Sower*?
13   In Monopoly, how much is paid to the Hospital in Community Chest?
14   How many islands are in the Philippines group?
15   Where was the news presenter Pamela Armstrong born?
16   What is the name of Scotland's largest cave?
17   In which university was "A Very Peculiar Practice" set?
18   What are the Sudanese Dunka tribe recognized to be?
19   Who led the French Protestants known as the Huguenots?
20   Which UK paper size is 105 x 148 mm?
21   What is the only English anagram of SUBLINEAR?
22   Which bridge was opened by Lady Thatcher in Hong Kong giving access to the airport of Lantau Island?
23   Which star sign links the sportsman Bill Beaumont and the presenter/singer Cheryl Baker?
24   In which US state would a Hoosier be a native inhabitant?
25   From which language does the word "parallax" originate?
26   What was George Hamilton-Gordon's title when he was UK prime minister?
27   Who invented contact lenses?
28   Belonophobia is the fear of what?
29   What was the first British Top Ten hit for Depeche Mode?
30   The airline Bell-Air is based in which country?

1. Other than being his wife what relation was Eleanor Roosevelt to Franklin D.?
2. What was the profession of Roger Moore's father?
3. What is the real name of the author Nigel West?
4. Which celebrity photographer wrote *My Royal Past*?
5. Who captained the first all-female crew to sail round the world?
6. Who was Mia Farrow's second husband?
7. What relation is Jonathan Aitken to Lord Beaverbrook?
8. What is David Bailey's middle name?
9. Which contest was Kiki Haakonson the first winner of?
10. Which MP competed at the Tokyo Olympics and was UK 100m record holder from 1967-74?
11. Which son of the late US Ambassador to Paris, Pamela Harriman, has been a British MP?
12. Who wrote a book of comic verse called *I Have No Gun But I Can Spit*?
13. Which 13-year-old gained a First in maths at Oxford in 1985?
14. Which Earl of Lichfield is the photographer Patrick?
15. Which Guinness heiress died of a drink/drugs overdose at Oxford University in the 80s?
16. Who is Wath-on-Dearne Comprehensive School's most famous old boy?
17. What was US President Nixon's wife called?
18. How was the designer Miss Mountney of Merthyr Tydfil better known?
19. Who said she was famous first as someone's daughter, then someone's wife, and probably finally as someone's mother?
20. Which ex-Tory Party chairman is the son of the actress Dinah Sheridan?
21. What relation, if any, is Vanessa Redgrave to Jemma Redgrave?
22. What is the first name of Martin Luther King's widow?
23. Who was Britain's youngest-ever city councillor at 21, and youngest - then - MP aged 28?
24. What are Prince Edward's four given names?
25. Where was Pierre Cardin born?
26. How was Vera Jane Palmer better known?
27. Who tried to assassinate Pope John Paul II in 1981?
28. Who was the first woman general of the Salvation Army?
29. Which prime minister was a former football referee and coach?
30. Whose second shop was called Nostalgia of Mud?

Screen Greats (see Quiz 64)

1 *Grand Hotel*. **2** Clark Gable, Jean Harlow. **3** James Stewart. **4** Claudette Colbert. **5** Robert Mitchum. **6** *Thoroughbreds Don't Cry*. **7** *Blue Skies*. **8** Rita Hayworth. **9** Orson Welles. **10** Olivia de Havilland. **11** *Stromboli*. **12** Spencer Tracy & Katharine Hepburn. **13** *Flying Down to Rio*. **14** Claude Rains. **15** Susan Hayward. **16** Paramount. **17** Deborah Kerr. **18** Lola-Lola. **19** Donald O'Connor. **20** Debbie Reynolds. **21** Joan Crawford. **22** Humphrey Bogart. **23** Gene Kelly. **24** Neath, Wales. **25** W.C. Fields. **26** *Safety Last*. **27** Lita Grey. **28** Mack Sennett. **29** Ginger Rogers. **30** Rita Hayworth.

Quiz 63 Pot Luck 32

LEVEL 3

1   What was the first British Top Ten hit for Booker T. and the MGs?
2   What is the only English anagram of ALARMING?
3   In which part of London were parking meters first introduced?
4   In Monopoly how much does it cost to buy Whitehall?
5   Who invented the contraceptive pill?
6   Which US state is known as the Apache State?
7   Which star sign links the TV presenter Michael Aspel and the botanist David Bellamy?
8   Who was the first Briton to win the World Show Jumping Championships?
9   From which language does the word "fuselage" originate?
10 Which singer moved to the USA for an acting role in "McKenzie"?
11 Cabrera and Formentera are in which island group?
12 Who wrote the poem "After Apple Picking"?
13 Sir John Houblon was the first governor of what?
14 Who had his jaw broken in 1973 by Ken Norton?
15 What was the work of Fulgence Bienvenue in Paris?
16 What is the approximate distance of Tokyo airport from London in miles?
17 Who designed the Sydney Opera House?
18 Who was the first person to swim the Channel underwater?
19 What was Jacques Offenbach's real name?
20 In which century was Alexander the Great born?
21 How many chromosomes are there in a normal human body cell?
22 Who had an 80s No. 1 with "Nothing's Going To Stop Us Now"?
23 At the scene of which of his pictures did Van Gogh shoot himself?
24 In which country was the actress Lynda Bellingham born?
25 The international car registration WAN applies to which country?
26 Who officially opened the Panama Canal?
27 Who was the first Englishman to climb the Matterhorn?
28 What law did Margaret Thatcher specialize in when she studied for the Bar?
29 Which two Formula One Drivers lost their lives at Imola in 1994?
30 Who did Sheila Hancock play in *Mr Digby, Darling*?

Quiz 64 Screen Greats

LEVEL 3

Answers - see page 302

1   In which movie did Greta Garbo say, "I want to be alone"?
2   Which two Hollywood greats were the stars of *Red Dust* in 1932?
3   Which Oscar-winner in 1940 received the DFC and the Croix de Guerre?
4   How was Lily Cauchoin better known?
5   Who did Ernest Borgnine say was "the best two-fisted drinker I've ever known"?
6   In which film did Judy Garland first team with Mickey Rooney?
7   What was the second film in which Bing Crosby co-starred with Fred Astaire?
8   Who starred opposite Fred Astaire in *You'll Never Get Rich*?
9   About whom did Marlene Dietrich say, "People should cross themselves when they say his name"?
10 Who played Maid Marian to Errol Flynn's Robin Hood in 1938?
11 What was the first Ingrid Bergman film directed by Roberto Rossellini?
12 Who were first teamed in *Woman of the Year* in 1942?
13 In which film were Fred Astaire and Ginger Rogers first together?
14 Who played Ingrid Bergman's husband in *Notorious*?
15 Who was born Edythe Marrener?
16 Which studio signed Gary Cooper in the late 20s?
17 Whose promotion for her first Hollywood film advised Americans that her name rhymed with "star"?
18 Who was Marlene Dietrich in *The Blue Angel*?
19 Who played the title role in *The Buster Keaton Story*?
20 Who had a career in films after being crowned Miss Burbank 1948?
21 Who married the chairman of Pepsi-Cola in 1955 and remained on the board of directors after his death?
22 Who played Captain Queeg in *The Caine Mutiny* in 1954?
23 Which film star first found fame playing the lead role in *Pal Joey* on Broadway in 1940?
24 Where was Ray Milland born?
25 Who replaced Charles Laughton as Mr Micawber in the 1935 film *David Copperfield*?
26 In which 1923 film did Harold Lloyd hang from the hands of a skyscraper clock?
27 Which wife was not mentioned by name in Chaplin's autobiography?
28 Whose life story was told in the 1939 movie *Hollywood Cavalcade*?
29 Who played "Anytime Annie" in *42nd Street*?
30 Whose pin-up photo was on the atomic bomb that was dropped on Bikini?

Quiz 65 Pot Luck 33

Answers - see page 307

LEVEL 3

1   At which Formula 1 Grand Prix circuit are the Tamburello and Acque Minerale?
2   Which fictitious bus company was featured in "On The Buses"?
3   What was Willie Carson's last ride to win the Derby?
4   In Monopoly, how much is won for second prize in a beauty contest?
5   Which shipping forecast area is east of Fair Isle?
6   If A is Alpha and B is Bravo what is U?
7   Dromophobia is the fear of what?
8   Who had a 50s No. 1 with "Hernando's Hideaway"?
9   Where did Shirley Williams become a professor when she left politics?
10 How many countries competed in the first soccer World Cup?
11 What is the capital of the US State of Kentucky?
12 In Scrabble what is the letter M worth?
13 What was Dorothy Parker's real name?
14 John Solomon represented England at which sport?
15 From which language does the word "cherub" originate?
16 In fiction, who was David Copperfield's first wife?
17 When did the Bank of England move to Threadneedle Street?
18 What was the first British Top Ten hit for Bow Wow Wow?
19 Which character was played by Jane Asher in *The Mistress*?
20 Who invented corrugated iron?
21 Ailsa Craig and Dobies Allrounder are types of what?
22 On which river does Lisbon stand?
23 Marlon Brando was born on the same day as which US actress/singer?
24 If it's noon at GMT, what time is it in Karachi?
25 How many islands are in the Dodecanese group?
26 Who replaced Accrington Stanley in the Football League?
27 What is the only English anagram of ANIMATED?
28 Which city on the signpost in "M*A*S*H" is 6,133 miles away?
29 In which country is Dalaman Airport?
30 Who wrote *A Tale of a Tub*?

Pot Luck 34 (see Quiz 67)

1 Tarragon. 2 Patricia Driscoll. 3 Joseph Conrad. 4 Winifred Atwell.
5 Taurus. 6 Cyclades. 7 Ralph Scheider. 8 Appeared on a set of stamps
(1991). 9 Dorothy. 10 5,000. 11 Eric Oliver. 12 1980. 13 Ali Baba.
14 Trinidad. 15 Rubens Barrichello. 16 Benjamin Franklin & George
Washington. 17 Spanish. 18 Park House, Sandringham. 19 "Mary Had A
Little Lamb". 20 *The Swan.* 21 Whitechapel. 22 "Make It With You".
23 11-1. 24 North Dakota. 25 Jack Giles. 26 Three. 27 Frank Zappa.
28 "The $64,000 Question". 29 Chance. 30 Hablot Knight Browne.

305

1   Which TV company was formed when ABC merged with Associated Rediffusion in the late 60s?

2   What was the BBC's first broadcast on June 7 1946 after the station had been closed down for seven years?

3   What is Rupert Murdoch's first name?

4   Which country has a national newspaper *B.T.*, founded in 1916?

5   Which company bought out NBC in 1985?

6   What is the Journal of the Society of Antiquities called?

7   Which BBC channel was launched in 1991?

8   Which newspaper is older - the *Daily Express* or the *Daily Mirror*?

9   What is ENG?

10 Who set up Britain's oldest daily trade newspaper?

11 In the US what does Nielsens show?

12 Which production company was founded by Lee Rich and Merv Adelson in 1968?

13 Where was the SECAM TV transmission system developed?

14 What is Britain's oldest national newspaper?

15 Which SES broadcast satellite was launched in December 1978?

16 In the 60s, what was an oater?

17 Which radio company set up NBC?

18 Which US cable channel was launched in 1980 specializing in foreign films?

19 What is the oldest weekly publication in the UK?

20 Which independent radio station began in the UK in March 1990?

21 Which town did Sky use as its UK satellite/cable testing ground?

22 Who was the first chairman of the Broadcasting Standards Authority?

23 What is the major daily paper of Denver Colorado called?

24 Which Sunday paper was founded in 1989?

25 In which three cities are Scotland's three major evening newspapers?

26 What is the full name of the Welsh fourth channel S4C?

27 Where was the Agenzia Internazionale Fides agency set up in 1926?

28 Which British city has produced a *News Letter* daily since 1855?

29 Which US TV network did Rupert Murdoch establish in the mid-80s?

30 What is Britain's oldest surviving provincial newspaper?

Quiz 67 Pot Luck 34

Answers - see page 305

LEVEL 3

1 What is the only English anagram of ARROGANT?
2 Who read the "Picture Book" stories on Monday afternoons?
3 Who wrote *An Outcast of the Islands*?
4 Who had a 50s No. 1 with "Poor People Of Paris"?
5 Which star sign links Eric Bristow and Joe Brown?
6 Tinos and Siros are in which island group?
7 Who invented the credit card?
8 What links the roses Silver Jubilee, *Rosa moyesii* and Harvest Fayre?
9 Who did Cheri Lunghi play in *The Monocled Mutineer*?
10 What is the approximate distance of Bejing Airport from London in miles?
11 Who was the first-ever world sidecar champion?
12 In what year did the sixpence cease to be legal tender?
13 Who had a female slave called Morgiana?
14 On which island was the children's presenter Floella Benjamin born?
15 Which lucky Formula 1 driver, who crashed heavily at Imola in 1994, escaped without injury?
16 Who appeared on the first two US adhesive stamps?
17 From which language does the word "cafeteria" originate?
18 At which house was Diana, Princess of Wales, born?
19 Which famous nursery rhyme was written by Sarah Josepha Hall?
20 What was the title of the 1994 book by the model Naomi Campbell?
21 Where in London was the first Salvation Army Revival Meeting?
22 What was the first British Top Ten hit for Bread?
23 What are the odds of rolling any combination totalling four in dice-throwing?
24 Bismarck is the capital of which US state?
25 Who won the first ten UK Closed Pro Squash Championships?
26 In Scrabble what is the letter B worth?
27 Who said, "Rock journalism is people who can't write interviewing people who can't talk for people who can't read"?
28 Which quiz show's questions were guarded by Detective Fabian?
29 On a Monopoly board what is between Angel Islington and Euston Rd?
30 What was Phiz's real name?

Answers

Pot Luck 33 (see Quiz 65)
1 Imola, San Marino. 2 Luxton. 3 Erhaab. 4 £10. 5 Viking. 6 Uniform. 7 Crossing streets. 8 The Johnston Brothers. 9 Harvard University. 10 13. 11 Frankfort. 12 3. 13 Dorothy Rothschild. 14 Croquet. 15 Hebrew. 16 Dora Spenlove. 17 1734. 18 "Go Wild in the Country". 19 Helen Mansel. 20 Pierre Carpentier. 21 Onion. 22 Tagus. 23 Doris Day. 24 5 p.m. 25 12. 26 Oxford Utd. 27 Diamante. 28 Toledo. 29 Turkey. 30 Jonathan Swift.

307

1 Which English monarch had a horse called White Surrey?
2 When was Paul Revere's ride to warn of the British advance?
3 What was the family name of Prince Albert of Saxe-Coburg-Gotha?
4 In which city did the Old Pretender die?
5 Which monarch communicated with his ministers in French?
6 Why did George V say *La Bohème* was his favourite opera?
7 Who was Napoleon Bonaparte's eldest brother?
8 Who was George V's elder brother?
9 Who was the first prime minister to occupy Chequers?
10 Who was George II's mother?
11 Who were the last two British monarchs to have two children who became British monarchs?
12 Who followed Sir Robert Walpole as prime minister of the UK?
13 Who was the first Hanoverian monarch to visit Ireland and Scotland ?
14 Which English king had the nickname Curtmantle?
15 Who was the father of the last Tsar of Russia?
16 Who attempted to assassinate Queen Victoria in 1849?
17 Which French painter was known as "Le Douanier"?
18 Who was the founder of the Standard Oil Company?
19 Who died in Britain's last public execution?
20 Who gave birth to Emile, Yvonne, Cecile, Marie and Annette in 1934?
21 Who was the first reigning pope to visit Britain?
22 Who was the first unmarried president of the USA?
23 Who opened Regent's Park Children's Zoo in 1938?
24 Who died at his Castle of Dux in Bohemia in 1798?
25 Which king was buried in Gloucester Cathedral in the 14th century?
26 Which British monarch had mistresses nicknamed the Elephant and the Maypole?
27 Who was the father of Edward VII's consort Alexandra?
28 Who founded Britain's first museum in 1683?
29 Who followed Herbert Henry Asquith as prime minister of the UK?
30 Where was Edward VIII born?

1 From which language does the word "bantam" originate?
2 In which country are the Anou Ifflis caves?
3 Who won the first "Pot Black" Trophy?
4 Who wrote *A Connecticut Yankee in King Arthur's Court*?
5 Which US state is known as the Panhandle State?
6 Who was prime minister of the UK in between William Pitt's two terms in office?
7 In Monopoly, how much is the income tax refund?
8 Which Scottish writer and statesman was the first Baron Tweedsmuir?
9 Who had a 50s No. 1 with "Whole Lotta Woman"?
10 What do the letters CS stand for in C.S. Lewis's name?
11 What is the capital of the Canadian province Yukon Territory?
12 In which country was the TV and radio presenter Katie Boyle born?
13 What did Hippolyte Mega Mouries patent in Paris in 1869?
14 Where in California is Disneyland?
15 Which character was played by Allyce Beasley in "Moonlighting"?
16 Eisoptrophobia is the fear of what?
17 Which star sign links Richard Baker and Thelma Barlow?
18 Who invented the automatic dishwasher?
19 What was Q's real name?
20 If it's noon at GMT, what time is it in Quebec?
21 Which Formula 1 driver has won the Monaco Grand Prix a record six times?
22 Who founded the Sûreté?
23 Where did the TV detective Jessica Fletcher live?
24 What is the only English anagram of PARTISAN?
25 What was the first British Top Ten hit for Tony Brent?
26 In which country is Findel Airport?
27 How did the Channel swimmer Matthew Webb perish?
28 How many islands are in the Pelagian group?
29 In Scrabble what is the letter G worth?
30 Whose 1987 autobiography was called *Little Wilson* and *Big God*?

Quiz 70 Children's TV

LEVEL 3

1   What were Roobarb and Custard?
2   Who narrated "Tales of the Riverbank"?
3   In the 50s, what name was given to the one-hour gap after children's and before adults' television programmes?
4   In which decade did "Watch With Mother" finish?
5   Which part did Letitia Dean play in "Grange Hill"?
6   Which female presented "Lift Off" in the 70s?
7   On which Farm did Worzel Gummidge live?
8   Who were the twins in "The Woodentops"?
9   Where did Torchy the Battery Boy live?
10 Who narrated "The Wombles"?
11 In "TISWAS" what was Bob Carolgees's punk dog called?
12 Who designed the Italian sunken garden on "Blue Peter"?
13 Who took over from Ringo Starr narrating "Thomas the Tank Engine"?
14 Where did Supergran's adventures take place?
15 Which two inventors invented Supercar?
16 Who was the Storyteller in the Channel 4 series?
17 In "Stingray" what did WASP stand for?
18 Who ran the sweetshop in the early days of "Sesame Street"?
19 What was the first weekend programme which Phillip Schofield presented regularly?
20 In "Rainbow" what colour were Moony and Sunshine?
21 Which humans appeared with Pussy Cat Willum?
22 What is the parish of the Reverend Timms?
23 Who were the first presenters of "Television Top of the Form"?
24 Who was the voice of Penfold in the "Dangermouse" series?
25 Which Tracy piloted *Thunderbird 2*?
26 Which clay model accompanied Tony Hart's programmes and who created him?
27 Who has presented "Screen Test" and "Blue Peter"?
28 What was the name of the Pogles' pet squirrel?
29 What were Bit and Bot on "Playschool"?
30 In "Vision On" what were Phil O'Pat and Pat O'Phil made from?

1 How many times did Graham Hill win the Formula 1 Monaco Grand Prix?
2 What was the first British Top Ten hit for Elkie Brooks?
3 How is Laszlo Lowenstein better known?
4 Tender and True and White Gem are types of what?
5 In which country is the city of Tashkent?
6 Which TV celebrity dressed as a waitress to promote Typhoo tea?
7 Which UK paper size is 148 x 210 mm?
8 What is the capital of the US State of Montana?
9 Who was said to have "loved mankind in general and women in particular"?
10 Who wrote *Der Steppenwolf*?
11 In which fictitious resort was "Hi-De-Hi" set?
12 On a French Monopoly board, what is the equivalent to Piccadilly?
13 The adjective vespine refers to which creatures?
14 Who were runners-up when Man. United first won a 90s championship?
15 Who joined the DJ Paul Burnett to become Laurie Lingo & the Dipsticks?
16 What was Ellery Queen's real name?
17 Who had an 50s No. 1 with "It's Almost Tomorrow"?
18 Who was the US Navy's youngest pilot in World War Two?
19 What is the only English anagram of ATELIER?
20 St Moritz is home to the world's oldest sporting club in what?
21 Whose second wife was Poppaea?
22 Roatan and Guanja are in which island group?
23 How had Tom McClean arrived in Blacksod Bay, Co Mayo, in 1969?
24 What is the partner of Phobos, the moon of Mars?
25 What is the approximate distance of Teheran airport from London in miles?
26 Who invented the pneumatic drill?
27 From which language does the word "poltergeist" originate?
28 What was Mindy's surname in the TV series "Mork and Mindy"?
29 Which star sign links the broadcasters Sue Cook and Jeremy Beadle?
30 Aside from floor and beam, what are the two other events for women gymnasts in the Olympics?

1 Who had a 1981 album *Hedgehog Sandwich*?
2 Which girl's name provides a track on *Bridge Over Troubled Water*?
3 On which album did Phil Collins make his vocal debut for Genesis?
4 "Can't Buy Me Love" first appeared on which Beatles album?
5 *Dark Side Of The Moon* was first released on which label?
6 Which album's sleeve featured David Bowie wearing boxing gloves?
7 Who recorded the soundtrack for the Oscar-winning film *The Piano*?
8 What type of surgery did Emerson, Lake and Palmer come up with?
9 Which Beatle holds a trumpet on the *Sgt. Pepper* album sleeve?
10 What are Gallagher and Lyle doing on the back cover of *Breakaway*?
11 What was Stevie Wonder's follow-up album to *Innervisions*?
12 Who is credited on the Worzels' first album?
13 Who recorded the album *Graceland*?
14 Which albums did Sarah Brightman and Andrea Bocelli release separately, each containing "Time To Say Goodbye"?
15 What was Sheryl Crow's debut album?
16 What colour stripe along with red and blue is on Police's *Synchronicity* sleeve?
17 What was the first original-cast recording of a show to top the charts?
18 "The Winner Takes It All" comes from which Abba album?
19 Whose first album was *No Secrets*?
20 Which album sleeve has the boxer John Conteh among the faces?
21 Who was the second British female artist to top the album charts?
22 Who was the narrator on Jeff Wayne's *War Of The Worlds*?
23 In 1994 whose CD won the Album of the Year Grammy in the US?
24 Which 60s character made a comeback in 1979 with *Broken English*?
25 Where was *Canto Gregoriano* recorded?
26 Who was the first solo artist to be a year's top-seller with a debut disc?
27 How many albums were in the first *Melody Maker* chart in 1958?
28 Pearl was a posthumously released album from which singer?
29 What was subtitled "The Best of the Boomtown Rats and Bob Geldof"?
30 What part of the body was on the sleeve of Pink Floyd's *Meddle*?

Quiz 73 Pot Luck 37

Answers - see page 315

LEVEL 3

1   What was Raphael's real name?
2   Who did Richard Wilson play in "My Good Woman"?
3   What is the only English anagram of ALLEGORIST?
4   Who had a 60s No. 1 with "You're Driving Me Crazy"?
5   In which country is General Manuel Marquez de Leon Airport?
6   In which century was Sir Humphrey Davy born?
7   In Scrabble what is the letter F worth?
8   Which shipping forecast area is south of Humber?
9   Which TV character's wives were played by Peggy Bates and Marion Mathie?
10 Which TV teddy was 40 in 1992?
11 In 1980 who described Ronald Reagan's monetarist policy as "voodoo economics"?
12 Actress Debra Winger was born on the same day as which Soviet gymnast?
13 How did the boxer Rinty Monaghan like to celebrate victory?
14 Who invented the electric oven?
15 From which language does the word "ketchup" originate?
16 How many islands are in the Falklands group?
17 Which team was Alain Prost with for his 80s hat-trick of Monaco wins?
18 Who wrote the novel *A Handful of Dust*?
19 In which country is the city of Tbilisi?
20 What do the letters LS stand for in Lowry's name?
21 What was the first British Top Ten hit for Bronski Beat?
22 In which sport were Wilfred and Herbert Baddeley famous?
23 In which country was the TV journalist Sandy Gall born?
24 Which star sign links Floella Benjamin and Judith Chalmers?
25 If it's noon at GMT, what time is it in Delhi?
26 Des Moines is the capital of which US state?
27 Ergasiophobia is the fear of what?
28 What is James Callaghan's first name?
29 Who was the only real-life comic to feature on the British "Smiles" stamps of the 1990s?
30 On which river does Munich stand?

Pot Luck 38   (see Quiz 75)

1 William Sturgeon. 2 A giant hedgehog. 3 The Overlanders. 4 David Niven. 5 Dutch. 6 Aquarius. 7 140. 8 Robert Gould Shaw. 9 Albania. 10 Athletics. 11 Georgia. 12 Richard Austen. 13 *The Old Curiosity Shop*. 14 Hayley Mills. 15 Cook. 16 Stagnation. 17 He had only one arm. 18 A Flower. 19 3,200. 20 "United We Stand". 21 Danielle Steele. 22 Colorado. 23 Pinza. 24 Joel Chandler Harris. 25 Marriage. 26 British India, now Pakistan. 27 Benjamin Disraeli. 28 Lord Byron. 29 Olivier Panis. 30 Northumberland Avenue.

Answers

313

1 Which 90s England player had the middle names Edward Riche?
2 Who was the first player to score over 200 in an English Sunday league game?
3 In what year did Graham Gooch make his county debut?
4 Who was the first England cricketer to be fined for conduct during a Test?
5 What sport - other than cricket - did Graeme Hick play for Zimbabwe?
6 Who scored the first fifty in a one-day international?
7 Who is the only player to represent both Australia and South Africa?
8 What is Ben Hollioake's middle name?
9 In 1996's NatWest Final Glen Chapple took six for how many?
10 Which England spinner shared his debut with Shane Warne's test arrival in England?
11 When did Essex first win the county championship?
12 Which one cap Neil took 2 for 148 and hit 38 runs in his one innings?
13 Where was the England bowler Andy Caddick born?
14 The Oval and Lord's were the first English test grounds - which was the third?
15 Who was the first keeper to make 10 test dismissals?
16 Which England cricketer was named after the Australian Neil Harvey?
17 Who in 1966, aged 16 years, 180 days, became Northants' youngest-ever player?
18 Bob Willis's eight for 43 ended the Ashes third test of 1981, but how many wickets did he take in the first innings?
19 Which team were the first after Lancashire to win the John Player League?
20 Which England player had the middle name Cleophas?
21 Who scored the first century in a one day international?
22 In which decade did Derby first win the county championship?
23 How many wickets did Neil Mallender take in his two test matches?
24 Which was the one county in 1997 not to have a player whose surname began with a W?
25 At which ground did Jim Laker take 19 test wickets in 1956?
26 And how many runs did Laker score in that fourth test against Australia?
27 How many times did Ian Botham skipper England in tests?
28 What is David Gower's middle name?
29 Who were the opposition when Mike Atherton played his first test?
30 Who took the catch that gave Fred Trueman his 300th test wicket

Quiz 75 Pot Luck 38

Answers - see page 313

LEVEL 3

1   Who invented the electromagnet?

2   What was Dinsdale in "Monty Python's Flying Circus"?

3   Who had a 60s No. 1 with "Michelle"?

4   Who was classed as "Anglo Saxon Type 2008" when he first went to Hollywood?

5   From which language does the word "schooner" originate?

6   Which star sign links Michael Bentine and Bamber Gascoigne?

7   How many degrees are there in each internal angle of a nonagon?

8   Which character was played by Pierce Brosnan in *Nancy Astor*?

9   In which country is the city of Tirana?

10   In which sport was Emmanuel McDonald Bailey famous?

11   Which US state is known as the Empire State of the South?

12   What were R.A. (RAB) Butler's first two names?

13   In which Dickens novel does Sampson Brass appear?

14   Which actress's first film was *Tiger Bay*?

15   Mangaia and Palmerstone are in which island group?

16   What is the only English anagram of ANTAGONIST?

17   In "Robin's Nest" what disablement was suffered by the dishwasher?

18   What is a Rafflesia the largest of in the world?

19   What is the approximate distance of Bahrain airport from London in miles?

20   What was the first British Top Ten hit for the Brotherhood of Man?

21   Who wrote *Thurston House" Palamino* and *Fine Things*?

22   Which US state is directly north of New Mexico?

23   On which horse did Gordon Richards have his only Derby success?

24   What was Uncle Remus's real name?

25   Juno was the Roman goddess of what?

26   In which country was the TV presenter Gordon Honeycombe born?

27   Who wrote *Vivian Grey*?

28   Who in 1812 said, "I awoke one morning and found myself famous"?

29   Who gave Ligier their first Formula 1 Grand Prix win since 1981 when he won at Monaco in 1996?

30   In Monopoly, if you were on Income Tax and got double five, where would you land?

Pot Luck 37 (see Quiz 73)

1 Raffaello Santi. 2 Rev. Martin Hooper. 3 Legislator. 4 The Temperance Seven. 5 Mexico. 6 18th. 7 Four. 8 Thames. 9 Horace Rumpole's. 10 Sooty. 11 George Bush. 12 Olga Korbut. 13 Sang "Danny Boy" in the ring. 14 Bernina Hotel, Switzerland. 15 Chinese. 16 Over 200. 17 McLaren. 18 Evelyn Waugh. 19 Georgia. 20 Laurence Stephen. 21 "Smalltown Boy". 22 Tennis. 23 Penang, Malaya. 24 Libra. 25 5.30 p.m. 26 Iowa. 27 Surgery. 28 Leonard. 29 Stan Laurel. 30 Isar.

1   What was Vivaldi's only oratorio called?

2   Where was the composer William Walton born?

3   What was Shakespeare's first tragedy?

4   For how many instruments is Xenakis's *Pithoprakta* for?

5   Who wrote the text for Benjamin Britten's *On this Island*?

6   Who is the subject of Jean Anouilh's play *L'Alouette*?

7   Which major European orchestra is the oldest?

8   Who wrote *Where the Wild Things Are* in 1980?

9   Who first used the organ in a symphony?

10 Who wrote the earliest concerto for flute?

11 What is the nickname of Mahler's Symphony No. 1 in D?

12 Who founded the Australian Ballet?

13 Who wrote the controversial opera *Lulu*?

14 Which Austrian wrote around 250 operas before his death in 1835?

15 Who wrote the earliest concerto for piccolo?

16 Which company for black dancers did Arthur Mitchell form in 1969?

17 Who gives Tony Awards?

18 Who wrote *Marlene* about Dietrich?

19 What was Shakespeare's first comedy?

20 How many symphonies did Bruckner write?

21 Who won the Leading Actor Tony in 1991 for *Shadowlands*?

22 How was the classical dancer Sydney Healey-Kay better known?

23 Where is the Santa Cecelia Academy Orchestra based?

24 Which instrument was invented in 1821 and had the first concerto written for it in 1951?

25 What is the nickname of Shostakovich's Symphony No. 7 in C written during World War Two?

26 What did the Festival Ballet change its name to?

27 Who wrote *The Duchess of Malfi*?

28 For which play did Margaret Tyzack win the Feature Actress Tony in 1990?

29 Who wrote the opera *Punch and Judy*?

30 Who was the founding choreographer of the New York City Ballet?

1 Which character was played by Jimmy Jewel in "Nearest and Dearest"?
2 What was Frank Richard's real name?
3 Who had a 70s No. 1 with "Double Barrel"?
4 The Spanish Formula 1 Grand Prix is held on the outskirts of which city?
5 How many main islands are in the Novaya Zemlya group?
6 Gatophobia is the fear of what?
7 In which town in Texas was Roy Orbison born?
8 On which Isle was the entertainer Rod Hull born?
9 Which parliamentary constituency did William Hague first contest?
10 If it's noon at GMT, what time is it in Honolulu?
11 From which language does the word "khaki" originate?
12 Who wrote *Love and Mr Lewisham*?
13 Who replaced Barrow in the Football League?
14 Which US state is north of Wyoming?
15 Shaft, Meteor and Onward are types of what?
16 In which country is Varna International Airport?
17 Who invented the endoscope?
18 What are the odds of rolling any combination totalling ten in dice-throwing?
19 Who in 1952 wrote *Water Music*, in which the pianist blows whistles under water?
20 In which fictitious village was "Oh No! It's Selwyn Froggitt" set?
21 In which sport was William James Bailey famous?
22 Which star sign links the entertainer Max Bygraves and the journalist Sandy Gall?
23 What is the only English anagram of CANE CHAIRS?
24 Niels Henrik Abek pioneered several branches of modern what?
25 Who won Emmy awards as an actor, writer and director of "M*A*S*H"?
26 The adjective aquiline refers to which creatures?
27 What is the capital of the US state of Idaho?
28 What is Shari Lewis's best-known puppet called?
29 Who was Mohammed Reza Pahlavi?
30 What was the first British solo Top Ten hit for Bobby Brown?

Quiz 78 Movie Comedies

LEVEL 3

Answers - see page 320

1   What was the second *Road* film?
2   Which comedy included the song "Somewhere in My Memory"?
3   In which city does *Sister Act 2* take place?
4   Who was turned down for the Spencer Tracy role in *Father of the Bride*?
5   Which two performers won BAFTAs for *A Fish Called Wanda*?
6   What is the name of the jewel thief in *The Pink Panther*?
7   Who starred opposite Michell Pfeiffer in *One Fine Day*?
8   What was the Doris Day remake of *My Favorite Wife* called?
9   In which film was Chaplin's Little Tramp seen for the last time?
10 Who wrote the books on which the *St Trinians* films were based?
11 What was Morecambe and Wise's first film called?
12 What is Nicole Kidman's job in *To Die For*?
13 Which classic comedy won BAFTA best film in 1951?
14 What was the first film the Marx Brothers made in Hollywood?
15 After which 1923 film did Harold Lloyd marry his leading lady Mildred Davis?
16 What was the follow-up to *A Fish Called Wanda* called?
17 In which 1936 film did Laurel and Hardy each play their own twins?
18 In which 1983 movie did Dan Aykroyd team with Eddie Murphy?
19 What was Woody Allen's first film as screenwriter and actor?
20 Who was the bungling Sherlock Holmes in *Without A Clue* in 1988?
21 Who wrote and starred in *L.A. Story*?
22 How was the screen comedian Louis Francis Cristillo better known?
23 What was the second *Carry On* film?
24 Which *Pink Panther* sequel mentions neither the Pink Panther nor Inspector Clouseau in the title?
25 Which comedy team first appeared in *One Night in the Tropics*?
26 Who played opposite Debbie Reynolds in *Tammy and the Bachelor*?
27 Who was the witch in *Spellbinder*?
28 Which 1982 film told of a concert party in Singapore in 1948?
29 Who wrote *Ghostbusters* with Harold Ramis?
30 Which was the first of the Rock Hudson/Doris Day comedies?

Quiz 79 Pot Luck 40

LEVEL 3

1   In Monopoly how much does it cost to buy Bow Street?
2   Which "EastEnders" actress appeared in the comedy "Split Ends"?
3   In which country is the city of Tripoli?
4   From which language does the word "elastic" originate?
5   In what year were the British Halley's Comet stamps issued?
6   In which sport was Edwin Percy Baker famous?
7   How was Giovanni Battista Montini better known?
8   Who had an 70s No. 1 with "No Charge"?
9   Who invented obstetric forceps?
10 Which Formula 1 racing driver gave his name to the Grand Prix circuit in Montreal?
11 What is the only English anagram of MARASCHINO?
12 On which river does Indianapolis stand?
13 Which star sign links Carol Barnes and Johnny Briggs?
14 In cricket, what name is given to 111 runs?
15 Which US State is directly east of Arizona?
16 Which "Emmerdale" animal was called either Jenny or Amos?
17 Which newspaper editor said, "Comment is free, facts are sacred"?
18 Who wrote the novel *Death in the Afternoon*?
19 What is the approximate distance of San Francisco airport from London in miles?
20 What do the letters JB stand for in J.B. Priestley's name?
21 If you are crapulous, what are you full of?
22 What is the name of the ship sailed by Captain Pugwash?
23 In which country was the presenter Kenneth Kendall born?
24 Annapolis is the capital of which US state?
25 Who did Honor Blackman play in *Never The Twain*?
26 In which country is the mineral cryolite found?
27 What was the first British Top Ten hit for James Brown?
28 What would a Cypriot call his capital of Nicosia?
29 Which volcano has the capital Quito, Ecuador, on its edge?
30 New Britain and Admiralty are in which island group?

Pot Luck 39   (see Quiz 77)

1 Eli Pledge. 2 Charles Hamilton. 3 Dave and Ansil Collins. 4 Barcelona.
5 Two. 6 Cats. 7 Wink. 8 Isle of Sheppey. 9 Wentworth (Yorks). 10 2
a.m. 11 Hindustani. 12 H.G. Wells. 13 Hereford. 14 Montana. 15 Pea.
16 Bulgaria. 17 Pierre Segalas. 18 11-1. 19 John Cage. 20 Scarsdale.
21 Cycling. 22 Libra. 23 Saccharine. 24 Mathematics. 25 Alan Alda.
26 Eagles. 27 Boise. 28 Lamb Chop. 29 The last Shah of Iran.
30 My Prerogative.

1 Who bought the Windsors' house in Paris in 1986?

2 Who was Nelson Mandela's companion on his July 1997 trip to London?

3 Who wrote her memoirs in "What Falls Away"?

4 Whose family estate is at Hyannis Port?

5 What did Goldie Hawn ride to open Harrods sale in January 1997?

6 After being Countess Spencer which title did Raine have?

7 Which singer was the celeb Isabel Preysler married to?

8 Which fashion house did John Galliano first design for in 1997?

9 What is Kate Capshaw's married name?

10 Who lives at Ray Mill House?

11 Which daughter of Joan Collins married in 1997?

12 Who owns a motor yacht called *Talitha G*?

13 Who was Naomi Campbell staying with in the Canaries when she was rushed to hospital in 1997?

14 Pamela Anderson won a court case over her withdrawal from which film?

15 What was the name of the Elton John documentary made by David Furnish?

16 What is the name of the Clintons' cat?

17 Who did the supermodel Vendela replace as UNICEF international spokesperson?

18 Who is Mrs James Keach?

19 How did Frances Roche become widely known?

20 Which actress is the granddaughter of the designer Elsa Schiaparelli?

21 In which capacity did Jane Makim attend Prince Andrew's wedding?

22 Whose family home is at Barnwell Manor?

23 Who was awarded the second-highest civilian medal for bravery in 1997?

24 Which interior designer was the son-in-law of Lord Mountbatten?

25 Who was Earl Spencer's best man who was jailed for fraud?

26 Who produced six offspring in the Lincoln Bedroom at the White House?

27 Which rich divorcee did Riccardo Mazzucchelli marry?

28 Which royal family name was Princess Stephanie born with?

29 Which rock star has granddaughters called Assisi and Amba?

30 Which ex-royal's family home was at Nymans in Sussex?

Quiz 81 Pot Luck 41

Answers - see page 323

LEVEL 3

1   Which shipping forecast area is south of Forties?
2   In which sport did Charles Smith make a fourth Olympic appearance aged 45?
3   How many islands are in the Faroe group?
4   In motor racing, what is the ECU?
5   Which character was played by Johnny Briggs in "No Hiding Place"?
6   If it's noon at GMT, what time is it in Bombay?
7   From which language does the word "cigar" originate?
8   In which US state would a Downeaster be a native inhabitant?
9   In which country is Trivandrum Airport?
10 Who had an 80s No. 1 with "99 Red Balloons"?
11 What is a dasyure?
12 The botanist Gregor Mendel belonged to which order of monks?
13 What did Howard Keel sell before he won a singing scholarship?
14 In which country, as well as Spain, is the city of Valencia ?
15 What name is given to a plant that doesn't have leaves?
16 In Scrabble what is the letter K worth?
17 What did Wonder Woman's lasso always make people do?
18 Helminthophobia is the fear of what?
19 How many main islands are in the Hawaiian group?
20 Who had *The Battle of the Books* published in 1704?
21 What did Shevardnadze call the idea that "each country should construct its foreign policy on a 'My Way' basis"?
22 What was the first British Top Ten hit for Joe Brown and the Bruvvers?
23 Which star sign links Henry Cooper and Bob Carolgees?
24 What was Henry John Temple's title when he was UK prime minister?
25 Which US state is directly south of Georgia?
26 In which sport was Gerald Matthews Balding famous?
27 Gene Wilder was born on the same day as which racing driver?
28 Which UK paper size is 420 x 594 mm?
29 Whose first book was called *Jigsaw*?
30 What is the only English anagram of INTERLACED?

Pot Luck 42 (see Quiz 83)
1 135. 2 The Four Pennies. 3 Reinvented. 4 Electric Company. 5 Nero.
6 Casablanca. 7 Pisces. 8 Philippines. 9 The *Daily Mail*. 10 "Word Up".
11 Venezuela. 12 Owens Illinois. 13 T.E. Lawrence. 14 Jezebel. 15 Clara
Danby. 16 Golf. 17 Minnesota. 18 Arthur Conan Doyle. 19 200. 20 Con
Brio. 21 Tuscany Valley. 22 Babar the Elephant. 23 Mintonette. 24 1,600.
25 17th. 26 Malay. 27 Arkansas. 28 Comoros. 29 Potato. 30 1989.

Answers

Quiz 82 World Tour

LEVEL 3

1 Allegheny and Blue Ridge are in which mountain range?
2 Where is the N'Gorongoro Crater?
3 The Commonwealth of Australia set up in 1901 comprised two territories and how many states?
4 Flores, Corvo and Pico belong to which group of islands?
5 Which city had a street called The Bowery?
6 Who links the Cenotaph in London and New Delhi?
7 What do the straits of Magellan separate?
8 On which river does Adelaide stand?
9 What is the capital of the Canadian province Manitoba?
10 Fagatogo is the capital of what?
11 What are the three volcanic islands of the British Virgin Islands?
12 Avarua is on which of the Cook Islands?
13 What are the Monte Titano peaks made from?
14 Who owns Bouvet Island?
15 How many official languages does South Africa have?
16 In which country is the largest expanse of sand in the world?
17 The Fouta Djallon mountains are to the south of which country?
18 On which river does Nashville stand?
19 Lake Kivu forms much of the western boundary of which country?
20 What is the former name of Nizhny Novgorod?
21 Where is the Kara-Kum Desert?
22 Doi Inthanon is the highest point of which country?
23 What is the capital of Anguilla?
24 Where is the largest phosphate deposit in the world?
25 Flying Fish Cove is on which island?
26 Which country lies between Guyana and French Guiana?
27 What does the Nile split into at Khartoum?
28 Aruba is off which country's coast?
29 Which islands were annexed to the Clunies-Ross family until 1978?
30 In the US which state is immediately west of Colorado?

Answers

Musicals (see Quiz 84)
1 Hair. 2 South Pacific. 3 Sweet Charity. 4 Frank Loesser. 5 Smokey Joe's Cafe. 6 Always. 7 "Oh What A Beautiful Morning". 8 Blood Brothers. 9 The Shadows. 10 Cats. 11 "With One Look". 12 Steve Harley. 13 Buddy. 14 Memories. 15 Martin Guerre. 16 Chess. 17 Grease. 18 Judi Dench. 19 Phantom of the Opera. 20 Funny Girl. 21 Marti Webb, Wayne Sleep. 22 Charles Hart & Richard Stilgoe. 23 Stephen Fry 24 Patti LuPone. 25 Cameron Mackintosh. 26 Dr Barnardo. 27 Anita Dobson. 28 Marvin Hamlisch. 29 Joseph and the Amazing Technicolor Dreamcoat. 30 Fagin.

Quiz 83 Pot Luck 42

Answers - see page 321

LEVEL 3

1   How many degrees are there in each internal angle of an octagon?
2   Who had an 60s No. 1 with "Juliet"?
3   What is the only English anagram of INTERVENED?
4   On a Monopoly board what is between Pall Mall and Whitehall?
5   What was the name of the caterpillar in "Dangermouse"?
6   Which port is known in Arabic as Dar el-Beida?
7   Which star sign links the author Jilly Cooper and the presenter Andy Crane?
8   In which country was the actress Susan Penhaligon born?
9   What was launched by Alfred Harmsworth and Viscount Northcliffe in 1896?
10 What was the first British Top Ten hit for Cameo?
11 The international car registration YV applies to which country?
12 Who invented industrial glass fibre?
13 What was T.E. Ross's real name?
14 In the Bible, who was King Ahab married to?
15 Which character was played by Pauline Collins in "No, Honestly"?
16 In which sport was John Ball famous?
17 Which US state is north of Iowa?
18 Who wrote *The White Company*?
19 How many 2.5 mile laps are completed in the car race, the Indy 500?
20 What term is given to a piece of music played vigorously?
21 In which valley was "Falcon Crest" set?
22 Which animated animal was married to his cousin, Celeste?
23 What was the original name of volleyball?
24 What is the approximate distance of Moscow airport from London in miles?
25 In which century was Daniel Defoe born?
26 From which language does the word "caddy" originate?
27 Which US state is known as the Bear State?
28 Moheli and Mayotte are in which island group?
29 Vanessa and Wilja are types of what?
30 Which year first saw red noses on cars in support of Comic Relief?

Pot Luck 41   (see Quiz 81)
1 Dogger. 2 Water polo. 3 22. 4 Electronic Control Unit. 5 Det Sgt Russell.
6 5.30 p.m. 7 Spanish. 8 Maine. 9 India. 10 Nena. 11 A marsupial.
12 Augustinian. 13 Aircraft. 14 Venezuela. 15 Aphyllous. 16 Five.
17 Tell the truth. 18 Worms. 19 Eight. 20 Jonathan Swift. 21 Sinatra
Doctrine. 22 "A Picture of You". 23 Taurus. 24 Viscount Palmerston.
25 Florida. 26 Polo. 27 Jackie Stewart. 28 A2. 29 Barbara Cartland.
30 Credential.

Answers

Quiz 84 Musicals

LEVEL 3

1   Which Broadway musical was the first to include nudes on stage?

2   Which musical opens on Emile de Becque's plantation?

3   "Big Spender" comes from which show?

4   Who wrote the lyrics for *Guys and Dolls*?

5   Which musical is based on the songs of Leiber and Stoller?

6   Which new 90s musical starred Sheila Ferguson, formerly of the Three Degrees'?

7   Which song opens the music for *Oklahoma*?

8   Which musical has the songs "Light Romance" and "My Child"?

9   Who next charted with "Don't Cry For Me, Argentina" after Julie Covington?

10   Elaine Paige's first Top Ten hit was from which musical?

11   What was Barbra Streisand's first hit from *Sunset Boulevard*?

12   Who duetted with Sarah Brightman on the chart single, "Phantom of the Opera" ?

13   Paul Hipp first played the title role in which musical?

14   Which album was subtitled "The Best of Elaine Paige"?

15   Which musical has the same theme as the Richard Gere film *Sommersby*?

16   Frederick Trumper was one of the heroes in which show?

17   Ian Kelsey of "Emmerdale" went on to star in which musical?

18   Whose withdrawal from "Cats" meant Elaine Paige starred in it?

19   Which Lloyd Webber show gave Cliff Richard a hit single?

20   Which musical does the song "People" come from?

21   Who were the first "Song" and "Dance" of *Song and Dance*?

22   Who wrote the lyrics of "Love Changes Everything"?

23   Which English comedian and novelist was said to have been made a millionaire in his 20s with his work on the West End hit *Me and My Girl*?

24   Who was the first Norma Desmond in *Sunset Boulevard* in London?

25   Who sponsored Oxford University's first professorship in drama and musical theatre?

26   Who was the subject of Rice and Lloyd Webber in *The Likes of Us*?

27   Who played opposite Adam Faith in the doomed *Budgie*?

28   Which musical writer wrote "Sunshine Lollipops And Rainbows" for Lesley Gore?

29   What was the longest-running show ever at the London Palladium when it finished in 1994?

30   Which role has been played by Barry Humphries, Jonathan Pryce and Russ Abbot?

Quiz 85 Pot Luck 43

LEVEL 3

1 On which river does Melbourne stand?

2 How did Barbara Betts become known in public life?

3 Who had an 80s No. 1 with "Save Your Love"?

4 Which character was played by Jane Seymour in "The Onedin Line"?

5 What was Saki's real name?

6 Lyon, Nord and Saint-Lazare are three stations on a French Monopoly board - what's the fourth?

7 What is the capital of the US state of Mississippi?

8 In which sport is Paul Jason Barber famous?

9 Who was the first indy car rookie to start from pole and win in 84 years?

10 In which country is the city of Windhoek?

11 What is the only English anagram of INTOXICATE?

12 The drunken midwife Sarah Gamp appeared in which Dickens novel?

13 What was the first British Top Ten hit for Canned Heat?

14 How many islands are in the Marquesas group?

15 If A is Alpha and B is Bravo what is K?

16 St Boniface is the patron saint of which country?

17 Who replaced Workington in the Football League?

18 In which country is Turku Airport?

19 Who wrote *The Once and Future King*?

20 Which US state is south of Kansas?

21 Who is the actress Catherine Oxenberg's mother?

22 In Scrabble what is the letter W worth?

23 Linonophobia is the fear of what?

24 In which country are the Siebenhengste System caves?

25 Which Swede did Frank Bruno beat in 1985 to become European heavyweight champ?

26 Which star sign links Steve Davis and Jim Bowen?

27 Who invented heat-resistant glass?

28 If it's noon at GMT, what time is it in La Paz?

29 Why was the 1961 world figure skating championships cancelled?

30 The adjective murine refers to which creatures?

Pot Luck 44 (see Quiz 87)
1 Archie Glover. **2** Claude-Joseph Rouget de Lisle. **3** Eiffel Tower. **4** 17.5-1.
5 Holography. **6** Triceratops. **7** Wyoming. **8** Scorpio. **9** Amandine-Aurore-Lucile (Lucie) Dudevant. **10** Pilot. **11** Bernard Bresslaw. **12** Hindi.
13 Oregon. **14** A Muster. **15** Floors Castle. **16** Bissagos. **17** Ayrton Senna.
18 3,200. **19** Dashiell Hammett. **20** "It Must Be Him". **21** Canadian Arctic Archipelago. **22** Four. **23** Maryland, Pennsylvania. **24** US Women's Open Golf. **25** Acton Town. **26** Rue de Courcelles. **27** Japan. **28** Terminates.
29 Hemingway. **30** Wrestling.

Answers

Quiz 86 TV: Stateside

Answers - see page 328

Answers - see page 328

LEVEL 3

1. Which role did Mr T play in "The A Team"?
2. Who was the local sheriff in "Twin Peaks"?
3. "All in the Family" was the US version of which UK sitcom?
4. In which state was "Thirtysomething" set?
5. Which actress has played Chris Cagney and Margaret Hoolihan?
6. "The Toast of the Town" was renamed what after its presenter?
7. Who were the two families in the US spoof "Soap"?
8. Which show's catchphrases included "You bet your sweet bippy"?
9. Which US TV network was founded in 1943 by Edward J. Noble?
10. Which blockbuster series, watched by over half of the US, had O.J. Simpson as Kadi Toura?
11. In which street did the Addams Family live?
12. Who was Executive Producer of "Star Trek: The Next Generation"?
13. Which non-profitmaking organization originally funded "Sesame Street"?
14. In "The Rockford Files" how much did Jim charge for a day's work?
15. To two years, when did "The Price Is Right" begin in the US?
16. Who owns the channel TNT?
17. Which sitcom was originally called "You'll Never Get Rich"?
18. What was the first US soap sold to Britain?
19. Who guest-starred as the judge in the final Perry Mason's case of the 60s series?
20. Who played the lead role in the US version of "Agony"?
21. On which US series was "University Challenge" based?
22. Which US network was the first to broadcast in colour?
23. Who transferred her radio role in "My Favourite Husband" to long-running TV success?
24. Which TV station was home to Ed Murrow and Walter Kronkite?
25. Which company did Lucille Ball create with her then real-life husband?
26. What was the name of "Play Your Cards Right" in the US?
27. Alan Alda hosted the US version of which UK satirical show?
28. What were the real names of the two known as Smith and Jones?
29. Which company bought the rights to "Prime Suspect" and didn't want Helen Mirren as the lead?
30. In the series where did Roseanne and Dan Conner live?

Answers

Olympics (see Quiz 88)

1 200m Individual Medley. 2 Marie-Jose Perec. 3 Cuba, Japan. 4 Lanier. 5 Belarus. 6 Renata Mauer. 7 Garmisch-Partenkirchen. 8 Tim Henman & Neil Broad. 9 Christa Luding, née Rothenburger. 10 Liechtenstein. 11 St Moritz. 12 Twice (1908, 1948). 13 Head garland of wild olive leaves. 14 Three. 15 Equestrian dressage. 16 Armenia, Azerbaijan. 17 Kenny Harrison. 18 Penny Heyns. 19 1994. 20 Carl Lewis. 21 Ian Walker, John Merricks. 22 Seppo Raty. 23 Mark Phillips. 24 Paul Palmer. 25 Steve Redgrave. 26 Mountain biking. 27 Over transport problems. 28 One. 29 Krisztina Egerzegi. 30 Eric Heiden (speed skating).

Quiz 87 Pot Luck 44

Answers - see page 325

LEVEL 3

1   Which character was played by Peter Bowles in "Only When I Laugh"?
2   Who wrote "La Marseillaise"?
3   The world's second TV service was beamed from which landmark?
4   What are the odds of rolling any combination totalling three in dice-throwing?
5   What was pioneered by the physicist Dennis Gabor?
6   What creature appeared on the most expensive of the British 1991 dinosaur stamps?
7   Cheyenne is the capital of which US state?
8   Which star sign links Sir Robin Day and John Cleese?
9   What was George Sand's real name?
10 Who had an 70s No. 1 with "January"?
11 Which *Carry On* actor was in "The Army Game" and "Secret Army"?
12 From which language does the word "jungle" originate?
13 Which US state is south of the State of Washington?
14 What term describes peacocks congregating together?
15 Which castle is the Scottish home of the Duke of Roxburgh?
16 Roxa and Caravela are in which island group?
17 Which Formula 1 driver won the Monaco Grand Prix each year from 1989-93?
18 What is the approximate distance of Lagos airport from London in miles?
19 Who wrote *The Thin Man*?
20 What was the first British Top Ten hit for Vikki Carr?
21 Banks and Baffin are in which island group?
22 In Scrabble what is the letter H worth?
23 The Mason-Dixon line is the boundary between which two states?
24 Patty Berg was the first winner of which major sporting event?
25 Alphabetically, what is the first station on the London Underground?
26 On a French Monopoly board, what is the equivalent to Euston Road?
27 In which country was the actress Victoria Principal born?
28 What is the only English anagram of MAIN STREET?
29 Which Ernest won the Nobel Prize for Literature in 1954?
30 In which sport was Edward Barrett famous?

Pot Luck 43 (see Quiz 85)

Answers

1 Yarra. **2** Barbara Castle. **3** Renée and Renato. **4** Emma Callon. **5** Hector Hugh Munro. **6** Montparnasse. **7** Jackson. **8** Hockey. **9** Nigel Mansell. **10** Namibia. **11** Excitation. **12** *Martin Chuzzlewit*. **13** "On The Road Again". **14** 10. **15** Kilo. **16** Germany. **17** Wimbledon. **18** Finland. **19** T.H. White. **20** Oklahoma. **21** Princess Elizabeth of Yugoslavia. **22** Four. **23** String. **24** Switzerland. **25** Anders Eklund. **26** Leo. **27** Carl Zeiss. **28** 8 a.m. **29** US team kiled in a plane crash. **30** Mice.

1   Which race gave Michelle Smith her third gold medal in Atlanta?
2   Who was the first Olympic athlete to win the 200m/400m double gold?
3   Who were the finalists in basketball in the 1996 Games?
4   On which Olympic lake did Steve Redgrave win a fourth gold?
5   With whom did Britain tie for 35th place in the medals table in Atlanta?
6   Who was the first gold medallist of the Atlanta Games?
7   Where were the 1936 Winter Olympics held?
8   Who were beaten by the Woodies in the 1996 men's doubles final?
9   Who was the first woman to win gold at winter and summer Games?
10 Which is the only country to have won winter but not summer gold?
11 Between 1928 and 1948 where were the winter Olympics held twice?
12 How many times have the Olympics been held in Britain?
13 What were victors given in the ancient Olympics?
14 How many of Mark Spitz's seven golds in 1972 were for team events?
15 In which event did Hilda Johnstone compete in the 1972 Games aged 70?
16 Which two countries beginning with A won first time medals in 1996?
17 Who beat Jonathan Edwards in the Triple Jump final in Atlanta?
18 In Atlanta who became South Africa's first gold medallist since 1952?
19 In which year were the Winter Olympics first held in the middle of the four-year cycle of the summer games?
20 Who was the second track and field athlete in Olympic history to win four successive titles in the same event?
21 Who won silver medals for Britain for yachting in Atlanta?
22 Who did Steve Backley beat into third place in 1996?
23 Whose horse Cartier forced him to withdraw from the Three-Day Event competition in 1988?
24 Who won Britain's first medal of the Atlanta Games?
25 Who carried the Olympic flag for the UK in Barcelona?
26 In which event, new in Atlanta, did Paolo Pezzo win gold?
27 Why did the Modern Pentathletes stage a sit-down protest at Atlanta?
28 How many people died because of the Centennial Park bomb?
29 Which woman won a record fifth individual swimming gold in 1996?
30 Who held the record from 1980 for most individual golds in one Games?

1   In which fictitious Manor House was "Mulberry" set?

2   Who gave Bill Wyman a walking frame when he married Mandy Smith?

3   Which country did Surya Bonaly represent at skating?

4   Who had an 80s No. 1 with "A Little Peace"?

5   Who invented the glider?

6   Mysophobia is the fear of what?

7   Which shipping forecast area is west of Dogger?

8   Who wrote *To the Lighthouse*?

9   In which country is the city of Aleppo?

10   What was Sapper's real name?

11   Mergoles and Kelvedon Marvel are types of what?

12   Where in Melbourne, is the Australian Formula 1 Grand Prix held?

13   Which US state is directly south of New Mexico?

14   Ernest Barry was a world champion which sport?

15   In Scrabble what is the letter P worth?

16   If it's noon at GMT, what time is it in Guatemala City?

17   Who was the last personality to be recorded on "This Is Your Life" before the death of Eamonn Andrews?

18   The athlete Carl Lewis was born on the same day as which royal?

19   What is the capital of the Canadian province Northwest Territories?

20   Which character was played by Patricia Hodge in "The Other 'Arf"?

21   What was the first British top Ten Hit for Ronnie Carroll?

22   How many islands and islets are in the Indonesia group?

23   Which star sign links actors Christopher Biggins and Lionel Blair?

24   Which US state is known as the Sooner State?

25   What is the only English anagram of MODERATORS?

26   In which country is Townsville Airport?

27   In which century was Franz Schubert born?

28   Who did Neville Chamberlain follow as prime minister of the UK?

29   On a French Monopoly board, how much is the fine on Impôts sur le Revenu?

30   In the TV series, what was Grizzly Adams's first name?

Answers

Pot Luck 46 (see Quiz 91)

1 "My Best Friend's Girl". 2 4,500. 3 Old Kent Road. 4 C.S. Forester.
5 Interlagos. 6 Joe Sugden. 7 Deer. 8 Nebraska. 9 Jukebox. 10 Sweet
Sensation. 11 120. 12 Harold Wilson. 13 Badger-digging. 14 Transience.
15 March 4. 16 A1. 17 Minnesota. 18 Taurus. 19 No play because of rain.
20 T.E. Lawrence. 21 Chonos Archipelago. 22 Germany. 23 Yashin.
24 1970s. 25 Arabic. 26 William Singer. 27 Stamped with a lion symbol.
28 Irving Berlin. 29 Golf. 30 St Paul.

1   How is Caryn Johnson better known?
2   Who was Woody Allen's date right at the end of *Annie Hall*?
3   Which actress's novels include *Delusions of Grandma*?
4   Which actress sang under the pseudonym Rainbo?
5   Who was the chain-smoking scientist in *Brainstorm*?
6   Who played the actress born Lucille Le Sueur in 1981?
7   Whose first Oscar nomination was in *The Sterile Cuckoo* in 1969?
8   Who won an Oscar without speaking in 1993?
9   Who was known as Anna Marno when she first went to Hollywood?
10   Who replaced Jean Harlow in the 1953 remake of *Red Dust*?
11   A film of whose wedding was released by MGM in Technicolor?
12   Who made her film debut in Hitchcock's *The Trouble With Harry*?
13   Who at 19 was Charlie Chaplin's oldest bride when he was 44?
14   Who married a French editor and wrote a book *Every Frenchman has One*?
15   Who was created Miss New Orleans 1931?
16   Which two films did Marilyn Monroe make after playing Sugar Kane?
17   In which TV soap did Demi Moore find fame?
18   Who was the daughter of Lana Turner who stabbed Lana's boyfriend to death?
19   Who played the investigator V.I. Warshawski on film and on Radio 4?
20   Who was the only female founder of United Artists?
21   Which film gave Elizabeth Taylor her third successive Oscar nomination in the 50s?
22   Which actress was called the Look on arriving in Hollywood?
23   Who was Honey Hornee in *Wayne's World II*?
24   Who was Warren Beatty's first wife?
25   Which actress had a son called Satchel?
26   Who was directed by her husband in *Rachel Rachel*?
27   Who played her sister as a child in *The Searchers* in 1956?
28   Whose autobiography was called *Goodness Had Nothing to Do With It*?
29   Who was born in 1932 as Edna Rae Gillooly?
30   Who played Jerry Lewis's child bride cousin in *Great Balls of Fire!*?

Answers

Animal World (see Quiz 92)
1 Vegetation above ground. 2 Capybara. 3 Barn Owl. 4 In its ear.
5 Insects. 6 Three. 7 Oxen. 8 Guanaco. 9 Live young. 10 Antelope.
11 30. 12 Red blood cell. 13 Highland collie. 14 London Zoo.
15 Bandicoot. 16 Colugo. 17 The Cat Fanciers Association of the US.
18 Strictly monogamous. 19 Madagascar. 20 Fisher. 21 Spiral. 22 When
they stand up on hind legs and tail. 23 Squid. 24 Squamata. 25 Cold-
blooded animal. 26 Snake. 27 Fox, badger or otter hunting. 28 Scaled
waterproof skins, shelled yolk-bearing eggs. 29 Venomous snake. 30 Great
Dane.

1 What was the first British Top Ten hit for the Cars?
2 What is the approximate distance of Bombay airport from London in miles?
3 In Monopoly, where would a double six from Piccadilly land you?
4 Who wrote *The African Queen*?
5 Which Sao Paolo suburb hosts the Brazilian Formula 1 Grand Prix circuit?
6 Who shot Kate Hughes's dog in the soap "Emmerdale"?
7 The adjective cerine refers to which creatures?
8 Which US state is directly south of South Dakota?
9 The Palais Royal Saloon, San Francisco, had the first what installed?
10 Who had an 70s No. 1 with "Sad Sweet Dreamer"?
11 How many degrees are there in each internal angle of a hexagon?
12 Who was the first Labour prime minister to meet a pope?
13 The dachshund was originally bred for what purpose?
14 What is the only English anagram of NECTARINES?
15 What is the latest date for Ash Wednesday in the 1990s?
16 Which UK paper size is 594 x 841 mm?
17 Which US state is the setting for "The Little House on the Prairie"?
18 Which star sign links Michael Barrymore and Dickie Davies?
19 What distinguished the first day of the first Old Trafford cricket test?
20 What was T.E. Shaw's real name?
21 Melchior and James are in which island group?
22 In which country was the actor Andrew Sachs born?
23 Puskas and who chaired Stanley Matthews off after his last game?
24 In what decade was Pluto's moon Charon discovered?
25 From which language does the word "minaret" originate?
26 Which character was played by Bernard Bresslaw in "Our House"?
27 What happened to British eggs for the first time in June 1957?
28 Who wrote the scores for the films *Easter Parade* and *Blue Skies*?
29 In which sport was Pamela Barton famous?
30 What is the capital of the US state of Minnesota?

Quiz 92 Animal World

LEVEL 3

Answers – see page 330

1 What does a browser forage for?
2 What is the largest living rodent?
3 What type of owl featured on the British Nature Conservation stamps of the 80s?
4 Where would a mammal have a malleus?
5 Echidna feed chiefly on what?
6 How many chambers does a camel have in its stomach?
7 What sort of creatures were the now extinct aurochs?
8 Which camelid is the ancestor of the llama and the alpaca?
9 What does a therian mammal produce?
10 In the animal world what is a bongo?
11 How many bones are there in the human arm?
12 What is an erythrocyte?
13 What is another name for the bearded collie?
14 Where is the world's largest zoological library?
15 Which marsupial has the highest reproductive rate?
16 What is another name for the flying lemur?
17 What is the world's largest pedigree cat registry?
18 Which unusual sexual characteristic does the Patagonian hare have?
19 The lemur is native to where?
20 Which species of marten can penetrate a porcupine's defences?
21 What shape are a bushbuck's horns?
22 In mongooses what is the tripod position?
23 What is the principal food of the sperm whale?
24 Which order of reptiles do snakes and lizards belong to?
25 What is a poikilotherm?
26 What is a taipan?
27 What were Dandie Dinmonts originally bred for?
28 Which two main features do reptiles have which amphibians don't?
29 What is a krait?
30 How is the German mastiff also known?

Hollywood Actresses (see Quiz 90)

Quiz 93 Pot Luck 47

Answers – see page 335

LEVEL 3

1 Which character was played by Jeremy Irons in "The Pallisers"?
2 On which river does Perth, Australia, stand?
3 What was the lowest value of a British Andrew-and-Fergie wedding stamp?
4 Which biscuit TV ad featured a Mexican singing "I can't stand it"?
5 Who had an 80s No. 1 with "Feels Like I'm In Love"?
6 In Scrabble what is the letter C worth?
7 Which star sign links the TV personalities Katie Boyle and Gordon Burns?
8 St Jude's Institute formed the soccer club now known as what?
9 In which country is the city of Constantine?
10 From which language does the word "hammock" originate?
11 In which century was Cyrano de Bergerac born?
12 Which city was home to the TV puppet owl, Ollie Beak?
13 Nosophobia is the fear of what?
14 Which US state is directly east of Minnesota?
15 Fresh breeze equals which number on the Beaufort Scale?
16 What was the first British Top Ten hit for CCS?
17 On a French Monopoly board, how much does it cost to buy a utility?
18 Pele was born on the same day as which English test cricketer?
19 In which country is Yundam Airport?
20 Selene is the Greek goddess of what?
21 Sammy Duvall was an 80s world champion in which sport?
22 What is the only English anagram of PERCUSSION?
23 If it's noon at GMT, what time is it in Rio de Janeiro?
24 What was Stendahl's real name?
25 How many islands are in the Mariana group?
26 Who did Steve Davis beat in the final when he first became world champion?
27 In which country was the actress Carmen Silvera born?
28 Dave Bickers was a British 60s champion in which sport?
29 What is the approximate distance of Johannesburg airport from London in miles?
30 Juneau is the capital of which US state?

Pot Luck 48 (see Quiz 95)

Answers

1 1981. 2 Graham Greene. 3 Tomato. 4 Canada. 5 Prettiness. 6 Canaries.
7 Earl of Liverpool. 8 Tennis. 9 Gary Davies. 10 Typically Tropical.
11 Frederick Walton. 12 Vietnam. 13 Isabel De Gines. 14 Scotland. 15 St
Bridget and St Eric. 16 Hutton and Washbrook. 17 £120. 18 "Hit The Road,
Jack". 19 French. 20 Idaho. 21 Capricorn. 22 Oxbridge. 23 Table tennis.
24 10,600. 25 A. 26 *Our Mutual Friend*. 27 Michigan. 28 "The Good Life".
29 New Zealand. 30 Thomas Straussler.

Quiz 94 TV: Cartoons

Answers – see page 336

LEVEL 3

1   In which show did Yogi Bear first appear?
2   Whose partners included Crazylegs Crane and the Aardvark?
3   Who was the most famous voice of Bugs Bunny?
4   What was Ding-A-Ling?
5   In "The Flintstones" what was Baby Rubble called?
6   Where did the Jetsons live?
7   What was Scooby-Doo's nephew called?
8   What was Bedrock's newspaper called?
9   In which series did Rock and Gravel Slag first appear?
10 What was the first name of Mr Magoo?
11 Who narrated Mr Benn?
12 What was the name of the four Banana Splits?
13 Whose gang included Brain, Spook and Benny the Ball?
14 Which vegetarian vampire was voiced by David Jason?
15 What was the racoon called in "Deputy Dawg"?
16 Who first produced the "Tom and Jerry" cartoons?
17 Whose catchphrase was "Drat and triple drat"?
18 Where did George Jetson work?
19 What were the first names of Hanna and Barbera?
20 What was Nero in "Dangermouse"?
21 Who created Frankenstein Jr in the 60s series?
22 Which cartoon character was first seen in "Le Petit Vingtieme"?
23 Hong Kong Phooey was the guise of whom?
24 For which railway company did Ivor the Engine work for?
25 Where was the series "Marine Boy" made?
26 In "The Flintstones" what was Wilma's vacuum cleaner?
27 What did Paddington's friend Mr Gruber do for a living?
28 In the Tin Tin stories what was Captain Haddock's ship called?
29 Who had purple hair and a dog called Alistair?
30 What was Yogi Bear's girlfriend called?

1   When did Italy adopt a double race format for Formula 1 at Imola and Monza?
2   Who wrote *The Third Man*?
3   Sioux and Sleaford Abundance are types of what?
4   In the TV series which country did Shelley's daughter emigrate to?
5   What is the only English anagram of PERSISTENT?
6   Hierro and Gomera are in which island group?
7   What was Robert Banks Jenkinson's title when he was UK prime minister?
8   In which sport was Blanche Bingley famous?
9   Which Radio 1 DJ was given the nickname Medallion Man?
10 Who had a 70s No. 1 with "Barbados"?
11 Who invented linoleum?
12 In which country is the city of Da Nang?
13 Which character was played by Sylvia Sims in "Peak Practice"?
14 Who were the opponents for Bobby Charlton's first international?
15 Who are the patron saints of Sweden?
16 In the 40s who were England's regular test openers?
17 In Monopoly how much does it cost to buy Pentonville Road?
18 What was the first British Top Ten hit for Ray Charles?
19 From which language does the word "chassis" originate?
20 Which US state is known as the Gem State?
21 Which star sign links Richard Briers and Keith Chegwin?
22 In which General Hospital was "Emergency Ward 10" set?
23 The Corbillon Cup is awarded in which sport?
24 What is the approximate distance of Sydney airport from London in miles?
25 On a six-string guitar, what note is played fifth fret, top string?
26 In which Dickens novel does Bradley Headstone appear?
27 Which US state is directly north of Indiana?
28 What was filmed in Kewferry Road, Northwood, Middlesex in the 70s?
29 In which country was the comedienne Pamela Stephenson born?
30 What was Tom Stoppard's original surname name?

Quiz 96 Communication

Answers – see page 334

LEVEL 3

1. In communications what does SONAR stand for?
2. What did Bardeen, Shockley and Brattain invent in 1948?
3. What is EFT?
4. How many megabits are there in a gigabit?
5. What is the full name of the computer language COGO?
6. What is a computer that links one network to another called?
7. What was the longest tunnel of any kind when it was finished in 1944?
8. Which Post Office clerk suggested roadside postboxes be erected in Guernsey?
9. What does EEROM mean?
10. What are the two extremities of the Pan-American Highway?
11. What was the first regular direct broadcasting system called?
12. What does ASCII stand for?
13. In 1997 which country had the cheapest postal service?
14. In which UK mainland county is the oldest postbox in daily use?
15. What were early tape recorders, pioneered by Poulsen called?
16. Where is the largest switchboard in the world?
17. What did Emile Berliner first demonstrate in 1888?
18. Which countries does the submarine telephone cable FLAG link?
19. What does the Interprovincial Pipe Line Inc. carry?
20. What postmark did the first undersea post office have?
21. What was the name of the first radio station in the USA?
22. What was the name of the huge telecommunications exchange at the Atlanta Olympics?
23. On the international E-road network what do three dots mean?
24. The first transatlantic radio message was sent from where to where?
25. Which country in 1997 had the greatest number of telephone subscribers per head of population?
26. Where in 1997 was the world's largest dish radio telescope?
27. Which British company pioneered stereophonic sound?
28. What is the name of the restaurant on Canada's CN Tower?
29. On which network is the Lovell telescope at Jodrell Bank?
30. What is MATV?

Answers

TV: Cartoons (see Quiz 94)
1 "Huckleberry Hound Show". 2 Pink Panther. 3 Mel Blanc. 4 Fox.
5 Bamm Bamm. 6 Orbit City. 7 Scrappy-Doo. 8 The *Daily Slate*. 9 "Wacky Races". 10 Quincy. 11 Ray Brooks. 12 Fleegle, Bingo, Drooper and Snorky.
13 Top Cat (in "The Boss Cat"). 14 Count Duckula. 15 Ty Coon. 16 Fred Quimby. 17 Dastardly. 18 Spacely Space Sprockets. 19 William, Joseph.
20 Caterpillar. 21 Buzz Conroy. 22 Tin Tin. 23 Penrod "Penry" Pooch.
24 Llantissily Rail Traction Co. Ltd. 25 Japan. 26 Baby elephant on roller skates. 27 Antiques dealer. 28 *Karaboudjan*. 29 Crystal Tipps. 30 Cindy.

336

1   Ochlophobia is the fear of what?
2   If it's noon at GMT, what time is it in Lima?
3   Who had a 50s No. 1 with "Hoots Mon"?
4   The actor Danny Glover was born on the same day as which member of the Eagles?
5   Which character was played by Christopher Biggins in "Poldark"?
6   In which country is the city of Chittagong?
7   From which language does the word "iceberg" originate?
8   What is the capital of the US state of Louisiana?
9   Which country lost their Formula 1 Grand Prix after 1981 but re-entered the staging in 1995?
10 What was Tintoretto's real name?
11 On a French Monopoly board, how much is the Taxe De Luxe?
12 Which shipping forecast area is east of Dogger and Humber?
13 Who replaced Gateshead in the Football League?
14 Which pop singer appeared in "Happy Days" as Leather Tuscadero?
15 In which country was the actress Angela Thorne born?
16 The adjective "leporine" refers to which creatures?
17 Teddy Bourne competed in three Olympics at which event?
18 How many islands are in the Kuril group?
19 What was the first British Top Ten hit for Glen Campbell?
20 Which actor was Adrian Mole's grandfather and in "The Army Game"?
21 Alice Perrers was the mistress of which monarch?
22 Which US state is North of Arkansas?
23 What is the only English anagram of SHATTERING?
24 Where was the first by-election held after the 1997 general election?
25 Who invented margarine?
26 In Scrabble what is the letter Y worth?
27 Which ape was played by Roddy McDowall in "Planet of the Apes"?
28 Which US state is known as the Wolverine State?
29 Which star sign links Danny Baker and Roy Barraclough?
30 In which country is Yoff Airport?

Answers

Pot Luck 50   (see Quiz 99)
1 "I Hear You Now". 2 108. 3 Morgan Beaudine. 4 Tiziano Vecellio.
5 Chagos. 6 Misconstrue. 7 Germany. 8 Sagittarius. 9 A bird.
10 M/A/R/R/S. 11 John Fowles. 12 Monaco. 13 Leon Brittan. 14 800.
15 Detective Inspector. 16 Super Tax. 17 Equestrianism. 18 November.
19 Percy Le Baron Spencer. 20 Michigan. 21 Blue and white. 22 John Le
Carré. 23 Friday. 24 Ted Ray. 25 Mazanares. 26 Scott Welch. 27 Ohio.
28 Italian. 29 Duane Eddy. 30 Four.

1   What was the last battle between Britain and America?
2   Who fought whom in the late 19th-century War of the Pacific?
3   In which war were Britain the victors in 1842?
4   What was the first battle in the American War of Independence?
5   Which British Army general was born at Westerham vicarage in 1788?
6   What was the largest carrier battle of World War Two?
7   Who was defeated at the battle of Pharsalus in 48 BC?
8   During which war was the battle of the Alamo?
9   In which battle were tanks first used?
10 Who was the German commander at Verdun in 1916?
11 What was the last major naval battle of World War Two?
12 Where did the Russians have their final conflict in Germany in World War One?
13 In which war did the Battle of Solferino take place in 1859?
14 In World War Two, the battle of Coral Sea stopped a Japanese attack on where?
15 The site of the battle of Koniggratz in 1866 is now in which country?
16 Canada fell under British control after which battle of the Seven-Years War?
17 Which treaty led to the withdrawal of US troops from Vietnam?
18 In which war was the battle of Tsushima?
19 Conflict between which two tribes brought about the Biafran war?
20 After which major battle did the French leave Vietnam?
21 At which World War One battle did the Germans use poison gas for the first time?
22 Which ships were involved in the first battle of the Atlantic in 1939?
23 Which British territory was captured on Christmas Day 1941?
24 Who was defeated at the battle of Lepanto in 1571?
25 Who fought the Romans in the Battle of Mons Grapius in AD 84?
26 Who was in charge of the Russian army when the Germans were defeated at Stalingrad?
27 Which war was precipitated by the rejection of the Nineteen Propositions?
28 Which treaty ensured the Boers lost their independence in 1902?
29 Which three countries along with Germany invaded Russia in 1941?
30 Which World War One campaign began with the arrival of Indian troops at Abadan?

Folk & Blues (see Quiz 100)
Answers

1 Judy Dyble. 2 Phil Ochs. 3 Paris. 4 Rolling Thunder Review. 5 "The Times They Are A-Changin'". 6 Blind Willie McTell (Ralph McTell). 7 The Humblebums. 8 Conor. 9 Travers (Peter, Paul and Mary). 10 Blind Lemon Jefferson. 11 *Rhymes and Reasons*. 12 Riley. 13 Troubador. 14 Elektra. 15 Martin Carthy. 16 John Lee Hooker. 17 Sandy Denny. 18 Alexis Korner. 19 Al Stewart. 20 *Basket Of Light*. 21 Wilson. 22 Chicago. 23 Cecil Sharp. 24 Macclesfield. 25 Al Kooper. 26 T-Bone Walker. 27 West Virginia. 28 Brain haemorrhage. 29 Bob Dylan. 30 Sam Hopkins.

1 What was the first British Top Ten hit for Jon and Vangelis?

2 How many degrees are there in each internal angle of a pentagon?

3 Which character was played by Kurt Russell in "The Quest"?

4 What was Titian's real name?

5 Banhos and Salomon are in which island group?

6 What is the only English anagram of CONSUMERIST?

7 In which country is the city of Duisburg?

8 Which star sign links Janet Brown and Christopher Cazenove?

9 One of the 1988 Edward Lear stamps depicted Lear as what?

10 Who had an 80s No. 1 with "Pump Up The Volume"?

11 Who wrote the book *The Collector*?

12 Where is the Autodromo Enzo e Dino Ferrari circuit?

13 Who was MP for Richmond, North Yorks, before William Hague?

14 What is the approximate distance of Madrid airport from London in miles?

15 What was Regan's rank in the last episode of "The Sweeney"?

16 On a Monopoly board what is between Park Lane and Mayfair?

17 In which sport was George Bowman famous?

18 What month did Channel 4 go on the air in 1982?

19 Who invented the microwave oven?

20 Lansing is the capital of which US state?

21 At half-time in 1995 Man. Utd changed shirts at the Dell from grey to what colour?

22 Who said, "Spies, like prostitutes, are always going to be with us"?

23 If March 1 is on a Monday in a leap year, what day was January 1?

24 The comic Charlie Olden was known by what name?

25 On which river does Madrid stand?

26 Who ended Joe Bugner's 1995 boxing comeback?

27 Which US state is West of Pennsylvania?

28 From which language does the word "manifesto" originate?

29 The theme tune for *Peter Gunn* was played by which lead guitarist?

30 In Scrabble what is the letter V worth?

Quiz 100 Folk & Blues

Answers – see page 338

LEVEL 3

1 Who was the original female vocalist in Fairport Convention?
2 Who wrote "There But For Fortune"?
3 In which city was Alexis Korner born?
4 What was Bob Dylan's 1976 tour called?
5 Which cover version sneaked in the charts for Ian Campbell in 1965?
6 Who did Ralph May take his stage name from?
7 What name did Billy Connolly and Gerry Rafferty sing under?
8 What was the name of Eric Clapton's son whose death inspired "Tears In Heaven"?
9 Who made up the trio with Yarrow and Stookey?
10 In the 1920s, who recorded "Match Box Blues" and "That Black Snake Moan"?
11 What was John Denver's first album called?
12 What is B.B. King's actual first name?
13 What was the name of London's leading folk club in the 60s?
14 Tom Paxton's *Ramblin' Boy* album came out on which label?
15 Simon and Garfunkel took the song "Scarborough Fair" from whom?
16 Who used the pseudonyms Birmingham Sam and Delta John?
17 Who wrote "Who Knows Where the Time Goes"?
18 Which blues man had a speaking part on Hot Chocolate's hit "Brother Louis"?
19 Who recorded the album *Bedsitter Images*?
20 Pentangle's "Night Flight" came from which album?
21 What was Woody Guthrie's middle name?
22 Smitty's Corner and Pepper's Lounge were blues clubs in which city?
23 Who published in 1907 *English Folk Songs: Some Conclusions*?
24 John Mayall comes from which untraditional birthplace of bluesmen?
25 Who played organ on Dylan's "Like A Rolling Stone"?
26 Who made the album *Stormy Monday Blues*?
27 According to John Denver which state is "almost heaven"?
28 How did Sandy Denny die?
29 Which folk hero played piano in Bobby Vee's band the Shadows?
30 What was Lightnin' Hopkins's real name?

Quiz 101 Pot Luck 51

Answers – see page 343

LEVEL 3

1   What was the first British Top Ten hit for Eartha Kitt?
2   On a French Monopoly board, how much does it cost to buy a station?
3   Who was the first British conductor to have his life dramatized on TV?
4   From which language does the word "typhoon" originate?
5   In which country is the city of La Plata?
6   Whose last Formula 1 Grand Prix race of his career was at Adelaide in 1985?
7   What was Robert Gascoyne-Cecil's title when he was UK prime minister?
8   Bert Turner got an FA Cup Final goal and an own goal playing for whom?
9   Which UK paper size is 841 x 1189 mm?
10 Who invented the parking meter?
11 In which country are the world's deepest caves?
12 Which star sign links the presenter Gavin Campbell and the comedian Jasper Carrott?
13 In which country was Alan Whicker born?
14 Mike Avory and Pete Quaife were members of which pop group?
15 What is the approximate distance of Frankfurt airport from London in miles?
16 What was Michael Angelo Titmarsh's real name?
17 How many clusters of islands are in the Maldives group?
18 In which US state would a Bay Stater be a native inhabitant?
19 Odynophobia is the fear of what?
20 Who had a hit in 1975 with "Loving You"?
21 If it's noon at GMT, what time is it in Riyadh?
22 Model White and Green Globe are types of what?
23 Which soccer club left the Scottish League in the 1960s?
24 Which US state is directly east of New Hampshire?
25 Which character was played by Julie Covington in "Rock Follies"?
26 What are Phoebe, Mimas and Rhea?
27 In which country is Spokane Airport?
28 What is the only English anagram of INTERSPERSE?
29 Who wrote books about the Wombles?
30 In which sport was Beryl Burton famous?

Answers

Pot Luck 52   (see Quiz 103)
1 Italian. **2** 18th. **3** India. **4** "Everybody's Got To Learn Sometime". **5** Kadi Touray. **6** Caisse de Communaute. **7** Stoneway. **8** Gemini. **9** Colorado. **10** H Rider Haggard. **11** The Battle of Wounded Knee. **12** Squash. **13** John Parrot (three). **14** 10. **15** Thomas à Becket. **16** Germany. **17** Cape Verde. **18** Sebastopol. **19** 3,400. **20** Tom Robinson Band. **21** Parliaments. **22** 19 minutes. **23** Nereid. **24** Berlin. **25** 1973. **26** Vatican City. **27** New York. **28** Graham Hill. **29** Vengeance. **30** Hawaii.

Quiz 102 Rugby

Answers – see page 344

LEVEL 3

1   Which country were the first to play in two union World Cup Finals?
2   As a player Willie John McBride went on how many Lions tours?
3   To five years, when did France first win the Five Nations outright?
4   Who won league's first Man Of Steel award?
5   What was the half-time score when Wigan beat Bath 82-6 in the cross code challenge?
6   Who is Argentina's leading all-time point-scorer?
7   Who didn't go and collect his loser's medal after the 1996 Pilkington Cup Final?
8   Keith Elwell played in 239 consecutive games for which league side?
9   Who scored 45 individual points for New Zealand against Japan in 1995?
10 Which university did Will Carling go to?
11 Who is the only person to captain the Lions and the English cricket team?
12 Who said at the wedding of the All-Black Glen Osborne, "I'm not the best man: I'm one of the security guards"?
13 Who scored most tries in the first Super League season?
14 Which country first completed the Grand Slam in 1968?
15 How old was Barry John when he retired from playing rugby?
16 Who said, "I'd rather play for Gloucester for 10p than go to Newcastle for £85,000"?
17 Rory Underwood began his senior career with which club?
18 What is Martin Offiah's middle name?
19 Gavin Hastings scored how many points in the 1995 World Cup game against Ivory Coast?
20 Ellery Hanley first won the Man Of Steel award while with which club?
21 In which decade were Orrell founded?
22 Which club did Gareth Edwards play for?
23 Who was Warrington's first player to win the Man Of Steel award?
24 In the 1995 World Cup which two players scored seven tries?
25 Who captained Wasps to the 1990 Courage League championship?
26 Which team won league's Challenge Cup before Wigan's eight-in-a-row run?
27 the full-back J.P.R. Williams played once in a 1978 international in which position?
28 Who was the first person to play in and later coach an England Grand Slam team?
29 Where was Tony Underwood born?
30 Who said, "There is no place for racial prejudice in the teachings of the Lord"?

Movies: Oscars (see Quiz 104)

1 Diane Ladd, Laura Dern. 2 Frank Borzage. 3 Sessue Hayakawa. 4 Costume design. 5 *Kitty Foyle.* 6 Sophia Loren. 7 Sally Field. 8 *Broadway Melody.* 9 Marlee Matlin (*Children of a Lesser God*). 10 Geraldine Page. 11 Spencer Tracy. 12 Ingrid Bergman. 13 *It Happened One Night.* 14 *Cimarron, Cavalcade.* 15 Greer Garson. 16 Glenda Jackson. 17 11 nominations, no winners. 18 *Mr Skeffington.* 19 "Somewhere in My Memory". 20 Deborah Kerr. 21 Joan Fontaine, Olivia de Havilland. 22 Charlie Allnut (*The African Queen*). 23 *Giant.* 24 *The Man Who Knew Too Much.* 25 Hollywood Roosevelt Hotel. 26 Margaret Rutherford. 27 Louise Fletcher (*One Flew Over the Cuckoo's Nest*). 28 *Going My Way.* 29 Hayley Mills. 30 *All About Eve* (14)

Quiz 103 Pot Luck 52

Answers – see page 341

LEVEL 3

1 From which language does the word "balcony" originate?
2 In which century was the US novelist James Fenimore Cooper born?
3 In which country is the city of Nagpur?
4 What was the first British Top Ten hit for the Korgis?
5 Which character was played by O.J. Simpson in "Roots"?
6 On a French Monopoly board, what is the equivalent to Community Chest?
7 What is Malcolm's surname in the TV series "Watching"?
8 Which star sign links Stanley Baxter and Joan Collins?
9 Which US state is known as the Centennial State?
10 Who wrote the novel *King Solomon's Mines*?
11 What was the last major conflict between native North Americans and US troops?
12 Don Butcher was a champion in which sport?
13 Which finalist has won the fewest frames since snooker's world championship became first to 18 frames?
14 Whole gale equals which number on the Beaufort Scale?
15 Who did Fitzurse, de Tracy, de Merville and le Breton murder?
16 In which country was Bruce Willis born?
17 Boa Vista and Sao Nicolau are in which island group?
18 In which fictitious terrace did Eric Sykes and his sister Hat live?
19 What is the approximate distance of New York airport from London in miles?
20 Who had a hit in 1977 with "2-4-6-8 Motorway"?
21 What is the only English anagram of PATERNALISM?
22 How many minutes did Brian Little's England-playing career last for?
23 What name was given to the second of Neptune's moons to be discovered?
24 In which city was André Previn born?
25 When did Denmark join the European Union?
26 The international car registration V applies to vehicles from where?
27 Which US state is directly west of Vermont?
28 Who was the first Formula 1 driver to win at Monaco in three successive years in 1963-5?
29 In Greek mythology, Attis is the god of what?
30 Where did Frank and Pat go for their honeymoon in "EastEnders"?

Pot Luck 51 (see Quiz 101)

1 "Under the Bridges of Paris". **2** F20,000. **3** Sir Thomas Beecham.
4 Chinese. **5** Argentina. **6** Niki Lauder. **7** Marquess of Salisbury.
8 Charlton (1946). **9** A0. **10** Carlton C. Magee. **11** France. **12** Pisces.
13 Egypt. **14** The Kinks. **15** 400. **16** William Makepeace Thackeray.
17 19. **18** Massachusetts. **19** Pain. **20** Minnie Riperton. **21** 3 p.m.
22 Turnip. **23** Third Lanark. **24** Maine. **25** Devonia Dee Rhoades.
26 Satellites of Saturn. **27** USA. **28** Enterprises. **29** Elizabeth Beresford.
30 Cycling.

1 Who were the first mother and daughter to receive simultaneous Oscar nominations?
2 Who won the first Best Director Oscar?
3 Who was nominated for his role as the prison camp commander in *The Bridge on the River Kwai*?
4 Milera Canonero won an Oscar for *Chariots of Fire* for what?
5 For which film did Ginger Rogers win her only Oscar?
6 Who was the first person to receive an Oscar for a role played entirely in a foreign language?
7 Whose second Oscar prompted her "You like me" speech?
8 What was the first talkie to win an Oscar?
9 Who won an award in her first film, based on a Mark Medoff play?
10 Which actress won her first Oscar after her eighth nomination?
11 Who was the first Best Actor in successive years?
12 Of all the star cameos, who won the only Oscar for *Murder on the Orient Express*?
13 What was the first movie to win Best Actor, Actress, Director and Film?
14 Which two 30s Best Films had one-word titles?
15 Which Irish actress had one win in seven nominations by 1960?
16 Who was the first Best Actress to win the award twice in the 70s?
17 In Oscar terms what links *The Color Purple* and *The Turning Point*?
18 For which 1944 film did Bette Davis win her fifth successive nomination?
19 Which song from Home Alone as Oscar nominated?
20 Who received an honorary Oscar in 1994 after six unsuccessful nominations in 12 years?
21 Which sisters were nominated for Best Actress in 1941?
22 Which character won Humphrey Bogart an Oscar in 1951?
23 For which film did Rock Hudson receive his only nomination?
24 In which film was "Que Sera Sera" an Oscar-winner?
25 Where were the first Oscars presented?
26 Who was Best Supporting Actress winner in 1963 for *The VIPs*?
27 Who won an Oscar playing Nurse Ratched?
28 In which film did "Swinging on a Star" win an Oscar?
29 In 1960 who received a miniature statuette for her "outstanding juvenile performance"?
30 Which 50s film had most Oscar nominations?

Quiz 105 Pot Luck 53

Answers – see page 346

1 Who had a hit in 1985 with "My Toot Toot"?

2 What were the names of Timothy Lumsden's parents in "Sorry"?

3 Which shipping forecast area is south of Shannon and Fastnet?

4 What is the only English anagram of PROCREATION?

5 Which city introduced Britain's first trolley-bus service?

6 Who was Nigel Mansell's teammate at the Newman Haas Indy Team?

7 Who invented the slide rule?

8 In which country is the city of Nanning?

9 In which hospital is the TV comedy series "Surgical Spirit" set?

10 Joan Rivers was born on the same day as which opera singer?

11 If it's noon at GMT, what time is it in Rangoon?

12 In Scrabble what is the letter N worth?

13 In which Dickens novel does Jeremiah Flintwinch appear?

14 How many islands are in the Laccadive group?

15 What blood group did the Vulcan Mr Spock have?

16 What was the first British Top Ten hit for the Trammps?

17 From which language does the word "skippe" originate?

18 On which river does Pittsburgh stand?

19 Which star sign links the comics Stan Boardman and Ronnie Corbett?

20 Who replaced Bradford Park Avenue in the Football League?

21 What is the approximate distance of Mexico City airport from London in miles?

22 Which county gave the setting to the TV series "Rich Tea and Sympathy"?

23 In which sport was Philip Mario Caira famous?

24 What is the capital of the US state of Pennsylvania?

25 Phagophobia is the fear of what?

26 If A is Alpha and B is Bravo what is U?

27 Who invented the car speedometer?

28 Which character was played by Sean Maguire in "Grange Hill"?

29 How much was the weekly family allowance when first introduced?

30 In which country is Pago Pago Airport?

The Last Round (see Quiz 107)

1 India. **2** William Golding. **3** "Hold Me Tight". **4** 11. **5** Nevada. **6** Ely. **7** Rationale. **8** Joseph Glidden. **9** Caroline. **10** 92. **11** New Lyne. **12** 35-1. **13** Leo. **14** Whitechapel. **15** Harry Longbaugh. **16** Cabbage. **17** Speed skating. **18** Frances. **19** Utah. **20** Arabic. **21** Chile. **22** Charles Farrar Browne. **23** Nurse Hilda Price. **24** Lyn St James. **25** Sir Winston Churchill. **26** Toaster. **27** South Africa. **28** Customs and Excise. **29** Musical Youth. **30** 2,200.

1 Who said, "Take it easy driving - the life you save might be mine"?
2 What was suggested that you "Buy some for Lulu"?
3 How much did "1001" clean your carpet for?
4 What did Patsy Kensit advertise in her first TV ad?
5 Pook's "Blow the Wind" was used to advertise what?
6 Which programme was interrupted with the first ever commercial on UK TV?
7 Who wrote "O Sole Mio", which advertised Wall's Cornetto?
8 Which brand of what featured in the first UK TV ad?
9 Who wrote "The Flight of the Bumble Bee", which urged us to buy Black & Decker paint-stripper?
10 Whose watches were advertised to the music of Ramirez?
11 Which Bobby Hodgens and Siobhan Fahey song hit No. 1 after being used in a VW ad?
12 Which Muddy Waters hit was reissued after it was used to advertise Levi's?
13 Which Mozart opera helped to sell the Citroën ZX?
14 Verdi's "Dies Irae" was used to advertise which newspaper?
15 Who were the original jingle artists for the song that became "I'd Like to Teach the World to Sing"?
16 Georgie Fame's "Get Away" started out as a jingle for what?
17 In 1960 the ad music for Strand cigarettes gave a hit to whom?
18 In the BT "EastEnders" ad what was the late Arthur Fowler doing?
19 Whose music was the theme from *Raging Bull* and used to advertise Heineken Export?
20 Whose wines were trumpeted to the sound of Pachelbel's *Canon in D Major*?
21 Which upmarket scent was advertised to Vivaldi's *Four Seasons*?
22 Which music by whom advertised Hamlet cigars?
23 Who wrote *The Force of Destiny* (*La forza del destino*), used for Stella Artois lager?
24 The Clash's only No. 1 was used to advertise what?
25 What was being advertised in the jingle which began "You'll wonder where the yellow went"?
26 Where did the spring water come from which was advertised by Elgar's Cello Concerto?
27 Which model ditched everything but her ex's VW keys?
28 What was Lorraine Chase advertising when she said "Nah, from Luton Airport"?
29 According to the ad, what did PAL stand for?
30 Which drink was advertised to the music of Offenbach's *Barcarolle*?

1 In which country is the city of Srinagar?

2 Who wrote the novel *Rites of Passage*?

3 What was the first British Top Ten hit for Johnny Nash?

4 How many sides has an undecagon?

5 Carson City is the capital of which US state?

6 Which cathedral's 800th anniversary was marked by a 1989 set of stamps?

7 What is the only English anagram of ALIENATOR?

8 Who first manufactured barbed wire?

9 Belau and Kusac are in which island group?

10 To five, how many league games did Gazza play for Newcastle?

11 Which electronics firm featured in the TV series "Making Out"?

12 What are the odds of rolling double one in dice-throwing?

13 What star sign links Michael Brunson and John Craven?

14 In Monopoly, if you were on Liverpool Street Station and got double four, where would you land?

15 What was the name of the outlaw nicknamed the Sundance Kid?

16 Hargenger and Spivoy are types of what?

17 In which sport was John Dennis Cronshey famous?

18 On TV, what was the name of Spender's wife?

19 Which US state is directly west of Colorado?

20 From which language does the word "sherbet" originate?

21 The airline Ladeco was formed in which country?

22 What was Artemus Ward's real name?

23 Who did Lynda Bellingham play in "General Hospital"?

24 Which female driver was the 1992 Indy 500 Rookie of the Year?

25 Which statesman won the Nobel Prize for Literature in 1953?

26 What kitchen aid did Charles Strite invent?

27 In which country was the TV Presenter Bob Holness born?

28 What did the people who appeared in "The Duty Men" work for?

29 Who had a hit in 1982 with "Pass the Dutchie"?

30 What is the approximate distance of Cairo airport from London in miles?

Answers

TV: Ads (see Quiz 106)

1 James Dean. 2 Smarties. 3 Less than half a crown (25p). 4 Bird's Eye frozen peas. 5 Orange phone. 6 "Channel Nine". 7 Di Capua. 8 Gibbs SR toothpaste. 9 Rimsky Korsakov. 10 Citizen. 11 "Young At Heart". 12 "Mannish Boy". 13 *The Marriage of Figaro*. 14 *Today*. 15 Hillside Singers. 16 Petrol. 17 Cliff Adams. 18 Working on his allotment. 19 Mascagni. 20 Thresher. 21 Chanel No. 19. 22 Bach's "Air on a G String". 23 Verdi. 24 Levi's. 25 Pepsodent toothpaste. 26 Buxton. 27 Paula Hamilton. 28 Campari. 29 Prolongs Active Life. 30 Bailey's Irish Cream.

HOW TO SET UP YOUR OWN
PUB QUIZ

It isn't easy, get that right from the start. This isn't going to be easy. Think instead of words like; 'difficult', 'taxing', 'infuriating' consider yourself with damp palms and a dry throat and then, when you have concentrated on that, put it out of your mind and think of the recognition you will receive down the local, imagine all the regulars lifting you high upon their shoulders dancing and weaving their way around the pub. It won't help but it's good to dream every once in a while.

What you will need:

- A good selection of Biros (never be tempted to give your own pen up, not even to family members)
- A copy of *The Best Pub Quiz Book Ever!2*
- A set of answer sheets photocopied from the back of the book
- A good speaking voice and possibly a microphone and an amp
- A pub
- At least one pint inside you
- At least one more on your table
- A table

What to do:

Choose your local to start with, there is no need to get halfway through your first quiz and decide you weren't cut out for all this and then find yourself in the roughest pub in Christendom 30 miles and a long run from home.

Chat it through with the landlord and agree on whether you will be charging or not, if you don't then there is little chance of a prize for the winners other than a free pint each and this is obviously at the landlord's discretion – if you pack his pub to bursting then five free pints won't worry him, but if it's only you and a couple of others then he may be less than unwilling, as publicans tend to be.

If you decide on a payment entry keep it reasonable, you don't want to take the fun out of the quiz; some people will be well aware that they have very little hope of winning and will be reluctant to celebrate the fact by mortgaging their house.

Once location and prize are all sorted then advertising the event is paramount, get people's attention, sell, sell, sell or, alternatively, stick up a gaudy looking poster on the door of the bogs. Be sure to specify all the details, time, prize and so on – remember you are selling to people whose tiny attention span is being whittled down to nothing by alcohol.

After this it is time for the big night, if you are holding the event in the 'snug' which seats ten or so you can rely on your voice, if not you should get hold of a good microphone and an amplifier so that you can boom out your questions and enunciate the length and breadth of the pub (once again, clear this with the landlord and don't let liquid anywhere near the electrical equipment). Make sure to practice, and get comfortable with the sound of your own voice and relax as much as possible, try not to rely on alcohol too much or "round one" will be followed by "rown' too" which will eventually give way to "runfree". Relax your voice so that you can handle any queries from the teams, and any venomous abuse from the 'lively' bar area.

When you enter the pub make sure you take everything listed above. Also, make sure you have a set of tie-break questions, that you instruct everybody who is taking part of the rules – and be firm. It will only upset people if you start handing out impromptu solutions and let's face it the wisdom of Solomon is not needed when you are talking pub quiz rules; 'no cheating' is a perfectly healthy stance to start with. Keep people happy by double-checking your questions and answers, the last thing you need is a mix up on the prize-winning question.

Finally, keep the teams to a maximum of five members, hand out your answer papers and pens and, when everybody is good and settled, start the quiz. It might not be easy and it might not propel you to international stardom or pay for a life of luxury but you will enjoy yourself. No, really.

ANSWERS

Part One

1 _____

2 _____

3 _____

4 _____

5 _____

6 _____

7 _____

8 _____

9 _____

10 _____

11 _____

12 _____

13 _____

14 _____

15 _____

16 _____

17 _____

18 _____

19 _____

20 _____

21 _____

22 _____

23 _____

24 _____

25 _____

26 _____

27 _____

28 _____

29 _____

30 _____

ANSWERS

Part Two	
1 _____	16 _____
2 _____	17 _____
3 _____	18 _____
4 _____	19 _____
5 _____	20 _____
6 _____	21 _____
7 _____	22 _____
8 _____	23 _____
9 _____	24 _____
10 _____	25 _____
11 _____	26 _____
12 _____	27 _____
13 _____	28 _____
14 _____	29 _____
15 _____	30 _____

ANSWERS

1 _____

2 _____

3 _____

4 _____

5 _____

6 _____

7 _____

8 _____

9 _____

10 _____

11 _____

12 _____

13 _____

14 _____

15 _____

Part Three

16 _____

17 _____

18 _____

19 _____

20 _____

21 _____

22 _____

23 _____

24 _____

25 _____

26 _____

27 _____

28 _____

29 _____

30 _____